The Story of the Lord's Dealings with Mrs. Amanda Smith

An Autobiography.
The Story of the Lord's Dealings with Mrs. Amanda Smith the Colored Evangelist;
Containing an Account of Her Life Work of Faith, and Her Travels
in America, England, Ireland, Scotland, India, and Africa, as an Independent Missionary:

By
Amanda Smith

With an introduction
By
Bishop J.M. Thoburn

The Story of the Lord's Dealings with Mrs. Amanda Smith

The Story of the Lord's Dealings with Mrs. Amanda Smith

AN AUTOBIOGRAPHY

THE STORY OF THE LORD'S DEALINGS WITH

MRS. AMANDA SMITH

THE COLORED EVANGELIST

CONTAINING AN ACCOUNT OF HER LIFE WORK OF FAITH, AND HER TRAVELS IN AMERICA, ENGLAND, IRELAND, SCOTLAND, INDIA AND AFRICA, AS AN INDEPENDENT MISSIONARY.

WITH AN INTRODUCTION BY

BISHOP THOBURN, OF INDIA.

"Hitherto the Lord hath helped me."

CHICAGO:
MEYER & BROTHER, PUBLISHERS,
108 WASHINGTON STREET,
1893.

**PREPARED FOR PUBLICATION
BY**
HISTORIC PUBLISHING

No part of this publication may be reproduced, stored in a retrieval system, or transmitted, in any form, or by any means, electronic, mechanical, photocopying, recording, or otherwise, without the prior consent of the publisher.

All Rights Reserved
HISTORIC PUBLISHING
©2017
(Edited Materials)

AN AUTOBIOGRAPHY
THE STORY OF THE LORD'S DEALINGS WITH MRS. AMANDA SMITH
THE COLORED EVANGELIST
CONTAINING AN ACCOUNT OF HER LIFE WORK OF FAITH, AND HER TRAVELS IN AMERICA, ENGLAND, IRELAND, SCOTLAND, INDIA AND AFRICA, AS AN INDEPENDENT MISSIONARY.

WITH AN INTRODUCTION BY
BISHOP J. M. THOBURN, OF INDIA.

"Hitherto the Lord hath helped me."

CHICAGO:
MEYER & BROTHER, PUBLISHERS,
108 WASHINGTON STREET,
1893.

Entered according to Act of Congress in the year 1893, by
AMANDA SMITH
in the office of the Librarian of Congress at Washington.

The Story of the Lord's Dealings with Mrs. Amanda Smith

PREFACE.

For a number of years many of my friends have said to me, "You ought to write out an account of your life, and let it he known how God has led you out into His work."

Sometime before that wonderful man of God, John S. Inskip, passed away, he said, "Amanda, you ought to write," and he kindly offered to assist me in getting the items together.

Many other friends in America, have said the same, and I have replied, "I could not do it, for I don't know how to go about it," and so would not entertain the thought.

Time passed on, and after I was in England a while, the friends there began to say the same thing, and as an inducement to commence, told me that it might be done much cheaper there than in America.

As I was constantly on the go, and had no time to think about it, and certainly none to write, things remained thus until after my return from Africa. Then friends in different places again urged me to do this, and being broken down in health, and so unable to labor as much as formerly, I began to think of it more seriously and prayed much over it, asking the Lord, if it was His will, to make it clear and settle me in it, and give me something from His Word that I may have as an anchor.

Asking thus for light and guidance, I opened my Bible while in prayer, and my eye lighted on these words: "Now, therefore, perform the doing of it, and as there was a readiness to will, so there may be a performance also out of that which ye have." (2nd Cor. viii: 11.)

I said, "Lord, I thank Thee, for this is Thy Word to me, for what I have asked of Thee. Praised be Thy name."

And from that moment, my heart was settled to do it. But as the time has gone, and so much has seemed to come if) to hinder, and several persons who had kindly offered to assist me, were called away in one direction or another, and I was so wearied and the task looked so big, my heart began to fail me, and I thought I could not do it.

Again I went to the Lord in prayer, and told Him all about it, and asked Him what I should do, for His glory alone was all I sought. He whispered to my heart, clearly and plainly, these words, "Fear thou not, I will help thee." (Isa. xli: 13.) Again I praised Him; so now I go forward with full faith and trust that He will fulfill His own promise.

My friends who know me best, will make allowances for all defects in this autobiographical sketch; and I believe strangers also will be charitable, when they know that my opportunities for an education have been very limited indeed.

Three months of schooling was all I ever had. That was at a school for whites; though a few colored children were permitted to attend. To this school my brother and I walked five and a half miles each day, in going and returning, and the attention we received while there was only such as the teacher could give after the requirements of the more favored pupils had been met.

In view of the deficiency in my early education, and other disadvantages in this respect, under which I have labored, I crave the indulgence of all who may read this simple and unvarnished story of my life.

AMANDA SMITH.

The Story of the Lord's Dealings with Mrs. Amanda Smith

INTRODUCTION.

During the summer of 1876, while attending a camp meeting Epworth Heights, near Cincinnati, my attention was drawn to a colored lady dressed in a very plain garb, which reminded me somewhat of that worn by the Friends in former days, who was engaged in expounding a Bible lesson to a small audience.

I was told that the speaker was Mrs. Amanda Smith, and that she was a woman of remarkable gifts, who had been greatly blessed in various parts of the country.

Having spent nearly all my adult years on the other side of the globe, my acquaintance in America was by no means an extensive one, and this will explain the fact that I had never heard of this devout lady until I met her at this camp meeting.

Her remarks on the Bible lesson did not particularly impress me, and it was not until the evening of the same day, when I chanced to be kneeling near her at a prayer meeting, that I became impressed that she was a person of more than ordinary power.

The meetings of the day had not been very successful, and a spirit of depression rested upon many of the leaders. A heavy rain had fallen, and we were kneeling somewhat uncomfortably in the straw which surrounded the preacher's stand.

A number had prayed, and I was myself sharing the general feeling of depression, when I was suddenly startled by the voice of song. I lifted my head, and at a short distance, probably not more than two yards from me, I saw the colored sister of the morning kneeling in an upright position, with her hands spread out and her face all aglow.

She had suddenly broken out with a triumphant song, and while I was startled by the change in the order of the meeting, I was at once absorbed with interest in the song and the singer.

Something like a hallowed glow seemed to rest upon the dark face before me, and I felt in a second that she was possessed of a rare degree of spiritual power.

That invisible something which we are accustomed to call power, and which is never possessed by any Christian believer except as one of the fruits of the indwelling Spirit of God, was hers in a marked degree.

From that time onward I regarded her as a gifted worker in the Lord's vineyard, but I had still to learn that the enduement of the Spirit had given her more than the one gift of spiritual power.

A week later I met her at Lakeside, Ohio, and was again impressed in the same way, but I then began to discover that she was not only a woman of faith, but that she possessed a clearness of vision which I have seldom found equaled.

Her homely illustrations, her quaint expressions, her warmhearted appeals, all possess the supreme merit of being so many vehicles for conveying the living truths of the Gospel of Jesus Christ to the hearts of those who are fortunate enough to hear her.

A few years after my return to India, in 1876, I was delighted to hear that this chosen and approved worker of the Master had decided to visit this country. She arrived in 1879, and after a short stay in Bombay, came over to the eastern side of the empire, and assisted us for some time in Calcutta. She also returned two years later, and again rendered us valuable assistance.

The novelty of a colored woman from America, who had in her childhood been a slave, appearing before an audience in Calcutta, was sufficient to attract attention, but this alone would not account for the popularity which she enjoyed throughout her whole stay in our city.

She was fiercely attacked by narrow minded persons in the daily papers, and elsewhere, but opposition only seemed to add to her power.

During the seventeen years that I have lived in Calcutta, I have known many famous strangers to visit the city, some of whom attracted large audiences, but I have never known anyone who could draw and hold so large an audience as Mrs. Smith.

She assisted me both in the church and in open-air meetings, and never failed to display the peculiar tact for which she is remarkable.

I shall never forget one meeting which we were holding in an open square, in the very heart of the city. It was at a time of no little excitement, and some Christian preachers had been roughly handled in the same square a few evenings before. I had just spoken myself, when I noticed a great crowd of men and boys, who had succeeded in breaking up a missionary's audience on the other side of the square, rushing towards us with loud cries and threatening gestures.

If left to myself I should have tried to gain the box on which the speakers stood, in order to command the crowd, but at the critical moment, our good Sister Smith knelt on the grass and began to pray. As the crowd rushed up to the spot, and saw her with her beaming face upturned to the evening sky, pouring out her soul in prayer, they became perfectly still, and stood as if transfixed to the spot! Not even a whisper disturbed the solemn silence, and when she had finished we had as orderly a meeting as if we had been within the four walls of a church!

In those days a well-known theatrical manager, much given to popular buffoonery, wrote to me inviting me to arrange to have Mrs. Smith preach in his theatre on a certain Sunday evening. I was much surprised on receiving the letter, and taking it to her told her I did not know what it meant. Several friends, who chanced to be present, at once began to dissuade her:

"Do not go, Sister Amanda," said several, speaking at once, "the man merely wishes to have a good opportunity of seeing you, so that he can take you off in his theatre. He has no good purpose in view. Do not trust yourself to him under any circumstances."

After a moment's hesitation Mrs. Smith replied in language which I shall never forget:

"I am forbidden," she said, "to judge any man. You would not wish me to judge you, and would think it wrong if any of us should judge a brother or sister in the church. What right have I to judge this man? I have no more right to judge him than if he were a Christian."

She said she would pray over it and give her decision. She did so, and decided to accept the invitation.

When Sunday evening came the theatre was packed like a herring box, while hundreds were unable to gain admission. I took charge of the meeting, and after singing and prayer introduced our strange friend from America.

She spoke simply and pointedly, alluding to the kindness of the manager who had opened the doors of his theatre to her, in very courteous terms, and evidently made a deep and favorable impression upon the audience. There was no laughing, and no attempt was ever made subsequently to ridicule her. As she was walking off the stage the manager said to me;

"If you want the theatre for her again do not fail to let me know. I would do anything for that inspired woman."

During Mrs. Smith's stay in Calcutta she had opportunities for seeing a good deal of the native community. Here, again, I was struck with her extraordinary power of discernment. We have in Calcutta a class of reformed Hindus called Brahmos. They are, as a class, a very worthy body of men, and at that time were led by the distinguished Keshub Chunder Sen.

Every distinguished visitor who comes to Calcutta is sure to seek the acquaintance of some of these Brahmos, and to study, more or less, the reformed system which they profess and teach. I have often wondered that so few, even of our ablest visitors, seem able to comprehend the real character either of the men or of their new system. Mrs. Smith very quickly found access to some of them, and beyond any other stranger whom I have ever known to visit Calcutta, she formed a wonderfully accurate estimate of the character, both of the men and of their religious teaching.

She saw almost at a glance all that was strange and all that was weak in the men and in their system.

This penetrating power of discernment which she possesses in so large a degree impressed me more and more the longer I knew her. Profound scholars and religious teachers of philosophical bent seemed positively inferior to her in the task of discovering the practical value of men and systems which had attracted the attention of the world!

I have already spoken of her clearness of perception and power of stating the undimmed truth of the Gospel of Christ. Through association with her, I learned many valuable lessons from her lips, and once before an American audience, when Dr. W. F. Warren was exhorting young preachers to be willing to learn from their own hearers, even though many of the hearers might be comparatively illiterate, I ventured to second his exhortation by telling the audience that I had learned more that had been of actual value to me as a preacher of Christian truth from Amanda Smith than from any other one person I had ever met.

Throughout Mrs. Smith's stay in India she was always cheerful and hopeful. In this respect, too, she differed from most visitors to our great empire. Some adopt gloomy views as they look at the weakness of Christianity, and observe the stupendous fortifications which have been reared by the followers of the various false religions of the people.

Some even yield to despair, and refuse to believe that India ever can be saved or even benefited, while only a very few are able to believe not only that India will yet become a Christian empire, but that Christ will yet lift up the people of this land, and so revolutionize or transform society as it exists to-day, as to make the people practically a new people.

Our good Sister Amanda Smith never belonged to any of these despondent classes.

She sometimes was touched by the pictures of misery which she saw around her, but never became hopeless. She was of cheerful temperament, it is true, but aside from personal feeling, she always possessed a buoyant hope and an overcoming faith, which made it easy for her to believe. that the Savior, whom she loved and served, really intended to save and transform India.

Soon after Mrs. Smith's visit to India, another Virginian visited Calcutta on his way around the globe. This was Mr. Moncure D. Conway.

These two persons, Mrs. Smith and Mr. Conway, were representative Virginians. They had been born in the same section of the country, brought up as Methodists, and were thoroughly acquainted, one by observation and the other by experience, with the terrible character of the American slave system.

Mr. Conway in early life was for several years a Methodist preacher, but by his own published confession he never comprehended what the true spirit of Methodism was. He was at one time a well-known and somewhat popular Unitarian minister, but finding the Unitarians too narrow and orthodox for a man of his liberal mind, he set up an independent church or organization of some kind, in London, and preached to an obscure little congregation for a number of years, until his last experiment ended in confessed failure.

His recorded impressions received in India were of the most gloomy kind. He saw nothing to hope for in the condition of the people, and looked at them in their helpless state with blank bewilderment, if not despair. He passed through the empire without leaving a single trace of light behind him, without making an impression for good upon any heart or life, without finding an open door by which to make any man or woman happier or better, without, in short, seeing even a single ray of hope shining upon what he regarded as a dark and benighted land.

Mrs. Smith, the other Virginian, without a tittle of Mr. Conway's learning, and deprived of nearly every advantage which he had enjoyed, not only retained the faith of her childhood, but matured and developed it until it attained a standard of purity and strength rarely witnessed in our world.

She also came to India, but unlike the other Virginian, she cherished hope where he felt only despair, she saw light where he perceived only darkness, she found opportunities everywhere for doing good which wholly escaped his observation, and during her two years' stay in the country where she went, she traced out a pathway of light in the midst of the darkness!

As she left the country she could look back upon a hundred homes which were brighter and better because of her coming, upon hundreds of hearts whose burdens had been lightened and whose sorrows had been sweetened by reason of her public and private ministry.

She is gratefully remembered to this day by thousands in the land.

Her life affords a striking comment at once upon the value of the New Testament to those who receive it, both in letter and in spirit, and upon the hopelessness of the Gospel of unbelief which obtains so wide a hearing at the present day.

A thousand Virginians of the Conway stripe might come and go for a thousand years without making India any better, but a thousand Amanda Smiths would suffice to revolutionize an empire!

I am very glad to learn that Mrs. Smith has at last been induced to yield to the importunities of friends and prepare a sketch of her eventful life. I trust that the story will be told without reserve in all its simplicity, as well as in all its strength, and I doubt not that God will crown this last of her many labors with abundant blessings.

J. M. THOBURN.

CALCUTTA, October 22, 1891

The Story of the Lord's Dealings with Mrs. Amanda Smith

CONTENTS.

- CHAPTER I. . . . 32
  BIRTH, PARENTAGE AND DELIVERANCE FROM SLAVERY THROUGH THE CONVERSION OF MY MOTHER'S YOUNG MISTRESS—MY PIOUS GRANDMOTHER.
- CHAPTER II. 41
  REMOVAL TO PENNSYLVANIA—GOING TO SCHOOL—FIRST RELIGIOUS EXPERIENCES—PERNICIOUS READING.
- CHAPTER III. 50
  SOME OF THE REMEMBRANCES OF MY GIRLHOOD DAYS—HELPING RUNAWAYS—MY MOTHER AROUSED—A NARROW ESCAPE—A TOUCHING STORY.
- CHAPTER IV. 60
  MOVING FROM LOWE'S FARM—MARRIAGE—CONVERSION.
- CHAPTER V. 75
  HOW I BOUGHT MY SISTER FRANCES AND HOW THE LORD PAID THE DEBT.
- CHAPTER VI. 83
  MARRIAGE AND DISAPPOINTED HOPES—RETURN TO PHILADELPHIA—A STRANGER IN NEW YORK—MOTHER JONES' HELP—DEATH OF MY FATHER.
- CHAPTER VII. 10
  THE BLESSING—ABOUT SEEKING SANCTIFICATION BY WORKS.
- CHAPTER VIII. 131
  MY FIRST TEMPTATION, AND OTHER

EXPERIENCES—I GO TO NEW UTRECHT TO SEE MY HUSBAND—A LITTLE EXPERIENCE AT BEDFORD STREET CHURCH, NEW YORK—FAITH HEALING.
- CHAPTER IX.....156
VARIOUS EXPERIENCES—HIS PRESENCE—OBEDIENCE—MY TEMPTATION TO LEAVE THE CHURCH—WHAT PEOPLE THINK—SATISFIED.
- CHAPTER X.....170
"THY WILL BE DONE," AND HOW THE SPIRIT TAUGHT ME ITS MEANING, ALSO THAT OF SOME OTHER PASSAGES OF SCRIPTURE—MY DAUGHTER MAZIE'S CONVERSION.
- CHAPTER XI.....185
MY CALL TO GO OUT—AN ATTACK FROM SATAN—HIS SNARE BROKEN—MY PERPLEXITY IN REGARD TO THE TRINITY—MANIFESTATION OF JESUS—WAS IT A DREAM?
- CHAPTER XII.....205
MY LAST CALL—HOW I OBEYED IT, AND WHAT WAS THE RESULT.
- CHAPTER XIII.....228
MY REMEMBRANCES OF CAMP MEETING—SECOND CAMP MEETING—SINGING—OBEDIENCE IS BETTER THAN SACRIFICE.
- CHAPTER XIV.....245
KENNEBUNK CAMP MEETING—HOW I GOT THERE, AND WAS ENTERTAINED—A GAZING STOCK—HAMILTON CAMP MEETING—A TRIP TO VERMONT—THE LOST TRUNK, AND HOW IT WAS FOUND.

- CHAPTER XV.....270
  MY EXPERIENCE AT DR. TAYLOR'S CHURCH, NEW YORK, AND ELSEWHERE—THE GENERAL CONFERENCE AT NASHVILLE—HOW I WAS TREATED AND HOW IT ALL CAME OUT—HOW THINGS CHANGE.
- CHAPTER XVI.....287
  HOW I GOT TO KNOXVILLE, TENN., TO THE NATIONAL CAMP MEETING, AND WHAT FOLLOWED.
- CHAPTER XVII....301
  SEA CLIFF CAMP MEETING, JULY, 1872—FIRST THOUGHTS OF AFRICA—MAZIE'S EDUCATION AND MARRIAGE—MY EXPERIENCE AT YARMOUTH.
- CHAPTER XVIII.....316
  PITTMAN CHURCH, PHILADELPHIA—HOW I BECAME THE OWNER OF A HOUSE, AND WHAT BECAME OF IT—THE MAYFLOWER MISSION, BROOKLYN—AT DR. CUYLER'S.
- CHAPTER XIX.....337
  BROOKLYN—CALL TO GO TO ENGLAND—BALTIMORE—VOYAGE OVER.
- CHAPTER XX.....359
  LIME STREET STATION, LIVERPOOL, ENGLAND, AND THE. RECEPTION I MET WITH THERE—PAGES FROM MY DIARY.
- CHAPTER XXI.....374
  VISIT TO SCOTLAND, LONDON, AND OTHER PLACES—; CONVERSATION WITH A CURATE—GREAT MEETING AT PERTH—HOW I CAME TO GO TO INDIA.

- CHAPTER XXII.....403
  IN PARIS—ON THE WAY TO INDIA—FLORENCE—ROME—NAPLES—EGYPT.
- CHAPTER XXIII.....423
  INDIA—NOTES FROM MY DIARY—BASSIM—A BLESSING AT FAMILY PRAYER—NAINI TAL—TERRIBLE FLOODS AND DESTRUCTION OF LIFE.
- CHAPTER XXIV.....451
  THE GREAT MEETING AT BANGALORE—THE ORPHANAGE AT COLAR—BURMAH—CALCUTTA—ENGLAND.
- CHAPTER XXV.....473
  AFRICA—INCIDENTS OF THE VOYAGE—MONROVIA—FIRST FOURTH OF JULY THERE—A SCHOOL FOR BOYS—CAPE PALMAS—BASSA—TEMPERANCE WORK—THOMAS ANDERSON
- CHAPTER XXVI.....498
  FORTSVILLE—TEMPERANCE MEETINGS—EVIL CUSTOMS—THOMAS BROWN—BALAAM—JOTTINGS FROM THE JUNK RIVER—BROTHER HARRIS IS SANCTIFIED.
- CHARTER XXVII.....523
  CONFERENCE AT MONROVIA—ENTERTAINING THE BISHOP—SIERRA LEONE—GRAND CANARY—A STRANGE DREAM—CONFERENCE AT BASSA—BISHOP TAYLOR.
- CHAPTER XXVIII.....548
  OLD CALABAR—VICTORIA'S JUBILEE—CAPE MOUNT—CLAY-ASHLAND HOLINESS ASSOCIATION—RELIGION OF AFRICA—TRIAL FOR WITCHCRAFT—THE WOMEN OF AFRICA.

- CHAPTER XXIX.....571
  HOW I CAME TO TAKE LITTLE BOB—TEACHING HIM TO READ—HIS CONVERSION—SOME OF HIS TRIALS, AND HOW HE MET THEM—BOB GOES TO SCHOOL.
- CHAPTER XXX..... 592
  NATIVE BABIES—VISIT TO CREEKTOWN—NATIVE SUPERSTITIONS—PRODUCTS OF AFRICA—DISAPPOINTED EMIGRANTS.
- CHAPTER XXXI.....609
  LIBERIA—BUILDINGS—THE RAINY SEASON—SIERRA LEONE—ITS PEOPLE—SCHOOLS—WHITE MISSIONARIES—COMMON SENSE NEEDED—BROTHER JOHNSON'S EXPERIENCE—HOW WE GET ON IN AFRICA.
- CHAPTER XXXII.....631
  CAPE PALMAS—HOW I GOT THERE—BROTHER WARE—BROTHER SHARPER'S EXPERIENCE—A GREAT REVIVAL.
- CHAPTER XXXIII.....660
  EMIGRATION TO LIBERIA—SCHOOLS OF LIBERIA—MISSION SCHOOLS—FALSE IMPRESSIONS—IGNORANCE AND HELPLESSNESS OF EMIGRANTS—AFRICAN ARISTOCRACY.
- CHAPTER XXXIV..... 667
  LETTERS AND TESTIMONIALS—BISHOP TAYLOR—CHURCH AT MONROVIA—UPPER CALDWELL—SIERRA LEONE—GREENVILLE—CAPE PALMAS BAND OF HOPE TEMPERANCE SOCIETY AT MONROVIA—LETTERS—MRS. PAYNE—MRS. DENMAN—MRS. INSKIP—REV. EDGAR M. LEVY—ANNIE WITTENMYER—DR. DORCHESTER—

MARGARET BOTTOME—MISS WILLARD—LADY HENRY SOMERSET.
- CHAPTER XXXV..... 700
RETURN TO LIVERPOOL—FAITH HEALING—BISHOP TAYLOR LEAVES AGAIN FOR AFRICA—USE OF MEANS—THE STORY OF MY BONNET—TOKENS OF GOD'S HELP AFTER MY RETURN FROM AFRICA.
- CHAPTER XXXVI..... 719
WORK IN ENGLAND—IN LIVERPOOL, LONDON, MANCHESTER, AND VARIOUS OTHER PLACES—I GO TO SCOTLAND AND IRELAND—SECURE PASSAGE TO NEW YORK—INCIDENTS OF THE VOYAGE—HOME AGAIN—CONCLUDING WORDS.

LIST OF ILLUSTRATIONS.

- MRS. AMANDA SMITH, ... Frontispiece.
- MR. SAMUEL BERRY, FATHER OF AMANDA SMITH,.
- MAZIE D. SMITH,
- MARKET PLACE, BOMBAY,.
- PREPARING A MEAL, BOMBAY
- HILL MEN. NAINI TAL,.
- NIANI TAL, BEFORE THE LAND SLIDE,
- NATIVE CHRISTIAN FAMILY, INDIA,
- COOPER'S WHARF, MONROVIA
- THE PAINE FAMILY,.
- ASHMAN STREET, MONROVIA
- MY FIRST SUNDAY SCHOOL, PLUKIE,
- HOME OF PRESIDENT JOHNSON
- NATIVE SOLDIERS, LIBERIA,
- HOME OF LATE PRESIDENT ROBERTS
- KATE ROACH, SIERRE LEONE
- ON THE ST. PAUL RIVER
- GENERAL SHERMAN'S HOUSE, MONROVIA, .
- FRANCES, NATIVE BASSA GIRL,
- BOB,
- BAPTIST MISSION STATION
- BOYS OF MISSION SCHOOL,
- MISSION SCHOOL, ROTIFUNK,
- CAPE PALMAS
- BISHOP TAYLOR HOLDING A PALAVER.
- THE RECEPTACLE FOR EMIGRANTS, LIBERIA

The Story of the Lord's Dealings with Mrs. Amanda Smith

AUTOBIOGRAPHY OF AMANDA SMITH.

CHAPTER I.

BIRTH, PARENTAGE AND DELIVERANCE FROM SLAVERY THROUGH THE CONVERSION OF MY MOTHER'S YOUNG MISTRESS—MY PIOUS GRANDMOTHER.

I was born at Long Green, Md., Jan. 23rd, 1837. My father's name was Samuel Berry. My mother's name, Mariam. Matthews was her maiden name. My father's master's name was Darby Insor. My mother's master's name, Shadrach Green. They lived on adjoining, farms. They did not own as large a number of black people, as some who lived in the neighborhood. My father and mother had each a good master and mistress, as was said. After my father's master died, his young master, Mr. E., and himself, had all the charge of the place. They had been boys together, but as father was the older of the two, and was a trustworthy servant, his mistress depended on him, and much was entrusted to his care. As the distance to Baltimore was only about twenty miles, more or less, my father went there with the farm produce once or twice a week, and would sell or buy, and bring the money home to his mistress. She was very kind, and was proud of him for his faithfulness, so she gave him a chance to buy himself. She allowed him so much for his work and a chance to what extra he could for himself. So he used to make brooms and husk mats and take them to market with the produce. This work he would do nights after his day's work was done for his mistress. He was a great lime burner. Then in harvest time, after working for his mistress all day, he would walk three and four miles, and work in the harvest field till one and two o'clock in the morning, then go home and lie down and sleep for an hour or two, then up and at it again. He had an important and definite object before him, and was willing to sacrifice sleep and rest in order to accomplish it. It was not his own liberty alone, but the freedom of his wife and five children. For this he toiled day and night. He was a strong man, with an excellent constitution, and God wonderfully helped him in his struggle. After he had finished paying for himself, the next was to buy my mother and us children. There were thirteen children in all, of whom only three girls are now living. Five were born in slavery. I was the oldest girl, and my brother, William Talbart, the oldest boy. He was named after a gentleman named Talbart Gossage, who was well known all through that part of the country. I think he was some relation of Mr. Ned Gossage, who lost his life at Carlisle, Pa., sometime before the war, in trying to capture two of his black boys who had run away for their freedom. I remember distinctly. the great excitement at the time. The law then was that a master could take his slave anywhere he caught him. These boys had been gone for a year or more, and. were in Carlisle when he heard of their whereabouts. He determined to go after them. So he took with him the constable and one or two others. Many of his friends did not want him to go, but he would not hear them. I used to think how strange it was, he being a professed Christian, and a class leader in the Methodist Church, and at the time a leader of the colored people's class, that he should be so blinded by selfishness and greed that he should risk his own life to put into slavery again those who sought only for freedom. How selfishness, when allowed to rule us, will drive us on, and make us act in spirit like the great enemy of our soul, whoever seeks to recapture those who have escaped from the bondage of sin. How we need to watch and pray, and on our God rely.

He did not capture the boys, but in the struggle he lost his own life, and was brought home dead.

But I turn again to my story. As I have said, my father having paid for himself was anxious to purchase his wife and children; and to show how the Lord helped in this, I must here tell of the wonderful conversion of my mother's young mistress and of her subsequent death, and the marvelous answer to my grandmother's prayers.

There was a Methodist Camp Meeting held at what was at that time called Cockey's Camp Ground. It was, I think, about twenty miles away, and the young mistress, with a number of other young people, went to this meeting. My mother went along to assist and wait on Miss Celie, as she had always done. It was an old-fashioned, red-hot Camp Meeting. These young people went just as a kind of picnic, and to have a good time looking on. They were staunch Presbyterians, and had no affinity with anything of that kind. They went more out of curiosity, to see the Methodists shout and hollow, than anything else; because they did shout and hollow in those days, tremendously. Of course they were respectful. They went in to the morning meeting and sat down quietly to hear the sermon; then they purposed walking about the other part of the day, looking around, and having a pleasant time. As they sat in the congregation, the minister preached in demonstration of the Power and of the Holy Ghost. My mother said it was a wonderful time. The spirit of the Lord got hold of my young mistress, and she was mightily convicted and converted right there before she left the ground; wonderfully converted in the old-fashioned way; the shouting, hallelujah way. Of course it disgusted those who were with her. They were terribly put out. Everything was spoiled, and they did Dot know how to get her home. They coaxed her, but thank the Lord, she got struck through. Then they laughed at her a little. Then they scolded her, and ridiculed her; but they could not do anything with her. Then they begged her to be quiet; told her if she would just be quiet, and wait till they got home, and wait till morning, they would be satisfied. My mother was awfully glad that the Lord had answered her and grandmother's prayer. As I have heard my mother tell this story she has wept as though it had just been a few days ago. Mother had only been converted about two years before this, and had always prayed for Miss Celie, so her heart was bounding with gladness when Miss Celie was converted. But of course she must hold on and keep as quiet as possible; they had enough to contend with, with Miss Celie. Mother said she sat in the back part of the carriage and prayed all the time. Alter coaxing her awhile she said she would try and keep quiet, and wait till morning. But when she got home she could not keep quiet, but began first thing to praise the Lord and shout. It aroused the whole house, and of course they were frightened, and thought she had lost her mind. But nay, verily, she had received the King, and there was great joy in the city. They got up and wondered what was the matter. They thought she was dreadfully excited at this meeting. They did all they could to quiet her, but they could not do much with her. But finally they did get her quiet and she went to bed. But her heart was so stirred and filled. She wanted to go then to where they would have lively meetings. She wanted to go to the Methodist church. Oh my! That was intolerable. They could not allow that. Then she wanted to go to the colored people's church. No, they would not have that. So they kept her from going. Then they separated my mother and her. They thought maybe mother might talk to her, and keep up the excitement. So they never let them be together at all, if possible. About a quarter of a mile away was the great dairy, and Miss Celie used to slip over there when she got a chance and have a good time praying with mother and grandmother. Finally they found they could do nothing with Miss Celie. So the young people decided they would get together and have a ball and get the notion out of her head. So they planned for a ball, and got all ready. The gentlemen would call on Miss Celie; she was very much admired, anyhow; and they would talk, and they did everything they could. She did not seem to take to it. But finally she said to mother one day, "Well, Mary, it's no use; they won't let me go to meeting anywhere I want to go, and I might as well give up and go to this ball." But my mother said, "Hold on, my dear, the Lord will deliver you." She used to put on her sunbonnet and slip down through the orchard and go down to the dairy and tell mother and grandmother; mother used to assist grandmother in the dairy. One day mother said she came down and said:

"Oh! Mary, I can't hold out any longer; they insist on my going to that ball, and I have decided to go. It's no use." So they had a good cry together, went off and prayed, and that was the last prayer about the ball. How strange! And yet God had that all in his infinite mercy—opening the prison to them that were bound. Just a week before the ball came off, Miss Celie taken down with typhoid fever. They didn't think she was going to die when she was taken down, but they sent for the doctors, the best in the land. Four of them watched over her night and day. Everything was done for her that could be done. She always wanted mother with her, to sit up in the bed and hold her; she seemed only to rest comfortably then. She seemed to have sinking spells. The skill of the doctors was baffled, and they said they could not do any more. So one day after one of these sinking spells, she called them all around her bed and said: "I want to speak to you. I have one request I want to make."

They said, "Anything, my dear."

"I want you to promise me that you will let Samuel have Mariam and the children." Then they had my mother get up out of the bed at once. Of course they didn't want her to hear that; and they said:

"Now, my dear, if you will keep quiet, you may be a little better." And then she went off in a kind of sinking spell. When she said this, and they sent my mother out, she ran with all her might and told grandmother, and grandmother's faith saw the door open for the freedom of her grandchildren; and she ran out into the bush and told Jesus. Of course my mother had to hurry back so as not to be missed in the house. Miss Celie went on that way for three days, and they would quiet her down. When the second day came, and she made the request, and they sent my mother out, she ran and told grandmother that Miss Celie had made the same request; then she ran back to the house again, and grandmother went out and told Jesus. At last it came to the third and last day, and the doctor said: "She can only last such a length of time without there is a change; so what you do, you must do quickly."

Mother was in the bed behind her, holding her up. She called them all again, and said, "I want you to make me one promise; that is, that you will let Samuel have Mariam and the children."

"Oh! yes, my dear," they said, "we will do anything."

My mother was a great singer. When Miss Celie got the promise, she folded her hands together, and leaning her head upon my mother's breast she said, "Now, Mary, sing."

And as best she could, she did sing. It was hard work, for her heart was almost broken, for she loved her as one of her own children. While she sang, Miss Celie's sweet spirit swept through the gate, washed in the blood of the lamb. Hallelujah! what a Saviour. How marvelous that God should lead in this mysterious way to accomplish this end.

I often say to people that I have a right to shout more than some folks; I have been bought twice, and set free twice, and so I feel I have a good right to shout. Hallelujah!

I was quite small when my father bought us, so know nothing about the experience of slavery, because I was too young to have any trials of it. How well I remember my old mistress. She dressed very much after the Friends' style. She was very kind to me, and I was a good deal spoiled, for a little darkey. If I wanted a piece of bread, and if it was not buttered and sugared on both sides, I wouldn't have it; and when mother would get out of patience with me, and go for a switch, I would run to my old mistress and wrap myself up in her apron, and I was safe. And oh! how I loved her for that. They were getting me ready for market, but I didn't know it. I suppose that is why they allowed me to do many things that otherwise I should not have been allowed to do. They used to take me in the carriage with them to church on Sunday. How well I remember my pretty little green satin hood, lined inside with pink. How delighted I was when they used to take me. Then the young ladies would often make pretty little things and give to my mother for me. Mother was a good seamstress; she used to make all of our clothes, and all of father's every day clothes—coats, pants and vests. She had a wonderful faculty in this; she had but to see a thing of any style of dress or coat, or what-not, and she would come home and cut it out. People used to wonder at it. There were no Butterick's patterns then that she could get hold of. So one had to have a good head on them if they kept nearly in sight of things. But somehow mother was always equal to any emergency. My dear old mistress used to knit. I would follow her around. Sometimes she would walk out into the yard and sit under the trees, and I would drag the chair after her; I was too small to carry it. She would sit down awhile, and I would gather pretty flowers. When she got tired she would walk to another spot, and I would drag the chair again. So we would spend several hours in this way. My father had proposed buying us some time before, but could not be very urgent. He had to ask, and then wait a long interval before he could ask again. Two of the young ladies of our family were to be married, and as my brother and myself were the oldest of the children, one of us would have gone to one, and one to the other, as a dowry. But how God moves in a mysterious way His wonders to perform. My grandmother was a woman of deep piety and great faith. I have often heard my mother say that it was to the prayers and mighty faith of my grandmother that we owed our freedom. How I do praise the Lord for a Godly grandmother, as well as mother. She had often prayed that God would open a way so that her grandchildren might be free. The families into which these young ladies were to marry, were not considered by the black folks as good masters and mistresses as we had; and that was one of my grandmother's anxieties. And so she prayed and believed that somehow God would open a way for our deliverance. She had often tried and proved Him, and found Him to be a present help in trouble. And so in the way I have already related, the Lord did provide, and my father was permitted to purchase our freedom.

>"In some way or other
>The Lord will provide;
>It may not be my way,

It may not be thy way,
And yet in His own way,
The Lord will provide."

CHAPTER II.

REMOVAL TO PENNSYLVANIA—GOING TO SCHOOL—FIRST RELIGIOUS EXPERIENCES—PERNICIOUS READING.

After my father had got us all free and settled, he wanted to go and see his brother, who had run away for his freedom several years before my father bought himself. The laws of Maryland at that time were, that if a free man went out of the state and stayed over ten days, he lost his residence, and could be taken up and sold, unless some prominent white person interposed; and then sometimes with difficulty they might get him off. But many times poor black men were kidnapped, and would be got out of the way quick. For men who did that sort of business generally looked out for good opportunities. My mother's people all lived in Maryland. She hated to leave her mother, my dear grandmother, and so never would consent to go North. But when my father went away to see his brother, and stayed over the ten days, she thought best to go. Poor mother! How well I remember her. After a week how anxious she was. She used to sit by the fire nearly all night. It was in the fall of the year I know, but I am not able to tell just what year it was. After my father's death, my sister, not knowing the value of the free papers, allowed them all to be destroyed. We were all recorded in the Baltimore court house. Many times I had seen my father show the papers to people. They had a large red seal—the county seal—and my father, or any of us traveling, would have to show our free papers. But those I have not got, so cannot tell the, year or date. But, by and by, the ninth day came. I saw my mother walk the floor, look out of the window, and sigh. I used to get up out of my bed and sit in the corner by the fire and watch her, and see the great tears as she would wipe them away with her apron. She would say; "Amanda, why don't you stay in bed?"

I would make an excuse to stay with her. Sometimes I would cry and say I was sick. Then she would call me to her and let me lay my head in her lap; and there is no place on earth so sweet to a child as a mother's lap. I can almost feel the tender, warm, downy lap of my mother now as I write, for so it seemed to me. I loved my father, and thought he was the grandest man that ever lived. I was always the favorite of my father, and I was sorry enough when he was away, and when I saw my mother cry, I would cry, too. Ten days had passed, and father had not come yet.

Every day some of the good farmers around would call to see if "Sam" had got home yet. My father was much respected by all the best white people in that neighborhood, and many of them would not have said anything to him; but, "If nothing was said to Insor's Sam about going out of the state and staying over ten days, why all the niggers in the county would be doing the same thing!"

So this was the cause or the inquiry. Oh! no one knows the sadness and agony of my poor mother's heart. Finally the day came when father returned. Then the friends, white and black, who wished him well, advised him to leave as quickly as possible. And now the breaking up. We were doing well, and father and mother had all the work they could do. The white people in the neighborhood were kind, and gave my mother a good many things, so that we children always had plenty to eat and wear. We had a house, a good large lot, and a good garden, pigs, chickens, and turkeys. And then my mother was a great economist. She could make a little go a great ways. She was a beautiful washer and ironer, and a better cook never lifted a pot. I get my ability in that (if I have any) from my dear mother. Then withal she was an earnest Christian, and had strong faith in God, as did also my grandmother. She was deeply pious, and a woman of marvelous faith and prayer. For the reason stated my parents determined to move from Maryland, and so went to live on a farm owned by John Lowe, and situated on the Baltimore and York turnpike in the State of Pennsylvania.

My father and mother both could read. But I never remember hearing them tell how they were taught. Father was the better reader of the two. Always on Sunday morning after breakfast he would call us children around and read the Bible to us. I never knew him to sit down to a meal, no matter how scant, but what he would ask God's blessing before eating. Mother was very thoughtful and scrupulously economical. She could get up the best dinner out of almost nothing of anybody I ever saw in my life. She often cheered my father's heart when he came home at night and said: "Well, mother, how have you got on to-day?"

"Very well," she would say. It was hard planning sometimes; yet we children never had to go to bed hungry. After our evening meal, so often of nice milk and mush, she would call us children and make us all say our prayers before we went to bed. I never remember a time when I went to bed without saying the Lord's Prayer as it was taught me by my mother. Even before we were free I was taught to say my prayers.

I first went to school at the age of eight years, to the daughter of an old Methodist minister named Henry Dull; my teacher's name was Isabel Dull. She taught a little private school opposite where my mother lived, in a private house belonging to Isaac Hendricks (Bishop Hendricks' grandfather). She was a great friend of my mother's, and was very pretty, and very kind to us children. She taught me my first spelling lesson. There was school only in the summer time. I had about six weeks of it. I first taught myself to read by cutting out large letters from the newspapers my father would bring home. Then I would lay them on the window and ask mother to put them together for me to make words, so that I could read. I shall never forget how delighted I was when I first read: "The house, the tree, the dog, the cow." I thought I knew it all. I would call the other children about me and show them how I could read. I did not get to go to school any more till I was about thirteen years old. Then we had to go about five miles, my brother and myself. There were but few colored people in that part of the country at that time, to go to school (white school), only about five and they were not regular; but father and mother were so anxious for us to go that they urged us on, and I was anxious also. I shall never forget one cold winter morning. The sun was bright, the snow very deep, and it was bitterly cold. My brother did not go that day, but I wanted to go. Mother thought it was too cold; she was afraid I would freeze; but I told her I could go, and after a little discussion she told me I might go. She told me I could put on my brother's heavy boots. I had on a good thick pair of stockings, a warm linsey-woolsey dress, and was well wrapped up. Off I started to my two and a half mile school house,—John Rule's school house on the Turnpike. The first half mile I got on pretty well, a good deal up hill, but O how cold I began to get, and being so wrapped up I couldn't get on so well as I thought I could. I was near freezing to death. My first thought was to go back, but I was too plucky, I was afraid if I told mother she wouldn't let me go again, so I kept still and went. When I got to the school house door, I found I couldn't open it and couldn't speak, and a white boy came up and said, "Why don't you go in?" Then I found I couldn't speak, as I tried and couldn't. He opened the door and I went in and someone came to me and took off my things and they worked with me, I can't tell how long, before I recovered from my stupor. There were a great many farmers' daughters, large girls, and boys, in the winter time, so that the school would be full, so that after coming two and a half miles, many a day I would get but one lesson, and that would be while the other scholars were taking down their dinner kettles and putting their wraps on. All the white children had to have their full lessons, and if time was left the colored children had a chance. I received in all about three months' schooling.

At thirteen years of age I lived in Strausburg, sometimes it was called Shrewsbury, about thirteen miles from York, on the Baltimore and York turnpike. I lived with a Mrs. Latimer. She was a Southern lady, was born in Savannah, Georgia. She was a widow, with five children. It was a good place, Mrs. Latimer was very kind to me and I got on nicely. It was in the spring I went there to live, and sometime in the winter a great revival broke out and went on for weeks at the Allbright Church. I was deeply interested and impressed by the spirit of the meeting. It was an old-fashioned revival, scores were converted. No colored persons went up to be prayed for; there were but few anywhere in the neighborhood. One old man named Moses Rainbow, and his two sons, Samuel and James, were the only colored people that lived anywhere within three or four miles of the town. This meeting went on for four or five weeks. When it closed a series of meetings commenced at the Methodist Church.

One of the members was Miss Mary Bloser, daughter of George Bloser, well known through all that region of country for his deep piety and Christian character, as was Miss Mary, also. She was powerful in prayer. I never heard a young person who knew how to so take hold of God for souls. She was a power for good everywhere she went. How many souls I have seen her lead to the Cross!

One night as she was speaking to persons in the congregation, she came to me, a poor colored girl sitting away back by the door, and with entreaties and tears, which I really felt, she asked me to go forward. I was the only colored girl there, but I went. She knelt beside me with her arm around me and prayed for me. O, how she prayed! I was ignorant, but prayed as best I could. The meeting closed. I went to get up, but found I could not stand. They took hold of me and stood me on my feet. My strength seemed to come to me, but I was frightened. I was afraid to step. I seemed to be so light. In my heart was peace, but I did not know how to exercise faith as I should. I went home and resolved I would be the Lord's and live for him. All the days were happy and bright. I sang and worked and thought that was all I needed to do. Then I joined the Church. I don't remember the name of the minister, but I well remember the name of my class leader was Joshua Ludrick. I liked him for his lung power, for I thought then there was a good deal of religion in loud prayers and shouts. You could hear him pray half a mile when he would get properly stirred. He was leader of the Sunday morning class, which convened after the morning preaching. My father and mother, to encourage me in my new life, joined the Church and the same class, so as to save me from going out at night. Mrs. Latimer's children, three of them, went to the Sunday School, and I must get home so as to have dinner in time for the children to get off, but I was black, so could not be led in class before a white person, must wait till the white ones were through, and I would get such a scolding when I got home, the children would all be so vexed with me, and Mrs. Latimer, and my troubles had begun. I prayed and thought it was my cross. I thought I will change my seat in the class, maybe that will help me, and sat in the first end of the pew, as the leader would always commence on the first end and go down. When I sat in the first end, then he would commence at the lower end and come up and leave me last. Then I sat between two, thinking he would lead the two above me and then lead me in turn, but he would lead the two and then jump across me and lead all the others and lead me last. I told my father I got scolded for getting home so late and making the children late for school. Father said he would speak to Mr. Ludrick about it, but if he did, it made no change, and it came to where I must decide either to give up my class or my service place. We were a large family, and father and mother thought I must keep my situation, so I had to give up my class. It did not do me much good, anyhow, to be scolded every time I went, so I became careless and lost all the grace I had, if I really had any at all. I was light hearted and gay, but I always would say my prayers and read my Bible and good books and meant to get religion when I knew I could keep it. I wouldn't be a hypocrite, no, not I, so I went on, wrapped up in myself. Then I began to watch defects in professors, which is a poor business for any one. That is not the way to get near to God. I saw many things and heard many things said and done by professors that I would not do, I was much better than they were, so I went on in my own way for a while.

It has been years ago. While living at Black's hotel, in Columbia, I remember reading a book. I forget the title of it, but it was an argument between an infidel and a Christian minister. As I went on reading I became very much interested. "Oh," I thought to myself, "I know the Christian minister will win." It starts with the infidel asking a question. The minister's answer took two pages, while the question asked only took one page and a half. As they went on the minister gained three pages with his answer; and the infidel seemed to lose. And then it went on, and by and by the minister began to lose, and the infidel gained. So it went on till the infidel seemed to gain all the ground. His questions and argument were so pretty and put in such a way that before I knew it I was captured; and by the time I had got through the book I had the whole of the infidel's article stamped on my memory and spirit, and the Christian's argument was lost; I could scarcely remember any of it. Well, I was afraid to tell anyone. Oh, if any one should find out that I did not believe in the existence of God. I longed for someone to talk to that I might empty my crop of the load of folly that I had gathered. And I read everything I could get my hands on, so as to strengthen me in my new light, as I thought. Yet I wanted to forget it, and get out of it. But it was like a snare; I could not. A year had gone. I talked big and let out a little bit now and then. How beautiful the old hymn:

> "When Jesus saw me from on high,
> Beheld my soul in ruin lie,
> He looked at me with pitying eye,
> And said to me as he passed by,
> 'With God you have no union.' "

Oh, how true! I longed for deliverance, but how to get free. The Lord sent help in this way: My aunt, my mother's half-sister, who now lives in Baltimore, and whom I loved very much, came up to York, and then to Wrightsville, to visit father and us children. I lived in Columbia; and I went over to see her and had her come over with me. "Now," I thought, "this will be my chance to unburden my heart. Aunt lives away down in the country in Quaker Bottom, or in the neighborhood of Hereford, Md., and I know no one there, and no one knows me; I shall never be there; and just so that no one knows around here, that is all I care for."

My aunt was very religiously inclined, naturally. She was much like my mother in spirit. So as we walked along, crossing the long bridge, at that time a mile and a quarter long, we stopped, and were looking off in the water. Aunt said, "How wonderfully God has created everything, the sky, and the great waters, etc."

Then I let out with my biggest gun; I said, "How do you know there is a God?" and went on with just such an air as a poor, blind, ignorant infidel is capable of putting on. My aunt turned and looked at me with a look that went through me like an arrow; then stamping her foot, she said:

"Don't you ever speak to me again. Anybody that had as good a Christian mother as you had, and was raised as you have been, to speak so to me. I don't want to talk to you." And God broke the snare. I felt it. I felt deliverance from that hour. How many times I have thanked God for my aunt's help. If she had argued with me I don't believe I should ever have got out of that snare of the devil. And I would say to my readers, "Beware how you read books tainted with error." There are enough of the orthodox kind that will help you if you will be content with them, and the Book of books. Amen.

CHAPTER III.

SOME OF THE REMEMBRANCES OF MY GIRLHOOD DAYS— HELPING RUNAWAYS—MY MOTHER AROUSED—A NARROW ESCAPE—A TOUCHING STORY.

The name of my father's landlord was John Lowe, he was a wealthy farmer, lived between New Market and Shrewsburg, Pa. Pretty much all the farmers round about in those days were antislavery men; Joseph Hendricks, Clark Lowe, and a number of others. My father worked a great deal for Isaac Hendricks, who used to keep the Blueball Tavern. I and the children have gathered many a basket of apples out of the orchard, and many a pail of milk I have helped to carry to the house, and often at John Lowe's as well; I used to help them churn often. And then old Thomas Wantlen, who used to keep the store; how well I remember him. John Lowe would allow my father to do what he could in secreting the poor slaves that would get away and come to him for protection. At one time he was Magistrate, and of course did not hunt down poor slaves, and would support the law whenever things were brought before him in a proper way, but my father and mother were level headed and had good broad common sense, so they never brought him into any trouble. Our house was one of the main stations of the Under Ground Railroad. My father took the "Baltimore Weekly Sun" newspaper; that always had advertisements of runaway slaves. After giving the cut of the poor fugitive, with a little bundle on his back, going with his face northward, the advertisement would read something like this: Three thousand dollars reward! Ran away from Anerandell County, Maryland, such a date, so many feet high, scar on the right side of the forehead or some other part of the body,—belonging to Mr. A. or B. So sometimes the excitement was so high we had to be very discreet in order not to attract suspicion. My father was watched closely.

I have known him to lead in the harvest field from fifteen to twenty men—he was a great cradler and mower in those days — and after working all day in the harvest field, he would come home at night, sleep about two hours, then start at midnight and walk fifteen or twenty miles and carry a poor slave to a place of security; sometimes a mother and child, sometimes a man and wife, other times a man or more, then get home just before day. Perhaps he could sleep an hour then go to work, and so many times baffled suspicion. Never but once was there a poor slave taken that my father ever got his hand on, and if that man had told the truth he would have been saved, but he was afraid.

There was a beautiful woods a mile from New Market on the Baltimore and York Turnpike; it was called Lowe's Camp Ground. It was about three quarters of a mile from our house. My mother was a splendid cook, so we arranged to keep a boarding house during the camp meeting time. We had melons, and pies and cakes and such like, as well. Father was very busy and had not noticed the papers for a week or two, so did not know there was any advertisement of runaways. There were living in New Market certain white men that made their living by catching runaway slaves and getting the reward. A man named Turner, who kept the post office at New Market, Ben Crout, who kept a regular Southern blood-hound for that purpose, and John Hunt. These men all lived in New Market. Then there was a Luther Amos, Jake Hedrick, Abe Samson and Luther Samson, his son. I knew them all well. Samson had a number of grey-hounds. So these fellows used to watch our house closely, trying every way to catch my father. One night during camp meeting, between twelve and one o'clock, we children were all on the pallet on the floor. It was warm weather, and father and mother slept in the bed. A man came and knocked at the door. Father asked who was there? He said "A friend. I hear you keep a boarding house and I want to get something to eat."

Father told him to come in. He had everything but hot coffee—so he went to work and got the coffee ready. Father talked with him. The man was well dressed. He had changed his clothes, he said, as he had been traveling, and it was dusty, and he was on his way to the camp meeting. This is what he said to my father. So by and by the coffee was ready, and father set him down to his supper. This man had come through New Market, and Ben Crout and John Hunt, who had read the advertisement, saw this man answered the description and hoping to catch my father, told him to come to our house and all about my father having a boarding house and all about the camp meeting. It was white people's camp meeting, but colored people went as well; it used to be the old Baltimore camp, so called, and so that was the way the poor man knew so well what to say. He had come away from Louisiana, and had been two weeks lying by in the day time and traveling at night, but had got so hungry he ventured into this town, and these men were looking for him, but he did not know it. When they saw him they knew he answered the advertisement given in the paper, for it was always explicitly given; the color, the height and scars on any part of his body. Well, just about the time the man got through with his supper, someone shouted, "Halloo!" Father went to the door. There were six or seven white men, and they said, "We want that nigger you are harboring, he is a runaway nigger."

"I am not harboring anybody," father said. Then they began to curse and swear and rushed upon him. The man jumped and ran upstairs. My mother had a small baby. Of course she was frightened and jumped up, and they were beating father and tramping all over us children on the floor. We were screaming. There stood in the middle of the floor an old fashioned ten plate stove. There was no fire in it, of course, and as my poor frightened mother ran by it trying to defend father, she caught her wrapper in the door, just as a man cut at her with a spring dirk knife; it glanced on the door instead of on mother. I have thanked God many a time for that stove door. But for it my poor mother would have been killed that night. The poor man jumped out of the window up stairs and ran about two hundred yards, when Ben Crout's blood-hound caught him and held him till they came. When they found the man was gone, they left off beating father and went for the man. That was the first and last darkey they ever got out of Sam Berry's clutches. It put a new spirit in my mother. She cried bitterly, but O, when it was all over how she had gathered courage and strength. The good white people all over the neighborhood were aroused, but he was so close to the Maryland line they had him in Baltimore a few hours from then. And, poor fellow, we never heard of him afterwards.

Some time, about three or four months after this, along in the fall, we were sleeping upstairs. One night about twelve o'clock a knock came on the fence. My father answered and went down and opened the door. Mother listened and heard them say "runaway nigger." She sprang up, and as she ran downstairs she snatched down father's cane, which had a small dirk in it; she went up and threw open the door, pushed father aside, but he got hold of her, but O, when she got through with those men! They fell back and tried to apologize, but she would hear nothing.

"I can't go to my bed and sleep at night without being hounded by you devils," she said.

Next morning father went off to work, but mother dressed herself and went to New Market; as she went she told everybody she met how she had been hounded by these men. Told all their names right out, and all the rich respectable people cried shame, and backed her up. Dr. Bell, the leading doctor in New Market, who himself owned three or four slaves, stood by my mother and told her to speak of it publicly; so she stood on the stepping stone at Dr. Bell's, right in front of the largest Tavern in the place. There were a lot of these men sitting out reading the news. The morning was a beautiful Fall morning, and she opened her mouth and for one hour declared unto them all the words in her heart. Not a word was said against her, but as the spectators and others looked on and listened the cry of "Shame! Shame!" could be heard; and the men skulked away here and there. By the time she got through there was not one to be seen of this tribe. That morning, as mother went to New Market, this same blood-hound of Bell Crout's was lying on the sidewalk, and as mother went on a lady she used to work for, a Mrs. Rutlidge, saw the dog and saw mother coming. She threw up her hand to indicate to her the dangerous animal. They generally kept her fastened up, but this morning she was not. Mother paid no attention but went on. Mrs. R. clasped her hands and turned her back expecting every moment to hear mother scream out. She looked around and mother was close by the dog and stepped right over her. She was so frightened she said: "O, Mary, how did you get by that dreadful dog of Ben Crout's?"

Mother was wrothy, and said, "I didn't stop to think about that dog," and passed on. And this was the wonder to everybody around. It was the great talk of the day all about the country, how that Sam Berry's wife had passed Ben Crout's blood-hound and was not hurt. Then they began to say she must have had some kind of a charm, and they were shy of her. Ever after that nobody, black or white, troubled Sam Berry's wife. It was no charm, but was God's wonderful deliverance.

About two years or more after this, the papers were full of notices of a very valuable slave who had run away. A heavy reward was offered. He had by God's mercy got to us, and by moving the poor fellow from place to place he had been kept safe for about two weeks, as there was no possible chance for father or any one to get him away, so closely were we watched. My father was a very early riser, always up and out about day dawn. Our house stood in the valley between two hills, so that the moment you struck the top of the hill, either way coming or going, you could see every move around our house. Just on the opposite side of the road there used to stand two large chestnut trees, but these had been blown down by a great storm some time before, so there was no screen to hide the house from full view. This morning, while out in the yard feeding the pigs, he saw four men coming on horseback. He knew they were strangers. He could not get in the house to tell mother, so he called to her and said: "Mother, I see four men coming; do the best you can."

She must act in a moment without being able to say a word more to father. The poor slave man was upstairs. She brought him down and put him between the cords and straw tick. As it was early in the morning her bed was not made up. In the old-fashioned houses in the country we did not have parlors. The front room downstairs was often used as the bed-room. My little brother, two years old, slept in the foot of the bed. The men rode up and spoke to my father. He was a very polite man. "Good morning, gentlemen, good morning, you are out quite early this morning."

"Yes, we are looking for a runaway nigger." Just then my father recognized the high sheriff as Mr. E., who was formerly his young master. "Why, is this is not Mr. E.?"

"Yes, Sam, didn't you know me?"

My father made a wonderful time over him, laughed heartily and said: "What in the world is up?"

"Do you know anything about this runaway?"

Another spoke up and said: "We have a search warrant and we mean to have that nigger. We want to know if you have him hid away."

"Well," father said, "if I tell you I have not, you won't believe me; if I tell you I have, it will not satisfy you, so come in and look."

He didn't know a bit what mother had done, but he knew she had a head on her, and he could trust her in an emergency. The men hesitated and said: "It is no use for us to go in, if you will just tell us if you have him or know anything about him." And father said: "You come in, gentlemen, and look."

They said, "We have heard your wife is the devil," and then, speaking very nicely, "You know, Sam, we don't want any trouble with her, you can tell us just as well."

"No, gentlemen, you will be better satisfied if you go in and see for yourselves."

Just then mother, in the most dignified and polite manner, threw open the door and said: "Good morning, gentlemen, come right in." So they laughed heartily. Two dismounted and came in, went upstairs, looked all about while one looked in the kitchen behind the chimney, in the pot closet; and my mother went to the bed and threw back the cover (she knew what cover to throw back, of course,) there lay my little brother. She said: "Look everywhere, maybe this is he?"

"My! Sam," one of them said, "here is a darkey, what will you take for him?"

"No, you have not money enough to buy him," father said. Then mother said: "Now, gentlemen, look under the bed as well; you haven't examined everything here," and they laughed and ran out and said: "Well, Sam, we see you haven't got him."

And father said: "Well, now you are better satisfied after you have looked yourselves." So he didn't tell any lie, but he had the darkey hid just the same!

They mounted their horses and went off full tilt to York. We children were sharp enough never to show any sign of alarm. Poor me, my eyes felt like young moons. The man was safe. After they had got away, mother got the poor fellow out, and he was so weak he could scarcely stand. He trembled from head to foot, and cried like a child. Poor fellow, he thought he was gone, and but for my noble mother he would have been. We soon got him off to Canada, where, I trust, he lived to thank and praise God, who delivered him from the hand of his masters. I can't tell just how long it was after this occurrence, but it was in harvest time. My father had got home from work and was sitting out in the front yard resting himself; it was just beginning to get dusk. We children were all around playing. A tall, well-built man came up to the fence. Father said:

"Good evening, my friend." The poor man trembled, and said: "I don't know if you are a friend or a foe, but I am at your mercy."

"Don't fear," said father, "you are safe." Then he sat on the fence a while and began to tell his sad story. His feet had become so sore he could not travel. He had come away from New Orleans. He said his master owned a large sugar plantation and he was one of the head molasses boilers. His master was a very passionate man, and had threatened several times to sell him because he was a Christian and would pray, but he was a valuable man and so he held on; but he had committed a great offense this time. He said he was very tired, and, something he never did in his life before, he fell asleep from sheer weariness, and so burnt many. hogsheads of molasses, and this so enraged his master that he determined to sell him. He had a wife and three children, if I remember correctly. His master had him handcuffed and put in the cellar under the house, till the Georgia traders came. When the money was paid they generally had a great time drinking and gambling. He said he could not get to see his wife. O, how he prayed all day and all night. His young mistress, whom he had often nursed when she was a little child and whom he used often to carry about from place to place, was very much attached to him, as was frequently the case. She had been away North to school and was a Christian, and that may explain what followed. She was home from school just at this time, and like Queen Esther, when pleading for her people, she was made queen just in time. The evening before the morning he was to be taken away they were having a good jollification time. She waited till they were all full of excitement, and being a great favorite of her father's she managed to get the keys of the cellar and went in and unlocked his handcuffs and made him swear to her on his knees that if they ever caught him he would never betray her. Then she told him which way to go, to follow the North Star, which most of the slaves seemed to understand and travel by. She gave him a little money and something to eat. He prayed for God's blessing on her, and told her he would die if he was taken, but would never betray her; so he would. I shall never forget how he cried as he told this story to my father. He said he had traveled for three weeks, and after his food was all gone he lived on berries, blackberries were just ripe. He would lie by in the day and travel at night; kept in the woods, never traveled in day time, only when it would rain. We soon took him in and got water and bathed his feet. Mother got him a good supper. O, how the poor man ate; he was nearly starved. We kept him about two weeks, and then succeeded in getting him off to dear old Canada. O, how much this poor slave man went through for only the liberty of his body, and yet how few there are that are willing to make any sacrifice to secure the freedom of souls that Jesus so freely offers, for if the Son shall make you free then are ye free, indeed. Thank God, these days of sadness are past, never to be repeated, I trust. The poor man, I suppose, never heard of his wife and children, for this was years before the war and it was not likely they ever met on earth again, but I trust they will meet beyond the river where the surges cease to roll.

CHAPTER IV.

MOVING FROM LOWE'S FARM.—MARRIAGE.—CONVERSION.

After twelve years on John Lowe's farm, my father had an offer from a man named John Bear; it was between five and six miles from where we were. It was a small farm and my father had a better chance to help himself. He used to work a good deal in Strausburg then. Dr. Bull and his brother, Rev. Wesley Bull, lived in Strausburg. My oldest brother lived with the doctor a long time and took care of his horses. The doctor married a Miss Jane Berry, daughter of old Colonel Berry, of Baltimore. They first settled in Strausburg. I lived with them some time. How well I remember the old Colonel; he used to come to visit them, and was very kind to me. Would often speak to me about my soul's interest, but I was young and did not pay much attention at the time, but I never forgot it. After a time Dr. Bull moved to Baltimore, and Dr. Turner, who married Miss Julia Berry, Mrs. Bull's sister, lived in Strausburg, then I lived with Dr. Turner. How well I remember Dr. and Mrs. Turner. They were very fond of Maryland biscuit, and though I was young, I had the reputation of making the best Maryland biscuit and frying the nicest chicken of anyone around there, and the doctor used to say "Amanda can beat them all making Maryland biscuit and frying chicken." My! how it did please me! Somehow it is very encouraging to servants to tell them once in a while that they do things nicely; it did me good. I would almost kill myself to please them, and Doctor Turner's mother, dear Mrs. Flynn, what a good woman she was! She gave me the first Testament I ever had and used to come into the kitchen and read to me sometimes. She came several times on a visit to see Dr. and Mrs. Turner. After a time Dr. Turner moved back to Baltimore again, I went with them. It was my first time in Baltimore. We got in at night and I remember how I had never seen fine lights glittering in drug stores before, and as we drove along I thought I never saw such pretty houses in my life. O, I was thoroughly captivated. We had a long way to drive from the station then. Col. Berry lived at Poplar Grove, just a little out of Baltimore. Dear old Mrs. Berry, Mrs. Turner and the Doctor, and the old Colonel met us at the station. How well I remember the old home in the grove; it was the fall of the year; it was not late, but the fires were lighted and all was so cheery. I remember Mr. and Mrs. Hurst, the three children, Miss Petty and Missie, and little Berry and Mr. Somerfield, Miss Emily and Miss Eliza. Dr. Turner took a house in town on the corner of Franklin and Pearl streets, Baltimore. I remained till Christmas, then my mother came to see me and I went home with her. Some time after I that Dr. Waugh moved to Strausburg; Bishop Waugh's son. I remember the Bishop and Mrs. Waugh well. I always admired Mrs. Dr. Waugh so much; she never seemed to be cross about anything, nor at any time. The Doctor, too, was very gentle and quiet, but Mrs. Bishop was not so much so, though she was very nice. Mrs. Doctor did not like Strausburg, so they did not stay very long, but returned to Baltimore again. In the course of time Rev. Isaac Collis was appointed to the First Methodist Church, and I went to live with them a few months. My father used to do all their gardening. When their time was out they moved away. O, what changes have been since then; the most of these have gone to their reward, but some of their children and grandchildren still live. Dear Mrs. Turner's daughter, Mrs. Wilson now, whose husband is pastor of Wesley Chapel in Washington, is her mother right over again in kindness and amiableness of disposition. Mr. Wilson, her husband, is a noble man of God. I shall never forget their kindness to me last October, the time of the great Ecumenical conference. Mrs. Burres asked me to lead the holiness meeting that is held at the Wesley chapel every Wednesday at 11 o'clock, and when the meeting closed who should come and speak to me but dear Mrs. Wilson and her husband. Then she told me who she was, Mrs. Turner's daughter. She was married and had two lovely children. Mr. Wilson and she invited me to their home to lunch with them. Well, I thought that is a big thing to be invited to lunch, for I had walked about for two days and there was not a restaurant in the great capital of Washington where a colored Christian lady or gentleman could go and sit down and get a cup of tea or a dinner: and now to be invited here to lunch, I thought what does it really mean? Of course I accepted the invitation. I had thought Washington was like Boston or London. I had no such difficulty there. Thank God for real, practical, inright, outright, downright common sense; that is all I think people need on the color line. May the Lord give it to us quick. Amen. Dear Mr. and Mrs. Wilson lacked nothing in that line. God bless them! When I went I was shown into the parlor; my wraps were taken, and in a little while Mrs. Wilson came in. We had a pleasant little chat, then came her sister; I was introduced. She was so nice, then the dear little children. In a little while then Mr. Wilson came with a gentleman from the conference, then a lady and gentleman who were their guests. I was introduced to all as easily and naturally and common sense-like as possible. Then we went to lunch. The little girl took me by the hand and she and I led the way. The little thing was so nice she said, "Are you going to sit at the table with me?"

"Would you like me to do so?"

"Yes."

I don't suppose this was an everyday occurrence; it is not necessary that it should be so, but when occasions do come, all that is really needed is simple, real, manly, broad, Christian common sense. Mr. Wilson sat at the head of the table, I at the right, and the dear little girl next, and her little brother next and the others in order. We had an elegant lunch, and a very pleasant and profitable time together. We talked about India, Africa, Paris, Rome, Egypt, Scotland, Ireland, and the Isles of the Sea, and ended, I believe, with the Hero of the Congo, Bishop Taylor. We went upstairs, and after a little further chat Mr. Wilson asked me to sing and pray with them. I sang several songs. One was:—"The very same Jesus."

"The very same Jesus,
The very same Jesus,
O praise His name;
He is just the same,
The very same Jesus."

The other one was:—

"God is able to deliver thee
Though by sin oppressed;
Go to Him for rest,
Our God is able to deliver thee."

The Lord blest the singing to them, and our hearts were melted, then we knelt to pray. O, how the Lord helped me to pray. My own heart was overflowing with gratitude for the kindness shown me, for I recognized the hand of God in it all, and so praised Him. Amen.

In September, 1854, I was married to my first husband, C. Devine, by the Rev. Nicholas Pleasant, a Baptist minister in Columbia. My father did not object to my marrying, only on the ground that I was rather young, and I thought so, too, but still, like so many young people, I said, "But well, I know I can get on." Then there was the fellow saying all the nice things he would do for me, and I believed it all, of course. But it was not long before I wished I had not believed half he said, though in many things he was good. He believed in religion for his mother's sake. She was a good woman, he said, though I never saw her. He had two sisters who lived in Columbia. He could talk on the subject of religion very sensibly at times; but when strong drink would get the better of him, which I am very sorry to say was quite often, then be was very profane and unreasonable. We had two children. The first died; the other, my daughter Maze, is now married and living in Baltimore.

In 1855 I was very ill. Everything was done for me that could be done. My father lived in Wrightsville, Pa., and was very anxious about my soul. But I did not feel a bit concerned.

I wanted to be let alone. How I wished that no one would speak to me. One day my father said to me, "Amanda, my child, you know the doctors say you must die; they can do no more for you, and now my child you must pray."

O, I did not want to pray, I was so tired I wanted to sleep. The doctors said they must keep me aroused. In the afternoon of the next day after the doctor had given me up, I fell asleep about two o'clock, or I seemed to go into a kind of trance or vision, and I saw on the foot of my bed a most beautiful angel. It stood on one foot, with wings spread, looking me in the face and motioning me with the hand; it said "Go back," three times, "Go back. Go back, Go back."

Then, it seemed, I went to a great Camp Meeting and there seemed to be thousands of people, and I was to preach and the platform I had to stand on was up high above the people. It seemed it was erected between two trees, but near the tops. How I got on it I don't know, but I was on this platform with a large Bible opened and I was preaching from these words:—"And I if I be lifted up will draw all men unto me." O, how I preached, and the people were slain right and left. I suppose I was in this vision about two hours. When I came out of it I was decidedly better. When the doctor called in and looked at me he was astonished, but so glad. In a few days I was able to sit up, and in about a week or ten days to walk about. Then I made up my mind to pray and lead a Christian life. I thought God had spared me for a purpose, so I meant to be converted, but in my own way quietly. I thought if I was really sincere it would be all right.

I cannot remember the time from my earliest childhood that I did not want to be a Christian, and would often pray alone. Sometimes I would kneel in the fence corner when I went for the cows to bring them home. Sometimes upstairs, or wherever I could be alone. I had planned just about how I was going to be converted. I had a strong will and was full of pride. When I said I would not do anything, I was proud of my word, and people would say, "Well, you know if Amanda says she won't do anything, you might as well try to move the everlasting hills." And that inflated me and I thought, "O, how nice to have a reputation like that." I would stick to it; I would not give in; my pride held me. I went on in this course till 1856.

In a watch meeting one night at the Baptist Church in Columbia, Pennsylvania, a revival started. I lived with Mrs. Morris, not far away, and I could hear the singing, but I did not mean to go forward to the altar to pray: I didn't believe in making a great noise. I said, "If you are sincere the Lord will bless you anywhere, and I don't mean to ever go forward to the altar; that I will never do." So I prayed and struggled day after day, week after week, trying to find light and peace, but I constantly came up against my will. God showed me I was a dreadful sinner, but still I wanted to have my own way about it. I said, "I am not so bad as Bob Loney, Meil Snievely, and a lot of others. I am not like them, I have always lived in first-class families and have always kept company with first-class servant girls, and I don't need to go there and pray like those people do." All this went on in my mind.

At last one night they were singing so beautifully in this Church, I felt drawn to go in, and went and sat away back by the door and they were inviting persons forward for prayers. O, so many of them were going, the altar was filled in a little while, and though I went in with no intention of going myself, as I sat there all at once,—I can't tell how,—I don't know how,—I never did know how, but when I found myself I was down the aisle and half way up to the altar. All at once it came to me, "There, now, you have always said you would never go forward to an altar, and there you are going."

I thought I would turn around and go back, but as I went to turn facing all the congregation, it was so far to go back, so I rushed forward to the altar, threw myself down and began to pray with all my might: "O, Lord, have mercy on me! O, Lord, have mercy on me! O, Lord, save me," I shouted at the top of my voice, till I was hoarse. Finally I quieted down. There came a stillness over me so quiet. I didn't understand it. The meeting closed. I went home.

If I had known how to exercise faith, I would have found peace that night, but they did not instruct us intelligently, so I was left in the dark. A few days after this I took a service place about a mile and it half from Columbia, with a Quaker family named Robert Mifflins. This was in January. I prayed incessantly, night and day, for light and peace.

After I had got out to Mr. Mifflins', I began to plan for my spring suit; I meant to be converted, though I had not given up at all, but I began to save my money up now. There were some pretty styles, and I liked them. A white straw bonnet, with very pretty, broad pink tie-strings; pink or white muslin dress, tucked to the waist; black silk mantilla; and light gaiter boots, with black tips; I had it all picked out in my mind, my nice spring and summer suit. I can see the little box now where I had put my money, saving up for this special purpose. Then I would pray; O, how I prayed, fasted and prayed, read my Bible and prayed, prayed to the moon, prayed to the sun, prayed to the stars. I was so ignorant. O, I wonder how God ever did save me, anyhow. The Devil told me I was such a sinner God would not convert me. When I would kneel down to pray at night, he would say, "You had better give it up; God won't hear you, you are such a sinner."

Then I thought if I could only think of somebody that had not sinned, and my idea of great sin was disobedience, and I

thought if I could only think of somebody that had always been obedient. I never thought about Jesus in that sense, and yet I was looking to Him for pardon and salvation.

All at once it came to me, "Why, the sun has always obeyed God, and kept its place in the heavens, and the moon and stars have always obeyed God, and kept their place in the heavens, the wind has always obeyed God, they all have obeyed."

So I began, "O, Sun, you never sinned like me, you have always obeyed God and kept your place in the heavens; tell Jesus I am a poor sinner." Then when I would see the trees move by the wind, I would say "O, Wind, you never sinned like me, you have always obeyed God, and blown at His command; tell Jesus I am a poor sinner."

When I set my people down to tea in the house I would slip out and get under the trees in the yard and look up to the moon and stars and pray, "O, Moon and Stars, you never sinned like me, you have always obeyed God, and kept your place in the heavens; tell Jesus I am a poor sinner." One day while I was praying I got desperate, and here came my spring suit up constantly before me, so I told the Lord if he would take away the burden that was on my heart that I would never get one of those things. I wouldn't get the bonnet, I wouldn't get the dress, I wouldn't get the mantilla, I wouldn't get the shoes. O, I wanted relief from the burden and then all at once there came a quiet peace in my heart, and that suit never came before me again; but still there was darkness in my soul. On Tuesday, the 17th day of March. 1856, I was sitting in the kitchen by my ironing table, thinking it all over. The Devil seemed to say to me (I know now it was he), "You have prayed to be converted."

I said, "Yes."

"You have been sincere."

"Yes."

"You have been in earnest."

"Yes."

"You have read your Bible, and you have fasted, and you really want to be converted."

"Yes, Lord, Thou knowest it; Thou knowest my heart, I really want to be converted."

Then Satan said, "Well, if God were going to convert you He would have done it long ago; He does His work quick, and with all your sincerity God has not converted you."

"Yes, that is so."

"You might as well give it up, then," said he, "it is no use, He won't hear you."

"Well, I guess I will just give it up. I suppose I will be damned and I might as well submit to my fate." Just then a voice whispered to me clearly, and said, "Pray once more." And in an instant I said, "I will." Then another voice seemed like a person speaking to me, and it said, "Don't you do it."

"Yes, I will."

And when I said, "Yes, I will," it seeemed to me the emphasis was on the "will," and I felt it from the crown of my head clear through me, "I WILL," and I got on my feet and said, "I will pray once more, and if there is any such thing as salvation, I am determined to have it this afternoon or die."

I got up, put the kettle on, set the table and went into the cellar and got on my knees to pray and die, for I thought I had made a vow to God and that He would certainly kill me, and I didn't care, I was so miserable, and I was just at the verge of desperation. I had put everything on the table but the bread and butter, and I said, "If any one calls me I won't get up, and if the bread and butter is all that is to go on the table, Miss Sue (the daughter) can finish the supper, and that will save them calling for me, and when they come down cellar after it they will find me dead!"

I set the tea pot on the table, put the tea cady down by it, so that everything would be ready, and I was going to die; and O, Hallelujah, what a dying that was! I went down into the cellar and got on my knees, as I had done so many times before, and I began my prayer. "O Lord, have mercy on my soul, I don't know how else to pray." A voice said to me, "That is just what you said before."

"O, Lord, if Thou wilt only please to have mercy on my soul I will serve Thee the longest day I live."

The Devil said, "You might just as well stop, you said that before."

"O, Lord if Thou wilt only convert my soul and make me truly sensible of it, for I want to know surely that I am converted, I will serve Thee the longest day I live."

"Yes," the Devil says, "you said that before and God has not done it, and you might as well stop."

O, what a conflict. How the darkness seemed to gather around me, and in my desperation I looked up and said, "O, Lord, I have come down here to die. and I must have salvation this afternoon or death. If you send me to hell I will go, but convert my soul." Then I looked up and said, "O, Lord, if thou wilt only please to help me if ever I backslide don't ever let me see thy face in peace." And I waited, and I did not hear the old suggestion that had been following me, "That is just what you said before," so I said it again, "O, Lord, if Thou wilt only please to convert my soul and make me truly sensible of it, if I backslide don't ever let me see Thy face in peace."

I prayed the third time, using these same words. Then somehow I seemed to get to the end of everything. I did not know what else to say or do. Then in my desperation I looked up and said, "O, Lord, if Thou wilt help me I will believe Thee," and in the act of telling God I would, I did. O, the peace and joy that flooded my soul! The burden rolled away; I felt it when it left me, and a flood of light and joy swept through my soul such as I had never known before. I said, "Why, Lord, I do believe this is just what I have been asking for," and down came another flood of light and peace. And I said again, "Why, Lord, I do believe this is what I have asked Thee for." Then I sprang to my feet, all around was light, I was new. I looked at my hands, they looked new; I took hold of myself and said, "Why, I am new, I am new all over." I clapped my hands; I ran up out of the cellar, I walked up and down the kitchen floor. Praise the Lord! There seemed to be a halo of light all over me; the change was so real and so thorough that I have often said that if I had been as black as ink or as green as grass or as white as snow, I would not have been frightened. I went into the dining room; we had a large mirror that went from the floor to the ceiling, and I went and looked in it to see if anything had transpired in my color, because there was something wonderful had taken place inside of me, and it really seemed to me it was outside too, and as I looked in the glass I cried out, "Hallelujah, I have got religion; glory to God, I have got religion!" I was wild with delight and joy; it seemed to me as if I would split! I went out into the kitchen and I thought what will I do, I have got to wait till Sunday before I can tell anybody. This was on Tuesday; Sunday was my day in town, so I began to count the days, Tuesday, Wednesday, Thursday, Friday, Saturday, Sunday. O, it seemed to me the days were weeks long. My! can I possibly stand it till Sunday? I must tell somebody, and as I passed by the ironing table it seemed as if it had a halo of light all around it, and I ran up to the table and smote it with my hand and shouted, "Glory to God, I have got religion!" The Lord kept me level-headed and didn't make me so excited I didn't know what I was doing. Mrs. Mifflin was very delicate; she had asthma, and I knew if I said anything to excite her it might kill her, and the Lord kept me so I didn't make any noise to excite her at all. I didn't tell her; didn't feel led to tell her. There was no one in the house at the time, not a soul. She was on the front veranda and I had it all to myself in the kitchen. O, what a day! I never shall forget it; it was a day of joy and gladness to my soul. After I had been converted about a week I was very happy. One morning it seemed to me I didn't know what to do with myself, I was so happy. I was singing an old hymn,—

"O how happy are they, who their Saviour obey,
And have laid up their treasures above;
Tongue can never express the sweet comfort and peace,
Of a soul in its earliest love."

When I got to the verse:—

> "When my heart, it believed, what a joy I received,
> What a heaven in Jesus' name;
> 'Twas a heaven below, my Redeemer to know,
> And the angels could do nothing more
> Than to fall at His feet, and the story repeat,
> And the Lover of sinners adore."

O, how my soul was filled. Just then the enemy whispered to me, "There, you are singing just as if you had religion."

"Well, I have. I asked the Lord to convert me and He has done it."

"How do you know?"

"Well I know He did it, because it was just what I asked the Lord to do, and He did, and I know He did, for I never felt as I do now, and I know I am converted."

"You have a great blessing," the Devil said, "But how do you know that is conversion?"

"Well," I said, "That is what I asked the Lord to do and I believe He did it."

"You know, you don't want to be a hypocrite?"

"No, and I will not be, either."

"But you have no evidence."

"Evidence, evidence, what is that?" Then I thought, I wonder if that is not what the old people used to call the witness of the

Spirit. "Well," I said, "I won't sing, I won't pray until I get the witness." So I began and I held this point; God helped me to hold this point. I said, "Lord I believe Thou hast converted my soul, but the Devil says I have no evidence. Now Lord give me the evidence," and I prayed a whole week. Every now and then the joy would spring up in my heart, the burden was all gone, I had no sadness, I could not cry as I had before, and I did not understand it and so I kept on pleading, "Lord, I believe Thou hast converted me, but give me the evidence, so clear and definite that the Devil will never trouble me on that line again."

Praise the Lord, He did, and though I have passed through many sorrows, many trials, Satan has buffeted me, but never from that day have I had a question in regard to my conversion. God helped me and He settled it once for all.

This witness of God's spirit to my conversion has been what has held me amid all the storms of temptation and trial that I have passed through. O what an anchor it has been at time of storm. Hallelujah, for the Lord God Omnipotent reigneth. Ye shall know if ye follow on to know the Lord. Amen. Amen.

CHAPTER V.

HOW I BOUGHT MY SISTER FRANCES AND HOW THE LORD PAID THE DEBT.

It was in September, 1862. The Union soldiers were stationed all along the line, from Havre de Gras and Monkton, Md. My aunt, my mother's sister, lived about a mile and a half from Hereford, on the old homestead, where my grandmother lived and died. After the death of my mother there were six of us children at home with father. My aunt, who had been married about two years, wanted my father to let one of my sisters go with her to Maryland. She had but one child of her own at that time, and she wanted my sister to be company for her little child, and to look after him, as she worked out by the day very often. So my father gave her my sister Frances, who was then about ten years old. It was not very safe for colored people to pass up and down, but sometimes they could do it without being molested at all. My aunt used to come back and forth once a year to the camp meeting, as many of the colored people, roundabout did. The camp meeting was then called the old Baltimore Camp. It was held on Lowe's camp-ground. My sister was very anxious to go with my aunt. She promised to take very good care of her, so father was quite willing to have her go. She had been there about three years, I think; my aunt then had two children; and my sister took care of them while she would be away at work every day; of course things didn't always go on with children as they should, and then my aunt was very severe on Frances; several times she whipped her very severely, so that the neighbors interfered, and that made unpleasant feelings between the neighbors and my aunt. Word came to my father about it, but he could not go very well, nor did any of the rest feel that we could go; there was so much excitement about the war we did not like to risk it. After the war had begun, these soldiers were stationed, as I have said, and I had made up my mind that I would risk it, and go and see about my sister. Prior to this my aunt had written father that Frances had got very unruly, and when she would whip her she would run away, and that she had gone off somewhere, and he must come and see after her. I was living in Lancaster, Pa., with Col. H. S. McGraw's family. I got six dollars a month. I told Mrs. McGraw about my sister, and told her I thought it was safe for me to go now; that I would be safer under the protection of the Union soldiers. I got her to advance me fifty dollars and I started on my journey down to Monkton. I went to Little York, Pa., and from York to Monkton, Md. I got to my aunt's house about one o'clock in the afternoon. She was not at home. The children were there, and they told me Frances was living with Mr. Hutchinson. Well, I didn't know where Mr. Hutchinson lived, but by inquiring got on the right road. Finally I came to the man who had been magistrate in that part of the country; I wanted to see him, for I had heard in that time my sister had been sold, so I went in to inquire what could be done. My sister was born free—born in Pennsylvania—and my father and mother were free, and I wanted to see what could be done. He told me that Frances had run off from my aunt and come to their house, and as he saw she had been very badly treated, and as she was very kind to the children, his wife thought they would keep her. She came to him for protection. Well, just at that time they were selling black people; everyone they could pick up anywhere that could not prove they were free born, were sold for so much. My aunt was a little vexed, so she did not bother about Frances, and my father could not go and swear for her, consequently she was sold to Mr. Hutchinson for a term of ten years. He told me that all I could do was to see Mr. Hutchinson, and if he would consent to give her up, I could get her by paying him what he paid for her, He said there was nobody to come forward and swear for her, and he saw she was not kindly treated, but that was all he could do about it. He did not take much pains to give me satisfaction. Oh! those were times! However, after he told me what he did, I started for Mr. Hutchinson's. My! how I cried. How I thought of my dear mother. I was all alone. I walked and prayed. I had had nothing to eat all day. I was very hungry. I had passed several farm-houses, and wanted to go in and ask for a drink of water, but I was afraid. Finally I came to a very fine house, standing back from the road; beautiful grounds, green grass and trees, a beautiful white veranda, and an old lady in a white cap, sitting out on the veranda; there was a pump in the yard, with a nice bright tin cup hanging on it; but there was a large dog lying on the stoop, so I stood at the gate a moment; the old lady got up and walked to the end of the veranda, and I called out to her, "Madame, I'm very thirsty; will you please let me come in and get a drink of water?" She said "No, no; go on, go on." I nearly fainted for a moment, and I lifted my heart and said, "Now, Lord, help me, and take away the thirst;" and in an instant every bit of thirst and hunger left me; I had not a bit, no more than if I never had been thirsty. I walked on about a mile further in the sun; I got to Mr. Hutchinson's and saw my poor sister. I don't think I ever saw a heathen in Africa, that looked so much like a heathen as she did. I could hardly speak to her. She was busy at work, and seemed to be happy, but I was not. I told her I had come after her, and to see Mr. Hutchinson. Poor thing, she was so glad to see me!

I don't know how many black people Mr. Hutchinson owned; he was excited over the war; and while he was considered to be a very good man to his black people, yet he was rough when I told him what my errand was. When I told him my sister was freeborn, was not a slave and never had been, he simply said he had nothing to do with that; he had paid forty dollars for her, and he was not going to let her go for less. Well, I didn't know what to do. I cried, but he raved; he swore, and said Frances had not been of any use anyhow. At first he said he would not let her go at all. Then he went into the house. His wife was a very nice woman. How well I remember her. I cried, and cried, and could not stop. I was foolish, but I could not help it. She said something to him. He went into the house, and by and by he came back and said he was not going to let her go for less than forty dollars. Then my sister told me if I would go over to Mrs. Hutchinson's father's (I think his name was Matthews, and he was a Quaker), and see him, she thought he might help me. They were very nice people, and had always been kind to her. It was about a quarter of a mile across the fields. So I went over then and old Mr. Matthews told me I was to go on back, and next morning he would ride over. So, sure enough; next morning the old man came over. He pitied me, I saw, but he could not help me much. Mr. Hutchinson walked up and down and swore. I told Mr. Matthews that I had no money scarcely, and I did not know how to get back if I paid out the forty dollars. I would only have enough to get back to York, and how was I going to get from York to Lancaster, where I lived, and get my sister there besides? Well, Mr. Hutchinson said, he had nothing to do with that. So he told my sister she could get ready and go. I paid him the money. Then she got ready. She went to get her shawl, and he said to her she should not have anything but what she had on. They had given her a shawl, a dress and a pair of great big brogan shoes; and they let her take the dress (a blue cotton striped) she had on; madame had given her a gingham apron; that she was to leave. So we started; just what she stood up in, with one domestic dress under her arm, was all she had. He flourished the horse-whip around so I didn't know but we were both going to get a flogging before we left; but we got out without the flogging. But oh! wasn't he mad! I thanked the Lord for the old Quaker gentleman. But for him it would have been much worse. Then how I prayed the Lord would bless Mrs. Hutchinson. I believe she was good. There were a number of little black children around there, and Mr. Hutchinson was kind to them, and played with them, and put them on the horse and held them on to ride, and they seemed to be very fond of him. But then they were slaves. What a difference it made in his feelings toward them. My sister was free. He had not any business with her, and I had no right to pay him any money; and if I had had as much sense then as I have now, I would not have paid him a cent; I would have just waited till he went to bed, and taken the underground railroad plan. But it is all over now, and my poor sister has long since gone to her reward.

When I came back to Lancaster, to Mrs. McGraw's, she allowed me to bring my sister there, and she helped around with the work till I got her trained somewhat; for she had always worked in the field, and had very little idea about housework. Now I worked, as it were, for a dead horse; for I was in debt to Mrs. McGraw fifty dollars. She paid me my wages regularly, but there was this debt; and with Frances on my hands, I was not able to pay a cent of the fifty dollars. Oh! how it worried me. I hated to think of it; I hated so to have debt. But then I could not help it, and I had no one to help me. My sisters were all poor, and worked hard for themselves. Father was not able to help me. One day Mr. Robert McGraw, Col. McGraw's brother, came to spend some time with them in Lancaster. He was a man that had plenty of means, and was very generous. I was always very glad when Mr. Robert came to see them. I was always sure of two dollars and fifty cents or five dollars when he went away. We dined at three o'clock in the afternoon; had breakfast at nine. Mr. Robert had had his breakfast and gone down town. He went into a bank to get a bill changed. He had four one hundred dollar bills rolled together. He went into the bank and got one bill changed as he went down in the morning. He came back at three o'clock to dinner. After dinner was over he always came out in the kitchen to light his cigar. Mrs. McGraw's son, Henry, a boy of about ten years of age, had a very fine dog, and thought a great deal of him. I was very particular about my kitchen, and they would come out into the kitchen and get to playing, and would sometimes make my kitchen look pretty well upset. Of course I didn't say anything, for Mr. Robert was kind; but I did not like it. Now when he got the bill changed and went to put the three hundred dollars back in his pocket, instead of putting the money into his pocket, he slipped it inside his pants; and strange as it may seem, he had come all the way home and it was not lost on the street. But while he was playing in the kitchen with little Henry after dinner it slipped down and dropped on the floor. It just looked like a piece of paper he had twisted up to light his cigar. I saw it lying there, but did not bother to pick it up at first. He had gone away down street. It was a little rainy. After awhile the dog came running in to go upstairs after Henry. The middle door was shut and he could not got upstairs. As he came back past me I went to give him a send off with my foot, and kicked this roll of paper that lay there. Something seemed to whisper to me, "You had better pick that up and look at it. It might be a twenty dollar bank note." So I picked it up; and Oh, my! In all my born days did I ever have such a surprise. Three hundred dollars! Three one hundred dollar bills on the Baltimore bank! My! But I said, "This is Mr. Robert McGraw's." Mrs. McGraw was very kind, but I knew if I gave it to her that I would not get more than a dollar; but if I kept it and gave it to Mr. Robert I was sure he would give me five dollars. There was no one in the kitchen but myself. The other two servants were upstairs. So I said to myself, "Mr. Robert will be here in a few minutes." This was between half past four and five o'clock in the afternoon. I said nothing to anyone. Mr. Robert did not come till along about six or seven o'clock in the evening. I had not said a word to anybody. The suggestion came to me, "Now this is a good chance for you to get out of debt to Mrs. McGraw. None of these bills are marked, and you can take it to the bank and give it to somebody and you can get that money." I let all these thoughts play through my mind, and then I said, "Now, Mr. Devil, you lie, I don't mean to get into any trouble about that money at all." After awhile I heard some one coming, talking, and I saw two or three persons. Mr. Robert did not come in at the front door; he came around through the yard and came in at the side door. Two boys were with him, and they had lanterns, and they had looked all along the street for this money.

This is the way he missed it. He went into a barber shop to get shaved. After he was shaved he put his hand into his pocket to get the money to pay for it, and found that he had only the money that he had got changed. The other bills were gone. He was very jolly, and said, "I have lost three or four hundred dollars; I don't know which. I will give fifty dollars if I can find it." And of course they were all out looking for it. So he came into the yard.

"What is the matter, Mr. Robert?"

"Amanda," he replied, "I have lost three or four hundred dollars," and then saying a word with two d's in it, he said he didn't know which, and continued looking about with the boys. I said, "My, Mr. Robert, three hundred dollars?"

"Yes, three or four, I don't know which. I will give fifty dollars if I can find it."

As soon as he said, "I will give fifty dollars if I can find it," I said "Mr. Robert, what did you say?"

"I said I will give fifty dollars if I can find it." Then he looked up at me through his glasses, and I said, "I wonder if I can find it," and at the same time reached way down in my pocket.

"Amanda," he said, "did you find it?"

"Hold on; wait till I see." And making a desperate effort I hauled it out. There were the three one hundred dollar bills, My! weren't the boys surprised! He turned right around to the flour chest that stood in the kitchen and counted me out fifty dollars in ten dollar bills.

I got down on my knees right there and then and thanked the Lord, and Mr. Robert said, "Oh, Amanda, it's all right, it's all right; you are welcome to it."

And that is the way the Lord got me out of that debt. "In someway or other the Lord will provide." Amen. Amen.

CHAPTER VI.

MARRIAGE AND DISAPPOINTED HOPES—RETURN TO PHILADELPHIA—A STRANGER IN NEW YORK—MOTHER JONES' HELP—DEATH OF MY FATHER.

After my conversion I continued to live in Columbia, Pa., a year or two; then went to live at Colonel McGraw's in Lancaster, about ten miles from Columbia, where I remained some four or five years. In the meantime the civil war had broken out, and my husband, in common with so many others, enlisted and went South with the army, from which he never returned. From Lancaster I went to Philadelphia, where I remained at service with different families for several years. There I became acquainted with James Smith, a local preacher, to whom I was subsequently married.

When the first few months after my marriage to James Smith had passed, things began to get very unsatisfactory. My husband had one grown daughter, eighteen years of age, by a former marriage, and I had one daughter, about nine years old, by my first marriage. At times, things in the house were very unpleasant. I was greatly disappointed, perhaps I had expected too much of my husband. He was a local preacher and an ordained deacon in the A. M. E. Church. My first husband was not a professing Christian at all, neither was I when I married him. During the years of my widowhood I boarded my little girl, here a while and then there. Sometimes she was well taken care of and at other times was not; for I found that often people do things just for the little money they get out of it; and when I would go and see the condition of my poor child, and then had to turn away and leave her and go to my work I often cried and prayed; but what could I do more? I had not yet learned to trust God fully for all things.

One reason for my marrying a second time was that I might have a Christian home and serve God more perfectly. I thought to marry a preacher would be the very thing, though notwithstanding, I prayed earnestly for light and guidance from the Lord, and I believe, now, he gave it me, but I did not walk in it. How sorry I have been many times since. I told my husband how, since my conversion, I felt it my duty to be an Evangelist. He quite agreed to it all, and told me he was preparing himself to join the Conference and so go into the itinerant work. He explained and reasoned it all so well, and, of course, I had learned to love him, and that went a good ways towards making everything look very plausible, notwithstanding the light the Lord had given me. I said the Lord knows the deep desire of my heart is to work for Him, and I could help my husband so much in his work. I had seen and known the influence of a minister's wife, and how much she could help her husband or hinder him to a great extent in his work. Mr. Smith said that was just the kind of a wife he wanted. I remembered Rev. Joshua Woodland and his wife, how they used to go about among the people and make them feel they were of them, and all who know them loved them; and so with my pastor, Rev. L. Patterson and his wife. She would lead prayer meeting and pray with the sick and dying, and was a beautiful housekeeper with all, and all these just suited me, and I thought how nice it will be to be able to do so much good, and beside to be spoken of as "Rev. Mr. and Mrs. Smith." I thought I saw it clearly, and I said, yet after all, this looks like the Lord's will. At that very hour Satan had gained the victory over me and yet I did not know it was he. After I had given my consent I went to the Lord to have it ratified, but not a ray of light came. I felt sad, but what could I do? I said when the Conference comes and Mr. Smith gets his appointment I will begin work at once with the people, and I will then get light and liberty of soul and will be all right, so this cheered me; but O, the subtilty of Satan, how he can transform himself into an angel of light to deceive even to this day.

The marriage was over and the Conference came. For several weeks prior to the session of the Conference I saw that my husband did not seem to be interested and studious as he had been, and when I would speak to him about it he would be cold and indifferent. O, how indescribably sad I felt; I was frightened. Now I thought if he changes his mind and does not join the Conference, what will I do? I felt I could not stand the disappointment. My heart was sad, yet I tried to hope all through. I watched my husband, but he was still indifferent. One day he came home from the Conference quite out of sorts with the Bishop and all the brethren, and I knew from the way he expressed himself all was up for my good work as a pastor's wife; but I prayed with what spirit was left in me and hoped that at the last things would come out all right. Finally, the Conference closed and the appointments were read. I said to my husband: "Are you not going to-night to hear the appointments?"

"No, I don't want to hear them;" so I went out alone. It seemed to me I could scarcely walk to the church—old Bethel Church, on Sixth street, Philadelphia. I went in, sat down and listened to the long list of appointments read. James Smith's name was not there. I said, can it be I have heard rightly. I saw my mistake, Satan had deceived me. "O, Lord," I said, "what shall I do?" I went home and asked my husband all about it.

I shall never forget how he took me on his lap and kindly put his arm around me and said, tenderly, "My dear, I was afraid to tell you what was really in my heart, I was afraid you would not marry me."

"But how could you deceive me so?"

"I knew it was wrong," he said, "but you will forgive me?"

Of course, I would, and did, but the remembrance was grievous. The Lord sustained me and gave me His grace.

After a year Mrs. Colonel McGraw, with whom I had lived in Lancaster for some four years, came for me to go a few months to Wheatland, Md., where they had moved. They found it difficult to get a cook, and they thought I might go for a few months to get the house settled. After getting the consent of my husband, I took my baby, little Nell, six months old, and my daughter Mazie, and we went for the summer. O, what I went through during those three months! I had to do all the cooking for the house, and eight farm hands, beside helping with the washing and doing up all the shirts and fine clothes and looking after my children. How I did it I don't know. There were but two other servants in the house, chambermaid and waiter, so I had no help only as they were kind enough, at times, to lend a hand. My baby seemed to get along nicely for the first three weeks, then she was taken sick with summer complaint, and in six weeks I had to lay her away in the grave to a wait the morning of the Resurrection. Mrs. McGraw had gone to Lancaster, so was not there. Mr. McGraw was just as kind as he could be to make things as pleasant as possible. He made all the arrangements for the funeral, and bore all the expenses, but, in spite of all, my mother heart was sore and sad. My husband was at Bethlehem Springs and could not get there. Nevertheless, the Lord stood by me. Praise His name for ever and ever. Amen.

In the fall I returned home to Philadelphia, and went out to days' work and took washing, in every way to help my husband. In the course of time the Lord gave me another dear little boy, and I named him after Thomas Henry, whom I loved for his Christian, manly bravery in the dark days of slavery.

He was a member of the M. E. Church, and was a licensed preacher for a number of years at Hagerstown, Md., and left that church and joined the A. M. E. Church in 1834. The stewards and sometimes the preachers, in those days owned slaves, and as one of the stewards of the church he belonged to, sold a poor colored girl away from her child, he was sad about it, knowing them all as he did; so he went to the Presiding Elder and asked him about the clause in the discipline about buying and selling slaves. He told him that he had nothing to do with the Steward's property; and after still further inquiry the same answer was given. Then with Tom Henry forbearance ceased to be a virtue and he said no man whose hand is red with innocent blood shall ever put, the Sacrament in my mouth. He remained a worthy member of the A. M. E. Church, which he served nobly till he fell asleep in Jesus, about ten years ago.

I speak of him because he was a father to me, and so often comforted my heart when I would be almost overwhelmed.

The story of his life ought to be read by every Methodist preacher of to-day, for many of them have forgotten what the fathers had to go through in preparing a church for them to carry forward. What wonderful changes have been since then! Surely, God hath been good to Israel.

In 1865 my husband took it position at Leland's Hotel, and we moved from Philadelphia to New York. We were strangers, I, especially. My husband, James Smith, was a Mason and an Odd Fellow, so in that way knew many more persons than I. The New York people, both white and colored, seemed so different from the Philadelphia people. I could not seem to get into their ways. In Philadelphia my church relations were so congenial and spiritual, but here I was very lonesome. We found it difficult to get rooms. In Philadelphia, you could get a small house to yourself, but rents in New York were high, and there were many things in the way. I hoped my husband would go back again; but no, I must make the best of things till we got started and acquainted. That means something when one goes to New York a stranger, as I did, and with but little money. I took a situation as cook up town, Twenty-fourth street and Lexington avenue, with a Mrs. L. It was a very nice place; there I stayed about two months. My husband got a room in York street, and then I only went out to day's work, still finding the people with whom I met cool and unsocial compared with what they were in Philadelphia. I told my husband I did not like New York. Then he advised me to join some societies, then I would get better acquainted. All the leading high-toned church people were in society; so it was then, and is to-day. Well, I was high-toned in spirit,—always had been; I think I took after the white folks I lived with; they were aristocratic. So I thought that is a good idea and I will get to know all the nice people; so I joined three different societies.

I was greatly disappointed in the spirit that I saw manifested among the members, but I said I will have to get used to things, then it will be better, so I went on for a year. Then there was a new society started called the "Heroines of Jericho." None but Master

Masons' wives and daughters could join it, and this society was very high-toned, and as my husband was a Master Mason, he was anxious for me to join. He came home one night and told me all about it. Nothing would do but I must join this if I let some of the others go.

Well, after some weeks I did, and we had flashy times, all the tinsel regalia and turn out and money spending and show; it took all I could gather to keep up with it, and I had no chance to draw anything, for I had good health and was never sick; but still I must go on paying my dues regularly, as I had begun; and so I did till '68, then after God had sanctified my soul He opened my eyes to see the folly of all this and taught me how to trust in Him, and I came out of every one of them.

The more I prayed about it the clearer God made it to me that all these secret societies are the mothers of selfishness, pride and worldliness. I shall praise God forever that when I asked Him for light on these things He gave it to me, and as I walked in it He led me out into a place of broad rivers. Some of the sisters and brethren visited me and tried to persuade me. They said, "you were just come to where you would be in office, and you have paid so much money in, and you should not leave it now." When I did not yield they turned on me and treated me coolly, and said many unkind things about me. But thank God, I was out to go in no more. I treated everybody very kindly, and did pray for them all, for I knew God would give them light if they only would receive it.

After this I had my trials. My husband could not understand why I should take such a position, but I could not explain, I could only sing,

> "He leadeth me! Oh! blessed thought.
> Oh! words with heav'nly comfort fraught;
> Whate'er I do, where'er I be,
> Still 'tis God's hand that leadeth me."

One morning as I was over the wash-tub my heart was sore. Oh! what a night I had had. I felt I could not bear any more, and I said, O, Lord, is there no way out of this? And as I wept and prayed the Lord sent Mother Jones. I did not want her to catch me crying; I did not believe in telling all my little troubles, but there she was, and I was so full and had suppressed so long that I could hold in no longer. "Well, Smith," she said, "how do you do?"

"O, Mother Jones, I am nearly heart-broken; James is so unkind," and I began to tell all my good works; how I did this and how I did that, and all I could to make things pleasant, and yet he was unkind.

"Well," she said, "that is just the way Jones used to do me, but when God sanctified my soul He gave me enduring grace, and that is what you need; get sanctified, and then you have enduring grace."

"My," I thought, "is that what sanctification means? Enduring grace? That is just what I need; I have always been planning to get out of trials, instead of asking God for grace to endure;" and as she talked on, down deep in my heart I prayed the Lord to make her go so I could get sanctified and get enduring grace, before James came home. O, how I did want her to go! After a while she went.

MR. SAMUEL BERRY, FATHER OF AMANDA SMITH.

MR. SAMUEL BERRY, FATHER OF AMANDA SMITH.

The minute she shut the door I turned the key and ran into the bed-room and got on my knees and prayed, "O, Lord, sanctify my soul and give me enduring grace. O, Lord, sanctify my soul and give me enduring grace."

Oh! how I struggled and wept and prayed. I threw myself on the floor, on my face, then I got up and walked up and down the room, wrung my hands, pulled my hair and cried, "O, Lord, sanctify my soul and give me enduring grace."

I thought if I could only get it before James came home at night, for I could never go through another night like last night, then I would cry, "O, Lord, sanctify my soul and give me enduring grace." So I went on for an hour, and when I got through I did not have the great blessing; God had prepared a better way. I was in such distress that I never thought about faith; I was taken up with my desire and distress when seeking the blessing. Well, I did not get it then, of course, for faith without works is dead, so works, without real faith in God, are dead also.

> "I struggled and wrestled to win it,
> The blessing that setteth me free,
> But when I had ceased all my struggle,
> This peace Jesus gave unto me."

In this connection I will give a brief account of the closing years of my father's life, as doubtless some may desire to know how he who had fought the battle of life so bravely met the last great enemy—death.

After my mother's death my father married again, but his second marriage was not as congenial as the first, and father had got older, and was not patient and forbearing as he ought to have been; and mother's people and children and grandchildren all lived in Baltimore, so that she would be away often for months at a time. Father was old-fashioned, and did not like some of the new methods in church, such as fairs and festivals and the like; so that in speaking against these things, and not in the mildest spirit, I fear, he offended the pastor of the church he belonged to; it was the African Zion Church, called Big Wesley, in Philadelphia, on Lombard street, below Sixth. He was a class leader, but he had incurred the displeasure of the pastor and the people mostly; so things got to be very unpleasant, and his spirit got sour and he left the church.

The Quakers had a mission on St. Mary's street, for the colored people, and they did a great deal of good, and father used to go there regularly; he seemed to enjoy it; they were plain and very kind; they manifested such a kind spirit towards all the colored people, and looked after the poor so nicely in the whiter time. There were large and good Bible classes, and they had excellent teachers. But notwithstanding all this, my father had lost his spiritual life. Oh! how it grieved me to think of it. I wept and prayed for him, and would talk to him sometimes when he would let me; but the old-time people did not want much talk from the children; so I had to be very careful.

After the Lord had sanctified by soul, my burden for my poor father increased! Oh, how sad! I wept, and it seemed that the Lord must save him anyhow, whether or no. But, oh! how I learned that we cannot do anything by trying to drive God. He cannot be driven. "But, oh!" I said, "It is my dear father I want saved, and the Lord can and must save him."

He was working at that time on a large and high building, and I was so afraid if he were to fall and be crippled, or killed; I could not bear to think of it. So I prayed more fervently. One day I had an awful test while I was praying for him in New York; he was in

Philadelphia; and it came to me, "Would you be willing for your father to be lost?" Oh! my blood seemed to curdle at the thought; how I did cry to God. Then it came, "Suppose it was God's will, could you submit?"

"Oh! Lord," I cried, "You made him, and he is yours, and you have a right to do with your own what you please; but oh! save my father."

Then it came, "Suppose you were to hear that he had fallen off that building and was injured for life?" Just then it seemed I saw him fall, and saw the men bring him home, all mangled and bleeding. Oh! what horror! I held my breath, for it seemed it was really so.

"I cannot bear the thought of seeing him suffer," I said. "But, oh, Lord, if there is no other way, then let Thy will be done." And I let go of father and took hold of God; and though I cannot tell how, I rested so sweetly in God. His justice is right. His love is right. Two years after this passed away before my father died; but, oh! how sweetly the Lord seemed to bring him to Himself; took all the harshness out of him; sweetened him down so beautifully. I shall never forget.

I had been home to Philadelphia on it visit, and I had father come around one night to tea before I left; he seemed so changed and different from what he had been; he had been sick for several days, but not in bed. I was not there when he died. The morning he died; he got up as usual, was very weak, but dressed himself, put on all his Sunday clothes, went out and took a walk, came back and read his Bible, and then said to my sister, "I feel so weak, I think I will go upstairs and lie down." And they went up a little while after, and she saw he was dying; not a struggle or a groan. I never had an anxious thought about him from the time I sank down into the will of God. What else ought we to do, when we bring our friends, but to sink into the will of God, and put them into His hands, and trust Him? Amen. Amen.

I had three brothers in the late war. My youngest brother came home sick, and died in the hospital at Harrisburg, in September, '62. I did not hear of his sickness until it was too late. I went at once, but when I got there he was dead and buried two days or more. Oh, what a blow it was to me! He was my favorite brother. He was home on a furlough with his captain, and came to see me. He and I had talked of trying to buy a little home for father. He was rather wild and I wanted him to save his money and send it to me, and I would put mine with it. Poor boy! I wondered why he didn't write after he went away. But he was taken with smallpox and died, and I never saw him again. I saw the men that were with him while he was sick and dying, and his grave; that is all, till the morning of the Resurrection.

My next brother, Samuel Grafton, served three years. He lived at Towanda, Pa., and about a year ago he was drowned.

My oldest brother, William Talbert, served two years in the war, and died about eight or nine months ago at York, Pa. How glad I was that I went to see them all before I went to Africa, and talked and prayed with them, and helped them all I could. Out of a large family of thirteen children, two sisters and myself are all that are living. One of my sisters lives in Brooklyn, N. Y., and the other in San Francisco, Cal.

But I return to the story of my experiences in New York.

The rent in York street was high. We got a room on Broom street. I went out house cleaning then, but my condition was such that I could not get on very well, and after a few months the woman that I had the room with said I would have to move, she was afraid I would be sick, and she could not attend to me, and she was afraid I was not able to get any one. That was true. It took about all I could earn to pay rent and keep up our societies, so I heard that persons in my state were well cared for at the Colored Home. I told my husband I would go there until after my confinement. He consented, as we could get no suitable rooms, and I went; but oh! when I got there and saw how things were I could not stay longer than a week. My husband went to see a friend, Mrs. Harris, a Philadelphia woman. She lived in Grove street. She was taking care of some one's house uptown and was not home at her own house. Her husband only was in at night, so she told my husband I could come there. I went there from the Home.

When my baby was three weeks old I took a situation with a person that seemed to be a real lady; she gave me three dollars a week, with my baby. I had not been in the house long before I saw it was the wrong place. Several girls passing back and forth through the kitchen and laughing and behaving so rudely, I saw that they were not straight. Oh! how sad. I had gone for a week until she could get some one. What shall I do, shall I go? I need the money and I said I will stay this week, so I told the madame I would stay only for a week. She said she was sorry, but if I would only stay she would give me more wages. I told her she must get some one, I could not stay, I would go when my week was up; so when the day came she stayed out of the kitchen all day, and sent orders. Then she went out pretending to look for some one; got back very late, sent word if I would stay till the next day she would pay me, some one had promised to come, so she went on for several days. One night I wailed until nine o'clock; I sent up for the money; she wanted me to stay till morning; I said I will not stay in this house another night, I will leave here to-night if it is not till twelve o'clock. She sent the money, not as she promised, but with cursing. I was glad to take what I got and get out. I went to a friend, Mrs. N., on Sullivan street, and stayed all night; I slept but little. She had a house full of washing, but little room, so she made me a bed an all ironing board and two chairs. Next morning while my baby slept, I felt led to go around and see my old Philadelphia friend, Mrs. Harris, on Grove street, who had now got home again, to see if she could tell me of a room anywhere. On my way back the Lord seemed to direct me and I came through Amity street. I saw in the rear a furnished room to let. I went in. There, I met old Mrs. Anderson, who was very kind and said when I told her who I was, that she had heard her sons, Gus and Peter, speak of me. I had met them years before at Long Branch. She seemed so pleased; it was she that had the basement to let. She let me have the basement at six dollars per month, and I told my husband when he came in the evening from the hotel, and he said he would pay the rent! Oh! how glad I was. I did thank God; I knew He had led me.

There was a carpet on the floor, a good sized stove, a bedstead, three chairs, a table and a lamp. I ran away and got my poor baby and was soon back. It was rather damp and I had never lived in a basement before in my life, but I soon had a good fire, and then when my husband came he was glad and sent the things, what few we had, and in a week or two I began to feel quite at home. Persons began to bring in washing to me, a half dozen, then a dozen, etc., and so I went on. After the first two months Sister A. wanted the carpet off the floor; a day or two later she wanted the table. All right, I said, it was rather inconvenient, but still I gave it. Another month's rent paid. Two or three clays after she wanted the mattress off the bed, and I said, "Sister A., you let the basement furnished for six dollars a month."

"Well," she said, "I can get more than that for it, and I want the mattress."

"All right," I said, and gave it to her. Then I began to guess what New York sharpers meant. Next thing was a chair, then the next was the stove. She said she had a good chance to sell it. I begged her then to let me have the stove a little longer, and in time the Lord helped me and I got a stove. In the meantime some one moved out from the upstairs. I told James, and we moved upstairs. Four rooms at eight dollars a month. I kept two and rented out the two attic rooms, so that helped to pay my rent. Then I began to get in some families' washing and was getting on very nicely, so much better to be upstairs and out of the damp basement, and I was happy. Then a shadow. Little Tom Henry, my baby, was taken sick, and after several weeks of great suffering he died, and we laid him away in Greenwood Cemetery, there to await the glorious Resurrection morn. My poor heart was sad for days, but Oh! how the Lord comforted me and upheld me with all.

I still went on with my washing. Many nights I have stood at my wash-tub all night, from six in the morning till six the next morning, and so at my ironing table, night and day. I would get so sleepy I could hardly stand on my feet, then I would lean my head on the window ledge and sleep a little till the first deep sleep would pass off, then I would work on till daylight with perfect ease. I had to use all the economy I could, and I knew just how much ironing I could do with a ten cent pail of coal. If I lay down I would oversleep myself, and my fire would burn out, and my coal would be gone. I worked hard day and night, did all I could to help my husband, but he was one of those poor unfortunate dispositions that are hard to satisfy, and many a day and night my poor heart ached as I wept and prayed God to help me.

In the next rooms to me, on the same floor, a Mrs. J. lived; she was an old Philadelphian. She had known my husband, and I thought as she was an old Philadelphian, and she seemed so nice, I would have a true friend who would sympathize with me and help me. How often when we are passing through deep trials we look for human sympathy, and lean on the human more than on God. In this I have always failed; but still I had to learn by experience. She was a widow. She and her daughter lived together. I was as kind as I could be, and did all I could for her poor daughter when she was ill. Mrs. J. and I had the same landlady, Mrs. Bowen. She lived in the front house just above Sixth avenue on Amity street. She was far from being a Christian woman, but was kind and lenient about her rent.

We paid her, not always the first day of the month. She would take a dollar at a time just as she could get it and say nothing. Christmas time came. Mrs. B. sent over to ask Mrs. Johnson to come in and cook her Christmas dinner, and she would let it go on the rent, as she was behind, and so it would help her. Mrs. J. said she would do it, but in the evening another party came for Mrs. J. and paid her the cash, notwithstanding she had promised Mrs. B. she would go. She sent her daughter to Mrs. B. and she went where she would get the cash. This displeased Mrs. B. very much, when she considered how lenient she had been with her for so long. The girl was young and could not do the work as well as her mother, and Mrs. B. said, "I will not put up with Mrs. J. any longer; she shall move."

I tried to talk to her as best I could, and told her to see Mrs. J. and not put her out; it might be she would pay up all her back rent. No, she would go to Jefferson Market and have a notice sent her to move.

"Wait," I said, "till she comes home to-night and hear what she says." So when Mrs. J. came I told her she had better go in and see Mrs. B. and not have her send the notice; but to my surprise Mrs. J. was quite spunky, and said if she wanted to send her a notice she could do so.

"Well, Johnson," I said, "you know Mrs. B. has been very kind, and I think you ought to go in anyhow and tell her why you did not come;" but she did not; so Mrs. B. had her summoned before the court of Jefferson Market. Saturday morning came. I had a large basket of gentlemen's shirts to iron. Mrs. J. came in and asked me if I would go to court with her. I said, "J., I have to get these shirts home by one, o'clock; the gentleman is going away, and I have promised, and if I go with you I can't do it." A friend of Mrs. J.'s was there, and I said, "Charlotte, can't you go?"

"Yes," she said, "I am going."

"O," I said, "then you don't need me; there is no use of so many going." She said, "yes."

I went to my work, and thought when they came back they would tell me how they came out; but no, neither of them came near. When I met Mrs. J. in the evening I said, "Good evening,

Mrs. J., is that you?" She did not speak. I was dumbfounded. I said, "That is Mrs. J., I know; but what is the matter?" A week passed. She went and came, and one evening as I was coming in I walked up to her and took hold of her and said, "But say, Johnson, what is the matter?" She pulled away from me, but never spoke a word.

O, how vexed I was at myself. I said the idea of my forcing people to speak to me when they don't want to, and I have done nothing to them. "I will never speak to her again while I live," I said. For two years after, God only knows what I had to undergo through that woman.

She had succeeded in paying up the back rent, and Mrs. Bowen was kind enough to let her stay. She lived next door to me on the same floor. Her daughter would speak, but she, never. Sometimes she would act as though she wanted to, but I was afraid to trust her, as she had acted so rudely before. She used to tantalize me by sending messages to me by people. When it would be my Saturday to scrub the long veranda and down the steps, she would wait on Saturday night till it was all done, and then would throw greasy bread crumbs all over the stoop and steps, and you know how grease will spread on soft pine. I would often cry, but said not a word.

A Sister Brown, to whom I had let my two rooms upstairs, and Mrs. J. got to be very special friends. In the spring I went out house-cleaning, and often when I would come home from work Mrs. B. would come in to talk and have a great story to tell me about what Mrs. Johnson said. I said nothing. I knew if I opened my mouth that both of those dear sisters would wish they were miles away. I prayed God not to let me speak; so one day I got home about four o'clock; a little while after Sister B. came in, so kind, apparently. After talking, she began about what Mrs. Johnson said. I said, "Look here, Sister B., I have no objections if Sister Johnson and you talk about me all you like. I work hard, and though I live beside Mrs. Johnson, I don't live off of her. I I don't owe her a cent"—(and she did owe me, for she had borrowed money from me and never has paid it yet). I said, "You must never tell me anything she says again while you live. I am next door to Mrs. Johnson, and if she wants me to know these things she must tell me herself."

These sisters were both in my own church. So poor Sister B. took offense at what I said and moved into Mrs. Johnson's. Mrs. Johnson moved into her two attic rooms and let Mrs. Brown have the lower rooms. I said nothing, but went on as if nothing had happened. My! what fine cronies they were; but it was not of long duration. After a few months Mrs. B. and Mrs. J. had a terrible falling out, and I had to take Mrs. B. to keep her from being set out in the street; and so had a chance to return good for evil. This greatly changed Mrs. B.'s spirit. We got on nicely till they were able to suit themselves better. Amid all this my soul cried out after God. I would talk to my husband, but he had no sympathy with holiness. He had had advantages far me, and was far more intelligent. He would always want to on this subject, and I could not keep up on that line and it would

throw me back, so I told the Lord one day if He would send James away somewhere till I got the blessing he would never get it away again, but that he hindered me from getting it. I knew he would often go away with his people for a month or two at a time. That was in my mind when I prayed; so, sure enough, in about a week after this prayer I looked out one morning and there came James back. When he came in I said, "My! James, what is up, are the folks going away?"

"No; they have got a young Irishman, just from the old country, a nephew of the cook who has lived in the family for a number of years, and they have taken him at fifteen dollars a month. He has been around me for two weeks, pretending he came to visit his aunt, but I see now he was only taking lessons how to manage the horses."

James got forty dollars, and a reduction to fifteen was a good deal in the employer's pocket. My heart throbbed. "O," I said, "if he should find out I prayed he would blame me," and I was afraid to talk much. He was like a fish out of water when he had no work. It was two weeks before he got a situation. Being a first-class coachman, he would not take less than forty dollars. Finally he got a situation at fifty dollars a month at New Utrecht, with a Mr. Roberts. He had only to drive twice a day. They had fine English horses, and they wanted them well cared for. They gave a comfortable house, rent free, two tons of coal for the winter, and a barrel of flour. This was the first of September. He went and wanted me to go, but having a right young baby I said, "No, James; I have got some nice families' washing in, and you go and try till spring, and I will save up and in the spring we will take a fresh start and we call have our garden and everything." But no, I must go right away. I reasoned every way I could, but he was determined I should go. At last I said, "James, I am afraid to go; you have done me so bad right here where I have just begun to get used to the people, and know how to turn around, and what will it be if I go there out in the country, no church near, and a stranger, and if I give up my washing what will I do? I can help myself a little now." But this did not please him, and I told him I would wait till spring.

The landlady died, and a new landlord raised the rent,—thirteen dollars. He paid the rent, but would do no more. His daughter was married and lived in Philadelphia, so he sent for them to come on and live

in the house, and he lived with them and would come home every other Sunday and stay till Monday. He came home regularly every fortnight. I said, "Now, Lord, while James is away do please give me the blessing I seek. I will be true, I will never let anything he may say or do get the blessing away from me."

One day while cleaning up my room I distinctly heard a voice say to me, "On Sunday morning go to Green Street Church and hear John Inskip."

"Yes," I said, "I will."

Then came such a quiet hush all over me, and I smiled. This was on Wednesday morning. So I went on thinking it over. Now, I was not definitely seeking the blessing as I had been. I thought when an opportunity offered and I could be baptized and come up to the Bible standard, then the Lord would have to sanctify me. How blind I was!

CHAPTER VII.

THE BLESSING—ABOUT SEEKING SANCTIFICATION BY WORKS.

I always got up as early on Sunday mornings as on other mornings. I got my breakfast, and cleaned up my house, and at nine o'clock my little Mazie went to Sunday School. While she was gone I would cook all my dinner and get everything ready. I did I not have time to cook much through the week, as I had often to dry my clothes in the house and I could not have the smell of cooking, so Sunday was the only day I would have a real good dinner, but I never stayed home from church to cook—so I gave my baby his bath and laid him in his cradle, then I got down on my knees and prayed the Lord to keep Will asleep till I went to Green Street Church, and to keep James in a good humor so he would not scold me, for I hated to be scolded, in the worst way. James was peculiar. If he came and I happened to be out, even though I went to carry clothes, he would be vexed. So after Mazie came I said, "Now you read your library book and be a good girl, I am going to Green Street Church this morning; it lets out before our church does, so I will be home in time. You can tell your pa, if he comes before I get back. If Will cries, don't take him up; just rock him."

She was a good strong girl, thirteen years old, quite able to take care of him and could manage him quite as well as I could, so I went and left them. On my way to Green street, it seemed the Devil overtook me. Just as I turned in Carmine street, I felt a Satanic influence walking by my side and whispering, "Now, you know, if James comes home and finds you are out, you know what you, will catch; you had better go to Bedford Street and hear John Cookman."

"Well, I will."

So when I got to the corner and was just going to turn down Bleecker street, a voice said, "No, go on." I went on. After I had gone about half a block Satan whispered again, "You are seeking sanctification?"

"Yes."

"Well, if James comes home and you are out, he will be very angry, and that will be a sin and you should not make anybody sin."

"No," I said, "I will not do it."

Then Satan said, "You had better go and hear that Presbyterian minister on the corner of Houston and Prince streets." I had heard how kind they were to colored people and I had promised several times I would go and hear this minister; the Devil had found that out some way; I can't tell how he knew it, but he did. "You had better go and hear him; then, it is nearer home, three blocks nearer, and you can get home quick."

"Yes," I said, "that is so."

When I got to the corner, as I was about to turn down, with a gentle pull a sweet voice whispered, "No, no, go on."

"Lord, help me!"

Oh, how will I ever praise God enough for His tender love and faithfulness to me in that awful hour. He gave power to my fainting spirit, and when I had no might, He increased strength. Hallelujah! Hallelujah! Praise the Lord!

I went on a little further and by and by the enemy seemed to approach me again fiercely He said, "Now, you are the biggest fool that ever was. You think you are going to hear John Inskip; he is not there, he is at the Five Points."

"O, if I thought Brother Inskip was not there, I would not go. I would go back."

I went on. When I reached the steps I shall never forget the thrill of joy that ran through my heart when I heard Brother Inskip pray. With what strength I had left I said, "Thank God, he is here and not it the Five Points." I seemed to feel the Satanic presence sweep by me and say, "O, she has found it out." Old Satan knew I had caught him in one of his biggest lies. I went into the church and sat down about three seats from the door. I had been to that church but once before and that was Brother Inskip's first Sunday. While I lived in York street I was very sick and could not walk away up to Sullivan Street Bethel Church where I belonged, so I went in there that Sunday. I sat in the

gallery. The people were so kind; one brother handed me a book and asked me to come again. I thank God for that spirit that was in Green street those days, even to colored people. The Sunday I got the blessing I did not sit upstairs, but O, how tired I was when I got into the church. I leaned my head forward and prayed God to give me strength. When Brother Inskip had finished his prayer he rose and made his announcements; the last hymn was sung, then came the text:— Ephesians, 4th Chapter 24th Verse,—"And that ye put on the new man, which after God is created in righteousness and true holiness." He said, "In preaching from this text this morning the brethren will observe I shall have to make some reference to a sermon that I preached a few Sabbaths ago on sanctification."

I was struck, for I had never heard a minister say that word in commencing his sermon before, and I said, "O, I have missed my chance; two Sabbaths ago I had such a drawing to come here and I did not do it; O, Lord, I have disobeyed that spirit and I am so sorry; do forgive me and help me, I pray Thee."

O, how I wept, for I had lost my chance and I am so hungry for the blessing; but, "Lord forgive me and help me to listen now."

I raised my head and fixed my eyes and thoughts on the speaker and got so interested it seemed he was preaching right to me, and I took every word. By and by I heard my baby scream out,—I heard him scream as distinctly as ever I heard a child scream. "You told Mazie not to take that child up, but she has done it and let him fall," Satan suggested.

For a moment the actual thing did occur, and it was before my eyes. My heart stood still and a voice said, "Trust the Lord."

"I will," I said, and fixed my mind again and listened, and as dear Brother Inskip warmed up and I was feasting, my baby screamed out again. I jumped, and it seemed that all the people in the church heard; it was so plain.

"There," the Devil says, "James has come home and Mazie has not done as you told her, and you will catch it when you get home."

O, I felt if I had wings I would fly. I wanted to scream out. A sweet voice said, "You said you would trust the Lord."

"So I did," I said, so I sat back and was listening and drinking in and thought all was well now. Again I heard my baby scream.

"There," said the Devil, "Mazie has let him fall and broken his back," and I got up and walked to the end of the pew.

"It is no use," I said, "I shall be tormented here; I will go home." And it was as though a person stood before me and said, "Didn't you say that you would trust the Lord with that child?"

"Yes," I said, "and I will trust the Lord, even if he is dead;" and I sat down. Just as I sat down Brother Inskip said: "There are a great many persons who are troubled about the blessing of sanctification; how they can keep it if they get it."

"Oh!" I said, "he means me, for that is just what I have said. With my trials and peculiar temperament and all that I have to contend with, if I could get the blessing how could I keep it? Now, some one has told him, for he is looking right at me and I know he means me." And I tried to hide behind the post, and he seemed to look around there. Then I said, "Well, he means me, and I will just take what he says." He used this illustration: "When you work hard all day and are very tired,—"Yes," I said, and in a moment my mind went through my washing and ironing all night,—"When you go to bed at night you don't fix any way for yourself to breathe,"—"No," I said, "I never think about it,"—"You go to bed, you breathe all night you have nothing to do with your breathing, you awake in the morning, you had nothing to do with it."

"Yes, yes, I see it."

He continued: "You don't need to fix any way for God to live in you; get God in you in all His fullness and he will live Himself.

"Oh!" I said, "I see it." And somehow I seemed to sink down out of sight of myself, and then rise; it was all in a moment. I seemed to go two ways at once, down and up. Just then such a wave came over me, and such a welling up in my heart, and these words rang through me like a bell: "God in you, God in you," and I thought doing what? Ruling every ambition and desire, and bringing every thought unto captivity and obedience to His will. How I have lived through it I cannot tell, but the blessedness of the love and the peace and power I can never describe. O, what glory filled my soul! The great vacuum in my soul began to fill up; it was like a pleasant draught of cool water, and I felt

it. I wanted to shout Glory to Jesus! but Satan said, "Now, if you make a noise they will put you out."

I was the only colored person there and I had a very keen sense of propriety; I had been taught so, and Satan knew it. I wonder how he ever did know all these little points in me, but in spite of all my Jesus came out best. As we colored folks used to sing in the gone by years:

> "Jesus is a mighty captain,
> Jesus is a mighty captain,
> Jesus is a mighty captain,
> Soldier of the cross."

> "Jesus never lost a battle,
> Jesus never lost a battle,
> Jesus never lost a battle,
> Soldier of the cross."

Hallelujah! Hallelujah! Amen.

I did not shout, and by-and-by Brother Inskip came to another illustration. He said, speaking on faith: "Now, this blessing of purity like pardon is received by faith, and if by faith why not now?"

"Yes," I said.

"It is instantaneous," he continued. "To illustrate, how long is a dark room dark when you take a lighted lamp into it?"

"O," I said "I see it!" And again a great wave of glory swept over my soul—another cooling draught of water—I seemed to swallow it, and then the welling up at my heart seemed to come still a little fuller. Praise the Lord forever, for that day!

Speaking of God's power, he went on still with another illustration. He said: "If God in the twinkling of an eye can change these vile bodies of ours and make them look like his own most glorious body, how long will it take God to sanctify a soul?"

"God can do it," I said, "in the twinkling of an eye," and as quick as the spark from smitten steel I felt the touch of God from the crown of my head to the soles of my feet, and the welling up came, and I felt I must shout: but Satan still resisted me like he did Joshua. But the Captain of the Lord's host stood close by and said, "Take off the filthy garments from him," and Satan was mad. again I yielded to the tempter and did not shout. Then I felt the Spirit leave me. I knew He had gone, and I said: "O, Holy Ghost, if Thou wilt only return I will confess Thee." I am so

glad God put the word confession in my mouth. I thought I would get ready, so when the Spirit came again I would shout; but before I knew it just as though some one threw a basin of water in my face, a great wave came and just as I went to say "Glory to Jesus!" the Devil said, "Look, look at the white people, mind, they will put you out," and I put my hands up to my mouth and held still, and again I felt the Spirit leave me and pass away.

Then Satan said: "Now, you have lied to the Holy Ghost, for you said if the Holy Ghost returned you would confess Him, and He did return and you didn't confess, and you have lied to the Holy Ghost."

O, shall I ever forget the horror of that hour? I thought I had committed an unpardonable sin, so was doomed forever. All hope was gone, and a horror of darkness swept upon my spirit. For about five minutes it seemed to me I was in hell, but somehow, I don't know how, I said, "Well, I know the Lord has sanctified my soul"—I felt so sure of it —"and I will go home to my church and give the witness."

Just then Satan says: "They will not believe you because you did not get the blessing there."

Then I knew there was a little jealousy and prejudice among some, so I said: "Well, no matter, I know the Lord has sanctified my soul, anyhow." And I went to get up to go out, but could not stand on my feet. O, I was so weak. My head seemed a river of waters and my eyes a fountain of tears. I put my hand in my pocket to get my handkerchief, but I could not get it out. Just then they arose to sing the closing hymn, that blessed hymn, "My latest sun is sinking fast." I tried to get up, but could not; then the Devil says, "No one knows you here, and they will think you are drunk."

"Lord, what shall I do," and a voice seemed to whisper in my left I ear, for Satan stood at my right, and would whisper his suggestions: "Pray for strength to stand up." I took hold of the pew in front of me and trembling from head to foot I stood up, but held on to the pew. Just as I got fairly on my feet they struck the last verse of the hymn,

> "Oh! bear my longing heart to Him,
> Who bled and died for me.
> Whose blood now cleanseth from all sin,
> And gives me victory."

And when they sang these words, "Whose blood now cleanseth," O what a wave of glory swept over my soul! I shouted glory to Jesus. Brother Inskip answered, "Amen, Glory to God." O, what a triumph for our King Emmanuel. I don't know just how I looked, but I felt so wonderfully strange, yet I felt glorious. One of the good official brethren at the door said, as I was passing out, "Well, auntie, how did you like that sermon?" but I could not speak; if I had, I should have shouted, but I simply nodded my head. Just as I put my foot on the top step I seemed to feel a hand, the touch of which I cannot describe. It seemed to press me gently on the top of my head, and I felt something part and roll down and cover me like a great cloak! I felt it distinctly; it was done in a moment, and O what a mighty peace and power took possession of me! I started up Green street. The streets were full of people coming from the different churches in all directions. Just ahead of me were three of the leading sisters in our church. I would sooner have met anybody else than them. I was afraid of them. Well, I don't know why, but they were rather the ones who made you feel that wisdom dwelt with them. They were old leading sisters, and I have found that the colored churches were not the only ones that have these leading consequential sisters in them. Well, as I drew near, I saw them say something to each other, and they looked very dignified. Now, the Devil was not so close to me as before; he seemed to be quite behind me, but he shouted after me, "You will not tell them you are sanctified."

"No," I said, "I will say nothing to them," but when I got up to them I seemed to have special power in my right arm and I was swinging it around, like the boys do sometimes! I don't know why, but O I felt mighty, as I came near those sisters. They said, "Well, Smith, where have you been this morning?"

"The Lord," I said, "has sanctified my soul." And they were speechless! I said no more, but passed on, swinging my arm! I suppose the people thought I was wild, and I was, for God had set me on fire! "O," I thought, "if there was a platform around the world I would be willing to get on it and walk and tell everybody of this sanctifying power of God!"

> "Of victory now o'er Satan's power,
> Let all the ransomed sing,
> And triumph in the dying hour
> Through Christ the Lord our King."

> "Oh! it was love,
> 'Twas wondrous love,
> The love of God to me,
> That brought my Saviour from above,
> To die on Calvary."

Somehow I always had a fear of white people—that is, I was not afraid of them in the sense of doing me harm, or anything of that kind— but a kind of fear because they were white, and were there, and I was black and was here! But that morning on Green street, as I stood on my feet trembling, I heard these words distinctly. They seemed to come from the northeast corner of the church, slowly, but clearly: "There is neither Jew nor Greek, there is neither bond nor free, there is neither male nor female, for ye are all one in Christ Jesus." (Galatians 3:28.) I never understood that text before. But now the Holy Ghost had made it clear to me. And as I looked at white people that I had always seemed to be afraid of, now they looked so small. The great mountain had become a mole-hill. "Therefore, if the Son shall make you free, then are you free, indeed." All praise to my victorious Christ!

> "He delivered me when bound,
> And when wounded, healed my wound.
> Sought me wandering, set me right,
> Turned my darkness into light."

Hallelujah! Hallelujah! Praise the Lord!

When I got home I opened the door; the baby was still asleep. I said: "Mazie, has Mr. Smith come?"

"No."

"Has Will slept all right?"

"Yes, he has not wakened up at all."

"Well, the Lord has sanctified my soul this morning," and she said, "Has he, mother?"

"Yes," I said, "and I want to go around and tell Auntie Scott." She was my good band sister. She lived in Clinton court, off Eighth street. When I got to the door, I knocked and opened at the same time. Brother Scott was lying on the sofa; he was assistant class leader to Brother Henry De Schield's, who was my leader. He believed in the doctrine of holiness, but had not the experience at that time, but, thank God, he believed in it and said

nothing against it, so that was in my favor. Brother Scott was "on the fence," sometimes he would seem to believe in it and talk as though he had it, at another time he would oppose it bitterly, so you never knew just when he would turn on you. When I went in that morning, I said: "Pop Scott, the Lord has sanctified my soul this morning."

He raised himself up, and said: "Did—did He?" (He stammered a little.) I did not wait for any more, I began to sing an old hymn that I had often heard sung in our love feasts and class meetings in the gone-by days, which seemed to be the real song of my soul. I had never felt such soul union with Jesus before in my life; so I sang:

> "I am married to Jesus
> For more than one year,
> I am married to Jesus
> For during the war."

The old man looked at me and smiled and got ready for an argument. The children all looked astonished. Sister Scott had not come in from church. When I had finished the verse, I said, "Good morning," and as I opened the door to go out, Sister Scott was just coming in. I said; "Oh, Scott! the Lord has sanctified my soul this morning."

I thought she would be so glad for she told me that years before in Canada, she had got the blessing through Mrs. Dr. Palmer. She never spoke of it definitely and clearly, so I never understood anything about it, but to my great surprise she very coolly said, "Well I hope you will keep it," and passed right in by me, and said not another word. I went out. Oh, what a shock!

"There," the Devil says, "She don't believe you have got the blessing."

"O Lord," I said, "Can it be that I am mistaken and will I have to go back and go all over the ground. I would rather die right here in my tracks."

As I was turning out of Eighth street in Sixth avenue, I cried out, "O Lord, help me, and if this blessing is not sanctification, then what is it?" And the Lord did help me. Quick these words came with power to my heart: "It is the power of God unto salvation to everyone that believeth." "Believeth," seemed to be so powerfully emphasized, and I said, "Lord, I do believe that Thou hast sanctified my soul," and the power of God came upon me so that my knees gave way under me and I dropped as though I were shot, right on Sixth avenue. The people were passing and looked at me and said nothing. I suppose they thought I was a little gone in the head, but God had turned my captivity and my mouth was filled with laughter. I scrambled up as best I could, for I did not fall prostrate, my knees gave way and I dropped on my hands, and every time I said the word which the Lord put in my month: "It is the power of God unto salvation to every one that believeth," another wave of power came upon me. Down I went again, and so three times, before I got home, I fell under the mighty power of God. Hallelujah! It is to-day the same, "The power of God unto salvation to every one that believeth," and I do believe God, and He has kept me saved magnificently. Hallelujah! There is a big triumph in my soul. I don't know where the Devil went, but I heard no more of him for a week, then he called on me and said, "When people get sanctified, everything gets better around them."

"Yes," said I."

"Well, you see James is not any better, if anything he is worse."

That was true, if possible, and I said I did think so too, and didn't understand it, for I thought he would be glad to know that I had got more religion.

"Then," said he, "You have no witness that you are sanctified."

"Well," I said, "I will have it, God helping me, right now."

It was Friday. I was ironing; I set down my iron and went and told Jesus. I said; "Lord, I believe Thou hast sanctified my soul, but Satan says I have no witness. Now, Lord, I don't know what to ask as a direct witness to this blessing, but give me something that shall be so clear and distinct that the Devil will never attack me again on that point while I live."

After a short prayer I waited a moment in silence, and said, "Now, Lord, I wait till Thou shalt speak to me Thyself," and a moment passed and these words came: "Ask for the conversion of Miss Chapel."

I said, "Lord, for a real evidence that Thou hast sanctified my soul, I ask that Thou will convert Miss Chapel between now and Sunday morning."

In a moment these words were flashed through my soul: "If thou canst believe all things that are possible to him that believeth." And I said, "Lord, I believe Thou will do it," and a flood of light and joy filled me. Oh, I praise the Lord. I arose from my knees praising God. I went to ironing; after a little while, Satan came again.

"You ought to go and see if the woman is converted before you are so sure."

"Well, yes, I would like to go, but then it is two miles away, and I am afraid Will might wake up and cry."

But the enemy urged me, "You had better not be too sure, you ought to go and see," and I was sorely tempted. I lifted my heart to God in prayer and said, "Lord help me, I believe that Thou wilt do it, and I will trust Thee." Then there came a still hush and quiet all over me and I went on ironing and singing. Praise the Lord!

Miss Chapel, referred to, was a very nice young woman, though not a Christian. She was a very upright, moral person. She was taken ill, and her sister, a very earnest Christian, was very anxious about her state, and asked me and others to come and pray with her. One day I went, and met Mother Jones and several others.

We sang and prayed with her and left her. And now a week had passed and I had not heard from her, and I had thought that was why the enemy attacked me so fiercely on Friday. Sunday morning came and I had persisted in believing and praising God, according to His word: "If thou canst believe all things are possible to him that believeth." I went to church, and as I sat in my pew after the sermon was over, and the collection was being taken up, Sister Jones, who sat in the opposite pew, got up and came over to me, and said "Smith, Chapel has got the blessing." I said, "Praise the Lord, when did she get it?" She said, "Yesterday afternoon." Then these words were spoken to my heart in power: "Now that is your evidence," and I said, "O Lord, I do thank Thee, Thou hast answered my prayer and given me this distinct witness that Thou hast sanctified my soul."

Many times since then my faith has been tried sorely, and I have had much to contend with, and the fiery darts of Satan at times have been sore, but he has never, from that day, had the impudence to tell me that God had not done this blessed work. Hallelujah! what a Saviour!

Everybody does not have direct witness to their sanctification nor to their justification in that way, but it is their privilege to have the clear, distinct witness of the Spirit to both justification and sanctification, and, as a rule, persons who do not get this distinct witness are unsettled in their Christian life, often waver and falter, and are more easily turned aside to new isms and doctrines; but, thank God, He has kept me in perfect peace while my mind has been stayed on Him and I have trusted in Him. Praise His name forever!

James did not come home for two weeks. When he came I sat down on his lap and put my arms around his neck and told him all about it. He listened patiently. When I got through he began his old argument. I said, "Now, my dear, you know I can't argue."

"O well," he said, "If you have got something you can't talk about, I don't believe in it."

"Well," I said, "I have told you all I can and I cannot argue." O, how he tantalized me in every way, but God kept me so still in my soul, and my poor husband was so annoyed because I would not argue. I knew what it meant, but praise God he saved me. I could only weep and pray.

Shortly after I was converted, I was deeply convicted for the blessing of heart purity; and if I had had any one to instruct me, I can see how I might have entered into the blessed experience. But not having proper teaching, like Israel of old, I wandered in the wilderness of doubts and fears, and ups and downs, for twelve years; and but for the Rev. John S. Inskip's having the experience himself, and preaching that memorable Sunday morning, September, 1868, in the old Green Street Church, New York, in all probability I might never have got into the blessed light of full salvation.

I shall ever thank God that the evidence of my acceptance with Him was so definite and clear when I was so deeply convicted for the blessing of heart purity. It was a hard struggle, anyhow; but if this point had not been settled so clearly it would have been much worse—the difference between the two convictions, pardon and purity. When I was convicted for sin I was under condemnation, and felt that I was a lost and wretched sinner. Now, when God in mercy had pardoned all my sins, he took away all condemnation and gave me joy and peace in believing. Hallelujah!

Now, when I was convicted for purity or sanctification, it was a deep conviction of want—an indescribable want; not condemnation. But, oh! that deep heart want. Like, after you have eaten a good hearty breakfast, and have worked hard all day, and get very hungry for your dinner or supper. Well, my heart cried out and longed as one that "Longeth for the morning." And yet I had no means, no words to express just what I wanted. One day a friend came in to see me. I was then living at Col. S. McGraw's, in Lancaster. She was quite a high-toned colored lady, for everyone knew the Porter family, and they were always considered one of the leading families among the colored people. The father was a large farmer in Kent county, and the sons were all fine young men, and pretty well educated, as was also the daughter. She had been a school teacher for many years, but was now married to Rev. Lewis Hood, who was pastor of the Union Church in Lancaster. So I thought I could open my heart to her, and she would be able to help me. So I said to her, "Sister Hood, I don't know what's the matter with me. Somehow I feel like I wanted something, but I can't tell just what. I pray, but I do not get help just as I want."

"Well," she said, "What's the matter with you? Aren't you converted?"

"Oh! yes," I said, "It isn't that."

"Well, haven't you got the witness of the Spirit?"

"Oh! yes; it isn't that."

"Well," she said, "If you keep on you will be crazy."

Then I was frightened, and said, "Oh! she does not understand me; and now if she tells anybody what I said they will not understand it, and will think I have backslidden; and here I am leading class, and the leader of the female prayer meeting."

So as soon as she was gone I ran down into the cellar and got down on my knees, and asked the Lord to take out of the mind of Sister Hood all that I had said, so she would not repeat it. I was in sore distress.

Several days after this I was reading my Bible, and I turned to the forty-second Psalm, first verse, "As the heart panteth after the water brook, so panteth my soul after the living God." My heart leaped. "Oh!" I said, "That's what I wanted—God! Now if anyone asked me what I wanted, as Sister Hood did, I could tell them it was God I wanted." The more I read my Bible, and fasted and prayed, the deeper my hunger became. One day I went

to George James—I generally called him "Father James"—he was a tall, elderly man, very dignified in manner, but was kind. He was very black, his hair was while, and he was a leading local preacher, and deacon of the A. M. E. Church, in Lancaster, at that time, where I belonged. So I went to him, and I said: "Father James, I have been reading the Bible to-day, and I see this: 'Blessed are the pure in heart, for they shall see God.' What does that mean?"

"You know," he said, "That is in the Bible for you to come as near to it as you can. But God knows you never can be 'pure in heart.'"

Then he went on and explained to me in his way. Of course I did not get much light. And the Devil said to me as I went home thinking it all over, "You are seeking after something that's not for you."

"Well," I said, "People do have this blessing. There are Job Morris, and Polly Waters, and others, and they say they are sanctified, and everybody believes them."

"Oh! but they are almost ready to die. But you are young, and you cannot expect to have what they have."

"Well, perhaps so," I said.

"Then, you know, Father James said that the Bible did not mean that." But somehow my better judgment said he was wrong. "I believe what the Bible says, and there must be some way that this grace can be obtained, or God never would have left it on record." But how to get hold of it I still did not know. I would read my Bible, and pray, and pray on. No light—only the deep hunger. Of course I had comfort in doing my duty— attending my class meeting and prayer meetings, and I would go about and pray with the sick and dying, and work in revival meetings, and in all ways I could. After working hard all day many times I would be called up at twelve or one o'clock at night to go and pray with somebody that was sick or dying. I never refused to go, rain or shine, cold or warm; I felt it was my duty, and I was always glad to do it. Then I would come home,— sometimes at three o'clock—and have but very little sleep, and up and off to work again next morning, when I did not have work in the house. My meat and drink was to see souls coming to Christ. I had no fear to go into a congregation and speak to men or women, young or old. I hardly ever went for persons in a congregation, in time of extra meetings, but what they went forward, and many of them were converted. Praise God forever!

And yet at times my spirit was vacillating. Sometimes high on the mountain. When I would tell of the rapture and joy I felt, sometimes the older brethren and sisters would say, "Ah, child, I was that way, too, when I first got converted; but you wait till the Devil shoots a few bomb-shells at you and you will not have so much joy." Poor me! I tried to look out for these bomb-shells. Oh! why didn't they tell me of the land of corn and wine and oil, and that the God of Caleb and Joshua was able, and would bring me in if I would only trust in Him? But, dear souls, they did not know it themselves, so could not help me. So one day I felt I must go and talk with Father James, for I had been reading the fourth chapter of second Thessalonians and third verse, "For this is the will of God, even your sanctification." So I said, "Father James, I have been reading the Bible to-day, and I see this." Then I quoted the text.

"Oh!" he, said, "my child, don't you know when people die very happy?"

"Yes," I said.

"Well, you know, God does not sanctify you until just before you are ready to die. Of course you could not go to heaven unless you were holy, and sanctification makes you holy, and you could not live in this sinful world if you were holy. So if you were sanctified you would die."

"Yes," I said. "Well, if it is going to kill me, I don't want it. I don't want to die. The Lord has done a great deal for me. I can do a little for Him; so I will just go on and do the best I can." So on I went.

Sometime after this I was reading the fifth chapter of Matthew, and when I got to the eleventh and twelfth verses I said, "My experience does not come up to this: 'Blessed are ye when men shall revile you and persecute you, and shall say all manner of evil against you falsely for my sake.' 'Rejoice and be exceeding glad, for great is your reward in heaven.' I cannot rejoice when anyone lies on me; it's no use; I can't do it." Then came up all my good works. "I go to church; I attend to all my duties; I do not go about meddling with other people's affairs; I mind my own business; and when anybody says anything about me that is not true, I must have satisfaction. I am not going to stand it." I had not read, "They that love God in Christ Jesus shall suffer persecution." But, Oh! haven't I learned it since then. One day one of the dearest friends I had, as I thought, told a real lie on me. It made quite a stir. I wondered where all the coolness came about in different directions but did not know the real cause. So I made up my mind I would go and ask the parties what the matter was. So I got down and prayed that the Lord would give me the right spirit, and not let me get vexed, and not let the parties get vexed, and make them tell me what the matter was. So off I started a little after nine o'clock in the morning. I walked till about two o'clock in the afternoon, and found myself about as near the truth when I stopped as when I started. The first place I called I said to the friend, calling her by name, "I hear so and so; I came to ask you what about it?"

"All I know," she replied, "is what John B. said that Mary S. said that you said that I said that she said," and so on.

Well, I went to the next parties. They said the same thing: "Well, all I know about it is Ann So and So said that you said that she said that I said that they said," etc. I went the round, then started home, so ashamed and disgusted. As soon as I got home I took off my wraps, went down into the cellar and got down on my knees, where I always went to settle hard difficulties, and I said, "Oh! Lord, if you will help me, I will never, while I live, go after another lie." And thank God I never have, though sometimes I have been tempted; but the Lord has always delivered me. Praise His dear name! Amen.

Some months after this I got interested in the subject of baptism, and I thought if I were immersed it would help me to see the way better. So I went to Father James and told him I would like to be immersed. My father and mother had all of us children baptized, as the discipline of the Methodist Church required; but I thought if I could answer for myself it would be better. Then if I camp up to all that the Bible said as far as I knew, the Lord would be obliged to give me the great blessing I sought. Father James did not discourage me in this, but rather was favorable. So this helped me to think that I was on the right track now. There were four or five others who wanted to be immersed also; so I went around to see them, and it was decided to send to Philadelphia for a good brother and local preacher in the African Methodist Church, a sanctified man named Brother Jones. Some years before there was a great revival in Columbia, and some six or eight of the converts wanted to be baptized. So they sent to Philadelphia and got Rev. Bob Collins, who was a powerful preacher in his day, and a leading minister in the A. M. E. Church. It was in the dead of winter. The Susquehanna river was frozen over, and they cut the ice, and Brother Collins baptized eight, I think it was. And they shouted and sang. They stood on the shore, and all around on the ice by hundreds. It was six o'clock in the morning. Oh! what a time! Of course all the Baptists believed in that, and they were out, and rejoiced with them that did rejoice. Our minister at that time was Rev. Sanford. His wife's sister, Henney Johnson, had been very sick, and she had got converted. But she leaned toward the Baptists. So to save her to her church, she was baptized that Sunday, and she got well after that, which was a great wonder to many. Sister Harriet N. Baker was one of the strong members in the church. She was baptized the same Sunday morning. Lancaster was only twelve miles from Columbia, so that we in Lancaster got water struck! For most all the colored people in Lancaster would go to Columbia to quarterly meeting. Oh! how I have seen the power of God displayed in the salvation of souls. What men and women they were to pray in those days. How I remember Candes Watson, Sarah Henderson, Chris Stokes, Simon Morris, John Morris, Jake Snively, and a host of others. How they come before me now, as I think it all over. But all these have gone, though it seems but as yesterday.

But to return to my story. After I had seen the parties I went to Father James and asked him to write to Brother Jones and find out what the cost would be. He replied that we were to pay him twenty dollars and his traveling expenses from Philadelphia and back. I was willing to pay him a month's wages, which was six dollars, if the others would make up the balance. So they were to try. A few weeks passed, then one of the leading ones in the number, Sister Maxwell, was taken sick, and her husband would not let her go into the water. Brother Williams went away. I had got my dress ready, but the others all backed out. Then Father James was taken sick. So he said that March was a bad month to go into the water, so if I would wait until April or May he would perform the ceremony. But alas! Poor man! About the first of April I stood by his bedside and saw him die, and heard his last words.

It was Sunday evening, and after I had come from church I went to sit with Sister James, his wife. It was about half past ten or eleven o'clock P. M., and the old man seemed to be sleeping quietly. All at once he roused up and coughed and made a noise as though something was in his throat. I said, "Father James, what is the matter? Do you want a drink of water?"

"No," he said, "there seemed to be a big black man standing by me running red hot irons down my throat."

Oh! how disappointed I was. For I wanted him to get sanctified a few minutes before he died, as he had taught me. But now all was over, and I had no one to go and talk to, but must wander on in darkness. Not a ray of light could I see.

After a year or two I went to Philadelphia. There I was married to my second husband, James Smith. Then I had given up seeking the blessing definitely, and so went on. Several years later on, we moved to New York; and, after many more trials, that I have already referred to, I was deeply convicted again for the need of heart purity. And again I began to seek it by works. I read in the Bible, "If I, your Lord and Master, wash your feet, ye ought also to wash one another's feet," John, 13:15. There were four of us sisters who had united in a band to pray for mutual help to each other; Sister Scott, Sister Bangs, Sister Brown, and myself. I told them what the Bible said about it, and they all agreed. I did not tell them I was seeking the blessing of holiness. I was afraid they might say something to turn me aside, and I was so hungry. So I got ready, and I thought as there were only four of us, and we were trying to help each other, that it would be right for all four of us to be together at this time. But now I praise the Lord that He did not allow this to come to pass, though I did not know then that he was hindering them, as I do now. I was the only one that had a small baby. Sister Bangs and Sister Brown had no families, and Sister Scott's children were all grown. So I had them come and meet at my house every Monday afternoon. Sister Scott always came. Sister Bangs would be there one afternoon, and Sister Brown would not be there. Then when Sister Brown was there, Sister Bangs wouldn't be there. So they were never all there at once. Still I held on and thought it was best not to have this feet-washing done unless we were all together. So I told the sisters and they agreed with me that the four, ought to be together. We did not try get up a society of this kind, but just we four united for our own mutual help. After three or four weeks went on, and we were defeated every time, I decided not to do it. I prayed about it, and it seemed to come to me that I was not to do it. So that is how the Lord saved me from the mistake of seeking salvation by works. How I ever praise Him for His loving kindness, and for His tender mercy, and for His great patience and forbearance with me. I see now that if I had not been hindered as I was, that I should have gone about teaching that immersion, and the washing of feet, were necessary in order to be sanctified, which would have been a great mistake, but the Lord saved me from it. Praise His name. Amen.

CHAPTER VIII.

MY FIRST TEMPTATION, AND OTHER EXPERIENCES—I GO TO NEW UTRECHT TO SEE MY HUSBAND—A LITTLE EXPERIENCE AT BEDFORD STREET CHURCH, NEW YORK—FAITH HEALING.

For about three weeks after God had sanctified my soul, he seemed to let me walk above the world.

> "I then rode on the sky,
> Freely justified I,
> Nor did envy Elijah his seat.
> My glad soul mounted higher,
> In a chariot of fire,
> And the moon it was under my feet.
> I could not believe
> That I ever should grieve,
> That I ever should suffer again."

But the Lord knew I must be disciplined for service. He began by degrees to let me down, and the tempter seemed to be let loose upon me. I have said the Devil turned his hose on me, for it was as though a man was washing a sidewalk or carriage, Satan seemed to come at me in various ways, in such power. I settled down in God, I got where I could not make a single effort to pray or do anything. I was helpless—I could not get out of the way. Oh, what temptations! So I said, "Well, fire away, but I will trust in God, though he slay me." It was dark, but it was not long till light broke in and drove the darkness all away.

Why does God permit these fierce temptations? It is, I believe, first, to develop the strength and muscle of your own soul and so prepare you for greater service, and second, to bring you into sympathy with others, that are often sorely tempted after they are sanctified, so that you call help them. For example: After the dreadful temptation I have spoken of I met two persons that were suffering from the assaults of the old Accuser, as I had. One was at Sea Cliff, the other at Chester Heights Camp Meeting. The lady at Sea Cliff was a very interesting, intelligent lady. She was Assistant Superintendent of a Sabbath School, as well as a school teacher. She had a large Bible class of young persons and had great influence with them, and with the church, where she was a member. She came from Greenpoint or Williamsburg. I don't remember which. She had sought and found the great blessing of full salvation, and had walked in the blessed light and comfort of it for over a year, and was very helpful to many of her friends, and, especially, to her large Bible class of young people, a number of whom had been led to consecrate themselves fully to the Lord, and had come out into the clear light of this experience of perfect love through her instrumentality. Of course Satan would hinder her from such a work as that, so he cast a heavy black cloud over her soul, and she was in dreadful darkness for three months. She went over and over her consecration to see if she had taken anything back in any way. No, she knew she had been true up to all the light God had given her, still Satan accused her and told her there was something wrong or she would not have this cloud hanging over her. She was afraid to tell her young believers for fear she would discourage them, so she had to go on with her work testifying definitely to what God hall done for her, but only held on by naked faith. Many times after she would get home from meetings she would spend hours in her room weeping and praying before the Lord, but no help came. The tempter would assail her as being a hypocrite and testifying to what she did not feel in her heart, but

God helped her to stick to her facts. She had given herself to the Lord, and she was His, darkness or light, joy or no joy, it did not alter the fact, and she decided to declare it. When she came to Sea Cliff in this state of mind she was obedient. She would testify and tell just her state, then she came forward for help. As she would tell her sad story she would weep bitterly; then different ones would try and tell her what to do, and she said I am willing to do anything; so one and another would say do this or that; then she was asked to come forward. She would be the first one to go and kneel to get help and light. Everybody seemed to be in great sympathy with her and tried to help her. I saw where she was and knew she was under a temptation

of the Devil, but I was a colored woman, I did not like to push myself forward. I heard this young woman's story for three days, so I used to pray for her, but never got a chance to speak to her. One morning Sister Inskip was leading a young people's meeting in a tent on the upper part of the ground. I slipped in and sat down on one of the outer seats. I see now why the Lord seated me there. The tent filled up, and Sister Inskip talked and then asked others to speak. Again this dear young lady got up, and said she had got what she came for, she had got some help, but she had to go home that day, and she would rather die than go home as she was. Mrs. Inskip said, "Well, just give yourself to the Lord."

"Oh," I thought, over and over, "why don't she tell her to shout."

No one ever had intimated that it was a temptation from Satan. When they went to kneel down this young woman knelt right in front of me so that I did not have to move from the seat I had taken, and, while Mrs. Inskip was speaking and helping others, I leaned forward and said to this lady, "That is a temptation of the Devil; you praise the Lord and he will bring you out."

She looked up, and through her blinding tears, said, "Oh, Amanda Smith, were you ever so since you were sanctified?"

"Yes, my child, I was. I was shut up in prison for three weeks and only just got out the other day."

"Oh," she said, "I see it. Now Satan has been telling me that sanctified people never had a cloud."

"Don't you mind him," I said, "Praise the Lord."

"Glory to Jesus!" She sprang to her feet and cried, "I have got the victory, I am saved, I can go home, Jesus has set me free, O, Praise the Lord."

"Whom the Son makes free is free indeed." Hallelujah!

Then I saw that my experience in the weeks before, had been made a blessing to her, just as Job's experience was intended to be a blessing to men and women through all coming time.

I went to New Utrecht, to Mr. Roberts', to see my husband, James Smith. His son-in-law, John Bentley, was there when I went. Whatever had gone before, I do not know. I knew this young man. He had been at my house in New York. I had treated him well, and had done my very best for him, and his wife also. But that day he cursed me, and told me I had no business there. I thought it was strange he should talk so to me, and I believe he incurred the displeasure of God, as did Elymas, the sorcerer, who withstood Paul and sought to turn away from the faith Sergius Paulus, a prudent man who had called for Barnabas and Saul, and desired to hear the word of God. But this man withstood them. But Paul, being full of the Holy Ghost, set his eyes on him, and said: "Oh! full of all subtlety and mischief, thou child of the Devil, thou enemy of all righteousness, wilt thou not yet cease to pervert the right ways of the Lord? And now, behold! the hand of the Lord is upon thee. Thou shalt be blind, not seeing the sun for a season." "And immediately there fell on him a mist and darkness, and he went about seeking someone to lead him by the hand," (Acts 13:8-12.) So, that day in New Utrecht, John Bentley came in, as I was in the next room talking with James, my husband. I had gone over to see him. My rent was due, and he had not been over for two weeks, and had not sent me any money. I was not well, and my baby was sick, and I was insisting that James should give me some money, at least the sixty cents that it cost me to come over from New York. But he would not. I was crying and talking, for my heart was almost broken. So, when John Bentley cursed and swore at me, I turned to him quietly, and said: "Why, John Bentley, haven't I a right to come where my own husband is?" But he was fierce. I did not know but he was going to strike me. But I went up to him and looked him in the face, and said to him: "When you have been at my house, haven't I always treated you well? I have never laid a straw in your way in my life; and I don't know why you should speak to me in such a way."

He went on talking and abusing me terribly. There seemed to come an indescribable power over me, and I turned and lifted my hand toward him, and I said to him: "Mind, John Bentley, the God that I serve will make you pay for this before the year is out."

He said: "Well, I don't care if He does. Let Him do it."

He had not more than said the words when he seemed to tremble and stagger. There was a chair behind him, and he dropped down into the chair. I never saw him from that day. This was about two weeks before Christmas, and before the New Year came, John Bentley was dead and buried!

I always feel sad when I think of it, but I believe that God was displeased with that man for cursing me that day.

My husband, James Smith, was formerly of Baltimore, Md. He was for many years a leader of the choir of Bethel A. M. E. Church, in that city. Afterward he moved to Philadelphia, and was ordained deacon in the A. M. E. Church. He died in November, 1869, at New Utrecht, N. Y. Since then I have been a widow, and have traveled half way round the world, and God has ever been faithful. He has never left me a moment; but in all these years I have proved the word true, "Lo! I am with you always, even to the end."

> "Sometimes 'mid scenes of deepest gloom,
> Sometimes where Eden's bowers bloom,
> By waters still, or troubled sea,
> Still, 'tis my God that leadeth me."

Amen. Amen.

I had told the Lord I would be obedient and would do all he bade me, so one day while I was busy at work it was whispered to my heart, "You go to Bedford Street on Sunday."

"Yes," I said, "I will." I always liked to go and hear Rev. John Cookman, who was then pastor. Sunday morning came; it was

Easter Sunday. My friend, Sister Scott, and I went. Strange to say, but the usher took us up front, in what is or used to be called "The Amen Corner." I shall never forget John Cookman's text and sermon. The words were: "See that ye make all things after the pattern shown you in the Mount."

O, what a congregation, and what power the young man seemed to have in those days. He brought out holiness so clear and definite. I had got wonderfully blest as they sang the old Easter Anthem, as only Bedford Street could sing it in those days. O, how it thrills me now as I think it all over! As Brother Cookman went on with his sermon increasing in fervor and power, the Spirit whispered to me distinctly, "Raise up your right hand," and I was just going to do so, when the Devil said, just, as distinctly, "Yes, you look nice lifting up your black hand before all the people"—and I drew back and did not do it.

Then the Spirit said: "The other day you told the Lord you would do any thing He would tell you to do."

"O, yes," I said, "I did. O, Lord, forgive me and give me another chance and I will lift my hand for Thee!"

By-and-by the Spirit said again, "Lift up your right hand," and I did, and the power of the Spirit fell on the people and the whole congregation. There were "Amens," and "Amens," and sobs and weeping and "Praise the Lord," heard all over the house, and many were led out of prison by the simple act of obedience to God. He did not tell me to shout, but to lift my hand for Him, and the people shouted, and my own heart then filled with adoring praise. O, I would God I had always obeyed Him, then would my peace have flowed as the river, but many times I failed. Once on the car coming from New Utrecht, where I had gone to see my husband, I had a tract in my hand with a message for a lad that got in. I saw him look at me, and then turn quickly away as if he was afraid I would hand it to him. My heart was prompted to give it to him, but I kept hesitating. First, I said, "I will wait till some of the people get out." Then, I said, "I will wait till I get out." The car stopped, the lad got out and ran away as though I was after him. I looked after him and wanted to call him, but he was gone. Then these words came to me in such force that I have never forgotten them, "His blood will I require at your hand." I did nothing but pray to God for His pardoning and forgiving mercy from that hour till I got home; at last, I felt He forgave me and gave me peace in my heart.

Here I desire to record some things the Lord taught me about what is now called faith, or divine healing.

I think it was in October, 1868, not very long after I had got the blessing of sanctification. It seemed that my faith had increased and strengthened in this short time, so that I did not seem to find it difficult to believe God for anything I really needed. I had never heard of Dr. Cullis, Dr. Bordman, or Dr. Mahan, of Oberlin, Ohio. I had never read a book or paper of any kind. I believed what I read in the Bible about the miracles performed by the Lord Jesus, opening the eyes of the blind, unstopping the ears of the deaf, and healing the sick, but thought it belonged to the days of miracles especially, and it was to prove to the unbelieving Jews the Divinity of our Lord Jesus Christ. I had often prayed for sick people, and asked the Lord to bless means that were used, and so many times He did it, as I believe in answer to prayer; but I never made any time about it, as though it were some especial state of grace, so much higher than entire sanctification or holiness. So I went on claiming promises, quenching the violence of fire, escaping the edge of the sword, out of weakness was made strong, waxing valiant in fight, and really turning to flight the armies of the aliens. And so found out that there is no want to them that fear the Lord. But I did not feel led to make a special gospel of the great and deep things God had taught me. The Gospel of Jesus was so full and practical, and with good, common sense it seemed to cover all my need. Praise the Lord for that lesson. For I find, no matter what the state of grace attained to in this life, one may ever learn some new lesson. Learn to know one's own self. Learn to know one's weakness. Learn to know the beauty of love and power and sympathy of Jesus Christ, our Lord and Savior. And so on.

It was Saturday. I was very busy, as that is a busy day, especially with a washwoman. After I had swept my room I gave the dustpan to Mazie to carry out to the ash box that stood on the sidewalk. It was when I lived in the rear at 135 Amity street, New York. When she came in, she said, "O, ma, someone has thrown a lot of nice books into the ash box; some of them are almost new." She was very fond of reading, so she said, "May I bring some in?"

"Oh, no," I said, "Mazie; I have little enough room now, and I do not want any old books or trash brought in." But contrary to my orders, the child slipped three of these books into the house, and hid them in the little closet on the shelf behind the smoothing irons. In the bottom of this closet, on the floor, I kept my coal. I could put in about two pailfuls, which was about a half bushel, at a time. So on Monday morning after prayers, Mazie had gone to school, I went to put some coal in the stove and then was going to gather my clothes. But I noticed that my irons were not back on the shelf in their place properly. So I went to arrange them, and found these books.

"There," I said, "I told Mazie not to bring any of these books in; she has not obeyed me." But as I looked at them I said, "Perhaps I should not have told her 'no' until I saw them; for they really are almost new." I don't remember what the two were, but the third was a small-sized book, entitled, "Child's Book on Physiology." So I began to read it. I looked through it. As I read on, its explanations, simple and so beautiful, of the human body in all its parts, in a way that any child could understand it, I got so interested that I sat down, though I was in such a hurry. After reading and thinking, I turned to the first page. There was a cut of the human frame on the fly leaf. As I looked at it and studied it, I said, "Surely, as the Psalmist says, 'Man is fearfully and wonderfully made.'" Now, in my imagination, I covered that frame with flesh, and skin, and sinew, and blood, and pulse, and life. Then I got a pain, or rheumatism, in the left arm or back; and I said, "Now, there is a man suffering pain in his arm and back. I give him medicine in his mouth, and it must go all this round to reach that spot; when God, who made him, knows how to reach the difficulty direct." Now, all this was as I imagined. There was not a soul in the house but myself. So I said, lifting my eyes to heaven, "Oh! Lord, I will never take another bit of medicine while I live without you tell me to." And I got up and threw out all my medicines—I had a few simple remedies in the house—and for a year and eight months I never touched anything. Oh! what wonderful lessons the Lord taught me in that time. It did seem that He watched as a father would watch his child. Sometimes I would bring in a basket of clothes, and it would be so warm I would sit down between the window and doors so as to get the breeze quickly, and I would hear the Spirit whisper, as distinctly as a man, so gently, but clearly: "You are sitting in the draught." Often I have looked around to see if there was not really a person speaking. If I was prompt and moved, it was all right. But sometimes I would say, when the whisper came, "Oh, yes, but I'm so warm;" and I would forget, until I would feel a pain in my back, or neck, or somewhere. Then I would at once look up to God and say, "Now, Lord, teach me the lesson you want I should learn; and then do please relieve me of this pain." Can you understand the patience and forbearance of God? I cannot. Sometimes He would bless me so; I would be so happy, I would whirl round and round and laugh and say, "Oh! Lord, how beautiful. I will never have to take any more medicine, and I can save the money that I spent for medicine for other purposes." But the Lord knew how to teach me, praised be His name. So at the expiration of a year and eight months, it was in November, I think, I took a severe cold. I never knew how I got that cold, and if the grippe had been known then, as now, I would have said I had it in its severest form. I never thought of medicine. The Lord was my physician, and had done everything I had asked for myself and my child for a year and eight months, so of course He would now. So I prayed as aforetime, but still grew worse. Oh! how dreadfully ill I was. But I held on. Oh! how I did cry to God for deliverance. For three days and nights I could not lie down, my cough was so bad. I had a raging fever. My head ached, and every bone in my body ached. I still grew worse, until the morning of the fourth day. I tried to get my clothes on, but could not stand up long enough. "Oh! what shall I do?" I went in my bed room and knelt down by a chair. Oh! how I cried and prayed. "Oh! Lord, what is the matter? What have I done? Thou didst always heal me when I asked Thee; and now Thou seest I can hardly hold my head up, I am so sick. Oh! Lord, show me if I have done anything to displease Thee; make it clear to me, and forgive me, for Jesus' sake. Now, Lord, I will just be quiet till Thou dost speak to me and tell me what I have done, and why Thou dost not heal me as Thou usest to do."

So I waited a few minutes; I don't know how long; then it seemed as though the Lord Jesus in person stood by me; such a peaceful hush came all over me, and He seemed to say, so tenderly, Oh! so tenderly, "Now, if you knew the Lord wanted you to take medicine would you be willing?"

"No, Lord, you always have healed me without medicine, and why not now? What have I done?"

Then it seemed just as though a person spoke and said, "No, no, but if you knew it was God's will, would you be willing?" I said, "No, Lord; you can heal me without medicine, and I don't want to take it." Then the patient, gentle voice said the third time, "No, no," and putting the question a little differently, said, "If you knew it was God's will for you to take medicine would you be willing to do God's will?"

Oh! how I cried. I saw it, but I said, "No, Lord, I don't like medicine; but Thou canst conquer my will. I do not want to live with my will in opposition to Thy will. Thou must conquer."

Oh! what a battle. It took me one whole hour before my will went down. I held on to the chair, for I felt I must get up, but I said, "No, I will die right here." But I held right on to the chair. I said, "I will never rise from here until my will dies." And I knew when the death was given and when the victory came. I remained quiet, and thought it all over. And I said, "Lord, I thank Thee. Now tell me what I must do." For I felt if the Lord had said, "Now, you go over there on Sixth avenue to the drug store, and take all the medicine, bottles and all," I was willing! Oh! I was willing all through! It seemed wonderfully sweet to die to my own will, and sink into God. So just then it came to me to use a simple remedy that I had used a thousand times before, and in twenty-four hours I was as well as ever. I never got over a cold like that before in my life in so short a time; a cold like that would always be a three weeks' siege. But I seemed to see what it all meant. God showed me. I was worshiping my will.

Sometimes when I have told this strange experience to some of the good people in these days, they throw up their hands in holy horror and say, "Oh! I don't see how you could dare to say so." But I see the same spirit of will-worship in many of those who profess what they prefer to call "Divine healing;" the same spirit of will-worship that I had. But I do not think they know it. I am at no controversy with anybody on these lines. But, Oh! how I do thank and praise God for opening my eyes to see, and I think, understand His will concerning Amanda Smith. I do not believe in calling the doctor for every little thing, or making a drug store of one's self; but I believe it right when you need medicine or doctor, to use both, prayerfully, and with common-sense, with an eye single. But to say the use of means in sickness is contrary to the will of God, and that all Christians should have faith and trust the Lord to heal them without the use of means at all, even though their common-sense, which is as much God's gift to us as any other blessing, tells them to use the means, but must close their eyes, ignore all symptoms, and by the force of will, which they must call "faith," ride over everything;—now this is where the tug of war comes in, with Amanda Smith. My neighbor prays, and is wonderfully healed; she is a Christian; so am I; we have both been blessed of God; I pray, and am not healed; someone tells me it is a lack of faith on my part, or there is something wrong in my consecration, or there is something wrong in me somewhere, and that is the reason I am not healed. Now comes the question: "How do you know that? Who told you so?" So that I must either stand judged, or else I must judge, and where do I get my authority for so doing? The Lord help me. Amen.

The days of miracles are not past. God has healed without the use of means of any kind, as well as with; and why He does not now heal every case as He used to do, I do not think I have any right to say is because of a lack of faith on the part of some poor, weak child of God; and so consign them to perdition. Then there are some things God would have us do for ourselves. Not long ago I was at the home of a good minister, a man that knew the Lord, and for years had walked in the light and blessedness of full salvation. He had begun to get deaf in his right ear; it came on gradually; sometimes worse than at other times. So he prayed earnestly, and believed God, and held on about a year. Finally he seemed to grow worse. His wife, a good, saved, orthodox, level-headed woman, had often said to him he ought to see a doctor about it. But he had a pretty strong will of his own, and did not yield easily to her persuasions. But she was gentle and patient. One morning as he was sitting in the room talking with me, she came in and said, "Now, my dear, you must really go and see the doctor this morning about your deafness; let him examine it; you are getting worse all the time, and it will never do to have you going around deaf."

The good man looked at his wife, then he turned to me and said, smilingly, "Sister Smith, my wife is generally pretty clear when she decides upon a thing."

"Yes, Sister Smith," she said, "it would do no harm to go and see about it, anyhow."

"Sister M.," I said, "you are quite right; just what I say."

So off he went. He was gone about two hours. When he returned, I said, "Well, Brother M., what did the doctor say?"

"Oh! praise the Lord," he said, "I am all right; clear as a bell." So he told the story, and laughed heartily. I said, "What did the doctor do?"

"Oh," he said, "he told me to sit down and he would examine My ear; he said there was nothing serious the matter; the wax was very dry. So he took his instruments and took out about a thimbleful of wax, and put a little sweet oil or something in it, and it is all right."

"Yes," I said, "praise the Lord. Some people would have teased the Lord to have Him clean out their ears, when they might do it themselves, or get someone to do it to whom God had given the sense and ability."

CHAPTER IX.

VARIOUS EXPERIENCES—HIS PRESENCE—OBEDIENCE—MY TEMPTATION TO LEAVE THE CHURCH—WHAT PEOPLE THINK—SATISFIED.

One day I was busy with my work and thinking and communing with Jesus, for I found out that it was not necessary to be a nun or be isolated away off in some deep retirement to have communion with Jesus; but, though your hands are employed in doing your daily business, it is no bar to the soul's communion with Jesus. Many times over my wash-tub and ironing table, and while making my bed and sweeping my house and washing my dishes I have had some of the richest blessings. Oh, how glad I am to know this, and how many mothers' hearts I have cheered when I told them that the blessing of sanctification did not mean isolation from all the natural and legitimate duties of life, as some seem to think. Not at all. It means God in you, supplying all your needs according to His riches in glory by Christ Jesus; our need of grace and patience and long suffering and forbearance, for we have to learn how not only to bear, but also to forbear with infirmities of ourselves and others as well.

I return to my story. Thus as I thought, I asked again, "I wonder why the Lord did not sanctify me fully when he justified me? He was God, and He could have done it; He could have done it all at once if He had had a mind to." Then the question, "Well, why didn't He do it?" and I was blocked. I believe that question was from Satan; he intended to make me think unkindly of God. "Here you have been struggling all these years; God could have done it all at once; but why didn't He do it?" "Yes," I said, "that is so."

"Well, why didn't he do it?" And I was so sad I began to cry and said, "Lord, I don't know why you did not sanctify me wholly when you justified me freely; but I know you have not done it." Then the blessed Holy Spirit came so sweetly and answered my question by asking me another, "Why didn't Jesus make the blind man see the first time He touched his eyes?" After the first touch Jesus bade him look, and asked him what he saw. He said, "I see men as trees walking."

Then He touched him again and he said he saw every man clearly.

He was Christ with the same power in His first touch as He had with the second. He could have made the blind man see clearly the first time, but He did not.

"Why," I said, "Lord, I see it, and it is none of my business why you didn't sanctify me fully when you converted me; it is enough for me to know that you have done it." I came into light and liberty praising the Trinity. I quit asking God questions about His own work. I think it is impertinence, and yet how many do this very thing, and when they don't get an answer to satisfy themselves they become perplexed and then land in skepticism with regard to the whole doctrine and truth of this great salvation.

One of the first things I discovered after I came Into the blessed light and experience of full salvation was a steady and appropriating faith that I never realized before. I always believed the Bible and all the promises, but I did not seem to have power to appropriate the promises to my soul's need; but after the light broke in and my darkness had fled, power was given me not only to believe the promises, but to appropriate them.

"My!" I said, as I would read the promises, "that is mine, and that is mine;" and it was like when the sailors reef their sails; I took hold of them and wrapped them round me and walked up and down in possession of the land. All things are yours, and ye are Christ's, and Christ is God's. I sang:

> "All things are mine,
> Since I am His—
> How can I keep from singing?"

One day as I was busy about my room I seemed to feel the conscious presence of Jesus. I saw nothing with my eyes, but I seemed to be conscious of the presence of a Holy Being by me and around me, and I talked with Him, and I was saying, "Now, if anyone should ask me to tell the difference between justification and sanctification, how could I tell them? There is a difference; I know it; I feel it; but I don't know how to tell it." And the dear Lord Jesus seemed to answer my question by asking another. He said: "What is the difference between sunlight and moonlight?" In a moment I saw it. I knew the beauty of the lovely moonlight. I had read by its brightness, and had often sewed at night, and it was beautiful. That was my justified state. How many times, I did not understand clearly, as in the sunlight; but the deeper experience was in power like sunlight in the natural world. It penetrates all the dark corners. If there is even it small nail-hole in a door, or a crack anywhere, the sun finds it out and looks through; then it heats up everything all about it. There can be no frost where the sunlight is; but it is tropical all the time. There were deep recesses in my heart that the moonlight did not reveal, but when the great sunlight of sanctification came, how it seemed almost to eclipse the moonlight state of justification, save the abiding consciousness of the time when God wrought that first work in my soul. I no longer sang the old hymn,

> "The midsummer sun shines but dim;
> The fields strive in vain to look gay,
> But when I am happy in Him,
> December's as pleasant as May."

That means two distinct states as real as the moonlight and sunlight. I knew it was true, but, O, why should there be a December in my heart when I may have the beaming sun? When the Holy Ghost came to my soul in sanctifying power it was the inaugural of a perpetual May-day that shall go on increasing in faith, and light, and strength, and power, and thanksgiving, and praise, and rest, and peace, and triumph forever and ever and ever. Amen. Amen.

How true this old hymn of Charles Wesley's:

> "I find Him in singing;
> I find Him in prayer;
> In sweet meditation,
> He always is there.
> My constant companion,
> Oh, may we ne'er part,
> All glory to Jesus.
> He dwells in My heart."

One day I was meditating and thinking upon His goodness. My heart was full of praise as I thought of all the Lord had done, and I said, "Oh, I will not need to pray now, as I used to do." Just then these words came: "The children of Israel gathered manna fresh every morning." I said, "Yes, Jesus." I knew He meant to teach me that it must be daily bread my soul would need, and as my natural need was met each day, so my spiritual need must be met by prayer and the reading of His Holy Word and the appropriating of His promises. Without this all else would avail nothing.

How I marvel at God's patience with me when I think how He led me about to teach me how to be obedient, in spite of all Satan's devices.

I was working up town one day, as the lady wanted some blankets washed. The morning I was to go I had slept rather late. I was to have been there at seven o'clock. A long walk from Fourth street to Twenty-third street. I felt led to take some tracts. I always kept a lot on hand and would take them when I went out, generally looking over them so as to see and know just what I was giving away. This morning Satan seemed to hurry me. "You will be too late if you stop to sort the tracts."

"Yes," I said, "I am afraid so." Then the Spirit would seem to say, "Take the tracts." Then I picked up a handful and began to look over them. Then I got so nervous. Satan said, "You know that lady will not pay you if you are not there at seven."

"Yes," I said, "she is hard about money anyhow." So I laid the tracts down and started off, and it seemed to me I never saw so many opportunities where I could have given a tract as I did that morning. When I got to the house the lady said she would not have the blankets washed that day; I should come the next week. And I saw how Satan had hindered me. How sorry I was I did not listen to the good Spirit and take the tracts. God knew the washing was not to be done that day, and that is why He whispered so gently to my heart, "Take the tracts." I don't know who lost the blessing by my not giving them, but I know I lost a blessing by not obeying. O, it is so safe to obey even though it may be dark. A few days later on, I went, and as I had sorted my tracts, I prayed that the Lord would show me to whom to give them; and what a good time I had. I met a very fine looking man and as I looked at him I trembled; but as he drew near I said, "Now, Lord, help me." I had met some colored men and had given them some tracts and spoken a word, and the Devil said, "That is a white gentleman, and he will curse you."

But when he came near I said, "Pardon me, sir; will you have a tract?"

He seemed thoroughly astonished, but very pleasant and courteous. He took the tract and thanked me. A couple of weeks after, a friend said to me, "Did you give a tract to a young man on Sixth avenue last week?"

"Yes."

"Well," she said, "It was you, then. I was working for Mrs. A., and she told me that her son came home so happy and told her that a colored woman had given him a tract, and that he had never read anything that had done him so much good as that tract."

O, how the mother and son rejoiced together. Her dear boy that she had prayed for so long had found peace and joy in the Lord. How strange it should come about in the way it did, but God moves in mysterious ways His wonders to perform. On a little further, I passed two men: they were musicians. They stood talking, and as I came near them a deep feeling came over me to give those men a tract. My heart beat quickly, but just as I got near them they seemed to think what I was going to do, so they started and walked across on the side. I said, "Lord, if you want me to give that man a tract, if there is a word that Thou dost want him to have, make him cross the next corner back again." O, how I did pray! Sure enough he did cross over the next corner and met me face to face and took a tract, and thanked me and seemed deeply impressed. Praise God.

At another time. One night I was crossing on the ferry boat. I had a good religious paper in my hand, which had a good sermon in it and some experiences. I said I will take this and give it to someone, men are more willing to take a paper than a tract. On the boat a nice looking lad sat just opposite me, and as I looked at him the Spirit said, "Give him that paper." Again I looked and thought I will give it to him before we get out. Then something seemed to say, "Give it to this other man that looks more thoughtful."

"No," it came to me, "Give it to that lad."

I got up and handed it to him. He took it and threw it underneath the bench. Then said Satan, "Now you have made a mistake, you would better have given it to the man."

But I lifted my heart in prayer and said, "Now, Lord, if there is anything in that paper that Thou dost want that young man to know, make him pick it up. Lord, don't let him go out, make him pick up that paper." I continued to pray, and we were nearing the shore. I saw the fellow was very restless. O, how I did beg the Lord to make him pick it up, I felt it had a word for him. Just as the boat struck the dock, he stooped down and picked up the paper and put it in his pocket and ran away. Just then the grand old text came: "If ye shall ask anything in My name, I will do it." (John 14:14).

I think it was November, 1869. On my way home one evening from work, I met a friend on Sixth avenue. She said to me, "Smith, are you going to the Fair to-night?"

"No," I said, "I am tired and shall not go."

"I have two tickets, if you like to go I will give them to you."

"All right," I said, "If I feel better after I get home I will go. You know I never go to such places unless the Lord wants me to do something for Him."

"Well," she said, "I wish you would go."

I went to my home at thirty-five Amity street, and as I prayed and asked the Lord, it was very clear to me I was to go. It was a damp, rainy evening, and I would think, "Well, it is too damp and I will not go." Then it would come to me, "Go, take some tracts."

I knew I would be criticised, for I had become a speckled bird among my own people on account of the profession of the blessing of holiness. Remarks would be made, "There is Amanda Smith, with her sanctification again." So I knew all that would be said, but I said, "Lord help me, and I will go for Thee. Tell me what Thou dost want me to do."

I went in, and there were quite a number; all seemed to look at me, remarks passed, and then all went on as they would there. I walked about and spoke to several, then I sat down and lifted my heart in prayer, and said, "Lord, I have no business here, and why should I stay, make it clear what you want me to do;" and these words were spoken to my heart distinctly, "Go stand in the way." I got up and went and stood at the lop of the stairs where the people were coming up. Several persons passed up, then came two young men full of glee. The Spirit seemed to pick out one especially, and said, "Speak to that young man." I did; he was respectful as he could be, but said it was time enough for him, and with a toss of the head turned away.

I handed some tracts to several others, then the Lord seemed to say, "You may go home." I went out, and felt that I had done as I was told, but how strange that I should not do anything but that. I went home and bore this young man up to God. This, I think, was on Wednesday evening. On Saturday, as I was carrying some clothes home, I met some one on Sixth avenue and they said, "Did you hear that Charlie S. is dead?"

"No."

"Well, he is, he was found dead in his bed this morning; he was at the Fair the other night, well and hearty." I went and looked at him. There he was, dead, no sign of sickness, and the very young man that God had sent me to speak to. He looked as though he were asleep. O, how sad it was, and yet how glad I was that I had strength given me that night to obey the Lord, and do as I thought He led me, whether the young man would hear, or whether he would forbear.

I seemed to see the inconsistencies of the brethren and sisters so much more than I ever had before. I had seen some before, as I suppose most people do. I saw my own, and what the Lord had saved me from, and I wanted everybody to get saved right away.

Brother Patterson was pastor of the Sullivan Street A. M. E. Church at the time I got the blessing. He enjoyed the experience and preached the doctrine. But colored people are like some white people; although the church prospered under his administration, and we had a wonderful revival during the two years, and the church was built up and edified, yet many of them did not like him. After he left, Rev. Nelson Turpin was sent to us. He was fierce. He openly opposed and denounced the doctrine and experience of the blessing of full salvation, although there were a number in the church, some among the leading members, who claimed to have the experience. He was very popular with the great mass. The church was crowded. Then we poor souls who dared to testify definitely in a Love Feast, or in a General Class, might expect a raking; and especially on Sunday nights, when the church would be crowded, he, would take especial pains to tell some ridiculous inconsistency about some sanctified sister or brother that he used to know. Then, if a sister, he, would say: "They put on a plain bonnet and shawl and wear a long face, but they are sanctified Devils." Then all eyes would be turned on Sister Scott and myself, for we were about the only ones that dressed in the way described. Then there would be a regular giggle all over the house. How much I had to contend with. Hence my temptation to leave the church. Then I did not like fairs and festivals and all the rest of it. But God saved me from backsliding over any of those things. Then I was in bondage to my clothes; in bondage to other people's clothes. If they were not made just as I thought they ought to be it troubled me, and I did not care if I did not hear them speak and pray in prayer meeting. I had rather not kneel at communion with these dressed-up people. Then I was afraid of Brother Turpin. At first he was very kind; but after a little while he would always try to shun me. But I would follow him up, ask him to come to see me, and would go to see Sister Turpin and the children. But he would always be very formal and cold. My! how afraid of him I did get! So one day Mother Jones said to me, "Sister Smith, if I were you I would not say anything about sanctification. You see people do not like it, and they persecute you, and I do not like to hear them."

"Well, but Mother Jones," I said, "the Lord has blessed me so, and I can't help it." Then she laughed and took hold of me kindly, and said, "I would not say anything about it if I were you."

So I went home and thought how Mother Jones sympathized with me. So I began to be very indefinite in my testimony. I chose words that the people would like. I would say, "I am all the Lord's." They would say, "Amen!" Or, if I said, "Jesus saves me fully," or "The blood cleanseth," they would say, "Amen!" to that. But if I used the word "sanctify," then there was a rustling among the dry bones. Then look out for the next testimony, especially if in a General Class or Love Feast. Thank God, He led my class leader, Henry De Sheilds, into the experience in answer to prayer, just three weeks after I got the blessing. So while "Pop" Scott, who was assistant class leader, never came out clear, Brother De Shields was a power and a great help to myself, and to many. He still lives in New York, and at this writing is walking in the light of full salvation. Still, I was afraid of Brother Turpin. Then darkness came over me, and the joy and peace all seemed to be gone. I did not know what ailed me. So I set apart Friday to fast and pray, and find out the cause of this darkness. Satan suggested many things, but I held on and cried to God for light and help. So, about two P. M., though I had stopped my work and gone away and prayed a number of times that day, I took my Bible and knelt down to pray. And I said: "Oh! Lord, show me what is the matter. Why is this darkness in my mind? O! Lord, make it clear to me." And the Spirit seemed to say to me very distinctly, "Read." And I opened my Bible, and my eyes lighted on these words: "Perfect love casteth out fear. He that feareth has not been made perfect in love." Then I said: "Lord, if I am not, I will be now." Then I saw what was the matter. Fear! And I said: "Oh! Lord, take all the man-fearing spirit out of me. I thank Thee for what Thou hast done for me, but deliver me from fear. Take all the woman-fearing spirit out of me, and give me complete victory over this fear." And, thank the Lord, He did it. There was no especial manifestation, but there was a deep consciousness in my heart that what I had asked the Lord to do, He had done, and I praised Him. Then He came to me: "Will you go uptown to Union Church on Sunday and testify definitely?"

"Yes, Lord, if Thou wilt help me, and give me Thy strength, and go with me, I will go." So there was a calm and peace in my heart. Union Church, uptown, was a colored church. There was not a member in it that believed in the doctrine of holiness; and from that church there had been great criticism in regard to my professing such a blessing. Sunday morning came. The Love Feast was at 6 o'clock A. M. I had been but once before. I got ready and went. My heart trembled, and my knees trembled. But I went on, and I said, "Now, Lord, help me, and I will go." I got in and sat down. The church was well filled. A number of strange ministers sat in the altar. Every eye was turned on me. After the meeting opened the testimony began. The ministers urged everybody to be short, and in many of the testimonies there were remarks and insinuations thrown out to me. I sat still and prayed. Oh! how I did pray. Then they began to get very noisy. They shouted and praised. I said to the Lord; "Now, Lord, I will speak for Thee if Thou wilt make these people be quiet. Lord, make them be quiet. I can't talk when there is a great noise, and Thou hast sent me here to speak for

Thee, and I want the people to hear. Lord, make them be still." Sometimes there would be three or four on the floor speaking at the same time. The ministers would urge them on, and say: "The Lord can hear you all. Don't wait on one another." But I prayed, "Lord, still them, still them." Then there came a pause. Then I got on my feet. Then they began to shout again, and they drowned me out. So I stood still, and prayed, "Lord, still the people." And He did. They calmed down so that when I began, there was not another one spoke. I began and quoted several passages of Scripture bearing on holiness definitely, and on God's promise of this grace to those who sought it, and how it was obtained by faith. And they listened. The ministers touched one another. I went on talking, and by and by I came to a point when it seemed a finger touched my tongue, and the power of God came upon me in such a wonderful manner that I talked, it seemed to me, about ten minutes. The people looked as though they were alarmed. The ministers who sat in the altar, and who had looked so critical when I came in, began to shout "Amen! Lord Almighty, bless that sister!" And then the fire seemed to fall on all the people. When I had finished, I. sat down, feeling that I had delivered the message according to the will of the Lord. To His name be all the glory for the strength He gave me that day. Amen. Amen.

One day Sister Scott called and was so happy. She told me some white sisters had been at her house, and had prayed and sung, and that they were full of the Holy Ghost. They were dressed so plain and neat. They belonged to the Free Methodist Church, uptown somewhere in New York. And they asked her to come to some of their meetings. "Oh!" I said, "why didn't you bring them to see me?" She said, "I told them I would bring you up to their church sometime." So on Sunday I went with her. It was about two miles from where I lived. We started early, and, of course, we walked all the way. We thought it was a dreadful thing to ride on the street cars on Sunday. And I think still we should not do it whenever we can avoid it. But I am not in bondage even in this as I once was. Praise the Lord! We got to the church. Mr. Mackey, who was so well known all over New York, was then very popular and prominent in that church, and was a good friend to the colored people. For years he led meetings at the Colored Home in New York. When we went into the church he was there, and was so glad to see us. He shook hands, and seated us, and was so kind.

"My!" I thought, "how nice these people are." For such treatment as that in a white church was not common for colored persons. Then the church was so very pretty and plain. No stained glass, or cushions, no pipe organ and quartette choir. Then the sisters were all so plain. So was I. For before I got the blessing I dressed Quaker style, because I liked it, and it was a matter of economy. Then the preacher that Sunday morning was a Mr. James, and he had no gold studs in his shirt, no rings on his fingers. His face was placid and bright. And what a sermon he preached on Holiness. My soul was fed, and I prayed to the Lord to put it in the heart of the minister to ask persons to join the church. I felt I must join this church. It was a true church. And that kind of preaching I had heard my father talk about that they used to hear forty years ago. Well, I prayed. Always before when I had prayed, from the time I had received the blessing, somehow the Lord had answered me so quick. But this morning He didn't seem to answer; and yet, now, I see it was an answer. For sometimes when the Lord denies a request, it's as much an answer as when He grants it. Though I had been a member of the African Methodist Church for years, I was willing that morning to join without a letter, on probation. I said, "I can get my letter from my church, I know, but they will want to know all the reason why, and I don't want to tell. I just want to come into this church. These people seem so good! Just the right kind of people." So I prayed on. The sermon was finished. Then they had a prayer meeting, and Brother Irvin prayed. Oh! what a prayer. I shall ever remember it. He was well known, and a man of wonderful power. And I thought, "Will they close without asking if any one wants to join! I will get up and go and ask them to take me in. But then they will wonder why I have not brought my letter, and what will I say? The Lord help me!" And He did, but not as I wanted then, but as it is written, "Ye shall know if ye follow on to know the Lord." The meeting did close, and no one was asked to join. But the friends gathered around Sister Scott and me, shook hands, and said they were glad to see us. The minister shook hands and asked us to come again. They were all so nice. They shouted, and were so free, as the Free Methodists are. Brother Irvin came up to me, and gave me several tracts on the origin and doctrine of the Free Methodist Church. How that it separated itself on account of slavery and secret societies. All this was new to me, but suited me exactly. Then he gave me a tract on plain dressing. Oh! how I did peruse that. Brother E. lived on Dominick street downtown, not a great way from where I lived, on Amity street. He had a week night class at his house, so he asked us to come. On Tuesday night I went. It was warm, and there stood on the table a pitcher of water, and every now and then someone of the brethren would shout, "Glory to God," then take a glass of water. Well, I thought it was dreadful. For I thought, "We don't do that. We can stay at class until it is out without drinking water." Then I thought it was wrong to use a fan. So I suffered from heat rather than fan myself when in church. Then they made so much unnecessary noise. Just what I didn't like in my own people. And I thought it would be different.

But I had made up my mind to join this church. So the next week I went again and they were having a prayer meeting. They had a great big carman on his knees by a chair in the middle of the floor. A brother was on each side of him, one behind him, and another in front, and they were shouting and pounding and trying to make the man say he believed. "You believe! Say Hallelujah." "Praise the Lord." Then they would say. "Amen!" Then they got up, took hold of the man, stood him on his feet and said, "Praise the Lord." But he was heavy, and would not say it.

"Well," I said, "that's just what I find fault with my own people for. And these people are good people, but they have their failings, just like other people. So I might as well stay where I am." Then they told me there were no prejudices among them. That colored people were always treated well. And I was glad of that. So the next week I went again. Brother James led the class that night. He had thrown across his shoulders a very stylish shawl, such as gentlemen wore in those days, and in it was a very pretty steel pin and chain, which shone bright.

"Well," I said, "I did not think Brother James would wear that."

So a sister came in. When she saw Sister Thompson, whom I had got to go with me that night, and myself, she frowned and turned her back on us. "Well," I thought, "they say they have no prejudice. But she acts just like she had, anyhow. After all, perhaps I had better not join."

Then a dear lady got up and gave such a beautiful testimony, and was so sweet in spirit. How her testimony helped me. But, Oh! such a raking as Brother James gave her about her dress. She had on a plain fifty cent black straw bonnet, with a piece of black ribbon across the middle and a little bow on the side. Not a flower, or a bit of color of any kind. She said, "Well, Brother James, I never thought anything about it. I just got the milliner to fix it up to wear to market, and I put it on." I never thought anything about the bow he had so bitterly denounced. But he did not let her off. He picked her testimony all to pieces. How I felt for her. And I thought there was much more of self and spirit in his manner and in the swell shawl and the steel pin and chain that swung about, than there was in the sister he raked so. Next he came to the sister who turned her back. She spoke short, and kept her back to us. When he came to me, I arose and said: "I understood that you people have no prejudices against colored people."

"Yes," Brother E. says.

"Well, will it be right for me to speak just what I think?"

"Yes, certainly," said he. "We are Free Methodists, so you can speak your mind."

"Well," I said, "I think you have the spirit of prejudice among you just like other people. I do not think I am mistaken, for the spirit of this meeting seems very clear to me."

They had on the mantel three or four little stuffed birds. So I said, "I do not think it is right to have those stuffed birds there. The Bible says we are not to have pictures of anything in heaven, or on earth, or in the water." Well, I knew the quotation correctly then. So after I had said this, Brother E. said, "Well, Sister Smith, God bless you. About there being prejudice, you are mistaken; but about the images, you are right."

So then Brother E. led his wife, and he said to her "You don't pray as much as you used to, I know. Often when I used to be down town in my office I could tell when you were praying." Then he talked to her so before all the people.

When he got through she got up and went upstairs and slammed the door after her. And I said, "Well, that means what I used to mean when I slammed the door after me." But still he did say a lot of things to her that I thought he ought to have said to her alone. So I said, "Well, these people are just like my own. So I guess I will not join."

When we came out, one of the sisters came out with us. She was a good sister. She went up to me, took hold of me, and said, "Sister Smith, you are right about that prejudice part of it. That sister that you referred to has got prejudices, and she was so vexed, and she said to-night as she was coming she hoped the colored folks would not be there. She does not like it because they come." I said, "I knew I was right. But Brother E. does not know that, does he?"

"Oh! no, she does not say it to them; but she has said it to me, and I know her."

So I never went back again.

Then Rev. Joshua Woodland was pastor of the A. M. E. Church in Brooklyn. He was a man of God, and preached the Gospel. So I said, "As I cannot get real food for my soul in my own church, I will go to Brooklyn and join Brother Woodland's. Of course it will cost me something to go and come, but I will walk on this side and cross on the boat, and walk on the other side to church; and then a sermon once a week will help me, and I will still go to my class here in New York." So I prayed for light and guidance for three weeks. At last I said, one day, "Lord, show me by Thy Spirit through Thy Word, what I must do. Thou knowest I want to do Thy will only." And I opened my Bible, and as I looked, my eyes lighted on these words: "Fear not, stand still, and see the salvation of God." And there came a flood of light and peace to my heart. And I arose and praised the Lord. I never left the church, but I have seen sad results of many who have left and gone away. Some have done well, probably, but others have made sad failures. What a pity. I can call up a number of white people, young men and women, that I used to know in New York, and Oh! how they have failed in their lives, leaving one church and joining another. Thank the Lord he has kept me steady. Amen.

It is often said to me, "How nicely you get on, Mrs. Smith; everybody seems to treat you so kindly, and you always seem to get on so well."

"Yes; that is what you think," I said; "but I have much more to contend with than you may think." Then they said: "Oh, well, but no one would treat you unkindly." Then I said: "But if you want to know and understand properly what Amanda Smith has to contend with, just turn black and go about as I do, and you will come to a different conclusion." And I think some people would understand the quintessence of sanctifying grace if they could be black about twenty-four hours. We need to be saved deep to make us thorough, all around, out and out, come up to the standard Christians, and not bring the standard down to us; and as old Brother Cooper in Africa used to say, "Lord, help the people to see." Amen.

One day a lady asked me if I did not think all colored people wanted to be white I told her that I did not think so—I did not. I never wished I was white but once, that I could remember, and that was years ago. I was at a white Methodist Church in Lancaster; I sat in the gallery. The new minister had come. This was his first Sunday. I lived at Colonel Henry McGraw's, on Lime street, and the church was about two squares from where I lived. The colored church where I belonged and attended was quite a ways from our house. I always had a big dinner to cook on Sunday when Mr. McGraw was at home. He had a very dear friend, Mr. James Reynolds, whom he always liked to have dine with him. I generally liked to go to church on Sunday morning, but it was too far for me to go and get back so as to have my dinner in time. I was always very proud of being prompt with my dinner so that often on Sunday I would only get out at night. This Sunday I thought I would go and hear the new minister. All the young people generally sat upstairs, and a colored person was to them an object of game and criticism. I was careful to do nothing to provoke this spirit, but I generally got enough of it.

I don't remember what the text was; but O, how well I remember the power with which the preacher spoke, and the sweetness of his countenance. As he preached the Lord blessed me wonderfully, and I did want to shout "Praise the Lord;" and I remember saying "I wish I was white, and I would shout 'Glory to Jesus.' " They did not look at white people, nor remark about their shouting; for they did use to shout! I did not shout, but thought, "The willing mind is accepted according to what a man hath, and not according to what he hath not." And that was the only time in my life I ever wanted to be white. But, praise the Lord! I shout now whenever His spirit prompts. No, we who are the royal black are very well satisfied with His gift to us in this substantial color. I, for one, praise Him for what He has given me, although at times it is very inconvenient. For example: When on my way to California last January, a year ago, if I had been white I could have stopped at a hotel, but being black, though a lone woman, I was obliged to stay all night in the waiting room at Austin, Texas, though I arrived at ten P. M.; and many times when in Philadelphia, or New York, or Baltimore, or most anywhere else except in grand old historic Boston, I could not go in and have a cup of tea or a dinner at a hotel or restaurant. There may be places in these cities where colored people may be accommodated, but generally they are proscribed, and that sometimes makes it very inconvenient. I could pay the price—yes, that is all right; I know how to behave—yes, that is all right; I may have on my very best dress so that I look elegant—yes, that is all right; I am known as a Christian lady—yes, that is all right; I will occupy but one chair; I will touch no person's plate or fork—yes that is all right; but you are black! Now, to say that being black did not make it inconvenient for us often, would not be true; but belonging to royal stock, as we do, we propose braving this inconvenience for the present, and pass on into the great big future where all these little things will be lost because of their absolute smallness! May the Lord send the future to meet us! Amen.

At Ocean Grove a lady took me aside and said, "Now, Amanda Smith, I want to ask you honestly; I know you cannot be—."

"What now?" thought I.

"I know you cannot be white, but if you *could* be, would you not rather be white than black?"

"No, no," I said, "as the Lord lives, I would rather be black and fully saved than to be white and not saved; I was bad enough, black as I am, and I would have been ten times worse if I had been white." How she roared laughing. She was all right, but I think she just wanted to test me a little bit. Yes, thank God, I am satisfied with my color. I am glad I had no choice in it, for if I had, I am sure I would not have been satisfied; for when I was a young girl I was passionately fond of pea-green, and if choice had been left to me I would have chosen to be green, and I am sure God's color is the best and most substantial. It's the blood that makes whiteness. Hallelujah!

"The blood applied,
I'm justified,
I'm saved without, within,
The blood of Jesus cleanseth me
From every trace of sin."

CHORUS—"There is power in Jesus' blood,
There is power in Jesus' blood,
There is power in Jesus' blood
To wash me white as snow."

"Many years my longing heart
Had sighed, had longed to know
The virtue of the Saviour's blood,
That washes white as snow."

One day in New York I went into the Tuesday Palmer's meeting. A lady came in, and there was a very comfortable seat by me, and after looking about for some other place she finally decided to take the one by me; but I saw she was uncomfortable. She fanned and fidgeted and fussed and aired herself till I wished in my heart she had gone somewhere else. Before the meeting closed I arose and spoke; the Lord helped me and blessed the people. At the close of the meeting this lady turned to me so full of pleasant smiles, and said, "Oh, I did not know I was sitting by Amanda Smith; I feel myself highly honored." I looked at her and pitied her, but felt sick! I said in my heart, "From all hollowness and sham, Good Lord deliver us!"

One day at Oakington Camp Meeting there was a lady I heard giving her testimony. She said, "I have come over five hundred miles to this meeting to get the blessing of entire sanctification. I believe it is my privilege to enjoy this experience, but I have not got it. I have read all the works on the subject and sought earnestly day and night, and yet I have not got the light."

O, how I wanted to tell her it was not in the books. I arose to speak and tell her, as I thought the Lord wanted me to, but I was told to sit down, there were others who wanted to speak. I was a little sorry, for I was quite sure my desire to speak was the Lord's prompting; but I must needs learn obedience of the powers that be. Praise the Lord for the grace that enabled me to do so. Hallelujah! I also saw some things that were not what I called consistent with the profession of the sanctified life. It was unexpected, and I was young in the experience and was struck a little; but God saved me from backsliding from this principle, as many do when they meet with things in life that do not harmonize with the profession of holiness. There is much of the human nature for us to battle with, even after we are wholly

sanctified, so that we shall ever need the beautiful grace of patience." For ye have need of patience, that, after ye have done the will of God, ye might receive the promise." Hebrews, 10: 36.

CHAPTER X.

"THY WILL BE DONE," AND HOW THE SPIRIT TAUGHT ME ITS MEANING, ALSO THAT OF SOME OTHER PASSAGES OF SCRIPTURE—MY DAUGHTER MAZIE S CONVERSION.

It all came to me so clearly after I had received the baptism of the Holy Ghost. I saw that I had prayed from my earliest childhood this prayer, but had never understood it; but, Oh! when the Spirit revealed it to me I was so astonished that I had not seen it before. "Our Father," I said, "God is my Father. He has made me, and I am His child." How that word "Father" filled me with awe.

"Who art in Heaven, hallowed be Thy name." At these words a holy reverence passed through my whole being.

"Thy kingdom come, Thy will be done on earth as it is in Heaven." Like the angels do it in Heaven. Then I thought, "How do the angels do God's will. Do they hesitate? Do they question? Do they shrink?" And I said "No." Swift, prompt, loyal obedience by angels, and I asked God that I may do His will on earth like angels do it in heaven. When I saw this, I covered my face and wept, and laughed; so simple, and so great!

"Thy will be done." Oh! that word, and to say it from the heart. When you stand by your dear ones dying, with not two dollars for funeral expenses, with a husband and father away, and when he might have come, yet did not, with no one to go to, when the very heavens seemed brass, and the earth iron, and you and your own body exhausted from hard work and watching day and night, and with but little food to sustain the body, then to say, "Thy will be done," from the heart, is more than all burnt offerings and sacrifice; and this prayer prayed from the heart, is what is meant by being entirely and wholly satisfied. I did not understand this when I first learned it, but the time came a few months after.

The Lord took from me my dear little Will. He was the brightest and most promising of all the five children I had had, and when he was but three days old, I got on my knees by my bedside and consecrated him to God. I had not done so with the others, and I thought it was why the Lord took them away, but I did not know about consecrating children to God, only in baptism. Now I saw afterward there was selfishness in it, though I was really sincere. I did this, thinking the Lord would not take him. Then I promised I would train him prayerfully, and he should be a preacher of the Gospel. I said: "Lord, I give him to Thee, and I hold myself just as Thy servant, to raise him for Thee; he is not mine, I give him wholly to Thee, and now help me to raise him. When he is five years old I will have him reading, and I will work day and night to give him an education."

When I got through with my prayer I arose and lay down again. He grew and thrived beautifully till he was five months old. Oh, how bright he was. He had had several little sick turns, but I never once thought he would die, because I had given him to the Lord so fully, and now the Lord will let me have him. One morning I had cleaned up my room, and had my tubs all ready to go to washing, for this I always did, so that my house was in order if any one should come in. The next was to give my baby his bath and make him comfortable. Just after I had done this and laid him down on the sofa, and emptied his bath, he seemed perfectly well and was crowing and so bright. His sister, Mazie, was getting ready for school, and was calling, saying: "Be good, Will, till I come back." All at once she called out to me: "Oh Ma, look at Will," and he was stiff in a fit, and there was froth on his mouth and he was black in the face. My kettle of wash water was on, and in a moment I had him another bath ready. I stripped him. There was no one to call. I never lost my presence of mind a moment. I put him in his bath. I did not forget to put in the water a handful of salt and a little mustard. I don't know how I did it, God kept me so still in my soul. He soon came out of his spasm when I put him in the warm water. The dear little fellow, the first thing he did was to look up and say, "Mama," and pat me on the check with his little hand. He seemed all right and I dressed him and laid him down and went to my washing. He slept and took his food as usual till several days had passed, then he seemed poorly and fretful, and I took him to a doctor; he prescribed for him and said he would be all right in I few days; but another spasm. Then for five long weeks I worked and watched and never took off my clothes, only to change them. I did everything I could; had no one to help; had to do my washing between times as I could. It never entered my thoughts that he would die. One Wednesday morning, I had been watching all night; he was restless, but I had got him quiet about five o'clock in the morning. I stole away from him to finish hanging up my last clothes and finish my work. About six o'clock he awoke and cried, and I would call to him and he would wait to see if I was coming and then he would cry again. I would say: "Hold on, Will, I am coming." Oh, how I worked! I had to work quick. When I got through I went to take him up. I found he had kicked off one of his little socks. I picked it up cheerfully and said, "Oh, Will, you have lost one of your boots, old man." When I went to put it on I saw his little foot was swollen on top. I knew what that meant; an arrow went through my heart, and I could hardly lift him from the bed. I tried to say, "Thy will be done," but I could not. I thought, "After all, the Lord is going to take him, and I can't say 'Thy will be done.'"

I had heard of a wonderful doctor for children, a lady. I thought I would try this new doctor. I took him in my arms, and when I got to the doctor's I could not speak a word. She looked at him and said to me, "You must not feel so bad, his eyes are bright, and I think he will be better in a few days;" but I knew the sign of his feet was no mistake. I paid her one dollar, and a dollar and a half for the prescription, and had but fifty cents left; all I had in the world. I went home and did as I was told, but I could not say "Thy will be done." Oh! the agony of my soul. The Lord sent a dear friend in Minte Corsey. Oh, how glad I was she came. She lived at service and could only stay a day or two, but this was a great help to me. Friday morning came, still I could not say, "Thy will be done." I wanted to say it, and then I resolved that I would neither eat nor drink until I could, from my heart, say, "The will of the Lord be done." It took me from Thursday till Friday afternoon about three P. M. I got the victory. While I was alone pleading with God for power to say, "Thy will he done," all at once my heart seemed to sink into a deep quiet, and I said, "Lord, Thou hast helped me, and I can say, 'Thy will be done.' " Oh, how sweet it was; it seemed to me I could

taste it; it was sweet as honey; and a voice seemed to reason, "Now, Amanda, you can have your choice, if you say the life of your child you may have it as easy as turning your hand," and I said, "Lord, Thy will is so sweet, I only want Thy will;" and it came again, "Whatever you desire it is only to say," and I said again, "Oh, Lord, Thy will is so sweet, I only say Thy will be done." Then the joy sprang up in my heart. I was filled with joy, and I went out of that room saying, "Victory, victory, thanks be to God, He giveth victory, Hallelujah!"

This was Friday afternoon about four o'clock. About two o'clock the next morning little Will fell asleep in Jesus, in my arms. I washed the little body and laid it out myself; laid him on the little stand. No tears; God seemed to dry them up with joy! O, the greatness of His peace that passeth understanding!

Saturday morning I don't know how I got my clothes home, but I did. I got a young man to go for my husband, who was at New Utrecht, not far from Brooklyn, N. Y. I had but two dollars, that had come in from my washing, and I wondered what I would do, but my husband would be home, and I thought I could leave that. Just then a flood of sadness seemed to fill my heart. I could not understand it. I was sick and weak, and I said it is because I have lost so much rest. I sent my little girl to tell some friends to come in, and they sent word it was Saturday and they were all busy, so no one came. I lay down I few moments, then I broke into a flood of tears. "Lord, help me!" I said.

About ten o'clock the young man came back, whom I sent to see my husband. He sent word he was sick himself, and could not come, and had no money. I felt I must sink. I said, "O, Lord, help me!" I was so weak I had to lie down three times before I could get properly dressed, as I must go out in the street. I thought I would go and see a lady with whom I used to live, away uptown, Fortieth street and Madison avenue. I thought if they could help me get my baby buried, I would clean house to pay them again. While I was getting ready to go, my dear friend, Sister Nancy Thompson, who lived in Clinton court, near Eighth Street, sent a messenger to say I must come to her house at once.

"O," I said, "I can't. I must go uptown," but the child would not go without me.

She said, "Auntie Thompson says I must not come without you," and I went with the child. I thought after I had seen her,

MAZIE D. SMITH.

then I would go on uptown. When I saw this dear friend, Sister Thompson, she said, "Smith, I hear your baby is dead." I said, "Yes."

She said, "If twenty dollars will help you, I can let you have it." And I saw God, and wept!

"Sometimes, 'mid scenes of deepest gloom,
  Sometimes where Eden's bowers bloom,
  By waters still, o'er troubled sea,
  Still 'tis God's hand that leadeth me." Amen.

Dear Sister Nancy Thompson has gone to Heaven out of great tribulation, last January. God was so good to bring me back from Africa to see her and pray and praise with her on earth before he took her to himself.

"There the wicked cease from trouble;
  There the weary are at rest." Amen.

I went home and sent off to make arrangements for the funeral on Sunday. The undertaker was kind. I told him just my situation. I said if you will take fifteen dollars I will pay you the other fifteen in a week. He said he had a bill to pay next Thursday and if I would let him have it by then, he would do what he could. I told him I thought I could do it. O, how the Lord did help me. He was so reasonable. God, I know, was in it all. On Sunday, at one o'clock, the funeral. I waited for my husband till after three, then they said if we did not go the gates would be closed and I would have to come back with the body. O, I was so alarmed. I did not know this.

So the undertaker himself said, "I think I had better go myself." So he got on beside the driver, and they drove very fast and we got there just as they were closing the gates, and but for the undertaker's being with us we would have had to bring back the lifeless little body. I thought my husband would meet me at the cemetery, as it was but a short distance from where he lived. I hoped he would be able to come that far; but no, he was not there. O, I could not describe the feelings of that hour. God held me Himself. I thanked the kind undertaker, and we got home about half past six o'clock.

It was the Quarterly Meeting Sunday at the A. M. E. Church on Sullivan street. I knew I had many friends there. Brother George Smith was always a good friend. He was the Chairman of the Board of Trustees. I went to him, and as I was an honorable member of the church, and had always done my duty as far as I was able, financially and otherwise. I told him just my situation, and asked him if he would be kind enough to state it and ask the people for a collection of fifteen dollars, that I might pay the undertaker. He did so, and there was a cheerful response and about twenty dollars was given, but as I had said fifteen, I got that and no more. I was thankful for that. I went on Tuesday and paid the bill, and got the receipt. O, what a burden was lifted from my heart. The undertaker, too, was glad, and thanked me and said, "Mrs. Smith, you have done well."

All that fall and winter was deep trial, and O, what lessons He taught me of Himself. Praise His name. The summer came and I went to Long Branch to work. I thought it would do me good, as I was very much run down. Still deeper trials came, and various. I was at Congress Hall, Mr. Laird's. He and his wife were very nice.

The housekeeper that had charge of the hiring of most of the women help was front Philadelphia. She was a Miss Jordan. She had power to discharge any that did not suit her. She would give them an order to the office and they were paid off and discharged—chambermaids, scrubbers and laundry women. I went as private laundress for the family of four, and if I chose to assist when there was a rush, all right. The wages were fair, and I could take my little girl, and I went in the laundry. There were many professing Christians, but one, a quiet and elderly person, who was living on good works of her own, and looking and stumbling at the inconsistency of others who professed to be Christians. The head laundress, whom I had known in Philadelphia for years, was a good church member, and I thought a good Christian, but I found things were different. I would do all my work and would always help with the sheets and pillowcases or towels or table cloths, whatever was the need, but always got through so as to go to church on Sunday. I found, after the first two Sundays, it was giving offense, and there was much criticism and talk about some people who had so much religion they could go to church and couldn't work on Sunday. They would say, "I came down here to work; I go to church at home."

I said nothing but felt sad. Every day at twelve o'clock I would run up in my room just over the laundry and pray. I never was over five minutes, so as not to be missed. Remarks began to

be made about this: "I can't get time to sleep. Some people can stop and go to sleep. I came here to work." I said nothing. One day just as I got on my knees, some one of them came up and opened the door, and seeing me on my knees, slammed the door and went down laughing. "Some people get on their knees to sleep, pretending to be praying." Then the laughter.

I came down but said nothing, not a word. So Miss J., the housekeeper, was informed. She was always very nice to me, but this time she came storming in the laundry and said, "Mrs. Smith, you will have to help with the sheets and table-cloths."

"All right," I said, and when I got through I would. I would get up at four o'clock in the morning; by seven I would have twenty or thirty sheets out on the line. I did not talk. By and by some one would call out, "Miss J. says no one out of the laundry will go to church on Sunday; she is not going to have it. What will you do, Mrs. Smith?"

I said, "Well, Sunday is not here, yet; we will see when it comes."

Then I saw several of them look in washing to make extra money —white pants, coats and vests. I would do all my work, then they would ask me to help. I did help to iron several times, till eleven o'clock one Saturday night, then I quit. I felt it was not right, and saw why they really had to work on Sunday—not that Mr. Laird required it—and when I saw this I resolved by the grace of God I would not be a party to their maneuvers. Sunday came. Every eye was on me to see what I was going to do. I didn't say anything; I went on as usual getting ready, and went upstairs. I watched my chance and found Miss J. in another part of the house, out from the laundry, and I went to her. I had prayed that the Lord would help me to speak to her and make her willing to hear, for as a general thing she didn't stop to hear what you said when she had made up her mind you must do something. So I met her in the hall of the big house and I went up to her and said, "Miss Jordan, I want to go to church this morning. The work is all done excepting what the women want to do for themselves, and I will have nothing to do with it," and she said, "Quite right, Mrs. Smith, you go on; don't say anything about it."

I went down, got ready, dressed my little girl, said nothing to anybody at all,—didn't say what I had said to Miss Jordan, didn't say what Miss Jordan said to me,—and went to church; but O, the storm of remarks and criticisms.

As I sat in church I thought to myself, "I don't like these surroundings, I don't like these spirits; I don't mean to get into a controversy or quarrel, and I think I will just go on Monday morning to Mrs. Laird and tell her that I will go home," and I sat looking to the Lord about it. This was before the service began. By and by the services began. The Rev. Dr. Stratton was the pastor, and announced the first hymn, which was,

"Give to the winds thy fears—"

I shall never forget it—

> "Give to the winds thy fears,
> Hope and be undismayed;
> God knows thy sorrows, counts thy tears,
> God shall lift up thy head."

I praised him, and said, "Lord, if you will help me, I will stick."

One day I was very much tried again, and was really depressed in spirit. I tried to be kind to everybody, and as accommodating as I could. I had not had a word with anybody, didn't want to, and didn't mean to, though they had tried in various ways to draw me into little spats, but the Lord saved me and gave me grace. One day I was feeling a good deal depressed and cast down, because I could not understand why there should be so much unpleasantness; there was no necessity for it, as I could see. I went up and knelt down to pray, feeling that I must leave, yet I needed the means; I needed the money. While I was praying and asking the Lord to help me and show me what to do, it seemed as though an angel stood by me. His wings were plumed, and the ends seemed to be tipped with fire. It was a beautiful sight, a beautiful vision, and seemed very clear to my mind; and I said, "Lord, what does this mean?" and these words came to me: "The wings of Hope and arms of Faith shall bear you conqueror through." I thanked the Lord and rose from my knees and went down to my work. I said nothing to anyone. I went to Mrs. Laird and said to her, "Mrs. Laird, I think I will go home; I don't like the unpleasantness; I think a good deal of it unnecessary; I have not been accustomed to having words or quarreling, and it makes me feel very bad; I think I had better go home."

She said, "You do the clothes very nicely, and Mr. Laird and I like you very much—like your work." And I said, "I don't want to have any words with Miss Jordan." She says, "Never mind Miss Jordan. You need not mind anything Mary Jordan says to you; you come to me. You just go right on with your work, and if you are disturbed, come to me."

I thanked her and went back to my work. I said nothing to anyone. I stayed until the whole house was closed for the season.

So the Lord brought me off more than conquerer. That's just like Him. Blessed be His name!

"For this is the will of God, even your sanctification." As I thought it over, I reasoned like this: "If my father, when he died, had left me heir to a certain it mount, or estate, why, I should have claimed it. And if there were other heirs, and they had tried to get it from me, I would have contended for my rights out of the will. And as it was in my father's will, the law would have justified me in so doing." As I thought it all over, I remembered reading in the papers a suit in the Orphans' Court at Brooklyn just at that time. So it all seemed plain to me. When Satan would suggest, "You cannot expect such a blessing," I stood on these words, "But it is the will of God. He is my Father. And He said in His inspired word, through His Apostle Paul, it is the will of God. And I am one of His legitimate children and a rightful heir, and I propose to have my rights out of the will, if all the rest of the heirs get offended." When I anchored there, somehow I seemed to get help. No matter how the Tempter would come, I stuck to the word, and would say, "But it is the will of God." And it seemed every time I would say it, it was like a girdle to my faith. Oh! how Satan hates to have you believe God. How he tries to wrest His word from your grasp. But when we hold on by faith, even though we tremble, how we honor God, and how we triumph at last. Hallelujah! Hallelujah! Amen! Fear not, my trembling friend, whoever you are. Believe only, and thou shalt see the glory of God, and not only see, but feel His power."

It was in the winter of 1869, in New York. We were holding revival services at Bethel Church, Sullivan street, Rev. Henry Davis, pastor. There were several young people in the Sabbath School who were converted. Mazie was, I believe, soundly converted. She gave evidences in her spirit and life for a time, though they were hard days for us then. She went to school, and had to work hard at home as well, which did not hurt her. She always could sleep well; so many nights when I would be washing or standing ironing all night, she, poor child, could sleep. Saturday generally was a hard day; she had to carry the clothes home; we could not afford to ride, so she had to walk, often long distances. I tried to help her in her religious life all I could. We always had prayers night and morning. We didn't read the Bible at night, but always in the morning, we read verse about; then we would sing a verse of a hymn; she was a fine alto singer; then I would pray. The third or fourth morning after she had been converted, I said to her; "Now, Mazie, the Lord has converted you, and you are very happy; and now if you want to be a real, growing and strong Christian, you must learn to pray."

"Well," she said, "Ma, I do say my prayers; but I don't know how to pray."

"Well," I said, "if you ask the Lord He will teach you how to pray; so the sooner you begin the sooner you will get over the embarrassment, and the Lord will bless you. Now, there are only two of us, and always when we kneel to pray I will expect you to pray first, and *I* will follow. Then on Saturday night, when we have our little prayer meeting, no matter who is here, as soon as we kneel to pray, you pray first." She gave a little sigh; and then we knelt down, and she sighed again. I knew it was hard for her to begin, but I waited, and then another sigh; then in her childish way she begun to thank the Lord for what He had done for her, and ask Him to teach her to pray; it very simple little prayer, but, Oh, so earnest. How happy she was I knew she would be, if she would be prayerful and obedient. The heavy cross was taken up. When Saturday night came, a number of people, perhaps six or seven, came in to have a little prayer meeting. The Lord had made this clear to me, that I was to have a prayer meeting at my room for those who wished to draw nearer to the Lord. I never expected to do anything, more than this. But after He had sanctified my heart it was beginning at Jerusalem; so at Jerusalem I did begin. And though the little prayer meeting was of short duration, yet God put His seal on it, and souls were blessed and saved. To God be the glory. Amen' Amen!

My object in having Mazie pray first at this meeting, was, I thought after she had carried clothes all day, and done other work as well, that the child was very tired and sleepy, and she would likely fall asleep on her knees while others would be praying; and I knew the dear Lord would not blame her for being weary and sleepy. Of course, I never told her why I did it, so there was no chance of her taking advantage of it. But, praise the Lord, He blessed her and strengthened her. She seemed to get on nicely; for she loved the Sabbath School, and was a bright, active scholar, both in New York, and Philadelphia, where she joined at Allen Chapel, Rev. Mr. Whitney, pastor. As she had stood so well I thought there would be no danger of her being influenced at a Catholic school. And then they told me she could have her Bible and Hymn Book just the same; and so she did take them with her; but they very quietly took them away from her after she was there a while, and said they would take care of them for her, and gave her such a nice book that she would like to read, about some good saint or sister; and as she was so fond of reading she accepted it at once. But she never saw her Bible or Hymn Book again till she left. Sending my daughter to this school was a serious mistake, on my part, and one that is made by many parents who are ignorant, as I was, of the subtlety of Rome.

CHAPTER XI.

MY CALL TO GO OUT—AN ATTACK FROM SATAN—HIS SNARE BROKEN—MY PERPLEXITY IN REGARD TO THE TRINITY— MANIFESTATION OF JESUS—WAS IT A DREAM?

It was in November, 1869. God had led me clearly up to this time confirming His work through me as I went all about—sometimes to Brooklyn, then to Harlem, then to Jersey City. All this was among my own people, and our own colored churches, though I often went beside to old Second Street, Norfolk Street, Willett Street, Bedford Street, and to different white Methodist churches, to class meetings and prayer meetings; but very little with white people, comparatively. The most I did was among my own people. There were then but few of our ministers that were favorable to women's preaching or taking any part, I mean in a public way; but, thank God, there always were a few men that dared to stand by woman's liberty in this, if God called her. Among these, I remember, was Henry Davis, Rev. James Holland, Rev. Joshua Woodland, Rev. Joseph H. Smith, and Rev. Leonard Patterson, and others—but it is different now. We have women deaconesses, and leaders, and women in all departments of church work. May God in mercy save us from the formalism of the day, and bring us back to the old time spirituality and power of the fathers and mothers. I often feel as I look over the past and compare it with the present, to say: "Lord, save, or we perish."

As the Lord led, I followed, and one day as I was praying and asking Him to teach me what to do I was impressed that I was to leave New York and go out. I did not know where, so it troubled me, and I asked the Lord for light, and He gave me these words: "Go, and I will go with you." The very words He gave to Moses, so many years ago.

I said, "Lord, I am willing to go, but tell me where to go and I will obey Thee;" and clear and plain the word came, "Salem!" I said, "Salem! why, Lord, I don't know anybody in Salem. O, Lord, do help me, and if this is Thy voice speaking to me, make it plain where I shall go." And again it came, "Salem."

"O, Lord, Thou knowest I have never been to Salem, and only have heard there is such a place."

I remembered that five years before while living in Philadelphia, I was at Bethel Church one morning, and the minister gave out that their quarterly meeting was to be held at Salem the next Sunday. I could not go —I was at service—this was all that I had heard about Salem, or knew. I said: "O, Lord, don't let Satan deceive me, make it very plain to me, and if this is Thy voice, speak again to me, do Lord, make it clear, so as to make me understand it, and I will obey Thee. Now, Lord, I wait to hear Thee speak to me, and tell me where to go," and I heard the word coming, I was afraid, it seemed as though the Lord would strike me down, and I drew down as though to hide, and the word came with power, "Salem," and I said, "Lord, that is enough, I will go."

A few weeks passed. O, how I was tested to the very core in every way. My rent was five dollars a month, and I wanted to pay two months before I went. I prayed and asked the Lord to help me to do this. It was wonderful how He did. I needed a pair of shoes. I told the Lord I was willing to go with the shoes I had if He wanted me to, but they were broken in the sole, and I said: "Lord, Thou knowest if I get my feet wet I will be sick; now, if it is Thy will to get the shoes, either give me some work to do or put it in the heart of somebody to give me the money to get the shoes." And these words came from God to my heart: "If thou canst believe; all things are possible to him that believeth." And I said, "Lord, the shoes are mine," and I put them on as really as ever I put on a pair of shoes in my life! O, how real it was. I claimed them by faith. When I got up I walked about and felt I really had the very shoes I had asked for on my feet. O, how very true that blessed promise—"What things so ever ye desire, when ye pray, believe that ye receive them and ye shall have them." I know that truth. Hallelujah!

Some three days after I said to my friend, Sister Scott, "I want to go to Seventh street before I go away, for I have promised some friends ever since the Sing Sing Camp Meeting, and I have

never had the chance to go, and I must go before I leave." The day before was Thanksgiving day, and I was over in Jersey City helping Brother Lewis. He had a meeting in the church on that day, so at Seventh street we had a good prayer and testimony meeting. Rev. John Parker was pastor. The Lord helped me to speak, and I told them the Lord had told me I was to go to Salem, and I was going, and I had only come to say, "How do you do, and good-bye." At the close of the meeting friends gathered around me and said, "Why, Sister Smith, where were you yesterday? We looked for you. We had a grand Thanksgiving sermon." Another said, "Come to my class." I said, "Thank you, but I, can't now; you must wait till I come back; I have got orders from above to go."

As dear old Father Brummell passed out he said, "Good-bye, Sister Smith." He shook my hand and put something in it. I thanked him and put it in my pocket, and so went home. As I sat by the fire and was warming myself—I had read my chapter in the Bible, and I was sitting thinking about the meeting—I began to get very drowsy and sleepy. "Well, I thought, I must get ready to go to bed."

Just then the thought came to me, "You had better see what that money is Father Brummell gave to you."

"Yes," I thought. "I had forgot that."

I put my hand in my pocket and took it out; there was one two dollar bill and three one dollar bills. I spread it on the table and counted it. It was the first time I ever had that much money given me in my life, just for nothing, like, and I thought I must have made a mistake in counting it, so I counted it again. Yes, it was really five dollars. Then I said, "Surely I have made a mistake; I am asleep, I guess;" so I rubbed my eyes and walked up and down the floor and went back and counted it again. Yes, it really was five dollars, and I said, "Well, how is it?" Just then a voice whispered, "You know you prayed about your shoes."

"O," I shouted, "Yes, Lord, I remember now. Praise the Lord! O, Praise the Lord!"

I was so happy I could hardly go to sleep. It was the Lord's doing, and it was marvelous. Amen.

After I had decided to obey the call and was getting ready to go, Satan fiercely attacked me as I stood ironing and praying earnestly to God. He said: "When Jesus sent out His disciples He sent them out two and two, and now you are going alone; they will say you are going to look for a husband, like others."

Then I thought of several that I knew who had gone out and really did get married, after a time; but what business was that to the old Accuser, and what had he to do with it? But the thought was so foreign from me that I cried out, "Thou knowest that is a lie. Thou knowest I only want to do God's will."

The Tempter harassed me so that I set my iron down and went into the room and got on my knees and said, "Lord help me, and choose somebody to go with me, if Thou dost want me to have a companion. Lord, I would like Sister Scott to go; I know her and love her; could get on so nicely together; but she has a family and she cannot go. Then there is Sister Bright, in Philadelphia, and others I know. If I were to choose them we might not be congenial spirits, and so would not get on together; so, Lord, if Thou wilt direct me to whom Thou wouldst, all will be well; and now, Lord, I wait before Thee earnestly to hear Thy word to me." And these words of Jesus were whispered as distinctly as a father's voice to his child, and it said: "Did I not tell you that I would with you?" And in a moment I remembered what He had said before—"Go and I will go with you."

"O, yes, Jesus," I said; "so you did." I had forgotten it; and I arose filled with joy and peace. Praise the Lord for victory!

A few days later I was off to Salem, New Jersey. I stayed a week in Philadelphia, and came near giving up and not going; notwithstanding God had clearly answered prayer, and made all so plain to me. O, the weakness and frivolity of poor human beings. Lord, pity us for Jesus' sake. Amen.

Oh! how much one has to unlearn in order to learn God's will more perfectly, I left New York for Salem, where God first sent me, in November, 1869, and returned in June. During these months of absence my friend, Sister Scott, had passed through deep trials—greatly complicated—could not be explained; only those that have had them know about them. I knew a good deal. She and I corresponded, and I would pray and advise her to stand fast; God would help her. But things got worse, and I think Satan got her frightened. Her husband, when in a passion, would make threats that frightened her. When she wrote to me and told me, I said, "The Devil wants to scare you; I don't believe anyone is going to kill you; stand firm."

She thought I ought to come home and stand by her, but I knew the Lord did not want me to meddle in man and wife trouble, so it was all right I was away. I said, "Scott, every eye is on you to see how you stand, and if sanctifying grace is good for anything, this is your time to test it. Don't you leave your home." This was the way I wrote, and I think it was not what she expected. From that time the spirit of her letters to me seemed to be greatly changed. I felt she was not the same in spirit. Then, encouraged by her son to leave her home, she did so and moved, with the three children, around in Minnetta street. While I felt she had changed, I loved her so well that I thought, "When I get home and see her and have a talk I can explain and clear up everything; she will understand me and will soon be all right." So in June I got to be full of hope and expectation, for I did not think I could live in New York without the former friendship and love of sister S. She had moved from Minnetta street to Dominick street, and after I had got a little straightened up in my room I could hardly wait to see her. I would smile to myself and think how glad she would be to see me, and what she would say; and it was all so real; but O, imagine my disappointment and surprise. When I went she was so cool and formal. O, how my heart sank. I told her everything that I knew used to interest her. She listened, and I saw she made an effort to be herself, and that hurt me so; I knew her so well. I told her why I wrote to her as I did, and I thought as she had been through so much for so many years she might have stuck to it a little longer, and I believed God would have helped her and brought her out conqueror. I saw that the Devil had made her believe that I did not care for her, and had no sympathy for her. We talked till twelve at night; then as we always prayed when we met, I said well, let us pray. We knelt; I prayed, but she did not. I went out with a heavy heart, and under an awful temptation.

"Oh!" I thought, "if Scott has turned against me after all these years of helpful friendship, what will I do?" and it was like Peter's walk on the water. I had got my eye off of Jesus, and I began to sink, and the more I thought of it the deeper I went. I called again and begged her to come and see me. I ran in again, and said, "I have been wishing you would come, that we might have a season of prayer together," but she made some excuse, which I knew was not like my old friend. How I wept and prayed; I thought it would kill me, but I see now what it meant. God was to separate me unto Himself and I must be weaned. O, what an ordeal. After a day or two she came in. I was ironing and she sat down on the doorstep. "Oh," I said, "come in," but she would not and went away without saying a word about prayer, and I was convinced that the real spirit of my dear friend of years had gone—only the woman was there. O, the sadness of that other spirit, how it lingers even to this day. I tried to cast my burden on the Lord with fasting and weeping and praying, but, O, for weeks I walked in darkness and Satan accused me. I looked over my mind to see if the advice I had given was the cause, no, I felt I was right. Well, to go and keep talking and trying to win my friend back to her former friendship—it seemed it was not what the Lord wanted me to do, but why had this darkness settled down over my spirit. I said, "O Lord, help me!" I did not seem able pray, I seemed to have no spirit in me. Yet I could not feel any clear condemnation, but, O, what a state I was in! I knew I had not taken anything back from God of my consecration, but, O, what was the matter with me, I could not tell. Other times when I would have these trials my friend would come and we would pray together and get deliverance, but now, I not a soul to help me, and I could not prevail. There are times when one needs help to prevail with God, but I had no help, and the Devil said, "You see, if you were sanctified fully, you would be able to pray, but you have grieved the Spirit in some way, and this is why God don't answer you."

O, how real it all seemed, and yet somehow I knew it was not so. I was afraid to tell anyone. Satan said, "If you tell anyone they will think you have backslidden, you never heard of anyone who was sanctified having darkness like that."

"No, I never did." So I went to meetings, and talked what I knew of the bright side for fear the people would think I had backslidden sure enough. I think sanctified people ought to tell the other side, for it is no sign that you are backsliding when there comes a shadow over your Spirit, even after you are wholly sanctified; but I was ignorant and did not know that these questions were from the Devil. O, how he can transform himself into an angel of light to deceive.

My little girl had gone to live in Philadelphia with a very nice family, and I was very busy finishing a dress so as to send it to her. I had just got a letter from her, and she was getting along very nicely. As I sat with a sad heart and at times wishing I really could condemn myself so as to get access to God, for I felt if I could feel any condemnation, then surely I could pray; all at once the thought came, go down to Dominick street to Mrs. Clark's holiness meeting. Sister Clark used to have this meeting every Thursday afternoon at her house. I said, "O, I am too busy, I want to get this dress done," but a deep conviction took hold of me and I felt I must go, so I got up and went. I began to feel a little lighter. I said, "I guess the Lord is going to bless me to-day."

I went into the meeting, there were a good many present, and about five minutes after I got into the room this awful avalanche of darkness came over me again, and I began to cry. O, how bitterly I cried; I was heartbroken. The hymn was given out. I was sitting by Sister Clark. Just before the last verse was sung, the Devil said, "Now they are going to ask you to pray, and you know you can't;" and I said, "No, I can't pray."

Sure enough, when they knelt down, Sister Clark said to me, "Sister Smith, pray." I had always been able to pray before and after I had been sanctified, but I tried, and broke down. Some one said, "Amen, Lord, bless Sister Smith."

They thought I had got blest and was very happy. So I tried the second time to pray, but could not. Then the third time, failed again. O, I could not pray.

"Sister Clark," I said, "you pray, I can't," and she did pray, as she could in those days, for she used to be mighty in prayer. Then we arose. I sat and sobbed like a baby, listened to the testimonies and hoped for just a ray of light to come to my mind, so dark. After several had spoken, I arose and made a confession of all I knew. I had gone to Philadelphia to see my sister who was very sick and not expected to live. I left on Saturday night by the twelve o'clock train and got in five o'clock Sunday morning; left again on Sunday night, at twelve, got to Jersey City at five A. M., so the Devil had told me, that was one of the causes of I darkness. Then I had gone out without taking my tracts several times, so he said that was another reason. Then I used to get up and pray once or twice in the night, but I had not done that for several nights, so he accused me of that. At another time, after I had worked hard all day, I was tired, and after I had read my Bible lesson I knelt down to pray and fell asleep on my knees, and did not wake till about two o'clock in the morning; so he accused me of that, but when I asked the Lord to forgive me for all of these, it seemed as if a voice would say, "No, that is not it," and I said "Lord, what is it?" So I told these sisters all this. "And now," said I, "I want to know if any of you have had such an experience, for I don't know what is the matter; do help me if you can. Do sanctified people ever have such an experience?"

"No," they said; they shook their heads and looked very solemn, and I sat down, and each sister that spoke in turn, joined with my accuser and condemned me. They said that no doubt that these things were very wrong and was the cause of this darkness, and strange to say while I wanted it so, yet something seemed to say, "That is not so," and I felt like saying to each one of them as they spoke, "It is not so."

There was one lady who sat over by the window. I shall never forget her, though I can't remember her name. She was formerly from England, and was a friend of Sister Clark's. She had very black hair; she wore it very plain, two little puffs each side; I used to know her so well at Mrs. Palmer's meeting and at Round Lake Camp Meeting. God bless her! She was the last to speak that day, they were all through but her, and all had condemned me, but when she rose to speak she looked at me and said so sweetly these words—I shall never forget it, she said: "The Lord has a controversy with Amanda Smith, and it must be settled between her and Him alone." And a flash of light went through my mind, and I said, "Thank you, I see it." God showed me that instant I was leaning on my friend, Sister S. O, how I was wrapped up in her, but the snare was broken. I went out, my captivity was turned, and I praised the Lord. When I got home I got on my knees and thanked God for the light to show me where I was, and then with tears I begged the Lord to cut me loose from Sister Scott. I said, "Lord, it almost kills me, but O, deliver me, cut me loose, if you have to kill me, cut me loose."

O, what a dying it was! It seemed my heart was bound around with cords and to let go would take my life, but I cried, "O, Lord, cut me loose," and it was as though someone snapped with a knife the cords around my heart, and I breathed freely, and said, "Thank God I have got the victory." I arose and praised the Lord, and walked up and down!

I was just going to sit down to my sewing when I thought, "I must go out and get a postage stamp and write to my daughter to-night, so that she can get it in the morning." Out I started to the drug store on the corner of Fourth street and Sixth avenue. Just as I turned out of Amity street in Sixth avenue, I glanced over the way on Cornelia street, and saw a person who looked just like my friend Sister S. She seemed to look at me, and I nodded my head, and was just going to call to her, when she quickly turned her head, and didn't seem to see me at all. I thought, "O, has Scott gotten to where she will not even speak to me?" A pang went through my heart, and Satan in a moment said distinctly, "You have got no joy now."

"No," I said, "not a bit."

"You are not happy, either."

"No, it's all gone." Then in a tantalizing manner he said, "Where is all your sanctification and holiness that you have been talking about?" And then for the first time I clearly realized that it was Satan himself that was accusing me, and I said, "Ah! Ah! Mr. Satan, it is you, is it? Well, now look here, happiness or no happiness, joy or no joy, sanctification or no sanctification, I belong to Jesus!" and I began to sing this hymn:—

> "The blood of Christ it cleanseth me,
> It cleanseth me, it cleanseth me,
> The blood of Christ it cleanseth me
> Just now, while I believe."

I did not sing loud. Some gentlemen and ladies were passing me. They looked at me rather strangely. As I sang I felt that hateful Satanic influence and power break and leave me, as really as I ever took a garment and laid it aside. I seemed to see the Devil in the shape of a little black dog, with his tail between his legs. He seemed to pass me down Sixth avenue. I don't know where he came from. There was nobody with him, but just as this power broke I saw this little dog pass.

The Lord had turned my captivity. I was like one that dreamed. My mouth was filled with laughter; I could not stop. I went into the drugstore, and the man in the store saw me laughing, so he fell in line and got to laughing to; he was stout, and he shook. I said, "O, sir, give me a three-cent stamp," and I laughed and he laughed, and I went out. He did not say a word to me, but, O, how he laughed. So did I. I turned to go home. I said,

"I will go down on this side and get me a spool of cotton while I am out," and just as I got opposite where I was attacked by Satan before, he had crossed over and was on the other side. He said, "O, you are very happy."

"Yes, praise the Lord!"

"You don't know how your child is coming on in Philadelphia."

"She is all right; I just had a letter."

"O, the people tell you that, but you don't know if it is true!"

"O, but I know if Mazie was not all right she would tell me."

"Well you want to go to the camp-meeting, too, and you have no money."

Then I recognized that old Accuser again, and I said, "Well, it is none of your business, I belong to Jesus," and I began to sing again,

"The blood of Christ it cleanseth me,
Just now, while I believe,"

and away he went, my adversary, and from that day to this I seem to be able to know him when he approaches, no matter in what shape he comes.

If you keep close to the blood he soon leaves, and nothing will put him on a run so quickly as a song or testimony of the power of the blood.

> "Glory to the blood that bought me,
> Glory to its cleansing power.
> Glory to the blood that keeps me,
> Glory, glory, evermore."

Amen! Amen!

Some time after the Lord had sanctified my soul, I became greatly exercised about the Trinity. I could not seem to under stand just how there could exist three distinct persons, and yet one. I thought every day and prayed for light, but didn't seem to get help. I read the Bible, but no help came. I wanted to ask some one, but I was afraid they would misunderstand me and think I was getting fanatical, as that spirit was being developed a good deal at that time. Brother Boole was pastor of Seventeenth Street Church. As I lived in New York I thought if I could hear him preach on the baptism of the Holy Ghost, that I would get light and help, but the Sunday he was to preach on this very subject I could not be there. I was engaged at Janes Street Church with Reverend Doctor Hamlin, so it went on for weeks after. I got through at Janes Street, and went to Williamsburg to help Brother Hollis. There the Lord blessed us very greatly The people were all very kind, but I met no one during the ten days that I felt I could trust to ask for this explanation. Brother Richard Ryan came over on Sunday afternoon, and he gave his experience of how he came into the blessing of sanctification. It was blest to many souls, and I got a little help on one or two points, but to understand the Trinity was still a great puzzle to me. We closed up grandly on Sunday night, and on Monday morning I went home to New York, 135 Amity street. My two little attic rooms were quite dusty, having been shut up for two weeks, so the first thing I did was to sweep and dust, and after a little lunch I said I will wash my dishes and will kneel down and pray, and I will stay on my knees till the Lord makes this thing clear. I had the dish-cloth in my hand, and as I walked toward the window a voice seemed to speak to me and say, "Every blessing you get from God is by faith." I said, "Yes,—and if by faith, why not now?"

I turned around and knelt down by an old trunk that stood in the corner of the room, and I told the Lord that I wanted to understand the Trinity, and that I was afraid of fanaticism, and I wanted Him to make it clear to me for His own sake. I don't know how long I prayed, but O, how my soul was filled with light under the great baptism that came upon me. I came near falling prostrate, but bore up when God revealed Himself so clearly me, and I have understood it ever since. I can't just explain it to others, but God made me understand it so I have had no question since. Praise the Lord! Then He showed me three other things. O, what a revelation. The wonderful fatherhood of God, the brotherhood of Jesus, the efficacy and broadness of the atonement. It seemed to sweep hard by the gates of hell. I saw how difficult it was for a soul to be lost, and how easy it was to be deceived by believing in universal salvation without repentance. I was awe stricken and wept. I durst not move. And now, as I think of it, I seem to feel the great waves of glory mingled with awe as they surged through my soul, so that my whole being seemed to throb with love and praise. All the points on these lines have been settled since that time, and like Elijah, I have been able to go on in the strength of this meat for more than forty days.

My soul was filled with His love. I seemed to be perfectly infatuated with Jesus. I said, "O, I must see Him with my own eyes;" but how? I said, "If I could die and go to Him I would, but suppose I should live twenty years and have to wait that long before I could see Him."

It seemed the thought was more than I could bear, so I began to pray this prayer: "O, Lord Jesus, reveal Thyself," and I said no other prayers day or night for a week. This one desire had eaten me up. I had three Band sisters. We used to meet once a week. I was afraid to tell them for fear they might say something to deter me, so when any one came to see me, while they were talking I would pray in my heart this same prayer, "O, Lord Jesus, reveal Thyself." I mourned as one would mourn for his mother. I wanted to see Him who had done so much for me. I said, "I must see Him, but how long must I wait?" A week had passed, my praying heart still longing to see Him. Monday morning came. I went from place to place to gather my clothes, praying at times, then wondering and now weeping, for I longed to see my beloved Christ. Twelve o'clock, my clothes were gathered, and I was all ready to begin washing on Tuesday morning at six o'clock. Monday afternoon my Band met at my house.

As I had a baby and could not go about very well, the three sisters, Sister Scott, Sister Banks and Sister Brown, all came to my house; but this day not one of them came but Sister Scott. She was a deeply pious woman, full of faith and the Holy Ghost, and was greatly crushed in her home life, like myself. We stood by each other through many a storm. Praise the Lord! It was her turn that afternoon to open the meeting. We generally took turns about; one would open by giving out a hymn, reading a chapter and then praying. Then we would tell each other our joys or sorrows, our victories and defeats, if we had any, and if Satan had buffeted us, how we bore up or if we yielded under the pressure, etc., and then we would advise each other and pray for each other. Sister Scott seemed to know so well how to approach the Throne of Grace, so that I always felt she would get hearing quicker, so I was glad it was her turn to pray that day, and all the time while she was praying the one cry of my soul was, "O, Lord Jesus, reveal Thyself." We kneeled with our backs to each other. Sister Scott did not know what I had been praying for, and while she prayed, all at once the room seemed to be filled with a hallowed

presence, and as she went on I felt she had got hold of God; it seemed like the rustling of wings, and Sister Scott cried out, "O, Lord Jesus, Thou art here." And He was; I saw Him; He came in at the door; it was open. O, can I describe Him, the lovely, beautiful Jesus! He seemed to stand about six feet high; loose flowing purple robe; His hair and beard as white as wool; His beautiful beard covered His breast to his waist; His face was indescribably lovely! O, it almost takes my breath as I see it all over! He came and stood by my side. He spoke not a word, but it was all in the expression of His lovely face. He seemed to say, "Now look at me; will that satisfy you?" I cried out, "Yes, Lord Jesus," and threw out my arms to embrace Him, but He vanished out of my sight. O, the glory of that hour I shall never forget, and as I think of the amazing condescension of God the Father to grant such a petition to so poor a worm as I, it seemed it would break my very heart!

> "He saved me from my lost estate,
> His loving kindness, O, how great!"

And now, like Job, I am willing to wait all the days of my appointed time till my change comes; and I shall go to be with Him and gaze on Him forever and forever.

Another time He manifested Himself in this wise: I had read somewhere in the Song of Solomon of my beloved being among the spices, and it seemed to me His presence was so consciously near that I felt as though a person was walking by my side. My heart was running over with love to Him as He talked with me of many things, and at times I would look around to see If I really could see Him; but no, I saw no one. One morning as I sat by the window thinking of Him and His great love to me, I raised my eyes, and as I looked through the venetian blind I seemed to see His lovely face peering through the blinds at me, and I cried out, "O, He looketh through the lattice at me; my heart is sick of love!"

"He satisfieth the longing soul, and filleth the hungry soul with goodness." 107th Psalm, ninth verse.

One night after much prayer I went to bed and soon fell into a doze of sleep. There seemed to be laid on my breast a beautiful white marble cross. It was cold. As the cross had pressed my forehead I felt the coldness, and the weight of it pressing me. "Oh," I said, "how beautiful;" but, my it was so heavy. In a moment I seemed to understand all it meant, and all my will seemed to be wrapped around it. I awoke, and it seemed as real as life itself.

As I meditated and asked the Lord to teach me and give me strength to bear the cross always, no matter how heavy it might be, I fell asleep again—and yet it did not seem as though I was really asleep; but I found myself in a strange place; it seemed like a church, and yet it was not. As I sat waiting, as for people to gather, there were seated three very stylishly dressed colored ladies and several finely dressed colored gentlemen. They were sitting in this large room. I thought they looked at me with a scowl of contempt on their faces as they eyed my dress from head to foot. Then they began to make remarks. I felt that they didn't want me in there; but I bowed to them and tried to be pleasant. They hardly noticed me. How cut I felt; and I said, "I wish I was out of here." Just then I seemed to hear a noise outside the house. There was a veranda that looked eastward, so I got up and walked out on the veranda. As I looked up, the moon was shining, and I looked just a little westward in the direction in which I had heard the seeming noise and I saw coming—it was like a great beam, though in shape, a perfect arm, as the right arm of a man! I called it a mighty arm. I wanted these persons to see it, but I did not dare ask them, so I moved and tried to get their attention by pulling my dress, thinking to attract them. They laughed, but did not come. As the arm got over my head—it was in the clouds, but I saw it distinctly. From the shoulder to the elbow was covered with down, beautiful, white. On this down seemed to lie the head of a beautiful bird, like the bill of a swan. It was buried in the down, and though the speed of the arm was so powerful, this head lay perfectly quiet and peaceful. It passed on eastward and was out of sight.

As I stood looking and wondering at the sight there seemed to spring up four great lions. Oh! how fierce they were! They came right towards me, and it seemed the next minute they would be upon me, as they leaped over the clouds on the way to destroy me. I trembled and cried out: "Help, Lord;" and in an instant it seemed two great clouds came together and swallowed them up, and I saw them no more.

Praise the Lord, that was it wonderful lesson to me; for shortly after this I had an experience almost identical. I had much to suffer, in and with my own people—for human nature is the same in black and white folks. They oppose the doctrine of personal holiness, so do white people; but God has a remnant among the old, and some of the young, both preachers and laymen, that believe and know the truth of this doctrine from the Bible standpoint experimentally, which is the top stone of all. Hath not God declared it that without holiness no man shall see the Lord? My prayer is, Lord, multiply the witnesses to the experience in life and power among preachers, bishops and laymen. It is the only hope for Methodism all over the land. May the Lord help us, white and colored! Amen.

But to turn again to my story. As I turned to go into the room I heard the most beautiful singing; it seemed miles away, but I never heard such singing on earth so beautiful, so smooth, and the heavenly sweetness I never can describe. As it neared me I knew the tune well, and as it drew still nearer I heard these words:

"Arm of the Lord, awake, awake,
Thine own immortal strength put on,
With terror clothed Hell's Kingdom shake,
And tread thy foes with fury down,"

And it passed on eastward, as the arm had gone. I could hear the singing away off, as it died away in the distance. I awoke. Oh, what peace and comfort filled my soul! I believe God permitted this to encourage my faith. How many ways He has to teach us to depend on Him, if we are only willing to learn. How sweet His own word, "Learn of me, for I am meek and lowly in heart, and ye shall find rest to your souls." Amen. Amen.

CHAPTER XII.

MY LAST CALL—HOW I OBEYED IT, AND WHAT WAS THE RESULT.

It was the third Sunday in November, 1890. Sister Scott, my band sister, and myself went to the Fleet street A. M. E. Church, Brooklyn. It was Communion Sunday. Before I left home I said to Sister Scott: "I wish I had not promised to go to Brooklyn." She said "Why?"

"Oh, I feel so dull and stupid."

We went early, and went into the Sabbath School. At the close of the Sabbath School the children sang a very pretty piece. I do not remember what it was, but the spirit of the Lord touched my heart and I was blessed. My bad feelings had gone for a few moments, and I thought, "I guess the Lord wanted to bless me here." But when we went upstairs I began to feel the same burden and pressure as I had before. And I said, "Oh, Lord, help me, and teach me what this means." And just at that point the Tempter came with this supposition: "Now, if you are wholly sanctified, why is it that you have these dull feelings?"

I began to examine my work, my life, every day, and I could see nothing. Then I said, "Lord, help me to understand what Thou meanest. I want to hear Thee speak."

Brother Gould, then pastor of the Fleet Street Church, took his text. I was sitting with my eyes closed in silent prayer to God, and after he had been preaching about ten minutes, as I opened my eyes, just over his head I seemed to see a beautiful star, and as I looked at it, it seemed to form into the shape of a large white tulip; and I said, "Lord, is that what you want me to see? If so, what else?" And then I leaned back and closed my eyes. Just then I saw a large letter "G," and I said: "Lord, do you want me to read in Genesis, or in Galatians? Lord, what does this mean?"

Just then I saw the letter "O." I said, "Why, that means go." And I said "What else?" And a voice distinctly said to me "Go preach."

The voice was so audible that it frightened me for a moment, and I said, "Oh Lord, is that what you wanted me to come here for? Why did you not tell me when I was at home, or when I was on my knees praying?" But His paths are known in the mighty deep, and His ways are past finding out. On Monday morning, about four o'clock, I think, I was awakened by the presentation of a beautiful, white cross— white as the driven snow—similar to that described in the last chapter. It was as cold as marble. It was laid just on my forehead and on my breast. It seemed very heavy; to press me down. The weight and the coldness of it were what woke me; and as I woke I said: "Lord, I know what that is. It is a cross."

I arose and got on my knees, and while I was praying these words came to me: "If any man will come after Me let him deny himself and take up his cross and follow Me." And I said, "Lord, help me and I will."

I did not know that I was so unwilling. But the Lord had showed me when I was at Oakington Camp Meeting in July, 1870. There was a gentleman there who lived at Espa, Pa. He made me a good offer, to give me a home in his family, as servant, as long as I lived, my little girl and myself. He said that his family was small; only himself and wife, and one son, a beautiful young man, who was with him at the meeting, and who also, with his father, urged me to go. He said his house was quite new, newly fitted up with all the modern improvements, and that he had a very nice colored man and family on the place, who was his farmer, and who was a good Christian man, and a local preacher, and that they held in his own house a holiness meeting once every week, so that I would not be lonesome; and as he had been asking the Lord about a person, he felt, and thought, I was the very person that would suit them, and he wanted me to break up housekeeping and come to live with them right away. I kept a small room in New York for myself and little girl.

He was a grand, good man, and talked so very nice, and it did seem at first glance that it was right I should do so, and I almost decided to go. But before I did decide, I spread it before the Lord, and asked the assistance and direction of His Holy Spirit,

and I soon found out that it was not the will of the Lord for me to confine myself as a servant in any family, but to go and work in His vineyard as the Spirit directed me. This the Lord had made very plain to me once before.

I worked out by the day and had a great deal to do, till the families I worked for went away out of the country, and the work got slack, and I had but one day out of the week, and that was at Sister Clark's, on Dominick street. So when my work was stopped, my revenue was stopped. I was reduced down to thirteen cents; and I did not know what to do. The enemy said to me, "You will keep on talking about trusting the Lord, and you will have to beg before you are done with it."

"It is none of your business," I said, "if I do. I belong to the Lord, and if He wants me to beg I'll do it."

And he left me a little while. But after a time he returned, and said, "You had better go to service and come home at night."

And I thought, "I could do that. My little girl goes to school, and when she was out she could come to where I was and stay till night, and then go home with me."

While I was thinking about it, my friend, Sister Scott, sent for me to go somewhere to work, but she had made a mistake in the number where I was to go, and I did not find it. I saw afterwards it was all the Lord's doings. I walked up and down for an hour. I went to the place with the number she gave me, but no such person lived there. On my way back I met a girl looking for a chambermaid in the family where she lived. She wanted me to go and see the lady at once; but I said, "No, if I do go now the lady will want me to decide when I can come."

"Oh, yes," said she, "for she wants some one right away."

"Well, I must ask the Lord first."

I went home and got down on my knees, and I said: "Oh, Lord, I am willing to go to service if Thou sayest so. But, Lord, Thou knowest I so love the Sabbath day, and if I go to service it will be taken from me."

Then these words were given me: "My grace is sufficient for you. If you trust Me you shall never be confounded."

"Now, Lord," I said, "for the evidence that I am not to go to service, send some one for me to go to work by the day."

And a little while afterward a little boy came and said that his mother had sent him to see if I could come next day and wash; and I said, "yes," and I had the evidence that I was not to go to service. I had but thirteen cents of money in the world. My little girl was at school, and when she came home the first thing she would say was, "O, Ma, I am so hungry; have you got any bread?" So I had done without any dinner, and saved the piece of bread I had, so that when my child would ask me for a piece of bread I might have it to give her. I thought I couldn't stand it, to have her ask for bread and have none to give her; so, though I was very hungry, I did without.

The grocer's name was Mr. Otten. His store was on the corner of Mannetta Lane and Sixth avenue. I always dealt with him. I never got anything on trust. When I had the money I would get what I needed, and pay for it. When I didn't have the money I would do without it. So I took the thirteen cents and went to Mr. Otten's store, and said to him, "Mr. Otten, I will tell you what I want; I want a loaf of bread, I want a quart of potatoes, I want three slices of salt pork, and I want a bundle of wood, and this is every cent of money I have between me and death." I showed him my money before I got the things. He looked at me.

"Well," he said, "thirteen cents is not money enough to pay for what you want."

"I know it, but that is what I want, and that is all the money I have."

And then he looked at me, and went and got the things and gave me back three cents.

Oh! how I praised the Lord. I hastened home. I made a nice little stew for dinner for Mazie and me. I was expecting this to last me a week. I didn't intend to eat much myself; I thought I could do without, but my child must have enough; and I had a faculty of piecing out a little to make it go a good ways.

Well, the next day I went to where I was to do the washing. It was not far from where I lived. I knocked, and the lady opened the door. She was a very rough, coarse woman. I said, "Good morning, Madame."

"Good morning. Are you the woman that's come to wash?"

"Yes, Madame."

"How much do you charge a day?"

"Well, Madame, I don't know, I believe the general price is one dollar and twenty-five cents."

"Well," she said, "I'm not going to pay any such price as that."

"Well," I said, "Madame, a dollar, then, I suppose."

"No, I won't pay a dollar. It is a three weeks' washing, but I can get it done cheaper than that."

"Well," I said, "Madame, seventy-five cents, if it is a three weeks' washing it ought to be worth seventy-five cents."

"Well," she said, "I'm not going to pay that. I can get it done for fifty cents."

So she turned and went away, and I said, "Good morning, Madame."

And just as I was crossing out of Fourth street into Sixth avenue, how Satan assailed me. I trembled from head to foot. He said, "Now you have been asking the Lord for a day's work, and the Lord has given you this work and you have refused it."

Then I thought, I will go back and tell her I will do it for fifty cents. And then something seemed to whisper, "Go on." So I went on a little further, and Satan attacked me again, and he accused me of not being obedient, and not walking in the way the Lord had opened up for me, and I thought, "I will go back and beg the woman and tell her I will do it."

I stopped still, and as I went to turn round a voice said to me, "No, no." And I said, "Oh, Lord, do help me. I don't want to be disobedient. I want to do Thy will only;" and I cried in the street!

Just as I was going in the rear of my own house, I met a lady coming out, and she said, "I have just been in the court looking for somebody to come and do a day's ironing. Call you come?"

"Yes; where is it?"

"Right up here in McDugal street."

She kept a boarding-house. She said, "I want you to come right away. We are very busy, and we are cleaning house, and I must have my ironing done at once."

So I laid down my things and went. It was about half a block from where I lived. I worked hard all day. Oh, what a day it was. It was in one of those boarding-houses that are on the scrimpiest order. There was a little fire in one end of the range, and it was not allowed to get hot enough to cook anything, scarcely on top. You would open a hole and set an iron in to get it hot, and perhaps you could iron a towel; then some one of the boarders would want some breakfast, and you would shut it up to try and get it hot enough to cook something, and that was the way it went,

I saw very soon after I got in there why it was she could not keep any help. However, I did the best I could; sometimes ironing a towel, sometimes washing a window, and then ironing a sheet or pillow case, then scrubbing a little, and managing in all sorts of ways. I endured it for two days; and she paid me my money—two dollars.

After that I never had any more trouble about days' work. I had all the work I could do, and more, at one dollar and twenty five cents to two dollars a day, until October, 1870, when I left my home at God's command, and began my evangelistic work. I did not know then that it meant all that it has been. I thought it was only to go to Salem, as the Lord had showed me. Shortly after this I was off to Salem. Got as far as Philadelphia, where I purposed leaving my little girl with her grandfather, while I went on to Salem. But strange to say, notwithstanding all the light, and clear, definite leading of the Lord, my heart seemed to fail me. I said to myself, "After all, to go on to Salem, a stranger, where I don't know a minister, or anybody. No, I will do some work here in Philadelphia."

So I got some tracts, went away down in the lower part of town, on St. Mary's street, and Sixth, and Lombard, and all in that region. I went into saloons and gave tracts; gave tracts to people on the corners; spoke a word here and there; some laughed and sneered; some took a tract. Then I went to the meetings, and sang and prayed and exhorted. I went about among the sick, and did all I could. And I said, "After all, the Lord may not want me to go to Salem."

After spending a week in Philadelphia I thought I would go home. Friday came, and I thought to myself, "Well, I will go home Saturday." But, Oh! there came such an awful horror and darkness over me. On Friday night, after I had come home front an excellent meeting, I could not sleep, all night. Oh how I was troubled. I did not know what to do, for I had spent all my money; father did not have much means, and when Mazie and I were at home I generally provided, not only for ourselves, but for all the family; so that my means went almost before I knew it; I had not much, anyhow. But it seemed to me I would die. So I told the Lord if He would spare me till morning, though I had not any money, I would go and see my sister, and if she could lend me a dollar so as to get on to Salem, I would go.

Saturday morning came. I borrowed a dollar, came home, and spent twenty-five cents of it for breakfast; then with what it cost me to ride down to get on the boat, in all about fifteen cents, I had left about sixty cents. My ticket on the boat was fifty cents; I had had some little hymns struck off; we colored people were very fond of ballads for singing.

A little while after I got on the boat, who should come in but Brother Holland, who used to be my pastor eight years before, in Lancaster, Pa. All this had come to pass in the years after I had known him; so that he did not know anything at all about it. He was very glad to see me, and asked me where I was going. I told him the Lord had sent me to Salem. Then I began to tell him my story. How the Lord had led me. How He had called me to His work. Dear old man, he listened to me patiently, and when I had got through he said:

"Well, Sister Smith, you know I don't believe in women preaching. But still, honey, I have got nothing to say about you. You go on. The Lord bless you."

I was dumbfounded; for I thought he was in the greatest sympathy with woman's work, though I had never heard him express himself with regard to it. But I was glad of the latter part of what he said.

It was quite a cool day, and the boat got in about two o'clock in the afternoon. There were no street cars then, as there are now. There was a big omnibus. They didn't let colored people ride inside an omnibus in those days. So I took my carpet bag and had to sit outside on the top of the omnibus.

They didn't let colored people off till all the white people were off, even if they had to go past where they wanted to stop; so I had to ride round on the omnibus at least three-quarters of an hour before I was taken to where I wanted to go.

The woman's name, where I had been told to go, was Mrs. Curtis. She was a widow, and owned her own house and grounds; she had quite a nice, comfortable little house. But she was a queer genius. Old Father Lewis, who had once been pastor of the A. M. E. Church at Salem, and at this time was pastor of the church at Jersey City Heights, N. J., had recommended me to Sister Curtis, because she was alone and had plenty of room, and he thought it would be so nice for me. It was more than a half mile from the locality in which the colored church was situated, and in which the majority of the colored people lived. But Sister Curtis seemed as though she was frightened at me. I told her who had sent me to her house, and how the Lord had called me to His work, and all my story of the Lord's doing. She listened, but was very nervous. Then she said she didn't know what in the world she would do, for she hadn't anything but some hard bread to give me to eat, and she hadn't any sugar; and I said, "Well, no matter for that. I can eat hard bread, and I can drink tea without sugar, if you can only accommodate me till Monday, at least."

Well, she said she could keep me all night, but she didn't like to leave any one in the house on Monday, because she generally went away to wash; and she generally had the cold pieces given her from the hotel where she went to wash dishes, and that was all she could give me to eat.

She knew how we colored people are about eating; we do like to eat; so I think she told me that thinking she would frighten me; but I agreed to everything. Then I asked her if she could tell me where Brother Cooper, who was then pastor, lived. She said, "Yes, it is about a mile and a half."

I asked her if she would show me which way to go. She did so, but did not give me anything to eat. I was very hungry, but I did not ask her for anything. So I started off about three o'clock, or a little after, and went to see Brother Cooper.

I was tired, and walked slowly, and it was about half-past four when I got up to the little village above. I inquired my way, and was told that Sister Johnson lived right close by Brother Cooper's, and if I would go to her house she could tell me, for it was just through her yard to Brother Cooper's house. So I went. I knocked at the door. The sister was in; several nice looking little children were playing around, and an elegant pot of cabbage was boiling over the fire. My! how nice it did smell; and I did wish and pray that the Lord would put it into her heart to ask me to have something to eat. I hinted all I knew how, but she did not take the hint. I knew by the sound of it that it was done and ought to come off!

I told her my story; told her about Brother Lewis; she was very glad to hear from him. I asked her if I could stay all night, because I felt so tired that I thought I could not walk back to Sister Curtis'. She said at once she could not possibly have me stay all night. Her mother had been dead about three months, and she had taken down the bedsteads, and she was so overburdened with her grief she had never put them up, and they were all lying on the floor.

I told her no matter for that; I could sleep on the floor just as well. No, she did not have room. She could not possibly do it.

Well, I stayed till it was pretty dark. It was after six o'clock. The more I talked the more she gave me to see that she was not going to ask me to have any cabbage, or to stay all night.

So I said to her, "Will you tell me where Brother Cooper, the minister, lives?"

"Oh, yes," she said, "I will send one of the children with you."

When I got to Brother Cooper's I knocked, and Brother Cooper came to the door; he was an awful timid man; so he stood at the door, holding it half open and leaning out a little ways, and asked me who I was. I told him that I was Amanda Smith; that the Lord sent me to Salem. Then I went on, standing at the door, telling him how the Lord had led me, and all about it. His wife, who was a little more thoughtful than he, heard me, and she called out to him, and said, "Cooper, why don't you ask the sister to come in." So then he said, "Come in, Sister."

I was awful glad, so I went in. Sister Cooper was getting supper. The table was set, and I thought, "Maybe, I will get something to eat now."

So I went on and finished my story, and they seemed to be greatly interested; and when the supper was quite ready, she said, "Will you have some supper, Sister Smith?" I thanked her, and told her I would.

While I was eating my supper who should come in but good Brother Holland, that had been on the boat. He said to Brother and Sister Cooper, "I am glad you have Sister Smith here. You needn't be afraid of her, she is all right; I have known her for years. I have not seen her since I was pastor at Lancaster."

Then they brightened up a little bit, and seemed to be a little more natural. My heart was glad. It was quarterly meeting, and Brother Holland was to preach in the morning and Brother Cooper in the afternoon. So Brother Holland said, as he was Presiding Elder, I might speak at night and tell my story.

"All right," I said.

After a little talk, Brother Holland left. Sister Cooper said she would be very glad to have me stay all night, but they had no room. They had not been long there, and had only fitted up one room for their own use. They thought they would make out with that for the winter. So then I was obliged to walk a mile and a half back to Sister Curtis'. I did hate to do it, but the Lord helped me.

So I stayed that night at Sister Curtis', and she gave me a little breakfast on Sunday morning, but it was mighty skimpey! But I found out that a good deal of praying fills you up pretty well when you cannot get anything else! On Sunday morning we went to Love Feast, and had a good time. Prior to this I had been asking the Lord to give me a message to give when I went to Salem. I said, "Lord, I don't want to go to Salem without a message. And now you are sending me to Salem, give me the message. What shall I say?"

Two or three times I had gone before the Lord with this prayer, and His word was, "It shall be made known to you when you come to the place what you shall say." And I said, "All right, Lord." So I didn't trouble Him any more till this Sunday morning. The Lord helped Brother Holland preach. When he got through preaching and the collection was taken, Brother Cooper made the announcement that I was there; he said, "There is a lady here, Mrs. Amanda Smith" (he had never seen me before or heard of me, and he was a rather jovial kind of a man, and in making this announcement he said, in a half sarcastic and half joking way), "Mrs. Smith is from New York; she says the Lord sent her;" with a kind of toss of the head, which indicated that he did not much believe it. Oh, my heart fell down, and I said, "Oh! Lord, help. Give me the message."

The Lord saw that I had as much as I could stand up under, and He said, "Say, 'Have ye received the Holy Ghost since ye believed?' " (Acts 9:2). That was the message; the first message the Lord gave me. I trembled from head to foot.

A good sister took me home with her to dinner. The people all seemed very kind. I felt quite at home when I got with them. We came back in the afternoon and had a wonderful meeting.

At night after Brother Holland had preached a short sermon, he called me up to exhort. As I sat in the pulpit beside him, he saw I was frightened. He leaned over and said, "Now, my child, you needn't be afraid. Lean on the Lord. He will help you."

And He did help me. There was a large congregation. The gallery was full, and every part of the house was packed. I stood up trembling. The cold chills ran over me. My heart seemed to stand still. Oh, it was a night. But the Lord gave me great liberty in speaking. After I had talked a little while the cold chills stopped, my heart began to beat naturally and all fear was gone, and I seemed to lose sight of everybody and everything but my responsibility to God and my duty to the people. The Holy Ghost fell on the people and we had a wonderful time. Souls were convicted and some converted that night. But the meeting did not go on from that.

Thursday night was the regular prayer meeting night. Brother Cooper said I was there, and would preach Thursday night. He was going to give me a chance to preach, and he wanted all the people to come out.

There was no snow, but Oh! it was cold. The ground was frozen. The moon shone brightly, and the wind blew a perfect gale. One good thing, I did not have to go back to Sister Curtis'. Another good sister asked me to her house to stay. She made me very comfortable, but said I would have to be alone most of the day, as she was going to some of the neighbors to help with the butchering, as they do in the country. I was very glad of that, for it gave me a chance to pray. So I fasted and prayed and read my Bible nearly all day. Oh, I had a good time. And then I thought I would visit a neighbor near by, another friend. So I did; and this was a good old mother in Israel. I told her a little of my experience, and then I told her the message the Lord had given me to speak about, and how it would lead to the subject of sanctification.

"My child," she at once said, "don't you say a word about sanctification here. Honey, if you do, they will persecute you to death. My poor husband used to preach that doctrine, and for years he knew about this blessing. But, Oh! honey, they persecuted him to death. You must not say a word about it."

Well, there I was again! So I went home, and the next day I prayed to God all day. I asked Him to give me some other message. If this message was going to do so much damage, I did not want it. But no, the Lord held me to it. Not a ray of light on anything else but that. I didn't know what to do, but I made up my mind it was all I ever would do, so I would obey God and take the consequences. I thought sure from what the dear old mother told me that the results would be fatal; I didn't know but I would be driven out. But not so. "Obedience is better than sacrifice, and to hearken than the fat of rams."

Thursday was a beautiful, bright day; but Oh! cold, bitterly cold. So I got down and prayed and said, "Lord, Thou hast sent me to Salem, and hast given me the message. Now for an evidence that Thou hast indeed sent me, grant to cause the wind to cease blowing at this fearful rate. Thou knowest Lord, that I want people to hear Thy message that Thou hast given me. They will not mind the cold, but the wind is so terrible. Now cause the wind to cease to blow, and make the people come out."

The wind blew all day; all the afternoon. I started to go across the field, about a half mile from where I was, to talk and pray with a friend. On my way back, about five o'clock, as I was crossing a ditch which ran through the field, bordered on either side by a row of hedge trees, and a little plank across it for a kind of a foot bridge, the wind wrapped me round and took me down into the ditch. I could not hold on, could not control myself. I expected to be thrown up against the trees, and I cried out to Him all alone, "Oh! Lord, Thou that didst command the wind to cease on the Sea of Galilee, cause this wind to cease and let me get home."

Just then there came a great calm, and I got up out of that ditch and ran along to the house. By the time we went to church it was as calm as a summer evening; it was cold, but not a bit windy—a beautiful, moonlight night.

The church was packed and crowded. I began my talk from the chapter given, with great trembling. I had gone on but a little ways when I felt the spirit of the Lord come upon me mightily. Oh! how He helped me. My soul was free. The Lord convicted sinners and backsliders and believers for holiness, and when I asked for persons to come to the altar, it was filled in a little while from the gallery and all parts of the house.

A revival broke out, and spread for twenty miles around. Oh! what a time it was. It went from the colored people to the white people. Sometimes we would go into the church at seven o'clock in the evening. I could not preach. The whole lower floor would be covered with seekers— old men, young men, old women, young women, boys and girls. Oh! glory to God! How He put His seal on this first work to encourage my heart and establish my faith, that He indeed had chosen, and ordained and sent me. I do not know as I have ever seen anything to equal that first work, the first seal that God gave to His work at Salem. Some of the young men that were converted are in the ministry. Some have died in the triumph of faith. Others are on the way. I went on two weeks, day and night. We used to stay in the church till one and two o'clock in the morning. People could not work. Some of the young men would hire a wagon and go out in the country ten miles and bring in a load, get them converted, and then take them back.

One night I was so weary they said they would get on without me, and I could have a rest. A Mr. Huff had asked me to go to his house. Two of his sons had been converted. He had been a member of the church, but had got cold and backslidden. His wife was pretty much in the same condition. They had three younger children, ten and thirteen years of age. So I went to their house to have a rest. Before we went to bed that night we had family prayer. They had got out of the way of that, Mrs. Huff told me. She had got stirred up, so was anxious about her husband. I read the Bible and explained the Word the best I could; then I sang; then I got down to pray. There was a young man by the name of Williams, Mr. Huff's nephew, about twenty-one years of age, with them at the house. We knelt down to pray. I told Sister Huff she ought to pray in her family. Poor thing, she had prayed so little for a long time, it was rather hard; but she did. After she prayed, I sang a verse, then prayed. Archie Huff, the son, had been converted two or three days before, wonderfully. I asked him to pray. So he prayed, as a young convert, simply and earnestly, though he was very hoarse; but the Lord helped him. When he got through praying I sang another hymn; and by that time old Mr. Huff had tumbled over on the floor and was praying out loud for the Lord to save him; so I began to pray; and while I was praying, the young nephew, Williams, fell out and shook the house. And there we were. And while these two brethren were praying, and Archie and I were praying, and the old woman was praying, (as it was out in the country we didn't whisper at all; we talked right out), these younger children, a little girl ten years old, and the boys, twins, about thirteen years old, got converted. The little girl was sitting up at the opposite side of the room (her mother had put her to bed), praying for the Lord to bless her. The two boys had got up and come down, and they were praying that the Lord would bless them. I said, "Oh, Lord, what will I do? I have no help but Thee only. Help, Lord!" I thought if I only had somebody to sing; but there was nobody—only Archie and I; and we had got so hoarse that we could not do much. But it was beautiful just to see God do it all!

The whole five of them were converted that night. Oh, what a time. And so we were into it till about twelve or one o'clock. Then I slipped off and lay down a little while.

The news got out through the neighborhood, so they sent for me to come to another house next day, about a mile and a half away. Old man Huff hitched up his team, and he and his nephew and Archie and I went over to the neighbor's. This man was a very moral kind of a man. He had been seeking the Lord, but he had got a little discouraged, so they thought if I would go and talk to him it would help him. I thought "I will have a quiet time over here."

I got there about four o'clock in the afternoon. We talked and had a pleasant time, and had supper; and I thought we would have prayers after awhile. Well, about eight o'clock one or two persons came in, neighbors; that made five or six of us.

"Dear me," I thought to myself, "I have not strength to talk any longer, so I will just give out a hymn, and we will sing and have prayers."

So I did, and we got down to pray. I asked somebody to pray. While we were praying, three or four more came in. When we got through that prayer some one else struck in, and two or three more came in; so we had twelve or thirteen persons, packed in like sardines in it box. And pretty soon this man that had been seeking, cried out for salvation. Oh, how he prayed! It was not long till he began to believe; and what always follows earnest faith is victory. When he shouted victory it struck terror to the others that were not converted, and that night there were five or six converted in that house. Oh! what a victory!

Next day we visited round through the neighborhood. How the shouts of praise and hallelujah to God seemed to be every where we went. So I went back to church, for I did not get any rest there, and we went on two or three weeks longer. From there I went to Millville, N. J., with similar results. I remember one

night at Millville, after Brother Leonard Patterson had preached, he said I was to take the services and go on indefinitely.

There had been some little misunderstanding between two or three of the members, so there was not a very good feeling existing all around; and while we had good meetings, we would come right up to a point and stick. So after I had gone on three or four nights, I proposed to have a day of fasting and prayer, which they all quite readily agreed to. I said: "Now, I don't want anybody to promise to fast that cannot; some people cannot stand it; but just you who think you can fast one day, and pray to God for the outpouring of His Spirit—I want you to stand up."

Among those who stood up was an old Brother Cooper; they called him "Father Cooper." He had enjoyed the blessing of sanctification for about forty years. Oh, what a grand man he was! When that old man prayed, something gave way. There were several old brethren that I did not expect would fast at all. So Father Cooper got up and I said: "Brother Cooper, you cannot stand it. I don't mean you."

"Oh," he said, "Honey, I don't mean to let the children outrun me."

Another old man got up and said: "No, indeed, the children can't get ahead of me; I'm going with them." So one or two of the sisters and I visited from house to house. We prayed and talked and sang. I was led to visit two white families. They were poor people. The Devil tried to scare me; told me they were Roman Catholics, and would put me out. I had quite a little struggle, but finally I got victory and went. I do not know whether they were Roman Catholics or not; but the Lord helped me to speak to them and pray. One woman was so glad; she had a sick child. I talked to her and comforted her.

That night when we came together the Lord helped me to speak to them, and He sent His Spirit. When I asked them to come forward to the altar, those that were seeking purity, and those that were seeking pardon, I asked Father Cooper to lead in prayer. I shall never forget that prayer. I seem to see it all, and hear it yet.

There were two that had been leading sisters in the church, that did not speak to each other, and were neighbors, were standing in pews close to each other. They did not come forward to the altar when the others came, but I saw the Spirit of the Lord had hold of them; and while rather Cooper was praying, the Holy Ghost fell on the people, and these two sisters were struck by the power of God like lightning. One of them walked out of her seat and went over to the seat of the other and shook hands and wept, and one of them, a few minutes after, whirled over the back of the seat and down on the floor, and she walked on her back clear down the aisle up to one side and into the altar. I think if anybody had told her to do it she never could have done it.

It was a marvelous time. I have never seen anything like it before or since. There was one man that had been seeking the Lord for eight years. Everybody thought he was converted. He lived with his mother, who was a widow. Everybody, white and colored, liked and respected him. He was a good man, always went to church, and so the people said he was converted; but he did not know it. So when they told me this a day or two before the day of fasting and prayer, I had this man, with some others, specially on my mind. After this great victory, we worked till about eleven or twelve o'clock. I said, "Well, we will take up these who are seeking. We will just have them rise now."

We colored people did not use to get up off our knees quick like white folks; when we went down on our knees to get some thing, we generally got it before we got up. But we are a very imitative people, so I find we have begun to imitate white people, even in that. The Lord help us.

This poor young man got up and put his overcoat on, and he was sitting down and looking so sad, as though he was nearly heart-broken. I had talked and prayed and tried to help him all I could; and there never was a soul prayed more earnestly and sincerely than he did. But there he stuck. I stood and looked at him for a moment. O, how they sang. At last I went up to him and said: "Look here, Charlie D., why don't you let go and shout?"

"Oh!" he wept, "Lord save me!"

"Well," I said, "The Lord does save you; but you won't believe Him." And I said, "Let go and shout!"

And the Spirit of the Lord seemed to fall upon him, just like you would sprinkle hot coals on any one. He sprang to his feet, and the light went all over him like fire, and it seemed as though he would tear himself to pieces for a minute. "Oh," he said, "I have found it, I have found it, I have found it!"

This sent a thrill through the whole church, and again there was a shout; such a shout you never heard nor saw. It was about one o'clock before we got out that night. I shall never forget that meeting at Millville. Praise the Lord! He does all things well. Amen. Amen.

CHAPTER XIII.

MY REMEMBRANCES OF CAMP MEETING—SECOND CAMP MEETING—
SINGING—OBEDIENCE IS BETTER THAN SACRIFICE.

My first national Holiness Camp Meeting was at Oakington, Maryland, July, 1870. When I saw the notice in the paper of this meeting, I thought I would like to go. But then I was a poor wash woman, and how could I go? I went to do a few days' work for Mrs. Margaret Clark, when she lived on Dominick street, and was one of the flaming members of the Duane Methodist Church, and was a camp meeting woman of the old fashioned stamp. She said to me one day, "Sister Smith, you ought to go to the camp meeting at Oakington."

I said, "I should like to go if I could get something to do, taking care of the lodging tent, or get a chance as waitress in the boarding tent, so as to earn a little something." My rent was six dollars a month, and if I lost two weeks, then what would I do? So I said, "You write and get me a situation."

"Well, yes," she said, "but you won't get much good of the meeting that way."

"Well," I said, "I can't go any other way." So she said, "All right."

I went home and prayed that the Lord would open the way for me, and hoped.

Next week when I went, I expected to hear favorably from Mrs. Clark's letter. She said she had not heard from her letter yet, but said, "Sister Smith, why don't you trust the Lord and go to get the benefit of the meeting?" I was struck with the thought, just what I would like to have done. Then I thought, "What, trust the Lord about my rent?" I had not heard of such a thing, certainly I had never done it. I thought a moment and then said, "I will."

Then Mrs. Clark said, "You can take your own bed-tick and have it filled, and you can have room in our tent to sleep, and you will only have our tent to look after." How my heart leaped for joy. Then she told me how to manage, and I worked away, gathered what I could together and so got enough to pay my round trip ticket and had just ten cents over. When the time came Mrs. Clark said, "Send your trunk down to our house and it call go with our things in the morning."

I did so, but when the man got there a little after six o'clock in the morning they were all gone. When I got to the Cortlandt Street Ferry, I found my trunk was not there, the man had taken it to Debrosses Street Ferry, so the old man told me I had better go up to Debrosses street, about two miles away. My heart beat, I didn't know what to do. I thought, "I can't walk, it is so far, and I am so weary." I thought I might catch the train, and so took the street cars. Then I thought, "If I pay the ten cents to go up and down, how am I going to get through the ferry?"

I got back, but of course missed the train. I had to wait from about eight o'clock till half past ten. It seemed that everything was against me. O, how earnestly I did pray. I found that I was twenty-five cents short when I went to buy my ticket, that is If I got an excursion ticket, so I didn't know what to do. I asked the Lord to let me see someone I knew, so as to ask them to lend it to me. There were a great many persons waiting to go by the same train, among them was Rev. Henry Belden, whom I had often met at the Palmer meetings; Rev. Mr. Wells, pastor of the Seventeenth Street Methodist Church; Mr. Faulkner, and a number of other members of the church. They were all very kind to me. I thought, "Shall I ask Brother Belden for the twenty-five cents?"

Just as I looked around, who should be there but Brother Clark.

"O," I said, "I thought you had gone."

"I will not go," he said, "till Saturday,"—this was Wednesday morning, I think,—"Mrs. Clark left something and I hurried back to get it, and when I got here the train had just gone, so you will take it."

"Mr. Clark, will you please loan me twenty-five cents?"

"I have no change," he said, "but a two dollar bill, I will give you that and you can give it to me when I come."

So I got my ticket all right. Now the gates open, and the rush and noise—it was all so new to me then. I got in at last and took my seat, and I sat thinking and wondering how I would pay good Brother Clark his two dollars when he came on Saturday. "Lord, help me," I said, "and open the way for me."

Then Satan said to me, "If you had not bought that package of tracts you wouldn't have had to borrow that two dollars."

A day or two before, I had bought at the Bible House, a package of holiness tracts—they cost thirty cents. I knew my money was short, but holiness was so sweet to me that I wanted everybody to get it, and these tracts set the truth forth in such a clear, reasonable light I thought I might do a little work for the Lord in giving them to persons, so that was why I got them. The Devil don't like holiness anyhow, and I was ignorant of his devices, and was among strangers. He tried his best to pick a quarrel with me. After a little while I got my pack and took out the tracts and began to read, and in spite of all, I felt happy, and felt I had done right in getting them. The train went on. In a little while someone began to sing. I was asked to join in the song, and a real pleasant going to camp meeting we had. After the singing was over, Mr. Faulkner came back to the seat where I was sitting and said: "What are you reading, Auntie?" I handed him the package of tracts.

"Ah, do you know anything about holiness?" he said.

My heart caught fire in a moment, and I began to tell what great things the Lord had done for me, and after listening a while, he said, "I want to give our pastor, Brother Wells, some of these tracts," and I think he said his daughter and some other ladies were interested in the subject.

"All right, sir," I said, "I am very glad to have you take as many as you like." When he got through he returned what were not used.

"They are very good, and you must pray that God will bless them."

Then he handed me a two dollar bill. "I don't sell them, sir," I said.

He smiled and replied, "But don't you buy them?"

"Yes, but I didn't pay that for them, sir."

"No matter," he said, "I guess you call use it, can't you?"

"O, yes, sir, thank you, praise the Lord." Then he went away.

I saw how God hall answered my prayer and paid the two dollars I had borrowed of dear Brother Clark. "It shall come to pass that before they call, I will answer; and while they are yet speaking I will hear." Isaiah, 65:24. So when Brother Clark came on Saturday, I was glad to hand him the two dollars.

That camp meeting I shall never forget,. How God gave me friends and blessed me. It was the first time I had ever been to a meeting of that kind. I had never heard such testimonials and such preaching on holiness. The Sunday morning Love Feast will never be forgotten. The Lord laid it on me to give my experience of how I found the great salvation, and as I spoke He blest me greatly and the people as well. At the close, Brother Inskip said they wanted five hundred dollars—I think it was that amount—for the expenses of the big tent. Some person proposed to divide the amount in shares, so there was a hearty and prompt response, for everybody seemed to he so happy, and in about ten or fifteen minutes they had the amount, and over. I wanted to give something, I was so glad and happy I thought I would like to give ten dollars if I had it, so I said, "Thou knowest, Lord, if I had it I would give it, do put it into somebody's heart to give it for me."

I had hardly uttered the prayer when dear old Brother John McGlynn stood up and said, "Ten dollars for that colored sister that just now spoke."

"Praise the Lord! thank you, sir," I shouted. O, I felt I could fly.

It was there I began to learn the deep meaning of the text, "Ask and ye shall receive, seek and ye shall find, knock and it shall be opened it unto you."

In the afternoon I went into the tent where Brother Purdy was leading a meeting; he was probing and testing those who were seeking full salvation, for all who know Brother Purdy and his methods know that no one slips through his fingers easy, who is seeking for pardon or purity. He probes deep, praise the Lord. I listened. I knew my own heart measured up to each of these tests and I could say, "Praise the Lord!" My soul was all aglow with holy triumph. I stepped up and said, "Brother Brady, would you like to try your probe on me?"

He was all taken back, but in his pleasant way said, "Yes, can you stand it, Amanda?"

"Yes, sir;" and I took up the different tests he had given

and went through with them. The power of the Lord came down upon us, and O, what a meeting: sinners were converted, believers sanctified. The meeting lasted long after the preaching began in the evening. People came from all parts of the ground.

There I first met Mr. and Mrs. Martyr, of Philadelphia, who afterwards were very good friends to me. They are both now in Heaven.

It was the first time that I saw Rev. B. F. Adams. He preached a wonderful sermon on Sunday morning, and gave his experience how he got the blessing of sanctification. The power of the Spirit was manifest. Brother Adams sat down in a tempest of glory. It was the very Sunday that Rome was declaring the infallibility of the

Pope. Brother Boole sprang to his feet, as by inspiration and said, as he only could say it:

"In Rome to-day they are crowning the Pope infallible; let's rise and sing, 'All hail the power of Jesus' name, and crown Him Lord of all,' in our hearts forever."

And the whole congregation rose in an instant as one, and I think I never heard such singing—never heard that old Coronation sung as it was that day. Yes, we crowned Him King of Kings and Lord of Lords. Hallelujah! for the Lord God Omnipotent reigneth!

As I had learned at Oakington to trust the Lord for temporal things, and He had blest me so wonderfully, I began to pray about going to Sing Sing, and the Lord sent help. A few days before the meeting opened, Brother Munson, of Twenty-fourth Street Methodist Church, where my friend, Sister Scott, and myself used to go at times to his class, was down town one morning, and the Lord sent him into 135 Amity street, where I lived, in New York.

"Well, Sister Smith," he said, "are you ready for the camp meeting?"

"I am asking the Lord to open the way for me."

"Well, here are two dollars to help you along."

I did praise the Lord for another indication of His loving kindness. Calling a brother's name who was a member of his class, he said his family would give me a place to sleep in their tent, if I liked, or I could have a corner in the large meeting tent. "Praise the Lord." I said, "He doeth all things well. Now, tell me how to go, and all about it."

He did so, and left. I had a good time after he had gone, thanking God for His wonderful love to me. It was all a new experience, but so beautiful because I saw the Lord's hand in all. The day came, and my little daughter Mazie and I were off to the camp meeting. The Lord gave me many friends, and taught me new lessons. I remember many dear ones of those days, though so many have gone to be with God. Rev. John Cookman, who was then pastor of Bedford Street Church, and Rev. Brother Head strum, that wonderful man of God, Brother Moorehouse, and a number of others, were there. How well I remember dear John Cookman; he was then a power. I have no objection to his going to Heaven when his work was done, but somehow I felt as though he might have gone as safely through the dear old Methodist Church, that his father and brother Alfred, of blessed memory, loved and served so long; but praise the Lord, anyhow there are no sects in Heaven. Hallelujah! Oh, the City will be full of blood-washed souls out of every kindred, tongue and people. "What a gathering of the people that will be."

Then there was Brother Tom Sherwood, and Brother Knox, and King. What times we used to have in the police tent meetings! Brother John McClain's tent was where the young people held their meetings. There I first saw and heard Laura Bowden (afterwards Mrs. Crane); she was then in her prime of power. How the Lord did use her testimony and exhortation to the saving of many, young and old. I had never seen or heard of a young people's and children's meeting till then. All this was so new to me, and yet was grand.

One day Mrs. Dr. Butler was to speak on the Zenana work in India, where she and her husband spent so many years. Miss Bowden was to have charge of the Young People's Meeting. Mrs. Butler's meeting was in a tent in another part of the grounds and for ladies only. I wanted to hear Miss Bowden so much, for she was so clear on the subject of holiness, and this was my heart's delight, then I wanted to hear Mrs. Butler on India. I had never heard a missionary address in my life. At that time we had no Woman's Foreign Mission Work in our church; but it is different to-day, thank God.

I thought it all over, and decided to go into Mrs. Butler's meeting; she was to leave, and Miss Bowden would be there longer, so I would have another chance to hear her. I went into Mrs. Butler's meeting; it was in a large tent, and full of nice and many richly dressed ladies, I slipped in at the door and sat down behind them. Mrs. Butler had a small table in front of her; and on it a number of different heathen gods, such as were worshiped in India, and I had never seen anything of the kind before, but I thought it can't be that human beings worship such hideous things for gods. My heart melted, and I wept bitterly and thought, "O, if I could only go and sing that very familiar old hymn, 'I am so glad that Jesus loves me.' " It was new then and I had sung it a great deal, and God had blest it to so many souls. I thought, "If I could go and sing this hymn they would all be converted right off," but O, how little I knew about heathen superstitious and customs.

Well, I had only two dollars and a half in the world, that was to get my little girl a pair of shoes. She had walked about in the grass and got her shoes run inside. She was caring for Mrs. Vico's little child, and I didn't like her to have on those uncomfortable walking shoes, so the next morning I was to send to the village after them. I sat listening to Mrs. Butler. She made an appeal to the ladies for the Zenana work, and told how small a sum would keep a Bible woman in the field a year. "O," I thought, "if I had it I would give twenty dollars."

There was a pause, and only a few responded to this appeal out of the great number in the tent. I thought it very strange. By and by two ladies elegantly dressed got up and went out. They had on fine Leghorn hats, trimmed with deep black lace, elegant black lace shawls. "O," I said to myself, "those ladies ought to give twenty dollars, they must be rich." Then, as Mrs. B. talked on, others got up and left, giving nothing. How sad I felt. Just then the Spirit said distinctly to me, "You give that two dollars," and I said, "I will."

"Yes," the Devil said, "you will look nice to go up there with just two dollars; if you had five it would be something like."

Then I felt ashamed to give two dollars, and thought if I could only get out.

Then he suggested, "If you had gone to that Young People's Meeting you would not have felt so bad."

"Yes," I said, "I wish I had gone."

"Give the two dollars," the Spirit said again.

"Your child needs the shoes and you have no more," the Devil said. "Your first duty is to your child."

How concerned he was for her then!

I thought I would go out, and as I started the Spirit said, "God knows why you are going out; it is because you don't want to give that two dollars."

O, I felt I could scream out, so I went up to Mrs. Butler, sobbing like a child, and said, "Mrs. Butler." She looked at me and I said, "Can I go to India?"

"I wish you could," she said so kindly.

"Well," said I, "will you take two dollars?"

"Yes, I will," she said, "I will give you a paper, too."

It was the "Heathen Woman's Friend." I had never seen it before, so I went and sat down, and O, such a wave of glory swept over my soul, and I said, "Lord, I thank Thee, for I believe I have done right."

Just then the Devil said, "He that provideth not for his own household is worse than an infidel." It was like a shot, for it was in the Bible, and I had read it, and I didn't know what to do. I closed my eyes and lifted my heart to God and said, "Lord, I don't understand it, but somehow I feel I have done right." Then the Lord sent another shower of blessing to my soul. O, it went all through me like oil and honey! How good the Lord was to me, and at just that moment. Hallelujah! What a Saviour!

At half-past two the bell rang at the stand for preaching. I walked down rather slowly, and when I got there some one was making a plea for twenty dollars or more for putting the water tanks on top of the hill, so as to be more convenient for the people. A gentle whisper came to me, "Give that fifty cents."

"You will be a fool to give that," the Devil suggested, "for some one might give you two dollars; then you would have the fifty cents so you could get the shoes."

"Yes," I said to myself, "I guess I have got in sympathy with things, looking at them and hearing them." So I shut my eyes and turned round so as not to look up as the basket passed. But the man came and passed the basket right under my face, and I rose up and threw the fifty cents in the basket and said, "Glory to God for nothing, and hallelujah for everything, for I have got Jesus yet;" and O, such a wave of salvation swept through my soul, and I said, "Lord, I thank Thee for helping me to do right."

By and by the preacher commenced. I listened. Rev. John Cookman preached one of his strong holiness sermons. I was greatly blest; but every now and then the Devil would assail me and I would say, "Lord, help me; I believe I have done right." And he blest me still further. It was a fight; but thanks be to God who giveth us the victory.

After the meeting was over I went to my tent to get our tea ready. It was now about six o'clock, and just as we were sitting down and had begun our meal a voice called from the outside:

"Mrs. Smith, Mrs. Smith, Grandpa says you and Mazie must come and get your supper."

It was good old Father Brummel's little grandson.

"Billy, tell your grandpa I thank him, but we are having our supper and will come some other time."

I thought he had gone, but in a few minutes more he called out again:

"Mrs. Smith, Grandpa says you and Mazie must come over and get your supper."

So Mazie said, "Well, Ma, we had better go."

We had some peaches cut down. I said, "What shall we do with our peaches?"

"O," she said, "let's leave them for morning."

"All right," I said. So when we got in dear Brother Brummell's tent he said, "Come, Sister Smith, sit here," pointing to the seat. I shall never forget his loving, kind face. We passed in and took our seats at the table. When I turned up my plate there were three one dollar bills under it, fifty cents more than I had given. So old Satan got whipped that time! Praise the Lord! That was why he assailed me so during the preaching service but how sweetly Jesus delivered me out of his hand. Praise His name forever!

And this is only one of the many times He has delivered me. O, Lord, I will praise Thee.

After I had given the two dollars to Mrs. Butler, I sent to town next morning and got the shoes for my little girl just as I had purposed. At one o'clock Sister Jane Fee said to me, "Let us go to some place where we can have a little quiet and prayer together."

We took our Bibles and went far from the ground, in an old apple orchard. We found a large tree out of sight of the people, and almost out of hearing. There we sat down and read the Word. Oh, how Sweet it was. We wept together, and prayed, and praised the Lord, and made our request known, and He heard

us. After spending an hour, we returned to the campground. As I had had only a slight breakfast, and it was now two o'clock, I was feeling quite hungry!

As we were going down one of the avenues two gentlemen were standing talking. When we got up to them one of them reached out his hand and said to me, "This is Sister Amanda Smith, I believe."

"Yes," I said, "I that is my name, sir."

"I have often heard of you. Well, Sister Smith, how are you getting on?"

"Oh, very well; the Lord looks after me."

"Well, have you had your dinner?" he asked.

"No," I said, "not yet."

"Here are two dollars. Go over there, (pointing to a tent); that is Brother C.'s tent. I have just had my dinner, and they have a good table."

I thanked him kindly, and praised the Lord.

"But," I said, "I will not eat all this two dollars up; there will be some change. Where can I find you?"

"Oh, never mind that," he said, "you can keep it; make it go as far as it will."

Thus the Lord was my shepherd that day.

At six o'clock there was a prayer meeting held at what was called the old Second Street, or Policemen's tent. Brother King, Brother Smith and a number of others took part. God was in the midst of us. The Lord helped in singing, praying and exhortation.

How blessed it is to remember our old friends. Brother Tom Sherwood, with his grand "Amen," and "Bless the Lord," and "Glory to God," as he would so often make the woods ring when he would shout it.

The next morning, at the close of the early prayer meeting, I stood talking with some one, when a gentleman came to me and said, "Have you had your breakfast?"

"No," I said, "not yet."

"Well, I am going home; I have some tickets, and I guess the Lord will have me give them to you. They will last till the camp meeting closes."

"I thank God, and thank you," I said; "but as I am a colored woman they may object to my taking my meals at that tent."

"I don't think they will," he said; "I do not think there will be any objection, but I will go and see."

So he did; and it was all right. They treated me and my daughter most kindly; and the secret of it was, they were earnest Christians.

These are some of the Lord's doings, and they are marvelous. Hallelujah! And I did sing with spirit, and with understanding.

> "In some way or other the Lord will provide;
> It may not be my way, it may not be thy way,
> But yet in His own way, the Lord will provide."

And I began to trust Him for temporal as well as spiritual blessings as I had never done before. And Oh, how faithful was my Lord. How He has blessed me, and all the little I have done for Him.

I had not been accustomed to take part in the meetings, especially when white people were present, and there was a timidity and shyness that much embarrassed me; but whenever called upon, I would ask the Lord to help me, and take the timidity out of me; and He did help me every time.

I remember one Sunday, between the hours of the morning and evening service, there was a great concourse of people. At that time I had a good voice, and could sing very loud. Mrs. L. asked me to go to her tent, and on my way many crowded round me and asked me to sing. Near by was a large stump. Brother Smith, a class-leader at old Second Street Church, New York, called out, "Sister Smith, step up on that stump so the people may hear you better. By that time there was a crowd around me of about four hundred people. After I had sung one or two pieces, one of which was very familiar and blessed to many—

"All I want, all I want,
Is a little more faith in Jesus."

Brother Smith said, "Sister Smith, suppose you tell the people your experience; how the Lord converted you."

And I asked the Lord to help me if it was His will that I should honor Him in acknowledging what He had done for me. And I felt He would help me, so I trusted in Him and ventured to speak. As I went on my heart grew warm, and the power of the Spirit rested upon me, and many of the people wept, and seemed

deeply moved and interested, as they had never been before. God, I believe, blessed that meeting at that big stump on the old Sing Sing Camp Ground. How real it all seems to me now as I think it over, though it was so long ago. A day or two more and the camp meeting was over, and I and Mazie were on the boat going home to New York, to my dear home, which was two small rooms in the rear of 135 Amity street, now called Third street, just above Sixth avenue. I call it my dear home because the Lord had so many times answered my prayer, and blessed my own soul, and made it the birthplace of many souls. Those two little attic rooms will ever be dear to me, and I feel like saying, as one of old: "If I forget thee, let my right hand forget her cunning; if I do not prefer thee above all the fine mountains in America, England, Scotland, Rome, Egypt, or Africa."

> "Here I'll raise my Ebenezer,
> Hither by Thy help I've come,
> And I hope by Thy good pleasure
> Safely to arrive at home." Amen.

CHAPTER XIV.

KENNEBUNK CAMP MEETING—HOW I GOT THERE, AND WAS ENTERTAINED — A GAZING STOCK—HAMILTON CAMP MEETING—A TRIP TO VERMONT— THE LOST TRUNK, AND HOW IT WAS FOUND.

I had met Brother Luce at Round Lake Camp Meeting. He was a strong holiness preacher. Among others who had asked me to go to different camp meetings, he had asked me. I was a young beginner yet, and knew the Lord was leading. But I generally prayed over matters a good deal before deciding. There was a Mrs. Brown, who used to live at Harlem, N. Y. She was a good woman, and I used to work for her. I liked her very much. They had a tent at Round Lake, also. So one day she asked me to bring her a pitcher of water.

I often did little things for the ladies, brushed and settled up their tents, or got them a pitcher or bucket of water. I never felt that it hurt my dignity.

After I had brought her a pitcher of water, Mrs. Brown said to me, "We have a camp meeting at Wesley Grove at such a time, and we are short of workers, and I believe, Amanda, the Lord would bless you if you would go to our camp meeting; and all the money you needed would be at your disposal."

"Thank you," I said, "there are several who have asked me about going to different camp meetings. But you know I have to pray about it. So if you give me the address I will know how to go when I get home and get still before the Lord, so as to know just where He wants me to go, for when one says 'Come here,' and another 'There,' I cannot tell which way or place the Lord wants me to go. But when I get home and get still I can know His voice."

So off I went at that. The day before the camp meeting closed I met Brother Luce again.

"Now, Sister Smith," said he, "I have a church at St. Johnsville, and our people have a large society tent, and you could stay in it, and I would like to have you come to our camp meeting. I will give you my address, and when I get home I will write you and give you all the directions how to come, so you will have no trouble."

"All right, sir; thank you," I said.

The meeting closed, and I never had heard such wonderful preaching on the line of holiness. I was filled and thrilled. So I went home and began to pray and ask the Lord where He would have me go. For out of all the places I had been asked to visit, I wanted to know just where He would have me go. And a deep conviction settled down upon me that I was to go to Kennebunk. I liked Brother Luce and Brother Munger, and their families were all so kind to me while at Round Lake. Then Brother Luce would send me word just how to come. But to my surprise, when the letter came Brother Luce said, "Sister Smith, I am not well, and our people have decided not to take our big tent; so you had better not come, as you are a stranger, and have no place to stop."

"Well," I thought, "all right. I will go to Wesley Grove, where Mrs. Brown wants me to go. Then I know her, and like to work for her. So it will be better than going to Kennebunk."

Then the conviction to go to Kennebunk seemed to deepen, and I did not understand it. I must go to Kennebunk. I went to the Lord and told Him. I said, "Lord, I would be willing to go to

Kennebunk, but Thou knowest Brother Luce has written and told me not to come. And Thou knowest it is not nice to go where you are told not to come. And if I do, it will look like impertinence after he has written and told me not to come. So I will go to Wesley Grove. Mrs. Brown says they need help there. Then I have worked for Mrs. Brown, and I am better acquainted with her, and that would be better for me."

This time Satan helped me a little bit. He said, "Yes, the reason you want to go to Wesley Grove is because Mrs. Brown offered you money, and that is all you are going there for—money."

Oh! how horrible it seemed as I thought of it. And I knew it was not so. And I said, "Now, Mr. Satan, that's a lie, and I will not go to Wesley Grove at all. I am going straight to Kennebunk where they told me not to come. And I will show you it's not money I'm after."

I didn't know how much it would take for me to go to Kennebunk. I had been only to Philadelphia. So on Friday night I went to old John Street Church. Brother Roberts was class leader there. When they held their fiftieth anniversary they had made me, with a number of others, a life member, so I often used to go to this class.

That night there was a Mr. Palmer there. He was a very nice man, and a very consistent Christian. When the meeting was over, this gentleman went to put me on the Sixth avenue cars. He said, as we walked along, talking, "Sister Smith, for years I have been seeking the blessing of heart purity, and your testimony to-night helped me. But why is it I do not seem to get out into the full light?

The Lord has blessed me," he added, "and I have some means. I am a broker on Wall street. But I have consecrated all to the Lord. And any time you need any help, you must just let me know."

"Well, sir," I said, "I never tell anybody but the Lord about my needs. He knows all, and I always tell Him to put it into the hearts of the people to help me when I need it, and then I leave it."

Now, somehow, I felt that the Lord wanted that brother to give me some money, for I did not have quite enough to go to Kennebunk. So I said good night, and got on the car and on I went. But I prayed all the way, and after I got home, that the Lord would trouble that man's heart, for I felt that he was disobeying the Spirit, and that was one reason why he could not come out into the light of full salvation. You must not keep back the full price of loyal obedience to God, and yet expect Him to bless you. And yet how often do we find persons doing this very thing. Then they wonder why they do not get on. The Lord help someone who reads this to see the truth.

I felt somehow all the time that that man was the one that was to help me out. So next morning I got down and prayed again. And then I got up and began to get my things ready. I was doing some ironing. All at once I heard someone come running upstairs very quickly. When he got to the foot of the stairs he called out, "Sister Smith!"

"Yes," I said. Who should it be but this very brother.

"I had an errand uptown this morning," said he, "and I thought I would run in and see you."

Now he had never been to my house before in his life. So I

said, "The Lord sent him." I said to him, "Sit down, Brother Palmer." "Well," he said, "I haven't much time."

But he did sit down a few minutes, and then he said, "I wanted to give you a little money."

"Amen," said I. "You might as well have done it last night. That's what the Lord told you to do."

"Well, yes," he said.

It was just enough, with what I had, to get me a round trip ticket to Kennebunk Camp Meeting. Praise the Lord!

Then we got down on our knees and prayed. I said, "Now, brother, you might just as well settle this thing. The Lord is willing to bless you. Why don't you let him? Why not be obedient now? The Lord can do it now if you will just trust Him."

So while kneeling it came to me to sing a verse or two of that old hymn of Charles Wesley's:

> "Come, O, Thou traveler unknown,
> Whom still I hold but cannot see.
> My company before is gone,
> And I am left alone with Thee," etc.

After singing I said to him, "Now, Brother Palmer, pray and let go."

So he did. My! how he prayed! The Lord broke him all down. He got blessed while he was praying. I prayed a little and then I sang the next verse:

> "In vain Thou strugglest to get free,
> I never will unloose my hold;
> Thou art the man that died for me,
> The secret of Thy love unfold.
> Thy mercies never shall remove,
> Thy nature and Thy name is Love."

Then the blessed Spirit fell upon him, and he launched out into light and liberty. Oh! how he praised the Lord. What a morning that was in that little attic room on Amity street. "And still there's more to follow."

In a few days after this I was off to Kennebunk. I left New York by the Fall River Line at five o'clock P. M. When I got on the boat, to my surprise whom should I meet but Sister Clark.

"Why," she said, "Sister Smith, where are you going?"

"I am going to Kennebunk Camp Meeting. Where are you going?" "Well, praise the Lord," she said, "there is, where I am going."

We had a very pleasant evening together on the boat. We talked and prayed and sang. There were a number of very nice ladies, who seemed to enjoy Sister Clark's talk and prayers. We should have got into Boston, at the old Providence depot, at eight A. M., so as to take the train there for Kennebunk. But on account of a fog the boat did not get in on time, so we were ten minutes late for the train. Then we had to wait till twelve o'clock, noon, before there was another train. Well, I was going to get my ticket and go on the boat from Boston. It was cheaper that way. But Sister Clark said:

"Now don't do that, Sister Smith. You will lose two days of the camp meeting if you do that. Go right on now with me."

Well, I thought I would like to do it, yet I didn't have money enough. But she said, "I think you had better do it. I think you had better go right on with me."

So after talking awhile I decided to buy my ticket and go with her. That left me only fifty cents. After I got my ticket and sat down, oh! how Satan attacked me. He said, "Now you have been getting on, and the Lord has been leading you all the way. But now you have got out of the Lord's hands. You have got into Mrs. Clark's hands. She is leading you now."

Oh! I felt dreadful. I wished I had not seen Mrs. Clark. I wished I had not come on the boat. Oh! to think the Lord had blessed me so much, and now I had got right out of His hands, and was in the hands of a woman. I do not suppose Sister Clark ever knew how bad I felt. I could have cried.

After I walked about a little while, I said to Mrs. Clark, "I have Miss Sarah Clapp's address."

She lived on Winter street, Boston. I had met her at the camp meeting at Round Lake, and she had given me this address, and told me if I ever came to Boston I must call and see her. So I said, "I think I will go and see Miss Clapp."

"Very well," she said, "I will stay here and mind the things. Be sure you get back in time."

"Yes," I said.

So I went out and took the car and went to Miss Clapp's. How glad she was to see me. She had got the blessing at the Round Lake Camp Meeting, and she was praising the Lord, and saying how nicely the Lord had kept her, and how she had been getting on since she had got back to Boston. She got me some lunch. We sang and had a little prayer together, then she brought something to me and said, "I want you to take this. The Lord wants me to give it to you. But you must not look at it until you get in the cars."

Well, I was in a fidget, because I wanted to see what it was. So she sent a little girl with me to put me on the right car that would take me right to the depot. Oh! how I did want to look at what she had given me. But she had made me promise not to look at it, so I did not. When I did look at it, lo and behold, it was a five dollar bill! So another triumph for Jesus.

We arrived at Kennebunk at nine o'clock P. M. Sister Clark had friends that were looking for her, so they met her at the depot. Of course when we got to the grounds the meeting was over, and all the people were in their tents. I had the company of Sister Clark and her friend as far as the stand, or auditorium. Then Sister Clark said, "Sister Smith, what are you going to do?"

"I don't know."

The lady was with her said, "I wish I had room for you, Mrs. Smith, I would take you in. But really I have only room for Sister Clark."

"If I could find the lodging tent," I said, "I might inquire whether I could get a place for the night."

But she said she did not know really where to direct me. So the man set my trunk down, and I sat down on the end of a long bench beside it. There was one or two lights burning.

"Now then," the Devil said, "if you had gone on the boat as you first thought, and had not followed Sister Clark, you would have got here in the day time, and it would have been much better. Then, besides, you might have done some good work for God on the boat. It is all well enough for Mrs. Clark. She had friends looking out for her. But no one here knows you." "That is so," I said, "and I am so sorry I did not go on the boat."

One might have thought he was wonderfully interested for the poor sinners on the boat. What a pity I had not gone and talked to those people as he said. Oh! how subtle his suggestions. How he likes to tantalize you about what you might have done, especially after the opportunity is past. He does it to get your eye turned on a mistake, or on the sadness of your heart, because you have made a mistake, and how many poor souls he brings into bondage right at this point. I sat there, and in my heart I cried. But somehow I felt I was right in coming. So I said, "Lord, help me to learn the lesson. I suppose I will have to sleep under the stand."

So in my mind I began to fix about which way I should lay my head. There was a great pile of leaves and some straw under the stand, to be kept dry in case it should rain. So my imagined bed was made. Then I thought, "I wonder if there are any pigs about here, and if they would disturb me."

Then I began to feel a little afraid, and I said, "Lord, help me and do, please send someone to me."

I had scarcely uttered the words when I saw a door open away at the upper part of the grounds; a man came out and walked to where I was sitting. A moment later, and out came a sister. She said, "Brother M., where are you going?"

"Oh!" he said, "I think I see someone here! so I am looking about."

By that time he was quite up to me. "Why, is this Amanda Smith?"

"Yes," I said.

"Sister A.," he called, "here is Sister Amanda Smith. Praise the Lord. Oh! now I see why the Lord sent me out here. I had no especial business, but it seemed I must come down here and look about. Praise the Lord."

We had a praising time of it. They took me, bag and baggage, to the tent. It was a large society tent, and there were several families together. They had a large upstairs, and they said they could accommodate me for the night anyhow. I was so thankful. I had an elegant bed, and was so comfortable. In the morning when they had all gone downstairs I got on my knees and said, "'Now, Lord, this seems like the very place where Thou wantest me to stay. But they have said they could accommodate me only to-night. Now if Thou dost want me to stay here, make them ask me when I go downstairs, to stay. Amen."

In the morning I arose and went downstairs. We had family prayers. What a time we had. It was not strange to have a baptism of the Spirit fall upon us in those days while at family prayers and praising the Lord.

When the breakfast was over I said, "Now can you tell me where the office is where I can go to inquire about getting a tent, and some straw to fill my tick and pillow?"

"Oh! you are not going away, are you?"

"Well, you know you were only to accommodate me till morning, as I was out of doors last night."

"Well, were you comfortable where you slept last night?"

"Oh! yes."

"Very well. You just stay where you are."

Oh! didn't I Praise the Lord for his goodness, and for his wonderful works to the children of men. No wonder Job said, "And these are only parts of His ways." Hallelujah!

Here I must speak of Sister Clark's help when I was greatly tempted because the people gazed at me and followed me about from place to place and just stared at me.

Under this trial I learned the meaning of the thirty-second and thirty-third verses of the tenth chapter of Hebrews.

It was one Sunday. There had been a great crowd all day, and everywhere I would go a crowd would follow me. If I went into a tent they would surround it and stay till I came out, then they would follow me. Sometimes I would slip into a tent away from them. Then I would see them peep in, and if they saw me they would say, "Oh! here is the colored woman. Look!" Then the rush! So after dinner I managed to get away. I went into a friend's tent and said, "Let me lie down here out of sight a little while."

"Yes," she said, "the people do not seem to have any manners. I never saw anything like it."

So I got down on the floor under the foot of the bed, and I would see them as they would pass by, and hear them say, "Where is she, the colored woman?"

"I don't know, but I think she is in here," someone would say. But I kept still. About five o'clock the people began to leave the ground. So about six I stepped out and went down to the spring. I met Sister Clark. She said, "Sister Smith, have you had your supper?"

"No," I said, "there is something the matter with me."

"What is it?"

"The people have followed me about all day, and have stared at me. Somehow I feel so bad and uncomfortable."

"Well," she said, laughing, "don't you know the Bible says, 'You are to be a gazing stock?' "

"No," I said, "is it in the Bible?"

"Yes."

"All right, I can settle it then."

She went to the dining hall to supper, and I went down in the woods by myself, and there I had it out. I told the Lord how mean I felt because the people had looked at me. I prayed, "Help me to throw off that mean feeling, and give me grace to be a gazing stock." And after I had prayed, I remained kneeling and thinking it all over. All at once a thought came to me: "The other day when you were carrying the clothes home you saw a crowd standing and looking in at a window on Broadway, New York, at a picture."

"Yes."

"And you went up with the crowd and looked at it too."

"Yes."

"You heard the remarks of the people, and the approvals and disapprovals."

"Yes," I said.

"Did that picture say anything?"

"No."

"Did it injure its beauty?"

"No, Lord; I see it."

I got up and went on double quick to the tent. I praised the Lord. I laughed, and cried, and shouted. It was so simple, and yet so real. The next morning at the eight o'clock meeting I got up and shouted, "I have got the victory! Everybody come and look at me! Praise the Lord!"

I was free as a bird.

> "What a wonderful Saviour is Jesus, my Jesus,
> What a wonderful Saviour is Jesus, my Lord!"

At this same camp meeting the Lord cured a good old brother, Jacob C., of prejudice. He was a well-to-do man, and had lived in Maine all his life. He said he had never seen many colored persons, and never cared to have anything to do with them when he could help it. If he had any business to do with them, he would always do it as quickly as possible and get away. So now, when he saw me about in the meetings he was much disturbed. But still he felt that he needed the blessing, and had come to camp meeting for that purpose. Whenever the invitation was given for those who wanted a clean heart, he would go forward and kneel down. But then the black woman would be in every meeting; would sing, or pray, or testify. He could not get on. Then the Holy Spirit had showed him the filthy use of tobacco, and he thought he never could give that up. He had used it from a boy ten years old; and he was now about sixty. He said he had never been without it a day all these years; and if he failed to get it on Saturday, he would go into a drug store on his way to church on Sunday morning and get it, and pay for it on Monday. What a slave! He was a class-leader, and he said he felt he needed to be fixed up a bit.

So he did, I should say. One morning under a powerful sermon by Rev. B. F. Pomeroy, of the Troy Conference, he was led to make a full surrender of himself. When Brother Pomeroy invited them forward, this man went. He had got the victory while praying in the woods, over his prejudice against me an hour or two before. But the tobacco stuck. He had it in his mouth, and when he knelt there the Spirit said to him, "Can you give up that tobacco?" And I saw him when he dug a hole in the straw leaves and took his tobacco out of his mouth, put it down, covered it over and got on it with his knees! It was not long before the Lord poured in his heart the blessing of full salvation. My! how he shouted!

It was a wonderful meeting that afternoon. The first thing he saw when he got up and stood on his feet, he said, was the colored woman standing on a bench with both hands up, singing "All I want is a little more faith in Jesus." And he said every bit of prejudice was gone, and the love of God was in his heart, and he thought I was just beautiful!

I saw him the next year, and he was still saved. And he sat down by me in the dining hall at the table and gave me two dollars and he said the past year had been the best year of his life. Oh, how happy he was! God bless him. Amen.

I think it was June 21, 1871. 1 remember the great railroad accident at Revier. I got into Boston from Martha's Vineyard. I was anxious to catch the five P. M. train. It left Boston, and stopped at Hamilton, about seven o'clock. Then the next train did not leave till seven thirty, and that would not arrive at the camp meeting till about nine o'clock; and as I had never been there I was anxious to get there as early as I could. But the man that I had got to take my trunk was late, and just as I had got into the station the train was moving out.

"Oh, my!" I said, "I wanted to go on that train." The porter said, "You are too late now."

"When will the next one go out to the camp meeting?"

"Seven thirty," he said, "and will arrive about nine o'clock."

"Oh," I said, "I'm so sorry. I wrote I would be on that train."

There were a number of persons who had come to say good-bye to loved ones, parents, and children, and friends; and as the train moved off, handkerchiefs were waved and kisses were thrown, and the last good-bye said, and the train passed out of the station, and I felt as though I would cry, I was so disappointed. But that disappointment saved my life. We left Boston on the next train, a lively company of camp meeting folks. A number were just going for the Sabbath. I met a number of friends who knew me, and we had some singing on the train, and I was feeling glad and happy, after all my disappointment. We went at full speed, and all at once the train suddenly stopped. We sang on and waited for it to start. We didn't know what the trouble was. A half hour passed; still we did not move on. Some of the men went out, and we thought when they came back we would know what the trouble was. Another half hour passed, and they did not come back. Then some of the women said, "Let's go out and see." So several of us got out and walked down the track and met several coming, who said there was a great accident at Revier. Our train had stopped about it mile away, this side of where the accident occurred.

I, with several others, walked to the scene, and as we drew near the fire was roaring, and the shouts for help and the groans of the dying and wounded were something beyond description. Revier was only a small way station; there was no drug store, and no houses to get any help from. They took off the doors of the few houses that stood round, and the shutters, and everything they could get hold of. Some were scalded; some were burned; others with broken limbs; and we were helpless; we had nothing. I could only weep and pray. I thought of the goodness of the Lord in not letting the man get my trunk in time, and then the words of this Psalm came to my mind with much force. "A thousand shall fall at thy side, and ten thousand at thy right hand; but it shall not come nigh thee." Oh, how I did praise my loving Father, God.

They succeeded somehow in getting the track clear, and our train passed on. We arrived at the camp-ground between twelve and one o'clock at night. Sunday was a sad day, though many who were on the ground knew nothing of the accident, yet it seemed to cast a shadow. But the Lord was with us and helped. How well I remember some of the dear friends. My home was with Mrs. James Musso, in their pretty cottage. The lovely meetings we had! I remember Mrs. McGee, of Boston, and old Father Waite, of Ipswich. One day, going into the dining tent, he introduced me to the people as the "Fifteenth Amendment." That was the first I had heard of that bill. I also remember Father Snow, of Boston, Sarah and Laura Clapp, and dear Beenie Hamilton, and the wonderful tent meeting. She asked me to go with her to a little quiet meeting in a cottage. It was not to be a large meeting; only a few hungry ones who wanted help specially. The meeting was to be held only an hour; but we never closed it from half past two till six o'clock, and we could hardly close then; and if ever I saw God take hold of a meeting and control it, it was that afternoon. More than a score of souls were swept into the fountain of cleansing. Some people were convicted for pardon and for purity on the spot, and yielded to God, and God saved. Truly it was realized, "Knock and it shall be opened; seek and ye shall find; ask, and it shall be given you, for every one that asketh, receiveth; and he that seeketh, findeth; and to him that knocketh, it is opened." The most of the time I stood on my feet and exhorted, and sang, and talked, and prayed. When I got out and went to start home, I could scarcely walk. I was thoroughly exhausted. I had a cup of tea, and lay down a while, and was ready for another pitched battle. Glory to God!

Those were wonderful days. One does not see it in that fashion now. Oh, how we need the mighty Holy Ghost power that they had at Pentecost!

> "It was while they all were praying,
> It was while they all were praying,
> It was while they all were praying
> And believing it would come,
> Came the power, the power,
> Came the power that Jesus promised should come down."

One day, just before the camp meeting closed, Rev. Dr. Cushman, who was then Principal of the Ladies' Seminary at Auburndale, Mass., came to me and said: "Sister Smith, have you ever been to Lindenville, Vt.?" I said, "No."

"Well," said he, "that is my home, not far from there. Our camp meeting begins such a day (naming the day), and I believe the Lord would have you go to that meeting. I think you would do us good. I have to leave to-night," he continued, "or in the morning, but I will give you the directions how to come." So I told the Lord if He wanted me to go to Lindenville, and would give me the money, I would take that as an indication of His will. So the money came all right.

On Tuesday morning, I think it was, I was off. I didn't stop to eat my breakfast; I thought I would wait till I got there. I left Hamilton about six A. M. for Boston, so as to get as early a train as I could. I had no idea where Vermont was, much less Lindenville. I was as green as a pea! I had never traveled any distance, and coming from New York to Boston, and then to Martha's Vineyard, was the biggest thing I had ever done. I expected to get to Lindenville about ten o'clock A. M. When I got to the station at Boston, I went to the ticket office and asked for a ticket to Lindenville, Vt. The man said, "You won't have time to get a ticket; the train is just moving out." I turned and said to the man, "Put on my trunk, quick!"

He pitched it on, and I got on. I think it was the eight-fifteen train in the morning. When the conductor came I told him I didn't have time to get a ticket, so paid him what he asked. I said to him, "I didn't get my trunk checked; will you please look in the baggage car and tell me if you see such a trunk?" describing the trunk as best I could. In a little while he came through, and said, "Madame, there is so much baggage piled up that I cannot tell, exactly, but from the description you give I think it is there; it will be all right." So I was contented. Ten o'clock came, and I was not at Lindenville. Eleven o'clock—twelve o'clock—not yet. Then I began to get hungry. I saw no place where I could get even an apple. Then I wondered if I had not made a mistake after all. So the Devil thought this was his chance, and he assailed me fiercely:

"You don't know if you are on the right train."

"No," I said, "I do not."

"You ought not to have come without getting a ticket."

"No," I said, "I suppose not." Then I thought, "Well, I asked the Lord about it," and then he said, "You prayed, but you didn't pray enough."

"Perhaps I didn't," I thought.

Then a gentleman got in, and he looked very pleasant, and I thought I would ask him if I was on the right train to Lindenville, Vt. So I went to him and said, "You will excuse me, sir, but I want to ask you if this is the train that goes to Lindenville, Vt.?"

He said very sharply, "I don't know." Then everybody seemed to look at me. All the people seemed so strange. It seemed to me I had never seen that kind of people before. And they seemed as though they had not seen many of my kind before! My! how they stared at me! After a while a lady got on, and I thought I would ask her. And I said, "Madame, will you tell me if this train goes to Lindenville, Vt.?"

She pulled herself up, and said, "I don't know." Then I thought I would ask the conductor, but he sailed through in such it rush that I couldn't ask him. Then the Devil said, "You think the Lord wanted you to go to Lindenville, Vt.; but if the Lord wanted you to go, somebody would know if you are on the right train, and be able to tell you." And I thought, "Yes, that is so; it does seem so." And imagine my surprise when I never got to Lindenville, Vt., till six o'clock in the evening. But about four o'clock in the afternoon we stopped at a station, and Rev. Mr. Luce and his wife and children got on, and they spied me, and Brother Luce came up, and said, "Why, Amanda Smith, where are you going?"

"To Lindenville, Vt., sir."

"Well," said he, "we go as far as St. Johnsville. Then we are going up to Lindenville on Sunday to the camp meeting."

I was so glad. Then he asked me if I had had anything to eat. I told him no, and they gave me some lunch, and that helped me.

When we got to Lindenville, Dr. Cushan was there and met me at the station, and hunted for my trunk high and low; but he could not find it; there was no such trunk there. And I had to stay just with the clothes that I had on, and had traveled in, up till the next Saturday.

Well, we went to the camp meeting at Lindenville. We had a good time. The Lord blessed me very greatly. It was very primitive, but the people were very hearty and kind.

I remember Rev. Mr. McCann was Presiding Elder, and had charge of the meeting. I shall never forget the lecture he gave me the morning I left. He was very much afraid that I would be spoiled; and I remember as I sat before him, he charged me with vehemence; when he told incidents where colored people had been made a good deal of, and how they came down, and how they were spoiled, and how it affected them, and hurt their influence. I smiled, and he went on with his charge. People pitied me for his great solicitude, and I felt that his labor was in vain. There I sat in the congregation, and it was his farewell remarks, as the camp meeting had closed that morning. I didn't know whether to stay for another camp meeting, or whether to go. Some laughed, and others seemed to feel sorry, I didn't know what to do; but I prayed mightily. But the Lord kept me, and none of these things have come upon me. How I praise Him!

On Saturday we went to Boston. Dr. Cushan went to the store and got me some things to help me through Sunday. I was entertained at the home of Dr. Hopkins, of Auburndale. I spoke several times on Sunday. Sunday night we had a very precious meeting at the Methodist Church; so that I went home cheered in heart, though I had no trunk. I went to my room, and just as I was getting ready for bed I thought to myself, "I must make a very special prayer for my trunk." So I knelt to pray, and the words of John 15:7 came forcibly to my mind: "If ye abide in me, and my words abide in you, you shall ask what you will, and it shall be done unto you." And I said, "Now, Lord. here is Thy word, and as far as I know, I believe that I am abiding in Thee, and that Thy word is abiding in me. And now, Lord, I'm going to ask you about my trunk. Grant me this petition, that I will either get my trunk, or hear from it to-morrow."

Then these words came to me: "If thou canst believe all things are possible with them that believe." And I said, "Lord, I believe I will get my trunk to-morrow."

Just then Satan said, clearly, "That trunk has been gone a week, and you have hunted for it high and low, and Dr. Cushan, and Dr. Hopkins, and other friends, have looked for it; you have sent telegrams, and you have not heard a word of it; and now, for you to say you believe you will get it to-morrow, is presumption; and when people are sanctified and not presumptuous, they never say anything till they know it."

And then I began to get a little frightened. I said, "Oh, Lord, Thou knowest I do not mean to be presumptuous. But somehow or other I believe I will get my trunk to-morrow;" and every time I said "I believe" to God, it seemed to me my faith was strengthened, and there was a sweet assurance and peace came over my spirit that did not come when the least shadow of doubt would try to enter my heart. But the Tempter harassed me. Oh, how he harassed me! I rose from my knees, and went over to the little stand in the corner, and I said, "Lord, give me some word to help me." Then I opened my Bible, and my eyes fell on these words: "A crooked and perverse generation seeketh after a sign, and there shall be no sign given them," and I shut the book, and said, "Lord, I don't want any sign. I believe I will get my trunk to-morrow." Then Satan seemed to leave me, and I went to bed in peace. I believed God all night.

The first thing in the morning the thought of my trunk came into my mind, and I said, "Lord, I believe I will get my trunk to-day."

I didn't tell anybody. I just kept it before the Lord. I went down to breakfast. Dr. Hopkins was such a kind gentleman. He read the Bible for family prayer, then he knelt down to pray, and asked the Lord so earnestly about my trunk. I did not say anything to him about what I had believed upstairs. At breakfast he said, "Sister Smith, we will go to town this morning, and have another search for your trunk." This was Tuesday morning. They had hunted everywhere Monday, and had no tidings.

When breakfast was over, he and I started for Boston. He said to me, "Now, Sister Smith, you can go to Miss Clapp's, and I will go to the baggage room and inquire if they have heard anything about your trunk."

So I went on to Miss Clapp's, 19 Winter street. She was busy in the outer room, and told me to be seated in the parlor. I did so.

After awhile she called out and said, "Sister Smith, have you heard anything about your trunk?"

"No," I said.

Then she in a very pleasant manner said, "Well, somehow I believe you will get it. I had a valise lost once, and it was gone three months, but I got it all right."

I thought to myself, "Three months, indeed; I cannot wait three months; I want my trunk now." Still I did not tell her how I had believed in God. As I sat in the chair I threw my head back and began to sing this little hymn, that had been blessed so wonderfully of God to so many souls:

> "All I want, all I want, all I want,
> Is a little more faith in Jesus."

I sang two verses; and as I was repeating the chorus of the last verse a knock came at the door, and as Miss Clapp was not in the room, I got up and went to the door: and when I opened it, there stood a great big Irishman, about six feet high, with my trunk. And as he wheeled it in, he said, "Here is a trunk for Amanda Smith," and I shouted, "Praise the Lord," and he looked as though he was frightened. He wheeled the trunk in and stepped back, and I said, "You needn't be afraid; I'm only believing in God. That is all. Glory!" And he cut down stairs and I have never seen him since!

Oh! how Satan tried to wrest my faith. But God stood by me as He stood by Joshua; so that when the Tempter comes in like a flood the Lord shall lift up a standard against him. "Fear not. Be strong and of good courage. Said I not unto thee if thou wouldst believe thou shouldst see the glory of God?" Amen. Amen.

CHAPTER XV.

MY EXPERIENCE AT DR. TAYLOR'S CHURCH, NEW YORK, AND ELSEWHERE—THE GENERAL CONFERENCE AT NASHVILLE—HOW I WAS TREATED AND HOW IT ALL CAME OUT—HOW THINGS CHANGE.

I think it was in October, 1870, or 1871. It was when Miss Sarah Smiley, the Quakeress, was very popular. She was giving Bible readings at that time in different churches—Dr. Cuyler's Church in Brooklyn, at the Methodist Churches, and others. I was holding meetings at Twenty-fourth Street Methodist Church, with Rev. Dr.—, and Miss Smiley was giving a series of Bible readings at Dr. Taylor's Church at the same time. Some ladies at Brooklyn, who had been attending the Twenty-fourth Street Church, came one evening and said to me, "Oh, Amanda Smith, have you been to hear Miss Smiley at Dr. Taylor's Church?" And I said, "No."

"Well," they said, "she is to be there to-morrow afternoon, and it is to be her last Bible reading. It is on such a subject," naming the subject, "Oh, yesterday it was grand. I thought of you, and wished you were there. So I made up my mind I would come and tell you to-night, and maybe you could go to-morrow afternoon."

I was not holding afternoon meetings, only evening meetings, myself, so I thanked them very kindly and thought I would go and hear Miss Smiley. So I did. I went early. There was quite a company gathered, though it was a half hour before the time. A number of gentleman were present, and ladies whom I had met some at Ocean Grove, others at Dr. Palmer's Tuesday meetings, and some of these ladies said to me, "Now, Amanda Smith, while we are waiting it would be nice if you would sing."

The "Winnowed Hymns" were very popular then; they were

new, and there were a number of pieces I knew very well. In those days I used to sing a great deal, and somehow the Lord always seemed to bless my singing. So these ladies were very anxious to have me sing. I told them I did not like to do so; I thought it might not be pleasant in this new church, and it was not a Methodist Church, and perhaps they might not like it. But they told me it would be all right. Several of these ladies were members of the church. They assured me that it would be no breach of propriety for me to sing. So when they urged me, I sang.

The Lord blessed the singing. When I got through with one piece, they asked me to sing something else. They made the selections; I do not remember just now what they were, but I sang another piece. And while they were selecting another piece, I said, "I think I had better not sing any more just now," and asked the Lord to help me and not let me be singing when Miss Smiley came in. I thought she might think I had put myself forward. And the Lord saved me from that mortification.

The ladies were still urging me, and said they knew Miss Smiley would be rather pleased. But I did not feel so. So Miss Smiley came in when there was no singing going on. A minute or two later, as they were urging me so, I presume I would have been singing. Oh, how glad I was that the Lord had kept me.

Miss Smiley got through with her Bible reading beautifully. It was very interesting and everybody seemed to enjoy it. The gentlemen came up and shook hands with me, and thanked me for the singing. The ladies who were in thanked me for the singing, and as I was very near Miss Smiley, I thanked her for the address and told her how much it had helped me, but I thought she seemed rather cool. Then I was frightened, and sorry I had said anything to her.

By and by I saw a lady, tall, with black hair and a very sallow complexion, and a tremendous air, and a countenance not brightened by sweetness—but still, she passed. I saw this lady go up to Miss Smile and begin talking to her, and I saw Miss Smiley shaking her head; but I did not know what it meant.

I did not rush out through the ladies; I quietly waited and kept behind, so as not to be in the way; and after this lady turned away from Miss Smiley, she looked at me with a scowl and a look of contempt on her face. She stepped inside of a pew and beckoned me and said, "Come here, come here."

So I went up to her with all the smiles and grace I was capable of, and she drew herself up in the most dignified manner and said, "Who told you to come here?" And she said it in such a tone that it frightened me. It went all over me, and I began to stammer—a thing I never do—and I tried to think of the name of the lady who had asked me—for I knew her very well—but to save me her name would not come. She was at the meeting, but had got to the door, and was speaking to some one; and I looked round and said, "Mrs.—, Mrs.—," but I could not think of the name. I told her some ladies had told me about Miss Smiley's meeting, and I thought I would like to come and hear Miss Smiley.

"Well," she said, "we have invited Miss Smiley here."

"Oh." I said, "I beg your pardon, madame."

"Never mind, pass right out, pass right out," she said, waving her hand toward the door.

"Oh," I said, "Madame—" and she said, "Pass out, pass out," and she drove me away.

Some of the ladies were passing, and they said, "Oh, my, this is too bad."

"What is the matter?" another said. And another, "Oh, that is a shame." "What is it?"

By the time I got to the door there was so much sympathy and pity for me that they almost killed me. I cried, almost to convulsions. I was nearly dead. If they had not pitied me and seemed to feel so sorry for me, I could have got on well enough.

I went up to Sixth avenue and got on the car, and some of the ladies got on the same car; and they sat down beside me and tried to comfort me, and they made it worse. I was ashamed of myself, but I could not help myself. It seemed to me I had lost all control of my feelings. I cried about that thing for about two days, every time I thought of it. And it made quite a stir. The ladies came from downtown to see me about it, and to inquire about it. And I prayed so much for the woman, for I thought she needed to be prayed for, and I did pray for her with all my heart. So I think that she got the worst of it in the end!

Sometimes people say to me, "Oh, Amanda Smith, how very popular you are."

"Yes," I say, "but I paid for it." I paid a good price for my popularity. I don't know whether the lady is living or dead. I have never seen her since. Poor thing, how I have pitied her! I suppose the Lord will get her through somehow. But that is the only time I was ever ordered out of a church from a religious meeting, or any other kind.

Again, it was in 1870 or 1871, when my dear friend, Mrs. Hannah Whitehall Smith, was holding those marvelous Bible readings in Germantown and Philadelphia that God blessed so wonderfully. I had often heard them spoken of, and read of them, and thought how I would like to go; but then I did not know whether they would allow colored persons to go. The Lord often would send me around among white people where there was a good meeting going on, that I might learn more perfectly some lesson from His Word.

One day I was on my way to West Philadelphia when Mr. Robert Pearson Smith, who had been off in California, doing some evangelistic work, I believe, and had got home just a few days before, got on the car, and after he had sat down a little while he looked over and recognized me. He came and said, "I think this is Amanda Smith?" I said, "Yes." He took a seat by me, and did not have any fear or embarrassment from my being a colored woman. How real, and kind, and true he was. He said, "Amanda Smith, has thee attended any of the meetings that my wife Hannah, has been holding?"

"No," I said, "I have thought I would like so much to go, but I did not know if they would allow colored persons to go."

"Oh, yes, Amanda," he said, "there would be no objection to thee going, and I think thee would enjoy the meeting very much. God has wonderfully blessed Hannah, and scores of ladies of rank have been led to consecrate themselves to the Lord, and have realized great blessing. She will hold a meeting at 1018 Arch street, on Friday. Thee must go."

I thanked him very kindly, and told him I would do so.

"Now," I thought, to myself, "the Lord has answered my prayer, and opened the way for me, and no doubt He has some blessed lesson to teach me from His Word; for Mrs. Smith is such a wonderful Bible teacher."

So I looked forward to Friday with great delight. When the day came I got ready and went, prayerfully. But somehow I seemed to have a little trembling come over me as I neared the corner of Tenth and Arch streets; and I said to myself, "I wonder what is going to happen; my heart has become so sad all in a moment."

Then I began to pray more earnestly that the Lord would help me and lead me. Sometimes these feeling of sadness, though unexplainable, are the omen of a great blessing from God; at another time they may indicate disappointment and sadness, so that in either case God permits them, and prepares the heart by prayer to receive the blessing, or to endure the sorrow or disappointment. Praise His name for this.

Just when I was about to turn the corner, I saw two ladies coming. I knew them, and they were on the way to the meeting. I thought, "I will let them pass, and I will follow close on behind, and go in just when they are fairly in." I always tried to avoid anything like pushing myself, or going where I was not wanted. And then I knew how sensitive many white people are about a colored person, so I always kept back. I don't think that anybody can ever say that Amanda Smith pushed herself in where she was not wanted. I was something like the groundhog; when he sees his shadow he goes in; I always could see my shadow far enough ahead to keep out of the way. But I thought as Mr. Pearson Smith had so kindly told me that it would be all right for me to go to this meeting, that I would not be intruding; no, certainly not. When these ladies got up to me, they stopped, and spoke to me very kindly; they said, "Well, Amanda Smith, how does thee do? Is thee going to the meeting?"

"Yes," I said, "I have heard and read a good deal about the meeting, and I thought I would go to-day."

I saw they looked a little nervous or queer, so I said to them, "I met Mr. Pearson Smith the other day, and he told me to go; there would be no objection, and the meetings were very wonderful in blessing, and he thought I would enjoy them."

"Well, Amanda," one of the ladies said, "the meeting will be very full to-day, and there will be a great many very wealthy ladies in from Germantown, and West Philadelphia, and Walnut Hills, and the meetings are especially for this class, and I think thee had better not go to-day; some other day would be better for thee." And then they politely bowed, and went on.

I never said a word. I was dumbfounded; and there I stood. I thought, "How is this? I have been praying about this meeting ever since I saw Mr. Smith, and I have been expecting a real feast to my soul to-day, and now these ladies feel it won't do for me to go, because I am a colored woman, and so many of the wealthy ladies will be there. They don't know but that the Lord may have sent a message to some of them through me." So I said, "I will linger about till I know the meeting is well begun, then I will go and stand at the door."

Now I felt in my heart it was right to do this instead of going back home. I did so. "And after all it may be I may hear the word the Lord has for me; for He meant something by my coming." So I slipped in quietly and stood at the door; there were a number of others standing up. Just as Mrs. Smith was in the midst of her good Bible address, sure enough the Lord had a message for me, and I got a great blessing as I stood at the door. Praise the Lord!

And now, the change is, instead of Amanda Smith, the colored washwoman's presence having a bad effect on a meeting where ladies of wealth and rank are gathered to pray and sing His blessing, they think a failure more possible if the same Amanda Smith, the colored woman, cannot be present. This is all the Lord's doings, and marvelous in our eyes.

At the close of this meeting as the ladies were passing out, one and another came to me and spoke to me, and shook hands; "Why, this is Amanda Smith."

"Yes."

"Oh, here is Amanda Smith; why didn't you sing?" And another, "Oh, I have heard you." And another, "Oh, I wish you had sung such a piece." And another, "Why didn't you speak?" And another, "I have heard you sing such a piece at Ocean Grove at such a time, or at Round Lake." I was glad of this, for I thought, "After all, I have not spoiled the spirit of the meeting."

But then, I was not so well known then, and many people were shy of me, and are yet. But I belong to Royalty, and am well acquainted with the King of Kings, and am better known and better understood among the great family above than I am on earth. But I thank God the time is coming, and we "Shall know each other better when the mists have rolled away." Hallelujah! Amen.

In May, '70, or '71, the General Conference of the A. M. E. Church was held at Nashville, Tenn. It was the first time they ever held a General Conference south of Mason and Dixon's line. I

had been laboring in Salem, where the Lord first sent me, and blessed me in winning souls; the people were not rich; they gave me a home, and something to eat; but very little money. So, before I could get back to New York, my home, I took a service place, at Mrs. Mater's, in Philadelphia, corner of Coach and Brown streets, while her servant, Mary, went to Wilmington to see her child; she was to be gone a month, but she stayed five weeks; and now the Annual Conference was in session, at the A. M. E. Union Church, near by where I was, so I had a chance to attend.

The election of delegates to the General Conference the next year was a very prominent feature of the Conference; of course every minister wanted, or hoped to be elected as delegate. As I listened, my heart throbbed. This was the first time in all these years that this religious body of black men, with a black church from beginning to end, was to be assembled south of Mason and Dixon's line.

But the great battle had been fought, and the victory won; slavery had been abolished; we were really free. There, were enthusiastic speeches made on these points. Oh, how I wished I could go; and a deep desire took possession of me; but then, who was I? I had no money, no prominence at that time, except being a plain Christian woman, heard of and known by a few of the brethren, as a woman preacher, which was to be dreaded by the majority, especially the upper ten. Fortunately I had a good friend in Bishop Campbell, knowing him so well years before he was elected to this office. Also Bishop Wayman, Bishop Brown, and Bishop Quinn, were friends of mine. I believe I always had their sympathy and friendship. But there was no opportunity for me to speak to them personally. So I ventured to ask one of the brethren, who had been elected delegate, to tell me how much it would cost to go to Nashville; I would like to go if it did not cost too much.

He looked at me in surprise, mingled with half disgust; the very idea of one looking like me to want to go to General Conference; they cut their eye at my big poke Quaker bonnet, with not a flower, not a feather. He said, "I tell you, Sister, it will cost money to go down there; and if you ain't got plenty of it, it's no use to go;" and turned away and smiled; another said:

"What does she want to go for?"

"Woman preacher; they want to be ordained," was the reply.

"I mean to fight that thing," said the other. "Yes, indeed, so will I," said another.

Then a slight look to see if I took it in. I did; but in spite of it all I believed God would have me go. He knew that the thought of ordination had never once entered my mind, for I had received my ordination from Him, Who said, "Ye have not chosen Me, but I have chosen you, and ordained you, that you might go and bring forth fruit, and that your fruit might remain."

I spoke to some of the good sisters who were expecting to go; they said they did not know what it would cost. So I went home, and prayed, and asked the Lord to help me; and the conviction that I was to go deepened, and yet it seemed so impossible. Just before, the Conference closed I ventured to ask another good brother, who had been elected delegate, and whom I knew very well, and he was so nice, I thought he would tell me. "Brother S.," I said, "how much do you think it will cost?" This was the uppermost thought then—the cost to go to Nashville. "Oh, my sister," he replied, "I don't know; it will take all of a hundred dollars;" and with a significant toss of the head shot through the door, and I saw him no more till I met him next year at Nashville; and that was a surprise, but he managed to speak to me, as we both stopped at the Sumner House, and sat at the same table.

I was quite a curiosity to most of the visitors, especially the Southern brethren, in my very plain Quaker dress; I was eyed with critical suspicion as being there to agitate the question of the ordination of women. All about, in the little groups that would be gathered talking, could be heard, "Who is she?"

"Preacher woman."

"What does she want here?"

"I mean to fight that thing."

"I wonder what day it will come up?"

Of course, I was a rank stranger to most of them; the bishops, and all those whom I did know, had all got there before me, and were settled, and I was not going to trouble them for anything. Then those of the ladies whom I knew, wives of ministers or bishops, were dressed to the height of their ability; I could not rank with them; so I was all alone; "And His brethren did not believe in Him." "The servant is not above his Lord."

No one but God knows what I passed through the first three days. God, in answer to prayer, had marvelously opened my way to go; through the kindness of my dear friend, Mrs. Kibbey, of Albany, N. Y., who is now in Heaven, I had my outfit; it pretty tan dress, with a drab shawl and bonnet to match. I thought I was fine; but bless you, I found I did not shine in that land, worth a nickel; for my people, as a rule, like fine show.

Before I left New York for Nashville, I had heard that the bishops were to have it certain number of tickets at reduced rates; so I wrote Bishop Campbell and asked him if he would get me a ticket. About two weeks after, he was passing through New York, and called to see me, and explained the matter. How very kind he was. God bless his memory. I gave him the money—thirty some dollars—and in a day or two he sent me the ticket. Now I thought I was all right, and so thanked the Lord. He had answered prayer up to this time in all that I had asked.

I was expecting when I got to Philadelphia to find several ladies who had told me they were expecting to go without fail; but when I got there, there was but one lady—Sister Burley—and her husband; there were about twenty or thirty preachers, and just two ladies.

Poor Sister Burley was glad I was going, as she was alone; and I was glad she was going, as I was alone. She and I kept together as much as her husband would allow her; brother Burley was a remarkably selfish man, and stout accordingly; if he dropped his handkerchief his wife must be by him to catch it before it touched the ground, or pick it up immediately, or get him a clean one.

Of course, I was only a visitor. We arrived three days before the opening of the Conference. This was to give all the delegates time to get in. I thought I would have no difficulty in getting a place to stop, and, perhaps, it would not have been so bad if I had been more stylish looking.

We arrived, I think, about two P.M. Friday; we were driven to a large church where tickets were given with the name and address where each one was to stop. Now, there were five or six ladies, but none whom I knew; they seemed to eye me sharply, but took no further notice; by and by, plans were settled, and two or three of these ladies, and six or eight ministers got in a 'bus and were taken to their places. I inquired of those who had charge, but they said they only had the names of those who were delegates. Poor me; I almost cried, and was tempted to wish I had not come.

Sister Burley felt sorry for me, and asked her husband if he could not help me; but he said I ought not to have come without knowing something about things before I came.

"That is so," I replied; "but I am quite prepared to pay for my board, if I can find a boarding house."

By this time the 'bus was there again, and the next crowd were off to their lodgings; a few minutes more and another 'bus came, and my only friend, Sister Burley, was gone. It was then almost five o'clock; the 'bus came the last time; the man asked me where I was going; I told him I did not know.

"This is the last load, and you hall better get in; I take these people to the Sumner House; when you get there they might be able to tell you where to go."

I thanked him, and got in. When we got there I saw Mrs. Sumner and told her how it was; she said they were full, but if I would put up with it she would do the best she could. God bless her. I thanked her, and thanked the Lord. She was so hind and motherly.

Now, all that time no one had paid the slightest attention to me, any more than if I had not me in the world; they were all strangers to me, and full of excitement; so I was quite alone.

I would walk out in the afternoon alone, and to and from church alone. Several times I got ready in time and called at the parlor and asked if any of the ladies were ready; "not yet," was the usual answer; so I would walk on. After awhile, in the greatest style, would tome these ladies with the good brethren.

The early mornings and the evenings were quite pleasant; so Monday evening about six o'clock, I thought I would take a little walk; and, without knowing it, I got on the street leading to the Fisk University. As I walked on I saw a lady coming toward me; she began to smile; I thought, "I ought to know that face, but who is it?" She came up to me and said:

"Is not this Mrs. Amanda Smith?"

"Yes," I said.

"Oh, how do you do?" she said; "I'm so glad to see you. We just got home a few days ago, and we were talking about you last night; we were all in the parlor having a little sing, and we were speaking of the piece you sang with us in Music Hall, Boston."

"Oh," I said, "the Jubilee Singers." just then I recognized her. "Why, am I anywhere near Fisk University, where the Jubilee Singers came from?"

"Yes," she said, "we are just out such a place; and you must come out and see us. Professor White is going to invite the Conference out on Wednesday, and you must come."

This was Miss Ella Sheppard, now Mrs. Moore, wife of the faithful pastor of Lincoln Memorial Church, Washington, D. C.

When the time came there was quite an excitement about who was going. Carriages were engaged; I offered to pay for a seat in one, but there was no room; I sent out and ordered my own carriage, and paid for it myself.

While I was getting ready, a certain brother took a lady and put her in my carriage; when I went out to get in, he said, laughingly, "Mrs. Smith, Miss So and So and I want to go, and as you have room in your carriage, I thought we would get in;" but neither of them offered to pay a cent. I had half a mind not to allow it; but it was a good chance to return good for evil.

When we got there the good brother, being a minister, took his lady and passed quite up in front and was seated. I took a seat where I could get it, back in the congregation. One or two of the bishops were on the platform, together with a number of ministers, and the fine choir of the Jubilee Singers.

The meeting was opened in the usual way—an address by one of the bishops, then a song by the choir, singing as they could sing. Miss Sheppard spied me in the audience, and told Prof. White. He looked and looked, and could not see me at first. Then he went and spoke to Miss Sheppard again. Then she pointed out the plain bonnet. Then he spied me and quickly came down and shook hands, and was so glad. They all looked astonished. Holding me by the hand, he escorted me to the platform and introduced me to the large audience, who, in the midst of overwhelming amazement, applauded. Then the good professor told how they had met me in Boston, and how I sang the grand old hymn, "All I want is a little more faith in Jesus," and what a burst of enthusiasm it created. And of all the surprised and astonished men and women you ever saw, these men and women were the most so.

While he was making these remarks, I prayed and asked God to help me. Then he said, "I'm going to ask Mrs. Smith to sing that same song she sang in Boston, and the Jubilee Singers will join in the chorus."

If ever the Lord did help me, He helped me that day. And the Spirit of the Lord seemed to fall on all the people. The preachers got happy. They wept and shouted "Amen!" "Praise the Lord!" At the close a number of them came to me and shook hands, and said, "God bless you, sister. Where did you come from? I would like to have you come on my charge." Another would say, "Look here, sister, when are you going home? God bless you. I would like to have you come to my place." And so it went. So that after that many of my brethren believed in me, especially as the question of ordination of women never was mooted in the Conference.

But how they have advanced since then. Most of them believe in the ordination of women, and I believe some have been ordained. But I am satisfied with the ordination that the Lord has given me. Praise His name!

I had no trouble after I had Prof. White's and Prof. Spence's kind recognition, and I had the pleasure of spending a week or more at the University with those good people. And as I would talk at several of the meetings, the Lord blessed the dear teachers and students I also spent a week at Dr. Braden's. They were very kind, and the Lord gave us blessing in some meetings. They have done, and are doing, a grand work among my people. May God bless them all.

I give this little story in detail, to show that even with my own people, in this country, I have not always met with the pleasantest things. But still I have not backslidden, nor felt led to leave the church. His grace has ever been sufficient. And all we need to-day is to trust Him.

> "Simply trusting every day,
> Trusting through the stormy way,
> Even when my faith is small,
> Trusting Jesus, that is all."

CHAPTER XVI.

HOW I GOT TO KNOXVILLE TENN., TO THE NATIONAL CAMP MEETING, AND WHAT FOLLOWED.

It was in September, 1872, just after the camp meeting at Williamsville. When I went to Williamsville I had not thought anything about going to Knoxville. But while there a number of the friends thought I ought to go to Knoxville. Well, I hadn't prayed anything about it, so didn't know. I stayed with Mr. and Mrs. Little, who had charge of the book store. There was a Rev. Mr. Ford, who was Presiding Elder, or Pastor, of the Methodist Church at Knoxville. He was making the arrangements about camp meeting, and about Brother Inskip's coming to Knoxville.

One day I came in and they were talking, and Mrs. Little said to me, a little while after, that she was not feeling at all pleased at some things she had heard them say, and that she did not care to go. "But," she said, "Henry is going, and I suppose I will have to go."

"What is it?" I said.

"Why," she said, "they don't want you to go, and say it will not do if you go, at all."

"Why," I said, "I was not thinking about going. I have not asked the Lord anything about going, and I do not know as He wants me to go."

"Well," she said, "I would like to have you go, but then it is down South, and they are afraid it will hurt their meeting if you go."

"I would not go for anything," I said. "I am so anxious for everybody to get the blessing of sanctification, I don't want to go and hinder anybody, not for the world."

At dinner time I went up to the tent of the lady who had invited me to dinner. When I got there I found dear Sister Inskip and several others talking over the matter. Sister Inskip was so true and outspoken. Some were insisting that I should go, and were willing to pay my expenses. Dear Sister Inskip turned to me, and said, "It would be very nice to have Sister Amanda go, but we think too much of her to have her go down there and not be treated properly, so we hope she won't go."

Then I began to think there was more in what Mrs. Little said than I had at first thought. So I said, "I want everybody to get blessed, and I don't want to go unless the Lord wants me to go."

So there was not any more said directly about it. But somehow after that I got a very deep conviction that I was to go. I was sorry, for I thought, "Now, if I go after what Sister Inskip has said, I am afraid they will think I have done it impertinently."

That night dear Brother Wells preached. It was on Saturday night. I heard a little of the sermon. Up to that time it had been pretty uphill work. There was a great deal of opposition on the subject of holiness all through that part of Illinois, that had grown out of some very grave inconsistencies on the part of some who had been prominent in the profession and exposition of this great and blessed truth.

There was a great deal of earnest praying to be done. The Lord helped Brother Wells to preach, but I got under such dreadful conviction about the way they were feeling about my going to Knoxville, that I left and went down in the woods. It was dark, very dark, and I got down by a big log and asked the Lord if He would make it clear to me whether I was to go to Knoxville. If He said "Go," all right.

"But, Lord, I want to know. I don't want to hinder anybody from getting the blessing; and if my going will hinder anybody, or hinder this blessed work, I don't want to go. Now make it so clear what Thy will is in the matter that I will not be mistaken. And now, Lord, I ask thee for this evidence. If it is thy will for me to go, put it into somebody's heart to get me fifty dollars."

The rest of the people, who were invited to go to help in the work, had their expenses provided; but they didn't provide any for me, for the reason I have already said. So I thought I would ask the Lord for this great sum, for I thought fifty dollars was a great deal to ask for, and if I would ask for that much I would

probably not get it; and it I did not get it, of course I would not have to go. But while I was praying, these words came to me; "All things are possible to him that believeth." And I said, "Lord, I believe, if you will give me the money, you want me to go." And I felt it settled.

Just as I went to got up from my knees, a suggestion like this came:

"You know the Kuklux are down there, and they might kill you."

Then I knelt down again, and thought it all over; and I said, "Lord, if being a martyr for Thee would glorify Thee, all right; but then, just to go down there and be butchered by wicked men for their own gratification, without any reference to Thy glory, I'm not willing. And now, Lord, help me. If Thou dost want me to do this, even then, give me the grace and enable me to do it."

Then, these words came: "My grace is sufficient for thee." And I said, "All right," and got up.

I came up to the tent where I was staying, at Mrs. Little's, with perfect triumph. I never said a word to her, or to anyone.

On Sunday morning at the eight o'clock meeting, which was always a very grand meeting, I arose, and the Lord led me to relate my experience; how the Lord sanctified my soul; and the Holy Spirit seemed to fall on the people in a very powerful manner as I related my experience. And the Spirit said to one lady, "Get Amanda Smith fifty dollars to go to Knoxville."

This lady was the wife of a minister, Rev. Mr. Gardner. She had had a wonderful struggle for the blessing of a clean heart, and she told the Lord when she was consecrating herself to Him, that she would do anything He told her. So when the Spirit suggested this to her, she said, "I'll do it."

This she told me afterward. I did not know anything about It at the time.

There was a Mrs. Reeves, of Girard, O., there, and her friend, a Mrs. Smith, who had come with her; I had met Mrs. Reeves before, at Urbana, O., and so knew her, and had been at her home. She said to me on Sunday afternoon, just after the afternoon preaching was over:

"Mrs. Smith and I are going down to Springfield to see Lincoln's monument tomorrow morning; we want to start away about eight o'clock; wouldn't you like to go?"

"Oh, I was delighted. I didn't know this was anywhere in the region where Lincoln's monument was. Of course I was glad of the opportunity, and went with them. We were gone all day. I went up into the top of the monument and wrote on the wall, "Rock of Ages."

I shall never forget that wonderful scene to me. I had never seen anything like it before in my life.

After we had visited round and seen what we could, we came back, and got back to the camp ground about half-past five o'clock. Brother and Sister Inskip, with a number of the other brethren and friends, had been invited to Mrs. Blank's tent to tea. Mrs. Little and I had been invited also. When I got there they were just through tea, and they said, "Oh, Mrs. Smith, we have been waiting for you, but we could not wait any longer."

"Oh, I'm so glad; I just this minute got here."

Mrs. Inskip was just going off to take charge of the Young People's Meeting; she said, "As soon as you are through, Mrs. Smith, I want you to come down and help me in the Young People's Meeting."

I noticed that a number of these young people kept smiling and laughing, and I could not tell what was up.

So Mrs. Inskip went on, and I sat down to have my tea. Then I noticed several of the gentlemen and ladies, and they talked and smiled, and I said, "What is up? You all seem to be so happy."

"Oh, well, Mrs. Smith," they said, "never mind; when you are through, come into the tent; we want to see you before you go to Mrs. Inskip's meeting."

They had along table spread in the rear of the tent, In the old-fashioned camp meeting style, loaded with good things.

Now I had not breathed to a soul what I had prayed about. No one knew but God the prayer I prayed In the woods on Saturday night before. When I got through my supper I went into the tent; and after a little pleasant passing of words, a gentleman arose and said, "Well, Sister Smith, Sister Gardner, and some other ladies, have got a little purse for you, and they want me to present it to you, for you to go to Knoxville;" then handing it over to me, he presented me with fifty dollars and fifty-five cents.

Well, there was my money for Knoxville. Mrs. Gardner told me she could have got a hundred dollars just as easy as she got the fifty; but the word of the Lord to her was, "Get Amanda Smith fifty dollars to go to Knoxville."

I didn't go till the meeting had been in session about three days. I thought I would give them a chance to see what the results were before I got there, and what the bad effects might be after I got there. But the Lord was on my side, now may Israel say, to give me a clear assurance, and to make it plain to others, that I had not gone myself, but that He had sent me.

It was terribly uphill during those three days. Prejudice against the doctrine was strong. There had been some blessing, but not what they called a break. And yet there were some that were a little afraid that any little indication that had been seen, would be retarded by my appearance. So some of the good folks said, when they heard that I was on the ground, they were very sorry, for I must not expect to be treated as I was treated at home; meaning the North; poor things!

I went straight to Sister Little's, for she told me if I did come, to come right to them; they would have room in their tent. They generally had a large tent, for it was the book store, and a kind of general office. And I had my bed-tick, and would generally get it filled, and then my sheet and quilt and pillows, I took along myself; so at night, when the offices was closed, we put up the partition, and I made my bed down on the floor, and it was beautiful. Then, I was up always early in the morning so as to be out of the way before the time to open the office and book store.

It was Saturday, about two o'clock, I think, when I got there. When the afternoon service was over, I saw dear Brother Grey, of Philadelphia, standing talking very earnestly to a brother. I did not know who the minister was; but they were very close to Brother Little's tent, and I saw that Brother Grey made several attempts to get away, and every way he would start this brother would get in ahead of him and hinder him. I knew Brother Grey, and knew he was a good man, and I felt sorry for him. At last I said to Sister Little, "Who is that man talking to Brother Grey?"

"Oh," she said, "that is Rev. Mr. So and So," calling him by name. "He is arguing on the subject of holiness. He is terribly bitter against the doctrine."

"What," I said, "and a preacher, too?"

"Yes," she said, "and he has had Brother Grey pinned up against that tree for more than an hour. I believe he is in some real estate business now, down South here. He is not in the regular ministry."

"Well," I said, "the Lord bless him. We will have to pray him loose."

I don't know when he lot poor Brother Grey off, but I know it, was very late; almost time for the evening service to commence.

I do not know who preached Saturday night, but my heart was burdened in prayer. On Sunday morning at eight o'clock, Brother Little was lead the Love Feast service. I was very glad Brother Little had charge of that meeting, as I knew he would not hinder me from speaking as the Lord might lead. Brother Inskip preached at eleven. So the Lord laid it on my heart very heavily that I was to relate my personal experience of how the Lord led me into the blessing of entire sanctification.

The brother that had been talking and arguing so with Brother Grey sat way back in the congregation. It was in the big tent; I shall never forget it. There was a side where the colored people all sat, specially. So I sat on that side, quite near the front, and I kept looking to the Lord to indicate to me when he wanted me to talk. The testimonies and songs went on. There was a beautiful spirit in the meeting. Finally the time came when the Spirit bade me speak. I arose; a good brother from Philadelphia, I forget his name, sat very near me, and he was watching this brother that had been such an opponent; so, as I related how the Lord had led me, and my struggles and difficulties, the Lord blessed me and gave me great liberty in speaking. My! how my soul triumphed. The Spirit of God seemed to fall on the people; it took hold of this brother; I suppose I talked about fifteen minutes, and when I got through I had not more than taken my seat when this brother sprang to his feet, and holding up his hand he said:

"Hold on, brethren, hold on, hold on!" and walked to the front, weeping like a child. Oh! how he wept! "I want to say one word."

The shouts and amens and hallelujahs were full and free. The brother turned round and faced the congregation, straightened himself up, and braced himself, so as to control his feelings till he could get a start. Finally he said, "Brethren, I have been a Methodist preacher for so many years; I was converted at such a time; I entered the ministry," etc. "I have had a great deal of prejudice against these brethren coming here, and I have fought this subject of holiness." And he went on with his confession. But such a confession! And he ended by saying, "This colored sister, who has given us her experience, God bless her." Then he

came over and took hold of my hand and said "Lord bless you, sister." Then he finished his testimony, as follows:

"When I heard this colored sister tell how God had led her and brought her into this blessed experience, the darkness swept away and God has saved me, and I see the truth as I never did before. Glory to God."

Oh! what a shout! From that time the tide rose and swept on. The last night of the meeting came, and I was in Sister Little's tent. It was eleven o'clock at night. Sister Little had not been very well, and I was getting ready for bed; but the curtain was down, and I was sitting by Sister Little's bed talking with her and rubbing her arm. Brother Inskip did not know I was in the tent, and he came in; and I heard him say to Brother Little, "We have had a grand day; the Lord has been with us; and, after all, I was mistaken in not wanting Sister Smith to come. I tell you, Brother Little, God sent her."

And Sister Little wanted to say, "Amanda Smith is here now;" but I said, "No, no, don't say it; don't let him know it." This I heard with my own ears; and I would not let Sister Little call Brother Inskip. God bless him, for I know he only wished me well, and his only reason for thinking I should not go, was for my own good, and that of the meeting as well. But how far God's ways are above our ways, and His thoughts above our thoughts. It is safe to obey always, even though you may not always be able to explain. Amen. Amen.

I remained a few days in town, and held some meetings with my own people, which the Lord greatly blessed. Quite a revival broke out, and a number were converted. On Saturday afternoon, after the close of the camp meeting, I was down street doing a little shopping. On my way home I heard singing in the Presbyterian Church, though I didn't know it was a Presbyterian Church, then. The singing was beautiful; it sounded so much like home. They were singing that dear old hymn! "Jesus, Lover of my Soul," to the old tune. I listened, and wanted to go in, but did not dare to. The church was on the same block with the Methodist Church. I said to myself, "If I didn't have this parcel I would go in."

Just opposite, on the other side of the street, a colored nurse girl was out in the yard with a little child. I said to her, "What kind of a church is that where they are singing so?"

"I don't know," she said, "but I think it is a Presbyterian."

"I would go in if I didn't have these parcels."

"I will keep them for you," she said; "I will be out here with the child for some time."

So I handed her my parcels, and I went into the church. When I went to go in, there lay right across the door a large Newfoundland dog. I stood for a minute, and I thought, "Well, he must be a pretty good sort of a dog to be at church on Saturday morning." I touched him with my foot. He quietly lifted his head, looked at me, and lay down again, and I stepped over him and went in and sat down on a seat just behind the door. The first thing that struck me was the face of the minister; it was as radiant as a sunbeam. How beautiful! His name was McEwen. After he had given out some notices he announced his text, Isa. 35:8: "A highway shall be there, and a way, and it shall be called the way of holiness," etc. And he preached a straight, clear, orthodox holiness sermon; and the Spirit of the Lord came upon him and upon all the people. He was not demonstrative; calm, but, Oh, deep and powerful! The people wept and sobbed. I wanted to shout "Glory to Jesus;" but I said, "Oh, Lord, help me, and hold me still;" for I knew they were not used to any such thing, and it would have embarrassed the minister and confused, if not frightened, the people; and the only good it would have done, if any, at that time, would have been to me only.

So the Lord turned the big gush of praise into oil, and a wave of blessing passed so sweetly over my soul. Oh! it was like honey and oil mingled. It was indescribably beautiful, and sweet and heavenly. I shall never forget it. Praise the Lord!

When the meeting closed the people passed out. I heard some ladies say, "What in the world was the matter with Mr. McEwen? I never heard him preach so before."

"Oh, wasn't that a wonderful sermon?" said one. And another said:

"I think he has been to that holiness camp meeting."

And so he had, and had found the pearl of greatest price, even the blessing of a clean heart.

A lady came up to me and said so kindly (for they did not seem to be surprised to see me), "You are Amanda Smith?"

"Yes."

"I saw you at the camp meeting the other day. Our minister has got the blessing."

"Yes," I said, "I know the ring."

"We have been praying for him for five years. He's such a beautiful spirit, you would enjoy meeting him."

So she appointed an afternoon, and I went to her house, and what a blessed afternoon I spent in her parlor, and that at Knoxville, Tenn. I sang for them, and prayed, and told them how the Lord led me into the blessed soul rest after years of wandering. And I believe the Lord made it a farther blessing to this dear mister.

So Mrs. McEwen, the lady who had invited me to her house, (for that was her name, though she and the minister were no relation to each other), and who was a beautiful Christian lady, told me that she had got the blessed experience of full salvation some years before, reading Mrs. Phebe Palmer's book, "The Way of Faith;" and for years she had taken "The Guide to Holiness." She said there was not one in their church, when she sought and found the blessing; but that there were two other ladies, friends of hers, and members of the same church, who, like herself, longed for a deeper experience, and their custom was to meet once a week, and pray for the minister, and pray for themselves.

One day she went alone into her garret, so as to be away from every one, and there, as she knelt and prayed, the Lord seemed to open the windows of Heaven to her soul, and she was flooded with light and peace. She said: "I was so filled, I praised the Lord at the top of my voice. I came down and put on my things and went to see my dear Mrs. Blank. She was delighted; and we had a good time rejoicing together. A few days later she came out clear. Then the other. Now, we must still pray more earnestly for our minister, that he may see the truth and get the blessing." She said he was such a good man, and everyone liked him; but still there was a lack of real unction in his preaching. But she said all these years they never breathed it to him that they were praying for him. She had told him about the "Guide," given him a copy several times when he made his pastoral call. but every week for five long years these ladies met and prayed for their minister, and kept quiet, and now the answer had come. Oh, how full of delight and joy they were!

I think there might be similar results if there were more praying in the closet for the preacher. Don't talk much, but united, pray.

> "Pray, if thou canst or canst not speak,
> But pray with faith in Jesus' name."

She said about a year or two after she had got the experience her husband failed in business, and they lost nearly everything they had. But she said "The Lord kept me so quiet in my soul; and I believe but for this grace I never could have gone through what I did." She said her husband could not understand it, and sometimes he would feel vexed with her because she did not worry. "He said I seemed as though I did not care. But Oh, how I had to hold on to God for him. It seemed he would lose his mind at times. Praise the Lord, He kept me. Oh, Sister Smith, what deep waters God brought me through. How true His Word."

> "Many shall be purified,
> And made white and tried;
> But the hand that purifies,
> Tries."

So we are quite safe. Only hold still. Amen.

CHAPTER XVII.

SEA CLIFF CAMP MEETING, JULY, 1872—FIRST THOUGHTS OF AFRICA—MAZIE'S EDUCATION AND MARRIAGE—MY EXPERIENCE AT YARMOUTH.

Persons often ask me how I came to think of going to Africa. While at this camp meeting I had my home at Mrs. Battershell's. Their beautiful cottage was the finest and largest there at that time. Mrs. Battershell was a cousin of Mrs. Inskip's. She had told me when I came to Sea Cliff she wanted the privilege of entertaining me at her new cottage, so I had a very pretty little room all to myself, and went in and out as I chose.

One day during the camp meeting they had a mission day, and as there were different speakers, some from India, some from China, some from Japan, and some from South America, I think, I went to the meeting. I heard all the speakers, and was very much interested in the meeting.

Just as they were about to close the meeting there came up a little shower of rain, and as I had no umbrella, I hurried out and on to my cottage. The meeting had made an impression on my mind, and as I walked along I kept thinking of what I had heard, and all at once it came to me that I had not heard them say anything about Africa. Then I remembered when I was quite young I had heard my father and mother talk about Africa. I remembered, too, that I used to see a large paper, away back in the forties, called "The Brother Jonathan Almanac," something like the Frank Leslie. It had large pictures, and Africans in their costumes and huts, and Indians in their wigwams, great boa constrictors, bears, lions and panthers; and some of the pictures were horrid, as I remember them now.

Well, all the old farmers round about where we lived used to take those papers, and once in a while father would bring home one of them for us children to look at, and my good mother would always see that it was not torn to pieces. So we had it to look at for a time, then she would carefully fold it up and put it away. I remember what a treat it was when she would say we could have it to look at again. We would spread it on the floor, and then all of us children would get down, and what times we would have over "Brother Jonathan."

So as I was walking along now, thinking of this missionary meeting, I heard some one call out, "Amanda Smith," and I turned, and a lady overtook me and said as she came up to me;

"Well, Amanda Smith, how did you like the meeting?"

"It was very nice, and I liked it. But I did not hear them say a word about Africa, and I have been wondering if all the people in Africa are converted. I remember hearing father and mother talk about them a long time ago, but I have not heard anything of them since, and I was wondering."

She smiled, and said, "Oh! I would to God they were. Have you never heard of Melville B. Cox, our first missionary of the M. E. Church to Africa?"

"No," I said, "what about him?"

Then she gave me the history as we went on together. As she told me the story, and then said what his last words were when he died at Monrovia, Africa,—"Though a thousand fall, let not Africa be given up," —Oh! what a deep impression it made on my mind and heart.

When we got to the corner she turned and want to her cottage. I went into Mrs. Battershell's and went straight up to my own room, locked the door, and got on my knees. What a time of consecration, what a struggle I had! I said, "Lord, Africa's need is great, and I cannot go, though I would like to. But Thou knowest I have no education, and I do not understand the geography, so I would not know how to travel."

For I thought that the next great qualification for African work, next to a full consecration and sanctification, which I knew I had, was to understand the geography, so as to know how to travel in Africa. Of course I was ignorant and green, and the Lord knew that, and had patience with me. So I said, "Lord, I am too old to learn now, but if you will help me I will educate my daughter, Mazie, and she can go."

Then it came to me, would I be willing to have her go? Oh, what a struggle!

I seemed to see a great heathen town. There were the great boa-constrictors, and there the great lions and panthers, and there was my poor child. Oh! how I wept. But I said, "Lord, somebody must go to Africa, and I am too old to learn, so I cannot go. But I can, I will, I do, consecrate my child to Thee for Africa. My heart aches, but, Lord, help me. I give her to Thee. She is Thine, and Thou canst take care of her."

I suppose I was there for an hour or two, but I never left my knees till I felt I had given her fully to God for Africa.

"Now, Lord," I said, "open the way for me to get her educated, so that she will not have the difficulty that I have if you want her to go. Lord, I don't want her to read books and get worked up in that way, but help me to educate her, and then sanctify her wholly and send her whither Thou wilt."

When I arose from my knees, my heart was calm and restful. And now my thought was to get her educated. I prayed, and watched every indication.

Several days later I chanced to meet that good man, Dr. Ward, and during our conversation I began telling him my experience, and how I was looking to the Lord about my daughter's education, and asked him where would be a good school for her.

"Oh!" said he, "I wish I had known this yesterday. I have just given away a scholarship to some one (calling the name), and if I had known of your wish I would have been so glad to give it to you."

Well, it seemed that all was lost. But still I hoped. This was the first of my thinking of going to Africa.

I had worked so hard, and helped Mazie. She had been at Oberlin for a year, and at Xenia, and got on very nicely. But I could not keep up the expense. But at that time I was only thinking to fit her for a teacher, and selfishly had planned in my mind that if I could help it she should not have to slave and work hard day and night as I had done. So I thought when I got old she would be in a position to help herself and me, and I could keep the home and look after everything while she was away teaching, and we could be so happy together, so that my last days would be happy.

But, alas! how disappointed I have been, even in the shadow of such a hope. Every wish in that direction has been swept away, and I have had to surrender that cherished hope. I thought

I could not bear it. Oh! how I had to cry to God for enduring grace. And He has given it, and I am wonderfully upheld by His almighty hand. His grace is sufficient, even when we are disappointed in our brightest hopes.

She is married and settled in her own home, and I am where I was when I first started, so far as that is concerned. And now my prayer before the Lord is, that He will save her soul in His own way. While her name is on the church record, yet like so many dear souls, I fear she has but little spiritual life!

Time went on, and I saw no way to get my daughter educated for Africa.

One summer we were at Ocean Grove with Mrs. Sanders. She had bought some lots, and they had a fine cottage right on the lake. So she invited me and Mazie to come down and spend the summer for the camp meeting. They had put up a large tent, which Mazie and I occupied, on one of these vacant lots, beautifully situated, near the lake. They had a great deal of company, so Mazie and I used to go in, and wait on the table, and help with the work.

One morning I was busy helping in the kitchen before I went to the meeting; Mazie had been waiting on the table in the dining room; and Mrs. Sanders said to me:

"Amanda Smith, come into the parlor; I want to speak to you."

I did so, and she said, "I see that Mazie is just as smart as a steel trap; now, why don't you get her into school?"

Then I told her my story, how I had been praying, and how I had been watching and waiting for the Lord to open some way. I told her I had done the best I could, and the expenses were so heavy I found I could not keep Mazie in school. I had done what I could for her for two years, so I thought she would have to do the next herself; I had given it up. But as she talked on I seemed to see this was the way the Lord was to answer my prayer.

It was just as the camp meeting was closing, so Mrs. Sanders said:

"Now, if you find a place for her to go to school, I will help you to get all her outfit, and send her, if you can do the other."

I thanked her, and told her I would do what I could. I had heard of a good school in Baltimore, and as my aunt lived there I wrote and asked her about it; she kindly replied, and spoke highly

of the school; so that what she said confirmed what I had heard before; and then she was where she could look after my child; so this decided me.

The next week Mrs. Sanders went to New York and bought all her outfit, everything, and I went to work and got her ready, and I think it was about the third week in September we were off to Baltimore. She was at that school a year. Strange to say, just before the close of the year I got a letter from the matron, and she said Mazie was very smart; she was getting along nicely. If I could only just leave her for one year longer it would be the making of her. It was a pity to take her just now. And I wondered if I could stand it another year.

I went to the Lord and prayed, and asked Him to help me and strengthen me, and to open the way for me to get the means to keep her just another year.

About two or three weeks after I had decided to let her remain another year, the Lord seemed to open my way clearly to go to England. I only expected to stay three months, and I thought how nice it would be, while she was in school, and was not losing any time, and would be well cared for, and under good discipline and control, and then my aunt could look after her.

Everything seemed to be favorable. So in July, 1878, after I had gone to Baltimore and spent a week with her, I left her, and went to England. Instead of getting back in three months, as I had thought and planned, I was away for over twelve years.

After I had been in England about three months, the Lord made it very clear to me that I was to remain longer; so I thought three months longer; but when six months had passed, my way seemed to be shut up to come home, but open to remain. Now, people say, "But how was that?" That is just what I say; for I do not understand it yet, and could not explain it; but I am just as sure that God was in it, as I am of my own existence. It is one of God's inexplicable dealings. I wrote and sent money home to my daughter, and had made all arrangements for her for two years.

Then she wrote and told me she thought I had paid money enough for her, and that she wanted to come out of school, and had an opportunity for a situation as teacher; so I agreed to that. I knew she was clever enough, and quite able to do this, if she chose. A little while later on she wrote me that a young man had proposed marriage to her. I told her I had rather she would not marry. She had quite time enough, and it would be so much better for her to come to England and spend at least a year or two first.

I saw that her teaching plan was pretty well upset when she got the marrying spirit; and she was like many other young people; they cannot hear reason or anything when they take a notion to get married. If I had been at home, I think I should have forbidden it; but being away, I thought if anything should happen I would always blame myself. But I urged her to come to England and wait a while; then she wrote me she had decided to do so. Many of my friends in England, who had been interested in her, were delighted. They had written to her, and she was all for coming to England. So I got the money all ready and was just about to send it for her to come. All the arrangements were made. But I thought to myself, "I will wait for a letter from Mazie before I send it." And when the letter came she wrote me very frankly that the young man had persuaded her to wait till after she was married, and then come to England.

"No," I said, "if you come to England married you won't belong to me; you will belong to some one else; and if you can risk losing the opportunity that not many colored girls have had, and that you will not have again, and think more of the man, and take him in preference after all I have said, I guess the safest plan is that you remain." And I think so yet. But she could not have got a kinder husband, or one that did a better part by her, if I had been living right here with her. It is wonderful how the Lord provided in that.

In answer to prayer, the Lord opened my way to attend Yarmouth Camp Meeting. There I heard for the first time of the landing of the Pilgrims on Plymouth Rock. It seemed the Lord had appointed that grove especially for a camp meeting grove. There I first saw the famous Hutchinson family. Mr. Asa Hutchinson, his wife, two sons, and a daughter, Miss Abbie, how well I remember them; their noble, kind-heartedness. They had me sing with them several times. Although all have passed away, the precious memory of them still remains.

Through the kindness of Rev. B. F. Pomeroy, of the Troy Conference, I had my quarters during the camp meeting in one of his little tents. I shall never forget how kind he and his dear wife were to me. He used often to sit down and tell me wonderful

things about God's dealings with him, which often strengthened my faith, and helped me. Praise the Lord! Many lights there are along the shore that never grow dim.

I had been asked by the pastor of the Methodist Church, at Martha's Vineyard, to go to Martha's Vineyard Camp Meeting. He said he believed God would have me go, and that they had a society tent that they would put up on the camp ground, "and," said he, "you can stay with us and we will look after you."

This was on Wednesday. He said he must leave on Friday, but I could come with his wife and children. So I told Brother Pomeroy about it. He seemed to think is was not just the thing for me to go. He said that years ago that used to be the great place, the power of the Lord used to come on that camp ground in the old-fashioned way. "They have but very little of the Spirit now-a-days. They go more as a picnic, not the Holy Ghost times of the past."

Well, he was always so good in his counsel that I thought it was the thing, of course, not to go; still, I thought that it they were so orderly and lifeless the more need there was for me to go, I might help a little.

At the close of the morning service at the stand that day the Presiding Elder called out to all the tent holders within the circle to close the front of their tent, and there was to be no walking inside the circle from half-past twelve till two, when the afternoon service would commence.

During this interval I took my Bible and went into the woods about a half mile away, all alone, to ask God about going to Martha's Vineyard, and there, as I prayed and told the Lord how I had been asked to go, that Brother P. was a good man, and he said he thought I had better not go, and I wanted He should show me His will.

"Lord," I said, "if Thou dost want me to take any message I will do it for Thee."

So it was, whispered to we to read, and I opened my Bible to see what the Lord would give me. Mal. 14, 1st verse: "And the Lord said go speak as I command you." I was afraid and said, "O, Lord, I am a stranger and a colored woman, and the people are proud and wicked, as has been told me," and I wept and trembled, but he said, "Go, do as I command you."

I arose from my knees and went back to the tent, but I did not dare to tell brother P. what I had done. So the last day came, and when Brother P. began to take down their tent they wanted me to go with them to another camp meeting, but I said, "No, the Lord bids me go to Martha's Vineyard." They said they thought I was mistaken. But I said nothing.

I prayed for the Lord to give me means. I would take it as an indication that I was to go. The next morning I went into Father Snow's tent. We had a wonderful meeting. After the regular meeting was closed, several people asked me to sing, and a crowd gathered around. Some were standing on the benches. Some one dropped a two dollar note in my lap; that was my first token for the money, and I looked up and praised the Lord. Then there came a one dollar bill, then another, and so on till I had seven dollars. Just then a strange lady turned to me and said:

"Have you ever been to Martha's Vineyard?"

"No."

"I believe the Lord wants you there, and if you will go I will give you a good place to sleep."

This lady's name was Mrs. Jenkins. She said her daughter was on from Baltimore, and had taken a cottage for the summer; that she had such a nice colored woman who was nurse for her. Then she wrote her name and address on a card and said, "I leave to-day and want you to come to our cottage, if you come." I thanked her and said, "All right, madam." When the day came I started off with Mrs.—and the children and servant. The Lord seemed to have ordered everything.

Going up on the boat I went to pay my fare, and some one said, "Your fare has been paid."

"Praise the Lord," but I said I did not know the parties, so that I could thank them. So several of us sat down to dinner; when I went to pay they said, "Your bill is settled," and so there was another, "praise the Lord!" I could see so far very clearly the hand of the Lord in it.

When we reached the camp ground, Martha's Vineyard, it was found that the society tent that the pastor had told me about had been exchanged and another sent in its place, and after all we did not have any tent, so what should we do. I said to the pastor's wife, "What shall I do?"

"I don't know," she said, "what we shall do now, we will have to see about sending it back and getting our own."

"Well," I said, "I will go up to Mrs. Jenkins, who gave me her address," and, sure enough, it seemed to be just the place, so that "In some way or other the Lord does provide."

Now it came Sunday. O, how the Lord supplied my needs, one dollar, two dollars at a time. I kept watching for the time to deliver my message.

In the afternoon I went into a large tent where they were holding meetings before the approaching service. I sat down quietly, and they sang and prayed. I do not remember the minister's name who was leading the meeting. Just before the close he called upon me to sing. I arose to sing, but the Lord said, "Deliver the message first;" so I quoted the passage of Scripture, Mal. 4th chapter, 1st verse: "Behold the day cometh that shall burn as an oven, etc."

There was a great crowd around as well as inside the tent, and as I lifted my hand and pointed my finger towards the door, repeating the text that was given me, the people looked astounded. Then I sang, "All I want is a little more faith in Jesus." The Lord put His seal on this message, also on the song.

A lady from Providence, R. I., was in this tent meeting. She had come with a very definite object, to seek the blessing of a clean heart. She was called a swell lady; she was one of the ones rather up, and did not condescend to things of low estate! So as I began to sing, "All I want is a little more faith in Jesus," she walked out of the tent and said to herself, as she passed out, "I came here to seek the blessing of a clean heart, I did not come to hear a negro ditty," and the blessed Holy Spirit said to her, "Is not that your need, 'a little more faith in Jesus?'"

Then her eyes were opened, and she said, "O, Lord, I see." Then she went into her tent and there prayed, and the Lord sent the baptism and gave her the desire of her heart.

Some time after this, when Brothers Inskip and McDonald were holding their meeting at Providence, R. I., one morning I went into the meeting about one o'clock, (testimony meeting) I didn't know of this lady's struggle at the time, but just as I got into the door, I heard this lady say, "Amanda Smith." Her back was to me. I sat down quietly to listen to her testimony. She went on and gave it in the words above.

Now about the message. About four months after this camp meeting closed, I was holding meetings in one of the Methodist churches in Worcester, Mass., and a gentleman who was Superintendent of a large Sabbath School, (a Mr. C.) said to me one day, "Amanda Smith, do you remember being at Martha's Vineyard at such a time?"

"Yes," I said.

"Do you remember the Sunday in the tent when you got up and quoted that passage from Malachi and sang?"

"Yes."

"Well," said he, "the Lord sent that message to me."

Mr. C. was head clerk in one of the largest dry goods stores in Worcester, and at the same time was Superintendent of a large Sabbath School, and he worked very hard, and was very tired, and he had gone to this camp meeting for his vacation, and he and his young people all went out there for a vacation more than for the purpose of attending the meeting. They would go to preaching in the morning, but would not attend any of the social meetings. In the afternoon they would generally go off for a game of croquet, or on the lake, boating.

When they heard the singing in this tent a whole party of them were just on their way to the croquet ground. They stopped at the tent door to see the colored woman, and to hear what she had to say. He just got there as I repeated the text and he said it came to his heart like an arrow. He went back to his tent and began to pray, and he said the Lord showed him how near backsliding he was, how far away, so that he was really alarmed, and that text saved him through God's mercy.

I praised the Lord that he enabled me to obey him. It was not a little thing, it was a trial, but see the blessing that came out of it to this brother. I then praised the Lord that the message was heard by the one, and the song by the other. It pays to obey.

CHAPTER XVIII.

PITTMAN CHURCH, PHILADELPHIA—HOW I BECAME THE OWNER OF A HOUSE, AND WHAT BECAME OF IT—THE MAYFLOWER MISSION, BROOKLYN—AT DR. CUYLER'S.

It was in '78. I was holding meeting, first at Manayunk, Brother Rakestraw's; then at Holmesburg, Brother Gillingham's; then at Camden, then at Norristown, Brother Day's. We had a good work at all these placers. Many souls were saved and believers built up.

Then I was called to Horton Street. Brother Robinson was pastor. There the Lord blessed us mightily. There was a sweeping revival. Every night for more than two weeks the church was packed, altar and pulpit. Some of the good folks really got tried because the people crowded so. I remember one Sunday night the aisles and pulpit steps were crowded. Poor old Brother Tasks,—now in heaven—had hard work to get into the pulpit, and when he did get there he was obliged to stand. He said he would not come again in such a crowd.

After the address was over we tried to make room for the altar service. It was not long till the altar was filled with seekers, some for pardon, some for purity. I noticed a young man who sat on a chair in the aisle and seemed to be deeply interested. He seemed as though he wanted to come forward; and then, there was a young lady with him. I watched him. All at once he got up and laid his hat and coat down and came forward, and just as he put his hand on the altar rail and was in the act of kneeling down, the Lord blessed him so powerfully that he clapped his hands and shouted, Glory to God, I am saved. He, like the poor man in the Gospel, the leper that came to Jesus, said, "Lord, if Thou wilt Thou canst make me clean," and Jesus said to him in return, "I will; be thou clean."

As he turned to face the congregation, his sister, that he had not seen for years, was just behind him. She had been praying for him, but she did not know that he was there, nor did he know that she was there. She sprang to him and threw her arms around his neck and they had a good time of rejoicing together. This had a marvelous effect upon the congregation. A number came forward, and many professed to be saved that night.

One dear woman that I met last fall at the Saturday night holiness meeting, told me she was converted at that meeting; also her husband and two children. She told me how she disliked me because I was a colored woman; how she went to church full of prejudice, but when God saved her He took it all out, and now she loves me as a sister and thinks I have a beautiful color! Of course, I call that a good conversion to begin with.

Some people don't get enough of the blessing to take prejudice out of them, even after they are sanctified.

Sometime after this I went to Pittman Church. Rev. George McLaughlin was pastor. The church was not finished. We held meetings in the lecture room, a fine large room that would hold over three hundred, I suppose, and every night it was packed. Here we had a grand time from the start. On Sunday afternoon we had a marvelous meeting. At that meeting dear Brother Alkhorn got the blessing of sanctification, after seeking it for thirty years, as he said in his testimony when he arose. I shall never forget that Sabbath afternoon. The Lord wonderfully helped me to speak for Him.

Brother McLaughlin was a grand, good man to work with, though he was not very definite on the line of holiness, but he said to me, "Sister Smith, you go ahead; I am with you." So he put no bands on and I had perfect freedom, thank God.

Brother Alkhorn was a local preacher; was a converted man and had been for years, and always longed for the blessing of full salvation. He was thorough Wesleyan as well as Scriptural in his views of the doctrine. He said he would preach it and sometimes would believe he had it, then he would meet with ministers that did not see it as he did, and declare that all was done at conversion. Then he would get in the dark again, and this was the way he went on for years.

He kept a bakery on Lumber street. I got to know him and the family very well. He was a member of the Western Methodist

Church, and I think Dr. Patterson was the pastor at the time of his death.

He sat that Sunday afternoon about three pews from the altar, while many testimonies were given—many of them very definite and clear—to the experience and power of this great salvation. Then we had an altar service, and I urged those who really desired to know the experience for themselves to come forward and kneel at the altar, and settle it then and there. A number came forward. I saw Brother A. get up deliberately, take off his overcoat, fold it together, and then take his hat and cane and walk forward and hand them to some of the brethren. And as he kneeled at the altar, he said, "Brethren, I want the blessing." And he began to pray like he wanted it, indeed; and in a little while he sank down into a calm, and said, "It is done, praise the Lord. The blood cleanseth; glory to Jesus." He arose and bore the testimony that I have already given.

In about a year, I think it was, after this, he met with a sad accident; was thrown from his wagon, and in a few days died. But, O, he triumphs over death, hell and the grave!

I lost a true friend when he was taken, that is, as the world would say, but I have a never dying friend in Jesus. Praise His dear name forever.

At the same altar, kneeling just a little further along from where Brother Alkhorn kneeled, a great big man, a Dutchman, was kneeling. He had been seeking the Lord for fifteen years, off and on, but never got into clear light. The people at the altar were all getting blessed, and rising one after the other, and it was getting late and time for the meeting to close. This poor man got into an awful struggle. He cried out, "Lord, save me." He wouldn't get up.

"Hold on," I shouted, "you are nearly out."

I felt things were giving way, and I said, "All you need, all you want, is a little more faith in Jesus," and his poor wife felt she could not hold on any longer. She came inside the altar and was just about to throw her arms around his neck. She was overcome with sympathy for him. I caught her and said, "Oh, what ever you do, don't touch him; you will hinder him."

"Oh," she said, "I have prayed so long."

I held on to her and kept her back, while the brethren were encouraging his faith. In a few minutes he sprang to his feet, shouting at the top of his voice, "I am saved, I am saved. Glory to Jesus! Glory to Jesus!"

I let his wife go and he caught her up in his arms, then he let her go and caught hold of some of the brethren. Oh, how he shouted! I kept out of the way; of course I wouldn't interfere. So this was a good start for our meeting for the week.

We went on for ten days, and there were scores converted. During all this time the interest never flagged one night.

Brother M. wanted me to stay longer, but I could not. I had an engagement at Long Island, with Brother Hollis. It was at this time my house in Philadelphia was planned for, without my knowledge. About two weeks after, I got a letter from Mrs. James Orr. She said, "Some friends are planning to buy you a house, but they don't want you to know it, so don't let on that I have told you."

I was dreadfully frightened, and as soon as I had read the letter I got on my knees and prayed that the Lord would not let them succeed in getting the house that they were planning for. I thought it was too much for me. I said, the idea of a poor woman like me having a house given to her! There must be something wrong about it. Oh, how I prayed!

Several days after this I got another letter, saying that the house they were looking at and wanted, they could not get. There was. something that was not just satisfactory in regard to the deed, so I thought the Lord had answered my prayer, and it was all right.

In a day or two I was off again, holding meetings. After ten days, I came home. A number of letters were waiting for me—two from Philadelphia. I opened and read them. The first was from the same person. She said, "Don't say I told you, for they want to surprise you. They have looked at another house and have made arrangements to buy, and will pay so much to close the bargain, such a day."

That was all done two days before I got home, as I saw by the date of the letter. Then I thought it all over. I said, I have never asked the Lord to give me a house, and I wonder if He really wants me to have it. It must mean something, for why should these people persist in getting the house for me? I am a colored woman, and they are all white, and they are strangers. So then I got down and prayed the Lord to bless and prosper those who had

undertaken it. The lady that wrote me had told me how that everybody was favorable to it, how much Chaplain Gibben and his wife were interested and had given quite a sum to start with. Well, it did look as though the Lord was in it.

Then I opened the other letters. There was one from the very gentleman who was the proposer, and who had set the thing going, Brother Andrew Marshall. He was well known in Philadelphia, one of the leading men in Pittman Church at the time, and a man doing a large business in the bakery and confectionery, and a good man, so I could but feel the Lord was in it. He told me all about it. The house was three thousand dollars, subject to the ground rent of sixty dollars a year. Two thousand dollars of this money had already been provided for through friends of Mr. Marshall's, so that I had nothing to do with this part of it in any way; I must only be ready to come at the time they said. So away I went for two weeks more.

When I returned there were letters. The house was bought, the deed was made out in my name, and I only to come on. They said you need not bring anything if you don't care to. Some of the ladies of Pittman, with Mrs. Orr, had gone to work and furnished two rooms, the front bed-room upstairs, and the front parlor downstairs; everything nice and comfortable. So I got ready and went.

I took a very few things; I had not many. My dear old irons and ironing-board, that had seen me through so many hard places in New York, I couldn't forget them nor leave them behind! Then the little, low, old chair that I had kneeled beside and fought such a battle, on the remembrance of the New York riot after I was sanctified! I said, "I must take these things anyhow."

It was late on Saturday evening before I got off, so I did not get to the house till about seven P. M. Then, sure enough, at 1817 Addison street, a nice little three story brick house, nice white marble steps in front, all lighted with gas!

It was very nice. Then there were a number of friends gathered, and a good warm fire. I didn't know what to do or say, and I praised the Lord, and thanked the people, and I said, "Is it really mine?" Then they handed me the deed. Then I said, "Let us pray."

That seemed out of order, for we were all too happy to pray, so we sang the Doxology.

"Let me walk up and down in it," I said; so we went upstairs in all the rooms; I looked in all the closets, everywhere, then we went down in the basement, then I had the nicest tea! The ladies had provided everything.

It all seemed very fine. Everything went on nicely for about a year, then came a trial.

The great Centennial had started hopes and expectations in many that were never realized; so it was with Brother M. In this extremity he got Brother Robinson, one of the leading members in Salem M. E. Church, to help him meet some liabilities which were urgent, which he did. Then it appears that Brother M. failed on his side, which caused great dissatisfaction and unpleasantness between these friends.

I knew but little about it. I didn't try to know. I felt that what they had done was out of real kindness to me, though bad luck came of it, as it often does out of our best motives. This placed me in a very embarrassing position. They were both Christian gentlemen and business men, and who was I to dictate to them about what they were doing so kindly for me.

It got into the papers, through Brother Wallace, that the friends in Philadelphia, had given Amanda Smith a house, and also one at Ocean Grove. Mr. M. called my attention to the fact. I said, "That is a mistake; all I have at Ocean Grove, is this: the committee are always very kind and they do not charge me for my tent and ground during the time I stay, but that is all."

"Brother M.," I said, "you can correct that; see Brother Wallace and tell him," for he was then editor of the "Home Journal," and it was in that paper that the statement was made.

"If I do it," I said, "it will look as if I were dissatisfied, or like casting some reflection on your management of affairs."

"Yes," he said, "I will see, Brother Wallace," but I don't know whether he did or not. From that time, according to the best I could learn, the donations to complete the payment on the house stopped; but so far as that was concerned, I had nothing at all to do. I had just one hundred and fifty dollars in hand. This the Lord had given me at different camp meetings during the summer. I had given the one hundred to Mr. M. I kept the rest. I had my house all papered and painted inside, and a tin roof put on; it was not very long till it was all done.

Always before this time I had managed, and had enough to get on with nicely, and I thought as the house was mine, it was right I should put it in good order, then I would not have to do it in a long time again; but this statement in the papers affected me personally, greatly. I went about holding meetings as usual, but, got but very little to what I had received before. People said, "She is all right, she has two houses, one at Ocean Grove, one in Philadelphia," so, of course, if I had two houses I was rich and needed nothing to eat or drink!

Well, I did not know what to do, but the Lord helped me to hold still. I came home from a tour in Ohio, and went to Ocean Grove Camp Meeting. I had been there two days when a telegram came, saying:

"Come home at once. Marshall."

"What in the world is the matter?" I wondered.

I got ready and went on, at about ten A. M. Went to the store, saw Brother M. He was bright and happy.

"What is the matter?" I asked.

Then he told me he was embarrassed, and it was necessary for him to meet a note at such a time.

"Well," I said, "what do you want me to do?"

"I thought I would ask you if you would sign a mortgage, then we could borrow the money out of the Building Association till such a time, and I would get straight."

"You know, Brother M.," I replied, "I don't know a bit about the Building Association, I never could get it through my head, I have never done anything but pay my rent, that is all. I can lead a prayer meeting now and then, and that is about all I know."

"This will be all right," he said.

"Well, if you say so, I will do it."

So he went and had the papers made out. I had made myself responsible to the Building Association for fifteen dollars a month. I had never paid so heavy a rent before; then, five dollars a month for my ground rent, made it twenty dollars a month, besides other expenses; but I did the best I could.

Mr. Cleg, who was the Secretary of the Building Association, was very kind, and I told him I didn't know how in the world I could ever carry it. He told me to hold on and it would be better after a while.

Some months had passed, I don't know how long, when Brother M. came to me again and asked me to help him meet another engagement. So I went again; the papers were made out.

When Mr. Marshall stated to the lawyer the object of our coming again, the lawyer turned to me and looked at me right in the face, and said to me, "Do you want to sign this paper?"

"Well," I said, "I suppose I will have to."

Then he gave a quiet grumble to himself, as it were, and began to write, and I was asked to sign my name. That look he gave me seemed to have an expression in it like this, "Well, you are a fool," and that is just about the way I felt, but still I signed the papers and became responsible still further to the Building Association.

Now, with my ground rent and taxes I must pay forty dollars a month. I told Mr. M. I could not do it, but he said he would take hold and help me out as soon as these urgent demands were met.

I must go on, only God knows how I did. Sometimes I didn't have money enough to get me a loaf of bread. I went to Mr. Cleg and told him he must take the house, I could not pay the dues. He was very kind.

"Hold on, Mrs. Smith, pay what you can, we will not push you," he said, "everything is dull just now," etc.

I got so little for my services, I could not get on, and the constant thought I had to carry all the time that I was getting still deeper in debt to the Building Association. I was ashamed to tell anyone, it would look to white people like bad management on the part of those who were my friends. Then I knew what some of my own people would say, and had said already, that I was a kind of a "white folks' nigger," and I knew they would say, "That is just what I told you it would all come to, can't tell me about white folks." They wouldn't see God in any of it, so here I was. What to do I didn't know. I could not speak of it publicly for the reason I have already mentioned.

One day I came home in great distress of mind. I was away in Jersey helping a good brother who wanted me so much to help him. I went. He told me the people were very poor and could not give me much, and, though I had a number of other calls where I could have expected more, I chose to go to this place and help this brother.

After two weeks' hard work they gave me six dollars; and my railroad expenses were three dollars the round trip. The people were poor, but kind and good, and the minister was a good man and had a large family, but they were poor. God bless them.

They got me a home with a sister, where I was comfortable as I could be, though, sometimes It was very cold.

I got home about ten o'clock in the morning. I slipped into the house, kept the front windows closed, opened one window In the back room, and got down on my knees. I said, "Now, Lord, you must help me, for I can't go another day with this burden." It was dark. I did not eat. I thought and planned in my mind, and thought. Then I would pray again. When I gave out, I got up and lay down on the sofa and studied what plan I should take. "If I go to Mr. Marshall, he will say just as he said before. If I go to Mr. C., he is so kind, and will say the same." Then, down on my knees again. I saw myself put out of the house with no place to go. I sat with my things all around me and the people looking, some were laughing and saying, "I told you so."

Oh, what a struggle it was. It all seemed as real as life itself. I died out completely on this point, and when the last pang was over I felt myself singing Brother John Parker's hymn:—

> "I am more than conqueror through his blood,
> Jesus saves me now.
> I rest beneath the shield of God,
> Jesus saves me now."
>
> CHORUS.—"Though foes be strong,
> And walls be high,
> I'll shout, He gives the victory,
> I'll shout, He gives the victory,
> Jesus saves me now."

This was about two o'clock in the afternoon. I arose from the place and took my things off, for I had only laid off my bonnet. I opened the house upstairs and down, hoisted the windows and sang all the hymns I knew of by heart, I sang loud and strong. Oh, what a victory! A short time after this, the Lord marvelously opened my way to go to England, yes, I say marvelously, for all told, it was really marvelous, indeed.

After I had been in England about six months, though I had written to Mr. Marshall and Robinson, also Mr. Cleg, the secretary of the Building Association, a letter from Mr. Robinson came to say I must come home at once, the taxes had not been paid, and, I suppose, to hurry me, he said the house could be sold for taxes if not paid by such a day.

I had no one to refer to, but these two brethren, that had trouble enough with it already. I was at Mildmay, in London, when this letter came. My head whirled for a moment. I was in the street when I opened and read the letter. I felt as though I could fly. I said, what can I do, this is Thursday. I thought I would go and pack my trunk and take the night train to Liverpool and so take the first steamer going out. My heart beat and my mind was so confused. I stood still and closed my eyes and asked the Lord to quiet me and tell me what to do. In a moment He took every thought and wish to go home out of me. I said I can write and say all I need to say, and the same steamer that I would go on will take the letter.

So I wrote to Brother Robinson, "I can't come, but sell the house or give it away, I don't wish it, get your money out, I don't want any."

I see now I might have done differently if I only had known how, but still it would have been a great burden and anxiety on me, for instead of staying three months I was gone twelve years.

Then after I went to India, while I was at Naini Tal, Upper India, they sent me papers to sign, and I went before a magistrate at Naini Tal, India, and in the presence of these witnesses I signed all rights and claim away. So the house was sold, and Amanda Smith was where she was when she first started, so far as having a house was concerned; and that ended the house that so many people think I still own.

I was sorry for the good people who had given the money, but could not help it. I had nothing to do with it from first to last, but to accept it, as I have before stated. After the house was sold, the people had to move. I wrote to them to take care of my things. I sent the money to help to move the first time, but they moved a number of times in twelve years, so I found it difficult to keep up to that.

Everyone knows that often in moving, even when one is right on the spot themselves to look after their things, it is difficult to save losses and come out straight, so what must I expect when I came home from Africa, I had no place to go. The people had stored the things and had gone away for the summer, and had not got home when I arrived. When they did come, they could not get a house large enough to accommodate us all, but a good friend in Brooklyn, Mr. Tom Gibson, and his wife, had written me in

England inviting me, to come and spend some time with them. On the day I arrived I sent a telegram to him from the steamer, and Mr. Gibson came to meet me and took me to his home, and I stayed with them two weeks.

Mrs. Gibson was quite ill at the time, and has since passed away. I had known them for twenty years. Mrs. Titus, her mother, gave me a place to stay in her tent the first time I was at Round Lake Camp Meeting, and, after that, good Brothers Hillman and Hartshorn always saw that I had a tent all to myself. God bless them.

After the two weeks I felt I must have a room, my trunk and things were in the way, and through a friend of Mrs. Gibson's I got a small back room, which I had to pay ten dollars a month for. I could not do better at the time, but the Lord knew I could not stand that long, but O, I was so weak and worn and I must have some place.

A number of friends In different places kindly invited me to come and stay with them, but all wanted me to hold some meetings, and I was too tired and weary to think sometimes, and then the Lord, who is ever a present help in time of trouble, put it in the heart of that grand woman, Mrs. Mary R. Denmen, of Newark, and she wrote to me and said for me to come to Newark, and she would give me a room in one of her houses. The house that her coachman lived in was a nice, comfortable little house, with seven rooms, and Joseph had but a small family, so I could have one room there free of rent. Oh, how I praised the Lord for His wonderful, loving kindness, providing for me.

Mrs. Denmen is a member of the Episcopal Church, but ever since I have known her, for over twenty years, I have never had a warmer and truer friend than she has been. Her friendship is so practical, only God Himself knows how many times she has helped me when I know that no mortal knew my need but the Lord himself.

I have enjoyed my cozy little room this winter, while I have been writing my book, though much of the time I am away, but there is no place like home when you are there. Surely, the eyes of the Lord run to and fro over the whole earth to show Himself strong in behalf of them whose heart is perfect towards Him, and now I don't know where I may, next be led, but no matter where I go I shall never forget No. 64 Park street, Newark, nor my beloved benefactress, Mrs. Mary R. Denmen. May God bless her and her dear family.

Mr. Beecher had two Mission churches in Brooklyn—Bethany and the Mayflower. I spent a week at each, in 1878. In both of these churches the Lord blessed us very greatly.

I remember very distinctly one special incident—the reconciliation between two brothers who had once been very dear friends. They were boys together, and were both in business in the same office, in New York. They were both professed Christians, members of the church. One was Superintendent of the Sabbath School. But they had some falling out, and had not spoken to each other for four or five years.

Both wanted to speak, but each was too spunky to speak first, and the longer it went on the more difficult it became, until at last Mr. B. said he was so miserable, he had resigned his position as Superintendent, and had quit going to church regularly, and was just making up his mind to withdraw from the church entirely. His wife begged of him, for the sake of the three beautiful children they had, and the influence it would have on them, not to leave, so he was holding on, but felt he would leave. Oh! how the Devil chuckles over anything like that.

Though they would not speak, they would make hateful insinuations and remarks about each other, so that each would get what the other said, without speaking; and how tantalizing that is. But God, who is so rich in mercy, will not let us be tempted above that we are able to bear, but will, with the temptation, also make a way of escape. It pleased the Lord to let me be at the Mayflower just at that time.

One night, while I was speaking on the forgiveness of our enemies, the Spirit of God got hold of this young man. At the close of the meeting he came up and said he wanted to talk to me, and he told me his story. I urged him to go to his brother and have a talk with him.

"I know he will not speak."

"But," I said, "you speak to him."

"But I know him so well," he said, "that I know if I do he will curse me, and I can't stand it."

I told him that God would help him if he would resolve to do right. After, a long talk and prayer he said he would go to him. I told him I would pray for him that night and all the next day, and in the evening he was to report about it.

And Oh! how I did pray for those two men. Only as a soul can pray when it feels that God is about to gain a victory. Next morning, somehow, I felt so quiet and joyful. And yet I did not know what had happened. Only I believed God had undertaken for them.

The evening came on. I went to church, and I saw this gentleman come in. His face was like a sunbeam. He was handsome, anyhow. But, Oh! now he was beautiful. I knew something had happened. The heavy, deep, gloomy countenance was gone. He made his way to me at the close of the meeting, and said:

"Oh! Sister Smith, praise the Lord, it is all right."

"Amen," I said. "I told you so. Well, now tell me about it."

"Well," he said, "I made up my mind last night that I would speak to Will anyhow, and if he would not speak, and would curse me, I didn't care. The Lord fixed it so nice. I prayed all the morning as I was going. I am generally at the office first. But this morning he was there. So I went in. There was no one in but him. I walked right up to him, and I said: 'Look here, Will, I think it is time you and I were done with this foolishness of ours,' and he sprang to his feet and took me by the hand and said, with, tears, 'Yes, Charlie, I have wanted to speak to you for a month, but I was afraid you wouldn't speak.' 'And Will,' I said, 'I have wanted to speak to you, but thought you didn't care to speak to me, and would curse me. But the Lord has blessed me, and now we are old friends again. Thank the Lord!' "

If nothing else was done at that meeting, surely it was a great victory; this long breach between these two brothers healed, and a reconciliation taken place. Satan would rather they had fought a duel. But the best way to fight a duel, in my opinion, is on your knees, surrendering to God, and getting a heart filled with love and forgiveness. Amen.

Monday night I was at Dr. Cuyler's Church, Tuesday at the Methodist Church, Wednesday night at the Baptist Church, and we ended our services the next Sabbath at Dr. Buddington's. The ministers all united and gave their churches, and all the collections, so the ladies were liberal with me, God bless them. They knew nothing of my expectation of going to England, so I could see it was all the Lord's doings, and was marvelous. I asked the Lord for everything I needed, direct.

The summer before, my good friend, Mrs. Saunders, had given me a very nice black silk dress, had, it made and all, and I had expected it to last me all my lifetime, so I put it away and had not worn it. Then when I was at Fleet Street, the ladies had given me a grey suit, dress and cape, so I had these two good dresses, and one other that I traveled in. Some one gave me a pair of kid gloves, then some one gave me some ruching for the neck of my dress; some pocket handkerchiefs were given me, and some one gave me stockings. Oh, it was wonderful how everything seemed to come in. So my wardrobe was complete, though not elaborate, and, of course, it did not take me long to arrange it in my trunk.

That night at Dr. Cuyler's Church they had the lecture room engaged and all lighted and warmed so nicely, but he was regretting that a meeting had been arranged for Monday night at his church, as he was anxious the ladies should have a good collection; also, owing to the old folks' concert that was to be held at Dr. Sudder's Church, that night was not so favorable. He was afraid it would affect the result of the meeting, but his great surprise was the fact that the meeting was to begin at half past seven P. M. I got there at a quarter past seven and the lecture room was crowded, and many outside, and the people were clamoring and saying we must open the church. I never got in at all till the church had been opened and a fire started. As soon as the church was opened the people rushed out of the lecture room into the church. Dr. Cuyler told me to wait in the lecture room till the people got settled.

This unsettled me a little, but I prayed the more that God would bless the people and help me to speak for Him, and I said, "Now, Lord, don't let anybody take cold," for the church could not be heated for some time, but as there had been fire all day Sunday, they thought it was safe to venture.

The Lord did help me speak for Him. It was wonderful that night how He helped me. When all was settled and the large church was filled and many in the gallery, Dr. Cuyler said, "Mrs. Smith, will you go in now?" How very kind he was!

I knew there had been some trouble some time before about a lady speaking in his church. I thought if they would make such a fuss about one so gentle and sweet and refined as Miss Sarah Smiley, what would they do with me? So I said to myself, "Well, I will do just whatever I am told to do."

"They will not dare to ask me inside the chancel," I thought, "so if they put a bench or chair in the aisle and ask me to stand on it and speak, I will do it."

Mrs. Johnson and Miss Ludlow and a number of the other temperance ladies were with me, so Dr. Cuyler asked me if I would go in the pulpit.

"My!" I thought to myself; "however, I will do just as I am told," so I walked up, and it was dreadful high. After he had seated me, he said, "Mrs. Smith, would you like to have one of the ladies sit with you?"

"If they would like to, sir, I should be pleased." So he went and asked them, but each declined. Then he came himself and sat by me and introduced me to the people so nicely. I sang and gave a Bible talk. I had perfect freedom, as if I had been in a Methodist Church. I talked an hour and not a soul budged to go out, and Dr. C. spoke highly of the meeting, and the people gave the ladies a real fat collection, just like people do when they are really blest!

CHAPTER XIX.

BROOKLYN—CALL TO GO TO ENGLAND—BALTIMORE—VOYAGE OVER.

I was in Brooklyn holding meetings at Fleet Street Church, Rev. J. I Simmons, pastor. Then at Mr. Beecher's Mission, "Mayflower." We had a good work, and also at the other mission, uptown. Friday afternoon the ladies' meeting in the lecture room of Plymouth. There were several splendid ladies there in those days, and are yet, no doubt.

These Friday afternoon meetings were the regular ladies' consecration meetings, and on Saturday afternoon we had young people's and children's meeting in the same room, and I believe a number of the dear young people and children gave their hearts to the Lord. I needed rest very much. I had been going on without a break all summer and all winter. I was dreadfully worn and tired, and as soon as I got through had purposed going to Ocean Grove to rest a little. Dear old Brother Tompkins, of Tompkins Cove, N. Y., had given me the use of a room at their little cottage, where I could go and stay as long as I chose. How good of the Lord to thus provide for me! How well I remember those dear friends, though they have long since gone to their reward.

Everything in the way of comfort and convenience was left for me to use, so I was anxious to get off. Rev. Lindsey J. Parker was then pastor of old Sands Street Methodist Church. He came after me to come to Sands Street for ten days. I was stopping with a family next door to Plymouth Church, whose name I can't remember, but I know he was a Baptist brother, strong in the faith, and he doctored me well on baptism. My! how many books he gave me to read! I am not half through yet; don't know as I ever will be He was very kind though, and so was his family.

Well, I tried my best to beg off from Mr. Parker—I told him how tired I was, and how much I needed rest. I told him I would give him the whole month of September if he would let me off.

No, he said, his official board told him he must have me come, if but for a week, and I told him I would let him know the next week. I prayed earnestly that the Lord would give me strength and help me through that week, and it was wonderful how He did help me as I have often asked Him before. So on Monday morning I went to see if I could prevail on Dr. Parker to let me have the rest, but no word I could say moved him from what he had said first.

Just when we were busy talking the bell rang, and Dr. Parker was called away. Then a Miss Price, a friend of Mrs. Parker's, was there visiting. She was an English lady; had been in this country about four years, and was expecting to go home in April. She was very pleasant, and I began telling her and Mrs. Parker how I was trying to beg the Doctor to let me off for a rest. So finally Miss Price said, "Well, you do need rest; you had better come and go with me to England next month; it would be just the thing for you. The great Parts Exposition is going on, and I would take you, and we would have a real nice time, and I know the trip would do you good."

"Yes," I said, "that would be nice."

"Well," she said, "pray about it; I believe the Lord would have you go."

Just then Mr. Parker came in again. No more was said about England. He fixed on the day I was to come to Sands Street. I closed my last meeting at the "Mayflower" on Saturday night. There was a blessed work done, the result of which eternity alone will tell.

On Sunday afternoon was our first meeting at Sands Street. The old church was crowded. Our first meeting was for the young people and children, and I began by asking the older people, strangers and all, here and there, all over the house, upstairs and down, as I would call them out, "Brother, how old were you when you gave your heart to the Lord?" Then I would ask a sister.

There were some real gem testimonies to the grace of God, and this encouraged and helped the young people very much, so when I began our altar service it was not long till the altar was crowded, and many of the dear young people and children professed to have

found peace in believing that day. I spent a week, putting in two Sundays, and the Lord was with us and gave us blessing all through. Praise His name!

At the close of this meeting Miss Price came up to me and spoke to me, and said, "Did you pray about what I told you?"

I didn't recognize her at first, and I said, "About what?"

"Don't you know Miss Price, that spoke to you on Monday about going to England?"

"Oh, yes, I do remember you now."

"Well, did you pray about it?"

"No," I said. "I did not."

"Well," she said, "you must; I believe the Lord would have you go."

So that night when I went home and got ready for bed, the thought came to me, "You know that lady told you to pray about going to England," I said, "Yes, that is so."

I thought a moment and said to myself:

"Go to England! Amanda Smith, the colored washwoman, go to England! No, I am not going to pray a bit; I have to ask the Lord for so many things that I really need, that I am not going to bother Him with what I don't need—to go to England. It does well enough for swell people to go, not for me."

So, after I had this little talk all to myself, I said my prayers and went to bed. On Tuesday afternoon I was invited to tea to Brother Parker's. There were several others, also. Dr. Parker's brother, a young man, had just come from the old country. The Doctor was well pleased to receive him safe, so we were having a pleasant chat at the tea table. The young man was telling of his pleasant voyage across the sea. Then Dr. Parker told what a grand time he had when he came. He said the sea was beautiful and calm as a mill pond. He told how they had danced—the passengers I think he referred to; as he was a Methodist preacher, I don't suppose he indulged in dancing.

I listened attentively to all, for I never knew the sea was calm. My idea of the great sea was that it was always rough and tossing. I know I used to sing that good old hymn:—

"Like the rough sea that cannot rest."

So that was my best idea of the grand old ocean. I have learned a great deal about it since then.

Miss Price sat opposite at the table, and as she had crossed several times herself, she said, "There, Mrs. Smith, you see what a pleasant time we could have on board the steamer."

"Yes, but it costs money to go to England, and none but swell folks can go."

"You need not trouble about that," she said, "if you say you will go, I will see to that part."

That was a new version of it, so that night when I went home, I knelt down and said, "Lord, if Thou dost want me to go to England, make it very clear and help me. I don't know what I would do there, I don't know anybody, but if Thou dost want me, Lord, I leave it all to Thee," and somehow—I can't explain it—but God made it so clear, and put it in my conscience so real and deep, that I could no more doubt that He wanted me to go to England, than I could doubt my own existence. I can't explain it, only I knew it, and I don't understand it now, but as high as the heavens are above the earth, so are His ways above our ways, and His thoughts above our thoughts.

When I was through at Sands Street, and was about to start to Ocean Grove, Miss Price said:

"Now, Mrs. Smith, I am going to Philadelphia to see a friend married, and I will be back such a day, and you can write me."

I went down to the grove, and I was so glad to get there and have a little quiet and rest. I swept and dusted my room and opened the windows, and it was very pleasant. It was the first of April, and, as I thought it over, "Oh," I said, "after all, I think I can get more rest here than I can by going to England."

Then as I looked out from my window and saw the great ocean, and heard the great waves roll in, I trembled. It came to me, "You need a good rest. Then there is Mazie, you can't leave her here alone."

"Yes," I said, "that is so, I guess I won't go." So I did my washing and ironing and began my little sewing, mending and darning, and getting my clothes in order, and resting a little, for I took my time and didn't hurry, and so I went on for several days.

Then a letter came from Miss Price, saying, "Let me know by return mail if you will go with me to England. If you will go, all right, if not, I will join a party of ladies who are going."

A deep conviction came over me that I must go, but I said I had not rested half enough, and I didn't sleep well at night, I went

to bed tired and got up tired, then, beside, it is so far, three thousand miles away. "O, dear, I will write and tell her no, she has got those ladies to go with, so that is all right."

I sat down to answer the letter, and there was such a deep dread came over me as though I ought not to tell her I would not go, I could hardly write my letter.

"Oh," I said, "what is the matter with me?" A whisper came to me:

"Don't write her, no."

"But I can't go, I must write." So on I went, and I never wrote a letter with such a dread on me before in my life. I finished it, and took it to the postoffice and threw it into the letter box, and was so glad to get it out of my hand. Now, I said, I am free, and it seemed I was lightened for a little while, no sad feeling in my heart, no burden, everything gone.

"Oh," I said, "how much trouble that letter has given me, that is it."

I made several calls before I went home, as I had been away for three months. Everywhere I called, the friends were glad to see me, and said, "Amanda Smith, tell us all about where you have been and about the work," and I had much to tell of what God had wrought. Then, to sing and pray.

I did not go home till half past six, so I felt all that sadness is gone, I will have a nice tea and go to bed early.

I had been in the house about half an hour, I suppose, and my tea was about ready, and, all of a sudden, as when a gas jet is turned off, an avalanche of darkness seemed to come over me like the horror of darkness that came over Abraham. My heart sank, and great dread took possession of me. Every bit of desire for my supper left me, and I wanted nothing.

"O, Lord," I said, "what is the matter with me? Do help me." Then I said. "I don't mean to sleep to-night till I know what ails me." So I locked the doors and fastened the shutters and turned down my lamp very low, and got on my knees, and I said, "Now, Lord, I don't know the cause of this darkness, and I must know before I sleep, I am in for it all night, and I must know what the matter is."

I wept bitterly, and prayed. Then I thought it may be I have grieved the Spirit in some way, in what I said, when I called. Then I went, in my thoughts, to each place, and went through all

the conversation, but, no, no condemnation there. Then I went through all my work, every place I had been, no, no condemnation; then, "Lord, what is it?" I prostrated myself full length on the floor, and wept and prayed as never before. I said, Lord, I must know what is the matter with me. A whisper, "Arise." I rose upon my knees by the chair, and said, "Now, Lord, I will be still. Tell me, I pray Thee, what the matter is," and, after a few moments' stillness, it was as though some one stood at my right side and said distinctly:

"You are going about telling people to trust the Lord in the dark, to trust Him when they can't see Him."

"Yes, Lord, I have done so."

"Well, you tell other people to do what you are not willing to do yourself."

"O, Lord," I said, "that is mean, and by Thy grace I will not tell anybody to do what I am not willing to do myself. Now, Lord, what is it?" And clear and distinct came these words, "You are afraid to trust the Lord and go to England, you are afraid of the ocean."

My! it took my breath, but I said, "Lord, that is the truth, the real truth." Of course it was.

In a moment, in panorama form, God's goodness seemed to pass before me, and His faithfulness in leading me and providing for me in every way, and answering my prayer a thousand times, and now, to think I should be afraid to trust Him and go to England. Oh, such a sense of shame as filled me. I prostrated myself on the floor again, I felt I could never look up again in His dear face and pray. I never can describe the awful sense of shame that seemed to fill me, and I cried out, "Lord, forgive me, for Jesus' sake, and give me another chance, and I will go to England."

Then I thought, "If I write and tell Miss Price that I will go, she is a stranger, and she may think I am fickle-minded and she won't know how to depend on me, but if the Lord will give me another chance, I will go alone. I pledge Thee Lord, you may trust me, I will obey."

"What about your child?"

Then I saw myself on the steamer in a big storm, and the ship wrecked; it was so real, I heard the timbers crack, heard the thunders roll, saw the lightning, saw and heard the people screaming. Oh, it was awful. Then a telegram came to say the ship was lost.

Then my daughter got the news, then I saw her frantic and wild with grief! It was all as real as life, and my head seemed to swim, and I cried, "O, Lord, help me, I give my child to Thee, Thou canst take care of her."

Then I thought if she should get sick—well, the quickest word I could get would be by telegram, and if I should get to England, and they should send a telegram that she was sick, I knew what that would mean, it would mean she was dead. Oh, how I felt!

Then I thought it all over, and said to myself, "What if she were to be sick and die, and I could not be with her to do for her while she was sick, and pray and help her. If she were dead there would be no use of my coming home, for she would be buried before I could get to her, and then there would be no need of my coming."

I saw it all, and I said, "Lord, help me, I will obey Thee."

All of my sisters and brothers that were then living, came before me, one by one, six in number, and I saw each sink and die, and I went to the funeral of each of them, there on my knees, as real as ever I went to a funeral in my life, and I said, "Lord, help me."

"But," I said, "to stay here and disobey God—I can't afford to take the consequence, I would rather go and obey God than to stay here and know that I disobeyed." Then this hymn came:—

> "Lord, obediently I'll go,
> Gladly leaving all below,
> Only Thou my leader be,
> And I still will follow Thee."

Then there came such a flood of light and sweet peace that filled me with joy and gladness, and I sang and praised the Lord, for I felt He had dealt bountifully with me in great mercy.

In the course of a week or so I went to see Miss Price off. She sailed by one of the beautiful ships of the White Star Line. It was like a floating palace. I had never seen anything like it on water; it was magnificent. I thought what a mistake I have made. "Oh, Lord, you may trust me, I will go alone if you will give me another chance." So I went home.

A week or two later I had a letter from Mrs. Mary C. Johnson, saying, "Mr. Johnson and I expect to sail for England such a day in May, and would be glad to take you under our wing."

"Well," I thought, "this is very nice. Mrs. Johnson is such a nice lady, and she and Mr. Johnson have always been so kind to me, and I don't know of anyone I would rather go with than with them."

From the date of the letter I saw it would only give me a little over a week to get ready and I could not do it; then I got down on my knees and spread the letter on a chair and said, "Lord, Thou knowest I will be true and go alone, but I can't get ready and go with Mrs. Johnson, though I would so like to do so. I want to go to Baltimore and see Mazie, and tell her about it;" and then I prayed the Lord to quiet her and prepare her so she could not feel she could not let me go, and He did it, praise His name!

I wanted to go and see my brother that I had not seen in thirty years; he was my oldest brother, living in York, Pennsylvania; and a younger brother I had seen a few months before; he lived in Tonawanda, but my brother William Tolbert I had not seen in thirty years; so I said it is all right. I will write and tell Mrs. Johnson to write me when she gets to England and tell me how things look.

Some time before, I was in Boston at Mr. Moody's meeting; it was the last week of his meetings. There Mrs. Johnson told me that she had a deep conviction that the Lord had a work for me in Great Britain, but I gave no thought to it, so that Mr. and Mrs. Johnson were off in a few weeks. As soon as she got to England she wrote me and told me of the Keswick Convention, which answers to one of our holiness camp meetings in this country, but there the phraseology is changed a little, and they call it a convention for the deepening of spiritual life. This meeting was begun by that good man, R. P. Smith, years ago, and they are held every year. God certainly blest him in starting this convention, if nothing else was accomplished.

Numerous other meetings all over the United Kingdom have been productive of marvelous good, the record of which is in eternity, only.

A sad night for me. I think if Satan ever did have anything to do with mosquitoes he certainly had that night. Sunday was another hot day; the heat was something fearful. I walked to and from church, about five miles' distance, I think, but it seemed much longer because of the intense heat.

"Well," I said, "I will not go out this evening." So I went up to my room and lay down and tried to rest; but here the mosquitoes and flies seemed to join together. Oh, I felt I should go wild. I tried to pray, but, Oh, the poisonous mosquitoes did nothing but sing, first in one ear and then the other, then a sharp nip.

"Oh, dear, I can't stand it." So up I got. I said, "It is too far to go down to Bethel Church to-night, I will go into this white Methodist Church."

I was so wearied, I said, "Lord, do help me." When I went downstairs my aunt said to me, "Where are you going?"

"To church."

"I thought you said you were not going out again."

"Yes, but I am going into this white Methodist Church, on Exeter street."

She was surprised.

"We never go to the white people's church here. I would laugh if they put you out."

"Well," I said, "they will have it to do to-night for I am going."

I was glad she did not want to go, for her skin was very thin, and I thought if there was any unpleasantness I could bear it better than she could; so out I went, a half an hour before the time. The church was beautiful; the lights were burning dimly and it was so cool and quiet. The sexton was very pleasant and spoke to me, but did not tell me to go into the gallery—the custom used to be where colored people went to church they went into the gallery—so, as he said nothing, I walked in and went three or four pews from the door.

"If they put me out," I said, "I will have a good strut, and every body can see me."

Well, in the quiet I began to think and pray. Somehow, I felt the Lord had sent me there to teach me some lesson, and I said, "Lord, what is it that Thou wantest me to learn, for surely Thou dost mean something by all this?" So there I sat, praying earnestly.

By and by, the people began to gather, then two very nicely dressed ladies walked in and stood at my pew. I turned and looked them squarely in the face so they could see I was of the royal black, but they looked pleasant, so I arose and they passed in.

There were plenty of vacant pews on the opposite side and further

ahead. I don't know why they preferred that one unless for the peculiar fascination that seems to gather about royalty!

After a while the minister came in, the lights were turned up. Oh, how pretty it was, and the minister passed up into the pulpit and prayed, then announced the hymn. They sang, then a very earnest prayer, and all the usual preliminaries. All this time I prayed the Lord to teach me the lesson He wanted me to learn. When the minister arose and announced his text, he said: "My text will be found in Philippians 4:19, 'My God shall supply your need according to His riches in glory by Christ Jesus;' and the Spirit said to me clearly, "That is the lesson for you," and the emphasis seemed to be on the need, "My Good shall supply all your need," and I saw it, what it all meant.

After I went home from church, in Baltimore, my aunt said to me, "Well, how did you make out?"

"The Lord has taught me the lesson He wanted I should learn," I replied, "I am so glad I went."

When I saw how near I came to breaking my covenant with God, I was alarmed; I slept very little that night.

Next morning I was up betimes and was off to the train. They said it was the nine-thirty that left Baltimore. They said it was the lightning express; its destination was York, Pennsylvania. It made but two stops, at Wilmington, Philadelphia, and York. I felt I never wanted to go in that train again. Oh, it was so swift, as I looked out of the window it seemed to me the trees and posts would cut my eyes out, the speed was something fearful. I held on to myself, and said, "Lord, if Thou wilt help me I will never disobey again."

I got to York, spent the night with my brother, next day held a meeting at one o'clock in the Methodist Church, and left at half past two for Philadelphia, got home, went out and bought my trunk and packed it, and at seven P. M. I locked my door and dropped my key in the letter box and started for Horton street to my friend's, Mrs. Kenney. I met Mrs. B. and told her I was going to England to be gone the months, and I wanted her to look after my house till I came back.

"All right," she said.

I bade her good-bye, and so passed on. The next morning, Wednesday, at eight o'clock, I went on board the steamer "Ohio," Captain Morris in command. He was a perfect gentleman and

very kind to me. Through my dear friend, Mrs. Kenney, I had got my ticket all right, seventy dollars first class, of course.

There were quite a number of aristocratic passengers, and I, being a colored woman and alone, there was quite a little inquiry who I was, what I was going to England for, etc. I must say I did feel somewhat embarrassed. Several of the passengers asked me if I had ever been in England.

"No," I said.

"Are you going on business?"

"No, not special."

"Do you expect friends to meet you?"

"Well, no."

Then such a critical smile and remark. They would go away and would talk it over with two or more others and pass comments, and after a while another would come and put the some question in another form.

"You are going to Paris, I suppose?"

"No, I don't expect to go to Paris."

"I suppose you are going to join the Jubilee Singers. No doubt, you find this an expensive passage, Mrs. Smith?"

"Yes, seventy dollars was what I paid for my passage."

"You have friends that will meet you in England?"

"Well, no, I don't know that anyone will meet me."

Then I would tell them of my friend, Mrs. Mary C. Johnson, and Miss Price, and how it all came about, and they would seem to be so astonished to think I would be such a fool as to go to England on such a testimony. An old Quaker gentleman was the only one that really seemed to know about the leading of the Spirit, and he spoke for me on one or two occasions. Some of the ladies remarked that I should have gone steerage, and it would not have cost me so much.

They didn't know but I was a suspicious being of some kind, so this worried me a little, and one day I went into my cabin and got down on my knees, and said, "Now, Lord, these people ask me so many questions. If I tell them that Thou hast sent me to England, they don't understand it; and now, Lord, don't let them ask me any more questions. Stop them; take the curiosity out of them; make them let me alone, for Jesus' sake. Amen."

I got up and went on deck, and not a soul from that hour asked me any more questions, not one the whole voyage. "If ye shall ask anything in my name, I will do it."

> "Are we weak and heavy laden,
> Cumbered with a load of care,
> Precious Saviour, Still out refuge,
> Take it to the lord in prayer." Amen.

We were all pretty sick the first two days. The third day one of the waiters, a very nice, kind lad, helped me on deck. When the captain saw me he came to me, and said, "How are you, Mrs. Smith?"

"I am feeling better, captain, thank you."

Then he took a seat by me, and said, "Mrs. Smith, have you had proper treatment?"

"Yes, captain, thank you."

He said, "If you have any unpleasantness from any one on this ship, I want you to report to me."

"I thank you, sir, I will do so."

But I had no complaint to make. The stewardess was very kind, which any one could not help appreciating when traveling on shipboard. She would bring my lunch or meals up on deck, just as she did the others, and I had many pleasant talks with her.

The first Sunday we were out nearly all the passengers were laid up by seasickness. Out of the twenty or more lady passengers, I think there was not one up on deck till late in the afternoon, but the following Sunday we were all well and up and out.

The Quaker gentleman and his son were the only two that really seemed to take much to me, outside the curious questions that were asked. Then the gentleman and lady that sat next me at the table—they were from Philadelphia,—were both very agreeable and made it very pleasant for me, and this I appreciated very much.

The Quaker gentleman and his son wore very much interested in me when they learned I was, as the Friends say, "a preacher woman." The old gentleman told me much about the usages among the Society of Friends. He said the friends had always stood clear on the part of female preaching, and he said he was very proud of them. I had never met him before, and he did not know that colored women ever worked in that sphere. He encouraged me, and told me to go forward. Then he spoke to the captain about holding services.

There were five doctors on board, and no preacher among them. Most of the passengers were Episcopalians and Presbyterians,

all very nice, but very aristocratic, so these gentlemen came and asked me if I would take the service. I told them I would if the captain thought it would be agreeable. I did not want to do any thing that would not be perfectly agreeable to all. Then they went around and inquired, and everybody was willing. They thought, anything to break the monotony and have a novel entertainment.

The captain came to me himself and said he would be very glad if I would take the service. He would have the saloon arranged. I told him I would do so if he thought it would be best. He assured me that it would be all right, so everything was arranged. First bell was rung; it did seem real churchified! How the smiles and whispers went around among the passengers, "The colored woman is going to preach." All were invited down into the saloon, then the second bell was rung. Many of the second cabin and some of the steerage passengers came in. Those from the steerage were most of them Romanists, but all behaved reverently except one or two poor, ignorant persons.

The Episcopal prayer and hymn books were placed all around the long tables, and I did not know a bit how to proceed with that service, so I turned to my Quaker friend, for he and his son stood by me ready to assist in anything but to sing or pray, and he spoke to the captain, who said I should go on in my own way. So I gave out a hymn that was familiar, and they all joined as I started the tune. If I had dared to ask some one to pray I would, but if I had it would only have been an embarrassment to anyone but an old time Methodist, so I looked to God for strength and prayed myself, then I sang from the Winnowed Hymns that beautiful song, "Jesus of Nazareth Passeth By."

The Lord blest the singing and it captured their attention, and before I got through I saw a number of them were touched, but how I prayed that morning for Divine help, and it surely came.

I opened my Bible at the 14th chapter of John, and said, "I will not preach, but I want to talk a little from this dear old chapter," so I talked on for over half an hour with perfect liberty and freedom. Then I prayed, and as I spoke to the Lord the several passengers came before me, those that were sick, and friends left behind, the captain and officers that had been so kind, and so on, as the Spirit prompted the prayer, so I prayed. When I got through we sang the Doxology.

Oh, how it changed the spirit of the passengers. Ladies and gentlemen that had not even said good morning to me before, came to me and thanked me for what I said, and especially for the prayer. They shook hands and were so interested, and said, "Lord bless you."

There was a great swell doctor who belonged to the United States Navy—he and his wife and two children were very nice, but from the remarks of some of the passengers he seemed to act as though he thought the passengers on that steamer ought to feel they were highly honored that so great a passenger as he, doctor in the United States Navy was aboard that ship.

The two little girls were sweet little things, aged, I should think, about nine and six years; they seemed to take quite a fancy to me. They had no nurse with them, so I would amuse them, and we had a pleasant time, but when ever the doctor was around he would call them away. He would seem to feel so uncomfortable that they should be so stupid as to notice a black woman. I used to smile as I would see his maneuvers.

When I got to Liverpool I knew nothing about the Custom House. All the ladies had gentlemen to look after their baggage, and as there is always a commotion when we get in, so I said, "Lord, I have no one to look after my baggage or do anything for me, now help me and keep me quiet, and just help me through with everything."

The good doctor seemed to take special pains to hinder me. He had a good deal of baggage to be examined, I had but one trunk, he had three officers. I waited; then I saw a chance, and I just spoke to one of the men, and pointed out my trunk; just then the good doctor stepped right in front of me, clapped the man on the arm, took him away so roughly, so I waited till all were pretty well through. The doctor got in his cab and was off. Then the man turned to me and said, "Madame, this is your trunk?"

"Yes, sir," I said.

"I suppose you have no tobacco nor cigars, nor books?"

"No, no," was my reply.

"Well, all right, where do you want to go?"

"Lime Street Station, sir."

He whistled for a cab, I locked my trunk, and a moment more I was off.

My cab overtook and passed the good doctor. As I passed I looked out and waved my hand with a polite bow and rolled by, leaving the doctor behind, and instead of smiling like a good fellow and bidding me God speed, he simply frowned and seemed to bite his lip. I have never seen him since, poor fellow!

CHAPTER XX.

LIME STREET STATION, LIVERPOOL, ENGLAND, AND THE RECEPTION I MET WITH THERE—PAGES FROM MY DIARY.

I had to wait about two hours. I went to Keswick, where the big Conference is held every summer. Cannon Battersby was the rector of St. John's Church, and was President of the Convention. A holy man of God, he was. Mr. and Mrs. Johnson were there. They had spoken of me, so that everyone seemed to be expecting me.

Just before we got to Keswick I had to change cars and wait about an hour. The day was beautiful, and this was about four o'clock in the afternoon. I was a curiosity. How the people did look at me. I thought I would buy me a newspaper, and then they wouldn't look at me so much, but, lo and behold, that only made it worse. They seemed to wonder what in the world I was going to do with a newspaper. Then I walked up and down, then they walked up and down, as though they wondered what I was walking up and down for. They were very respectful; they did not laugh and make remarks like they would have done in this country, but they seemed to look as though they pitied me. By and by the train came in, and two ladies got out and one of them walked up to me and said, "Why, Amanda Smith."

"Well," I thought, "who in the world here knows me." I said, "Yes, madam, that is my name;" and holding on to my hand, she said, laughingly, "Don't you know me?"

"I know your face, madam, but cannot place you."

She still laughed and said, "Look at me."

"Oh, madam, do please tell me who you are."

"You held meetings with me at Sea Cliff, and New York. You spoke at a ladies' meeting in New York that I held once at Dr. C.'s church one afternoon."

No, I could not think. Then she said, "You don't know Mrs. Dr. Bordman."

"Oh, dear Mrs. Bordman, is it you, the joy of my heart?"

"Where are you going?" she asked.

"To Keswick Convention."

"Why, that is just where we are going."

Then she introduced me to the lady that was with her and we had a beautiful time and pleasant journey to Keswick.

The house where Mrs. B. and her friend had lodged was full, but they said they thought to get me a place near by.

Of course no one knew I was really coming, I had got Mrs. Johnson's letter telling me all about how to come, but I had no time to write and tell her I had decided to do so, so, in a little while after we had got to the house, dear Dr. Bordman went to see about my lodgings. It was in St. John's Lane. The landlady told him she could accommodate me for the night, but the next day she was expecting two young men who had engaged the rooms. So I went off to my lodgings.

The lady was a very pleasant old lady, a widow. She was quite alone, but had such a pretty home, like so many one sees in

England. The room was large; everything was elegant and rich, but old-fashioned; high bedstead, with heavy curtains around. I was glad when the night came, to go to bed. I had never been so long in such close quarters as in the cabin on the steamer, and I longed to have a good, free time without shaking. It was July, dreadfully hot here in America, but so cool in England that I could sleep with the windows closed and under a blanket.

"My! I never knew the luxury of an English feather-bed till that night. Oh, it was so elegant, a great big English feather-bed, I had never seen anything like it, though I had seen many a large feather bed here in America. I lay all over it. I said, "I want to get the benefit of this feather-bed, I will only have it for one night."

My! what a nice sleep I had; how refreshed and rested I was the next morning; how full of praise my heart was to God for His kindness in bringing me safely to England and giving me such a token of His favor among the people that received me; I shall never forget it.

I got up next morning, did up my room, and was to go to Mrs. Bordman's to have my breakfast with them. Before going out I thought to myself how I should like to stay here; it just seems like as if this is the place the Lord wants me to be, but the lady has said she could accommodate me only for the night, and of course I can't ask her when she has said she expects the young men. Then I got down on my knees and said my prayers, and I said, "Now, Lord, this seems like the very place that Thou dost want me to stay; now, Thou canst manage so that I can stay here, and if it really is Thy will, put it in the lady's heart when I go down stairs to tell me I can stay. I don't want to ask her. She has been so kind, and I am a stranger; but, Lord, I believe that Thou canst manage it for me; surely Thou canst if it is Thy will, so I leave it with Thee. Amen."

Somehow, my heart was so quiet and full of peace, I felt the Lord would do it, and yet it seemed so strange that He should. I took my bag in my hand and went down. When I got downstairs I met the lady. She bade me good morning and asked me how I slept. I told her, beautifully; I was so refreshed from the comfortable night's sleep. Then she said to me, "I have just had a telegram from one of the young men that was to come, and he has met with a friend he has not seen for a long time, so he is going to stay with him, and the other young man is going with a friend of his; so the room will be vacant and you can stay."

Oh, I came near shouting right out, but I knew if I did she would think I was wild, so I did say, praise the Lord; but I wanted to dance for joy. Oh, how wonderfully God provided for me. I went down and told Mrs. Bordman, and we had a good time praising the Lord together.

The meeting was held in a big tent in an open lot. There were crowds of poople. As I walked down to the tent and heard the singing, it all seemed very much like home. I was introduced by Mrs. J. to Canon Battersby. No one acted as though I was a black woman, I don't suppose they would have treated Mrs. President of the United States with more Christian courtesy and cordiality than they did me. After the preaching service was over I was introduced by Canon Battersby, and was asked to lead the after meeting. There were clergymen and workers all around, and I felt at first a little awkward. I thought I would never get hold of the way they did things; and they told me just to go right on in my own way, just as I was accustomed to do in America, and they would stand by and assist in anything I wished them to do.

So after talking awhile, I asked those who wanted personal conversion and prayer to stand, and a great number arose all over

the tent. I was a little surprised, but I kept looking to the Lord; then I said to the workers and clergymen, "Now, there is a great work to do; these souls must be spoken to, helped and prayed with. I want that all of you should go around and speak to them." Then I said, "If there are those who would like to come forward and kneel here, they may do so," though I saw that that was not the custom.

A few came to the front, and in a moment the clergymen and workers were all out in the congregation kneeling and praying with the seekers. By and by one would call out, "Mrs. Smith, here is a soul that has found peace in believing in Jesus."

That one would stand up and say a word, and then another would call out, "And here is another who wants to say a word," another and another would call out "Here's another," so I praised the Lord; and I remember how I was taken back, for I struck in to sing the old Coronation the way we sang it in America, "All Hail the Power of Jesus' Name," but no one joined, and I thought it was so strange. I went on with the first verse. I knew how it would have rung out at home, but I could not understand why they didn't sing; surely they must know it. They did, but the tune they sing in England is entirely different from that which is sung here.

There was a good Wesleyan brother that was speaking to those that were forward, and I turned to him and said, "Why don't they sing?" He says, "They don't know the tune." Then I said, "You start it to the tune they all know." And so he did.

My! how they sung it! And I learned that tune, though I did not like it at first; but now I do. Of course it don't beat the American tune, but still it is grand. Praise the Lord.

I don't know just the number that professed to receive peace that night, but I know it was a goodly number. To God be all the glory. That was my first work in England.

A few days later on I met some ladies from Liverpool who were members of Christ's Church, Everton, where Rev. Hay Adken was formerly rector. They had a large mothers' meeting. This lady, Mrs. Stavely, wanted to know if I would come to Liverpool and hold some meetings. I told her I would see about it and let her know later on. She was very pleasant, and I got to know her afterwards very well. She is among the dearest friends I have in England to-day. Her house is one of my homes. She received the blessing of full salvation when Rev. John Inskip and MacDonald were in England and went on their tour around the world.

Then Mrs. Johnson introduced me to a Mrs. Stephen Menzes, of Eggleston Hills, just out of Liverpool. She is a wonderful lady, does a marvelous work for the Young Women's Christian Association, and was its first organizer, I think. She invited Mrs. Johnson and some other friends to the hotel to dine, and invited me to meet these friends. They were very much interested to know my history and birth—if I was a slave, etc.

Then Mrs. Menzes arranged for me to come to Eggleston Hills. They had a large hall and did great work among the laboring class.

A day or so after that Canon Hopkins came to me with a letter from Lord Mount Temple, of Broadlands, in which his lordship invited me to their convention, to be held in August at Broadlands. I thanked him very kindly, of course. I didn't know who Lord Mount Temple was. I didn't know anything about Broadlands. Then I said, "Oh, I have heard Mrs. Johnson and Mrs. Bordman speak of it; I suppose they are all going, and Miss Smiley."

He smiled and said, "You are invited, Mrs. Smith."

I knew they had all been there, so I thanked him. I went home and told Mrs. Bordman of it, and she was very kind, but said she didn't think it was at all the thing for me to go to this convention. Well, I didn't know. I knew Mrs. Bordman was a good woman, and she would only say what she thought would be best for me. She said the doctrines and truths that were taught there were rather deep, and it might do me harm, and she only wanted to shield me.

Well, I could not understand it. I went upstairs to my room, took my Bible, got on my knees and began to pray the Lord to show me what His will was in regard to it. Clear and plain as my right hand, though I can't explain, but God showed me it was right I should go, so I thought no more of it.

Afterwards I told Mrs. Johnson. Oh, she thought it was dreadful; surely I must not go by any means. I prayed on. Clearer and clearer it came I was to go. I was invited to a Mr. Brathwait's, at Kendall, a very wealthy Quaker gentleman. Miss Smiley and Mrs. Johnson were there at the same time.

One day Miss S. came into my room—it was next hers—and said she felt impressed to come and warn me by no means to go to Broadlands. The Lord had always kept me so simple, and she had known of some who had been there who had got into a good deal of confusion in regard to these deep truths; the teaching there was so deep. Mrs. Johnson went out one morning, and when she came back she said she had word from Mrs. Menzes and that she was looking for me, and that I must surely go; anyhow, it wouldn't do for me to go to Broadlands, she was quite sure the Lord didn't want me there.

I could not make them understand it, but the more I prayed about it the clearer it was to my mind. Oh, I can't understand why they should hinder me, but I knew they did. I had told Mrs. Menzes when she first spoke to me, that I had been spoken to about this place, but that I could give four days before I went, if that would do, but after Mrs. J. came back a telegram came to me from Mrs. Menzes, saying that they would expect me on such a train, that meetings were arranged, so I went.

Mrs. Menzes met me at the station in her carriage. To my surprise, the first thing I saw were large placards with my name on, up against the railway station: "Amanda Smith, the *converted slave girl*, will sing and hold gospel meetings in Victoria Hall," giving the days and dates which I saw directly interfered with the time I was to go to Broadlands Conference, so I saw I was entirely planned out.

I said to Mrs. Menzes, "I have promised to go to Broadlands Conference, I told Mr. Hopkins that I would go, I remember that I told you I had."

"Well," she said, "you are advertised now and you can't possibly go, it will injure your influence greatly as a stranger, here in England. We think a great deal of it if you do not go when you are advertised."

Oh, how bad I felt. I was greatly tempted, and felt if I had had the money I would like to come home, but this was only a temptation, though I didn't get to Broadlands that year; but the next year did. Lord Mount Temple and Lady Beechman, and a number of others, came to Mr. Charlton's East End Mission one night where I was holding services and invited me again in person, and then, through the kindness of Mr. Edwin Clifford, Esq., I got to Broadlands, according to the will of the Lord.

Oh, how He blest me, and, I believe, made me a blessing to the people. I shall never forget the kindness of his Lordship and Lady Mount Temple. I was their guest in their home. Oh, what a home it was! how spacious, a regular palace.

When I went into dinner, Lord Mount Temple walked up to me and gave me his arm, and saying, "We will lead the way," took me into dinner and seated me at his right, and there I was, amid all that throng of English dignitaries. It was all new to me, in a sense, and yet I neither saw nor felt anything that was worth while being a fool over, for God had long since saved me, I believe, from foolish pride.

I believe It now, as I always believed it, in the Book: "Pride goeth before destruction, and a haughty spirit before a fall," and if I ever prayed for God to save me from anything it was from the foolishness of pride. Thank God, I believe he does, he keeps me saved.

I remember one morning in the conservatory where the morning meeting was held, Rev. Mr. Jukes and Mr. Geo. MacDonald gave a Bible reading. I saw nothing strange in it, it was beautiful to me. After this was over the meeting opened for those to testify who had received any special blessing. Mr. E. Clifford and I had hold a very interesting Gospel meeting on the evening before, so that when the meeting was opened for testimony there were a number who testified.

I felt the Lord laid it on me to give a bit of my own personal experience, how God converted and sanctified my heart, so I spoke, and the power of the Spirit seemed to come mightily upon all the people. Oh, what a stir; they wept and sobbed, and one woman was so baptized that she cried out and could not restrain herself. How the Lord helped me that morning. This work was very real in many hearts; even after I came from Africa I met a woman in Liverpool one night in the train, who said to me, "Do you remember the morning you spoke at Broadlands and gave your experience?"

"Yes."

"Do you remember some one crying out?"

"Yes."

"Well," she said, "that was I. Oh, God filled me that morning and I have never gotten over it, the trials have been severe, but, Oh,

I have been saved and kept and I am full of praise to-day. I am glad to see you, praise the Lord."

Her face was beaming with joy. That is only one instance, I don't know how many more, but God does, and that is enough. Amen.

I met with some things that were a little strange, but they didn't affect me any; for example: One morning after the breakfast was over, and after the prayer, we retired to the drawing room. Dr. Moxey and several others were in a very interesting conversation in regard to advanced views of spiritual things. One young clergyman, whose name I don't remember now, was saying, that somewhere in the part of the country where he lived he and his wife had attended some meetings where they were praying for the conversion of the Devil. Some one turned to me and said, "What do you think of that, Mrs. Smith?"

"Well," I said, "anybody that wants to do that is quite welcome as far as I am concerned, but I think he has a pretty big job on hand."

"Well," said they, "don't you see what a good thing it would be, Mrs. Smith, if only the Devil could be converted; you, and—referring to another evangelist that was present—and many other persons who are working so hard to get people saved, wouldn't have your work so often destroyed, for after all your work, he often upsets it all."

"Yes," I said, "I guess I will wait and see how you all come out."

Now, I didn't see anything in that that was so mysterious. The most mystery I saw about it was that people should spend time in such foolishness, when there is so much they might do that would be of permanent good.

After I got to England, the first money that was given me, about three days after, was five pound sterling and something over, equal to about twenty-five dollars. Some ladies at Keswick, said to Mrs. Johnson, "Who supports Mrs. Smith?" Of course they didn't tell me this, but they asked Mrs. Johnson all about it. She told them that I just trusted the Lord to supply all my needs, and so it went around quietly.

Mrs. J. came to me one morning and said to me, "Amanda, it is wonderful how the Lord is putting it into the hearts of the people to help you financially. Several have come to me and put in my hand money for you."

I thanked her very much.

"Several ladies have said they would hand me something this afternoon, when I get it together I will give it to you."

So when she handed it to me it was the amount that I have spoken of. Then I saw it was in direct answer to prayer, as I had asked the Lord on my way.

"Lord," I said, "confirm my coming to England by putting it into the hearts of the people to give me some money to help me after I get there, I am a stranger, no one knows me except Mrs. J. "

This is what I said to the Lord while I was on the steamer, and, now, three days after I land, this is the result. Surely the Lord is good. It is all wonderful, but it is just like Him. Blessed be his name.

Friday, Sept. 26th, 1878. This is a day that I had to regret. I had been invited to Lord Mount Temple's, through Rev. Mr. Hopkins, to go to the Broadlands Conference. When I told it to my dear American friends who were there, they thought it would not do for me to go at all. They said the teaching at that Conference was so deep, and they were afraid I would be confused, and it would not be good for me. And then, besides, for one like me to be entertained where there was so much elegance and style, it might make me proud and turn my head. But, poor things! they didn't know that I had always been used to a good deal of that, though in the capacity of a servant; so that no style or grandeur affected me at all.

But notwithstanding this invitation to me came directly from Lord Mount Temple's, they protested against my going. I prayed about it, and the Lord made it very clear to me that He wanted me at Broadlands. But as I was a stranger, and they bad been in England longer than I had, I yielded, but thought quietly in my mind that I would go anyhow.

But they so arranged it that I was to go to St. Helens, and take some meetings at Victoria Hall, at Mrs. Menzes'. And when I got there they had advertised me beyond the date when I was to go to Broadlands. And though I told them I had promised to go to Broadlands before, Mrs. Menzes said it would not do at all, after I was advertised; I would lose my influence for good; that that was one of the things they were very particular about in England. I knew nothing about the advertisement myself, and had nothing to do with it; but that I could not explain. So I did not go to Broadlands till the next year.

Monday, 29th. Quite a party of us take a carriage drive to Buttermere mountains. Oh, such a sight my eyes never beheld. The beauty and grandeur beggar description.

Wednesday, 31st. Had a nice meeting. Took a sixteen mile drive. Went to see the old church—seventeen hundred years old. I never saw antiquities in such profusion before.

Thursday, Aug. 1st. Tired, but saved. Go to Kendal, to Mr. Brathwaite's. Mr. Brathwaite is a very wealthy Quaker gentleman. I shall never forget their beautiful home, and their kindness to me, a stranger. God bless them. There I met Mrs. Johnson and Miss Smiley. Dear Miss Smiley, how solicitous she was for me! She came into my room one day and said she felt impressed to say to me that she thought I should not go to Broadlands. The Lord had blessed me so much, and it would be such a pity if I were to go there and be spoilt. Poor thing, how kind she was!

Saturday, Aug. 3d. I leave Keswick to-day for St. Helens. Arrive about three o'clock in the afternoon. Mrs. Menzes met me at the station with the carriage. The first thing that struck me when I got out of the carriage was large bills pasted up, beautiful pink paper, with black letters: "*Mrs. Amanda Smith, the Converted Slave from America, will give Gospel Addresses and Sing in Victoria Hall for so many days.*" My knees felt very weak, but there I was in for it.

Sunday, 4th. My first day at the Hall. It is a large hall, holding from six to eight hundred persons. It was right in a Roman Catholic settlement, and I was quite a novelty, being a woman, and a black woman, at that. So at night the meeting was crowded. But of all the audiences that I ever spoke to, I never before saw one so mixed— women with shawls over their heads, some with nothing on their heads at all, some barefoot, men and women respectable looking, others far from it, but on the whole all behaved well. Then there was a crowd that had gathered at the door to see me when I came out, and they almost pulled the clothes off of me it took four policemen to get me into the carriage, while the driver sat on the box and cut right and left with his whip to keep the way clear while he started. Of all the unearthly yells I ever heard, they gave them. This was all new to me. I had been around a good deal in America, and had been to many large meetings where there were thousands, but I had never seen anything like this before.

Monday, 5th. Praise the Lord, Oh, my soul.

> "The peace of Christ keeps fresh my heart,
> A fountain ever springing;
> All things are mine since I am His,
> How can I keep from singing?"

To-day we have a large field meeting, as they call it in England, a kind of picnic. I stood in a cart in this great big field, in the midst of five or six hundred people, and tried to talk to them, and sing. It was a difficult job and all new to me, but I did the beat I could.

CHAPTER XXI.

VISIT TO SCOTLAND, LONDON, AND OTHER PLACES— CONVERSATION WITH A CURATE—GREAT MEETING AT PERTH—HOW I CAME TO GO TO INDIA.

I think it was in September, 1878. I had met Miss Amars, of Galishields, Scotland, at the Keswick Conference. She was a highborn lady, and a typical Scotchwoman; and a more thoroughly consecrated, self-sacrificing lady, I think, I never met. Her mother, too, was an earnest Christian, and a staunch Scotch church woman. Miss Amars had a large mothers' meeting, and did all she could in every way to help the poor. And being a lady of wide influence, and using it for God, she did much good.

She was generally consulted about an evangelist, if one was to come to the town; she gave her influence and threw herself right into helping in every way; by visiting, and inviting people. There was a large hall where Evangelistic services were held every Sunday and through the week. So after Miss Amars had gone home from the Keswick Conference, where she had got a fresh anointing of the Spirit, she went to work at once, and prepared the way for my coming.

This was wonderful; for the Scotch Presbyterians are so conservative: and for a woman to talk before a mixed congregation of men and women was not to be thought of in Scotland. Whatever they did in England, or in the United States, they in Scotland could not venture that far.

The brother who had charge of the Evangelistic meetings in the hall, was more liberal than most of the brethren; and then knowing Miss Amars, as he did, he could not well refuse her when he told him of me. He consented to let me speak in his hall. I went at the time appointed. They had arranged entertainment for me at a very pleasant home, near by the hall, as they lived quite a little ways off, themselves.

Of course, I was quite a curiosity, to start with. The hall was crowded. It would hold about three hundred, or four hundred. The first two meetings, I saw they were a little afraid that I didn't know what I was going to do. But I was judicious and careful, and the Lord helped me wonderfully. By the time I held the third meeting one could not have told from their manner, and the hearty Scotch co-operation and sympathy with which they stood by me, but what they had been accustomed, not only to women preaching, but to black women, all their days.

Every night there were crowds. Many were turned away; they could not get in. The Lord gave me great liberty in speaking for Him, and many during the meeting professed to have found peace in believing. The first three nights I talked more directly to believers; I saw they were full of the knowledge of the truth, which is a marked characteristic of the Scotch people. They know their Bibles; but they need to know the Holy Ghost to quicken the Word into life and power.

At the close of the meeting one evening, a good, old brother said to me, softly, in his beautiful Scotch accent: "Sister Smith, I think you had better speak more to sinners."

"Yes," I said, "but you know there are many sinners in Zion, and I want them to wake up."

I often find when the truth hits that some one is very anxious you should go for the poor sinners. It is generally a sign that they want to be let alone. But when the Lord leads it is all right.

One morning a lady called to have a talk with me about the great salvation. She knew her Bible well, and was a staunch member of the church, and had been for years; but she had no assurance that she ever was converted. As she went on and told me her state, with tears, I asked the Holy Spirit to help me; and as I talked with her the Lord sent light into her heart; and there in Mrs. Amars' parlor the Holy Spirit witnessed to her heart that she was born of God. We knelt together, and for the first time in her life she opened her lips to pray and thank God for His great mercy, and testify to the family before she left that she had the assurance of her salvation. Praise the Lord! This was a wonderful victory.

My last meeting was held in one of the chapels. We had a large crowd, and though it was a week day morning, about nine o'clock, the chapel was almost crowded. Oh, what a blessed time we had!

If I could have stayed longer, there were other places that were open to me. This was an entering wedge. There had never been such a thing known as a woman talking to a mixed congregation, and that in the hall was remarkable; but when a chapel opened its doors, that was a departure. These were some of the Lord's doings in beautiful Scotland.

While I was there, as the winter was coming on, and was my first winter in England, I needed a cloak, and I had been thinking about it. I had to send money home to my daughter, and I thought I could not see how I was going to spare the money to get me a cloak. So I prayed, and asked the Lord to open a way that I might get a jacket, or something comfortable, for the winter. A fur-lined cloak was what I would have liked to have; but they were four and five and six guineas, and I knew I could not afford to pay that. No one knew that these thoughts were in my mind but the Lord. Miss Amars, and Miss Knowles, her friend from England, proposed taking me to Edinburgh for a day. As the meetings were only held at night, I could go about anywhere in the day. Edinburgh was about an hour and a half's ride from Galishields. I was very glad to go.

It was a beautiful morning. We left about eight o'clock. I had read about John Knox, and his persecution by Mary Queen of Scots, and I thought I would like to see the house where he had lived, for I had heard it was still standing.

The first thing after we got to Edinburgh these ladies said to me, "We want to do a little shopping before we go around sightseeing." They asked if I would like to go into the shop. I said, "Oh, yes."

They had planned to get me a cloak, but I did not know it. So they took me into one of the large shops, and into the cloak department, and the first thing I knew they began to fit cloaks on me. I held my breath; for I thought it could not be that I was going to get a fur cloak. But Miss Knowles told me that she wanted to give me a fur cloak. And so they got me a very nice cloak costing six guineas. My! I walked out of there swell!

Then the next thing was to see John Knox's house; to get a view of this old home, we walked along High street, and into the famous Canongate. This is the best way. There are tall; wierd, old houses on either hand, and among them the narrow home of John Knox; a strange looking building, adjoining a church; there

were steps going up from the outside, rickety looking, wooden steps. There was a sign hanging out, with the picture of John Knox in the attitude of prayer. I stood and looked at it, and thought, "Can it be possible that after all these years God has permitted one like me to be on this very ground where that man walked, and to stand and look at his house?" And I thought of what God had done through that mighty man of faith and prayer, and that He had favored me with such a privilege.

Then we visited St. Giles and the old abbey, Holyrood Palace, and the castle. The palace is open to visitors, and contains many objects of interest. Among these are the apartments of the ill-fated Queen Mary. In going through these apartments and having different parts explained, I was greatly interested; they were old in style to what they would be now, yet the remains of grandeur and splendor were there. The bed that the Queen slept in, with its lace and curtains, was said to be just the same.

From there we went to the museum. Among the things of interest we saw there was the frame of the pulpit in which John Knox preached. That was the first time I had ever seen stocks. I had read of Paul being in stocks in prison, but I never knew what it meant till I saw them in Edinburgh. Another thing we saw there was a stool, which was connected with an incident both historical and amusing. When the liturgy of Archbishop Laud was introduced into Scotland, the south end of the transept, which was used as a kirk, was the scene of this incident. The Bishop of Edinburgh held services there after the form prescribed by Laud. He had just asked the Dean to read the collect for the day, when a woman named

Jennie Geddes attempted to stop him by hurling at his head the stool on which she was sitting. He dodged it, but the blow was fatal to the effort to force Episcopacy upon reformed Scotland.

The chief sight of Edinburgh is the castle. It stands on the summit of a lofty and abrupt hill, and commands the city and surrounding country. How many things I learned from what they told me about all these. The Scotch ladies, as well as the English, are so well versed in the history of their country that they can with ease detail almost any event of any time. I never had met anybody that could do this so satisfactorily as they did for me. If my memory could only have retained what they told me, I would have had quite a little store of history laid up. All the bits of

history I had read about were explained to me over and over again. How beautiful it all was, and what a pleasant time.

It was all very interesting to me as the ladies described and explained it as we went along. They were familiar with the names, and I was quite familiar with them from hearing so much while there, and I thought I would never forget them. But after having the African fever so much I find my memory is quite weak, and I am so sorry I have forgotten the names of so many places and things.

By this time it was noon, and Miss Knowles proposed that we go to the Y. M. C. A. She had a special desire to go there and once more stand on the spot where she first stood up, at the meetings Mr. Moody was holding, and decided for Christ.

She was a beautiful young lady, in high position, with all the worldly pleasure and enjoyment at her hand, and was much admired as a society lady, and when Mr. Moody was holding meetings at Edinburgh she thought she would go and hear him. She was on a visit at that time in Scotland. Her home was in Southport, England. And as Mr. Moody went on with his address the Spirit of the Lord took hold of her and she yielded her heart fully to God, and from that hour gave up all that seemed to be so dear, as the world would call it. But she never had a regret. She turned right away from it without a lingering look behind. How beautiful! She used to come to my room and ask me to pray for her. How often we have knelt down and prayed together!

> "When we are willing with all things to part,
> He gives us our bounty, His love in our heart."

Praise Him, praise Him, Jesus our wonderful Redeemer.

So we went into the hall. They were not having a meeting that day. Miss Knowles took me to the spot and showed me where she sat and where she stood, the very spot. Her face beamed with light and joy as she seemed to live it all over again. And how she thanked and praised the Lord for giving her the courage to take the step that day.

Then we called on some friends and had an elegant lunch, and after this beautiful day of sight-seeing we returned again to Galishields, and after a little rest we were off again to the meeting. I was very tired, but the Lord gave us great blessing that night in the meeting.

Sunday, Nov. 8th, 1878. My first Sunday in London. I go to Wesley Chapel, and, Oh, to see one pray out of a book in the Methodist Church was so different from what I had ever expected. I shall never forget the text and the sermon. Everything seemed so formal and dead in comparison with what I had been accustomed to in our Methodist Churches in America. Even the seating of the people seemed formal; or, in other words, to me, it seemed dead. What confirmed it more was, when the minister took his text from Rev. 14:13, "Blessed are the dead that die in the Lord, yea, even so saith the Spirit, for they rest from their labors, and their works do follow them;" and I said to my self, "I guess there is a funeral sermon to be preached." And I thought he would make some reference to the person who had died, though I saw no sign of any who might be taken to be the parties who had lost relatives, save here and there in the congregation was some one dressed in black. But he went on, and I concluded when he was through that there was nothing to do but to bury them, for they were all dead, and the funeral sermon was preached.

Wednesday, Dec. 11th, 1878. Prof. Harris, of Cambridge, called to-day. Had a nice season of prayer together. Invites me to Cambridge.

Tuesday, 24th. I get a number of letters written to-day. About six o'clock a knock comes at my door. A servant Comes and says the expressman has brought a hamper for me.

"No," I said, "it cannot be for me. Nobody would send me a hamper. Nobody knows me here. It is a mistake."

"Yes, it is for you, Amanda Smith."

"No," I said, "it cannot be. Go down and tell the man it is a mistake. I'm not expecting anything."

So off she went. By and by she came back, laughing. She says, "The man says you must come and sign the book. It is for you. He was to leave it here."

Well, I went downstairs, and, lo! and behold, there it was. It was the first time I had ever had a Christmas hamper sent me. And it was packed full of the nicest Christmas things I ever had. I was astonished beyond expression. We went to work to take out the things. There was a beautiful cake, fine French candy, almonds, nuts, raisins, everything elegant; and down at the side I saw a beautiful album, and when I took it out I saw the secret, for there was Miss Morris' photo and a letter, with the compliments of the season. Then I knew she had sent it. So characteristic of her to think of the needs of any one, and then to think of me, a stranger, in a strange land. I cannot tell how I felt. I have no language to describe my deep appreciation and thanksgiving. She met me first at Keswick, and I learned to love her then; and after I had been at her home, and shared her hospitality and the friendship or her sister, Miss Anna, and Mrs. Richard Morris, I shall never forget her. May God ever bless her memory.

One time in London a young curate came to me to have a talk. He wanted to convince me in regard to the transubstantiation. He said he was rather a good High Churchman. He said the dissenters were wrong. He believed some of them were good, and it was such a pity they should be so wrong in their views or knowledge in regard to the Holy Communion.

"Now," said he, "you take the wine and bread figuratively, but don't you know that you are to take it as the real literal body of Jesus and blood of Jesus? But your faith must so take it that it really is changed, while in the act of being taken into the real body of the Lord Jesus, and into the real blood."

Well, I could not understand it. He explained and explained, and explained! I told him I could not see it that way. Then he went on in a very elaborate manner to bring illustrations and evidences to show and prove. I listened. He talked to me two hours.

I did not know what else to say, or at least I felt I did not want to say anything, for surely I was tired and felt the whole thing sounded to me like bosh; but still I was patient, and prayed the Lord to give me grace to hold still. Finally I said to him, after a great explanation, "Oh, that is the way you understand it."

Then he drew up his chair, thinking he had convinced me thoroughly, to make his final conclusion.

"Well," I said to him, "there is only one thing about it that is hard for me to do."

"Now, what is that, Mrs. Smith?" with such an air of complacency, as though he could soon clear that away.

"Why, it has always been such a hard thing for me to believe what I know is not true."

My! he was thunderstruck!

"Well," he said, "Mrs. Smith, I feel so sorry to think that a good woman like you should be deceived; but I will come and have a talk with you again; I like to talk with you. Sometimes when I talk to persons they seem to get so tired and vexed; but you are so patient and quiet."

I thanked him very kindly, and he left. Then I got down on my knees and said, "Oh, Lord, Lord, don't ever let that man come back any more, for I don't want to talk any more; I am tired. Amen."

"Well," I thought, "if you knew how disgusted I felt inside, you would think I got vexed, anyhow."

So the good curate never came back again and I was free.

I met with many strange things in different places in England, strange views of all sorts. I don't, know whether it is worse there than here, but the isms and cisms and fanatics—dear me, where are they not? They are like the flies and frogs of Egypt, all over; but they that trust in the Lord shall be as Mount Zion, which shall never be moved.

August 9th, 1879, I leave Keswick for Darlington with Miss Fothergil. Miss Fothergil has a very large and interesting Bible class of young men She is a great worker and organizer of Christian work. So at nine o'clock in the morning we went to this Bible class. I suppose there were two hundred men. Of course there were other workers engaged as helpers. It was a beautiful sight to see these men—working men—all engaged in studying the Word of God for an hour on Sunday morning.

At eleven o'clock we attended at the Friends' meeting house; no singing, or praying, or preaching, unless the Spirit moves. But I felt quite comfortable to sit and be quiet.

Monday, August 11th. I leave Darlington to-day for Broadlands Conference, Lord Mount Temple's. As I had been disappointed in not getting to go the year before, Lord Mount Temple was very kind, and when I was holding meetings at Charington Hall, at Stepney, London, he, with a number of his friends, came one night to the meeting, and he invited me personally to come to the conference next year. It did seem as though I was to be defeated this time, as I had been before, in going. But my dear friend, Mr. Edward Clifford, felt so sure that the Lord wanted I should go there, that he kept writing and urging me to come; and I was well persuaded that he was not wrong.

I was royally entertained at Lord Mount Temple's home. And God gave me favor among the people, and great blessing in song and testimony. Though everything was done very differently in regard to the meeting from what I had been accustomed to in America, yet the Lord seemed to get me through.

I remember the first day of the meeting. It was a beautiful day, and there were great numbers of people; and as we came in from the beautiful orangery, the hall where the meeting was held, and went into the house to dinner, as I stood in the great, spacious hall, and the ladies and gentlemen were waiting to go to dinner, Lady Mount Temple came down stairs and came up to me and put her arms around my neck and kissed me before all the people.

I was a little embarrassed, though I felt it was real. But no one knew whether I blushed or not, or whether I was really embarrassed; so far as my color was concerned, they could not perceive it. One good thing— there is no chameleon about me!

Then when we were ready to go to dinner Lord Mount Temple came up to me and said, "Mrs. Smith, take my arm." And we led the way to the dining room.

My! I thought. It was the first time in all my life that I was ever escorted by a gentleman to dinner in such style.

Dinner was something that I had always managed to get to without any help! But then, this was the order of the day. I soon found that this was the custom in England, for many times afterward I had that honor, and I have also had the same honor conferred upon me in America.

How well I remember the first time. When Dr. Newman, who is now Bishop Newman, was pastor of the Metropolitan Church in Washington, and Brother Inskip held that great tent meeting, I was at that meeting. Dr. Newman invited Brother Inskip to hold their closing service at his church. So they did. There was a meeting arranged for nine o'clock in the morning, in the lecture room, for ladies; and at noon the ministers were invited to a meeting upstairs in the audience room, and at night Brother Inskip preached. Then they left the next morning.

I was invited next day by Mrs. Newman to dine with them. I went at the hour appointed. Mrs. Newman was very kind, and after I went upstairs and laid off my things, we went down to dinner. Brother McDonald and some of the other brethren were also invited. When we got down into the parlor Dr. Newman came and said, "Take my arm, Mrs. Smith;" and we led the way; and he gave me the seat of honor at his right.

How well I remember the pleasant time we had, and the excellent dinner. What a gentle, sweet spirit seemed to pervade their home at that time. After the dinner was through, we remained at the table, talking. Dr. Newman said to me, "Now, Amanda, here is our William;" (referring to the colored butler); "we are very interested for our William; he is not converted, and I want you to talk to him. I buried his sister about a week ago. She was a good Christian. And William ought to be converted."

Then I turned to William and began to talk. We talked awhile, and William stood and looked very serious; and then Dr. Newman suggested that I sing, and Brother McDonald suggested what he thought would be a good thing, and we joined and sang.

Just in the midst of our singing the bell rang, and William had to answer it. When he came in he spoke to Mrs. Newman and told her who it was, and Mrs. Newman went out into the parlor, and in a little while she came back bringing a lady with her, whom she introduced as her friend, Mrs. C. I had met Mrs. C. the day before. Mrs. Newman had introduced me to her, and told me how she was seeking the Lord. After she was seated, Dr. Newman said, "Now, Amanda, I think you had better sing us another piece." So something else was suggested, and we joined and sang.

While we were singing, I noticed that Mrs. C. could hardly control her emotions. I knew the Spirit of the Lord had taken hold of her heart. Then Dr. Newman said, "Now we will have, a season of prayer."

So right there in the dining room we just knelt and prayed around; each one prayed. And when it came my turn it seemed to me I never was so helped in prayer. I prayed especially for this lady. I felt that God would bless her. Sure enough, when we rose from our knees, her burden was all gone and she was happy. She wrote me a beautiful letter while I was in Africa, and told me the blessing she received that day, had remained with her; and, though she had passed through a great deal of trouble, yet she had never lost the peace and blessing that came to her that day.

I thought at that time how wonderful it was for Mrs. Newman to bring that lady into her dining room when I was there. I know some ladies who would have been ashamed to let it be known that I was in their dining room.

Then I went down stairs and had a little visit with the old servant. She, too, bore testimony to Mrs. Newman's kindness to them. She said to me, "I used to live with Mrs. Newman's mother. Miss—, (calling her by her maiden name) was always kind. She has not changed a bit. Sometimes when they have little evening parties, and have ice cream, after the people are all gone, Mrs. Newman will come downstairs and ask if there was any cream left for William and me; and if there was not, she will send out if it was ten o'clock at night, so we may have our part. This treatment to you is not put on. I know them." Of course, this was all before Dr. Newman was Bishop.

Thursday, August 14th. I leave Broadlands for Salisbury. Rev. Mr. Thwaites invites me to come to Salisbury and hold some meetings. I was entertained at Fisherton Rectory.

Monday, 18th. I leave for Eastbourne, Miss Mason's house of rest. Here I meet many of the workers who are there for a week's rest, or more. How good of the Lord to give me this privilege, and these few days of quiet and rest.

Friday, 29th. Leave Eastbourne. Spend the evening with Miss Drake, at Dr. Bordman's, Rochester Square, London. She is on her way back to India.

Sunday, 31st. Mr. Richard Morris arranges a meeting at the Y. M. C. A. The Lord gave me great liberty in speaking, and we had a good time.

September 1st, 1879. I leave Doncaster for the great Perth, Scotland, Conference. These meeting's are held annually, and are very marked for blessing. I was asked to come a week before the Conference convened, and hold some preparatory meetings, so as to add to the interest of blessing at the Conference. Mrs. Gordon, of Park Hill, Aberdeen, and Mrs. Douglas were among the prominent ladies in the church, and they had arranged for my entertainment. I was met at the station by three Christian workers. When I stepped out of the train they came right up to me, and were so cordial and kind, I felt quite at home with them. They never allow you to carry anything; they just take your hand-bag, and go at once and see after your baggage, so that everything is made so easy for you. For this, I always praises the Lord.

I noticed they had bundles of hand bills, and were giving them to everybody. So I said, "You are trying to advertise well."

"Oh, yes," they said: "The people are very hard to get out to a Gospel meeting."

"Is that so?" I said, "I thought the Scotch people turned out well."

"The fact is, Mrs. Smith, we people have had the Gospel so much that we have become Gospel hardened, I think. When an evangelist does come, he always has to work a week before the people get interested and come out in any numbers. So you must not be discouraged, Mrs. Smith. Mr. Scrogey, from Ireland, was here some time ago, and he always gets more out than anyone else, and yet it was a week before there was any marked interest in the meetings. The people were so tardy about coming out."

"Indeed."

"We have a small hall, that will hold about a hundred, and we thought we would commence there first; then, if the meetings increased, we have a larger hall close by; it holds about three hundred and fifty."

"Oh, my," I said, "I thought the Scotch people were people of great faith; but you only have got faith for two hundred people. You must do better than that."

They laughed and said, "But, Mrs. Smith, you don't know the people."

"No," I said, "but I know the Lord, and He says, 'ask largely.' "

"Well," they said, "we will see to-night."

"They don't know," I thought, "that I am God's bulletin board, and to be even a sign post for God has its reward. However, I will not tell them. We will see."

So, as we walked on, they said, seemingly to prepare me, and cheer me. "Of course, Mrs. Smith, you will not feel embarrassed, for there will only be women allowed in the meeting."

"Why?"

"Well, we supposed you were not accustomed to speaking before men; go there will be no men allowed in."

"Oh," I said, "I don't mind speaking before men at all. At some of our camp meetings in America I have talked to two and three thousand— men and women, girls and boys, young and old."

They were astonished out of measure. So nothing further was said on the subject.

When evening came we went to the hall. It was packed and crowded; and all outside the door and along the street, so that I never got in at all. They took me to a house near by to wait till they lighted up the large hall, which took about twenty minutes, till all was settled. Then I went in.

As I passed down the aisle I saw three men had slipped in, and they leaned forward so as not to let me see them; and I never let on. Poor fellows; they were waiting every minute to be told to go out, and they were quite ready; they would have moved out at a word.

I went on, gave out my hymn, and opened the meeting; after prayer, I began my address. I never referred to the men, or said a word about what I had been accustomed to in America. As I talked on, the men began to raise themselves up and sit erect. My! I shall never forget their faces. They seemed to look glad. The Lord helped me to speak.

The next night six men came in. I went right on, and said nothing to them whatever. The third day two ladies called to see me. They were much interested in the meeting, and were very wealthy, and so carried on the principal part of the finances of the mission. They were very kind indeed to me. They were maiden ladies, sisters. So they came in their carriage to protect me, and see that I was not intruded upon by the men coming in. When we got to the hall there were seven or eight men. I saw these ladies looked very sharp and surprised. I went on and opened the meeting with a lively hymn; and the Scotch can sing, depend upon it. Then I asked some one to lead in prayer; and one of the lady workers did so, but it was very faint. Poor thing, I knew it was a struggle; fortunately it was not lengthy. So we rose, and I gave out the next hymn.

While they sang I noticed a great deal of quiet whispering and uneasiness; these good ladies were very nervous; I was greatly amused. Just before I began my address, one of them said to me, "Now, Mrs. Smith, there are those men; and they know quite well this is a meeting for women only; and they know they should not be in here. If you would like, I will speak to them, and have them go out."

"Oh, no," I said, "I don't mind; I think they came with their wives; I saw one man bring the baby and give it to the mother; and it they behave themselves it's all right; I want to talk to the women about their souls, and their salvation; and that is what the men need as well."

"Then it don't embarrass you to have the men present?"

"Not in the least," I said. And she sat down, comfortably surprised; and I had no further trouble about the men coming to meeting with the women. They did seem glad. They would shake hands with me, and say, "Lord bless you," and they smiled, and I suppose they thought I had given them the best chance they had ever had to get into a mixed meeting.

The Sunday night of the great Conference, in the large town hall, holding eleven hundred or twelve hundred people, Lady Hope, wife of Sir James Hope, an excellent Christian lady, known all over England and Scotland for her earnest Christian work among the navvies and working men, for the first time in her life, after I had sung "Whosoever," addressed a large audience of men and women.

They listened with profoundest interest to the Gospel address. It was a new epoch in Scotch history, for a woman to speak before a company of that kind, on such an occasion. I held meetings for a week after the Conference had closed; and in that same hall on the following Sunday night, a hundred stood up for prayers, mostly men, with tears running down their faces, and trembling as they stood. They didn't pop up and down in a minute, as we often see it here, but they rose and stood. Oh, what a night that was! The workers, though there were a great number, seemed to be astounded, and didn't know what to do. The Lord of Hosts was with us and helped us.

I remember a dear old woman, with a white cap on, and her Bible open in her lap. I went to speak to her. She was weeping bitterly. She knew her Bible almost by heart; there was not a promise I could mention but she knew it. She said, "Yes, Mrs. Smith, I know that, and I have read it over and over; but I have never had the assurance of my salvation, and I don't know that I am saved. I want to know it."

"Well," I said, "God wants you to know it; and you do know His Word; but it is the Spirit that quickeneth; so ask the Lord to give you His Spirit, and quicken the Word in your heart."

"Yes," she said, "I think it may be that."

"Have you ever praised the Lard for His precious Word?"

"Well," she said, "I try to be thankful, but then I don't know as I ever have really praised Him."

"Well," I said, "praise Him for what He has done, and trust Him to give you His Spirit of assurance."

And she did right away, and in a little while was as happy as a bride. My! how beautiful! Oh, how the blessed Spirit came to her heart! filled her with peace and joy. Praise the Lord for His mercy.

Then the Rev. Mr. Blank asked me to take a week's service in his church. He had an assistant pastor, And he himself had to be away.

This was a very new thing; to be in a Scotch kirk; a woman, and a black woman; who ever heard of such a thing? But the assistant pastor was a very earnest Christian worker, and took right hold, and the Lord was with us. Every night the house was crowded; they had galleries all around, and they were filled. They used the Gospel Hymns to sing in, and then they had their own Book of Psalms. How many dear old people, men and women. How they cheered me! They all joined in these hymns and sang heartily.

The third night of the meeting, one old gentleman came up to me, and whispered softly, calling me aside; and in his beautiful broad Scotch, he said, "Mrs. Smith, the old people would be much better pleased if you would open the meeting and close with a Psalm. We are used to singing the Psalms. The young people like the Gospel Hymns; but just for the older people, I will just put that in your ear."

Then giving me a little pinch on the arm, he turned away. I saw it in a moment. I said nothing, but the next evening I opened the service by giving out a Psalm. I never did such a thing before, and never had heard of it, and hardly knew which to give out; but they knew them all, so I ventured. I think it was the one hundred and third Psalm. However, it seemed to be just the right one; and the faces of those old people lighted up; they thought I was the nicest kind of a woman! And I thought I had heard singing before, but when I struck that Psalm it was the most beautiful thing I ever heard. So I got converted over right then and there to Psalm singing; though I had not backslid over any of the old Hymns that I had learned in days of yore. And if I lived in Scotland I should learn how to sing the Psalms.

We went on with that meeting for a week. The Lord gave us great blessing. Many souls were strengthened and blessed, while some for the first time decided for Christ.

September 20, 1879. Leave Perth for Aberdeen. Sunday afternoon, Park Hill Chapel, Mr. Gordon's. Mr. Gordon had built a large chapel in the town, and employed an evangelist by the name of Mr. Anderson; a grand, good man. He often had evangelists come and help Mr. Anderson with the meetings. So this was a new field for a woman to work in, in a mixed congregation, as was also the case in Perth.

Then the Spirit of the Plymouth brethren was so very strong in every direction. Of course, Father Anderson himself was on the straight line.

I remember one afternoon it was with great difficulty that I got into the church; they had afternoon meetings, and the crowds were simply enormous. I was to give a Bible reading that afternoon. The Lord had given us great blessings in the evening meetings. A number of souls professed to have found peace in believing. We had glorious times.

The work seemed to be signally blessed of God. But the good Plymouth brethren did not see it at all, because I was a woman; not that I was a black woman, but a woman. Paul had said: "Let your women keep silence in the churches," and it was a great violation of Paul's teachings. They would try, in a nice way, to get me into an argument; but I always avoided anything of the kind; for it is like bodily exercise which profiteth little.

One afternoon, as I was in the crowd trying to press my way through, a number of these brethren were at the door waiting for me, and they handed me a great epistle, with passages of Scripture quoted in most every other line. My! they are tremendous on quoting Scripture! I took the letters, and, to their surprise, instead of reading them before I began to talk, I put them in my pocket and went on. What they meant was, that I was to read the letters, and then they had their questions all propounded. But I just went on. My! how the Lord helped that afternoon, and we had a good meeting. So I think they gave me up in disgust, for I heard no more of them after that.

And here let me tell how it all came about that I got to go overland, and so to see Paris and the continent.

It was through my dear friend, Miss Morris, and that grand, good man, Lord Mount Temple, and my true friend, Mr. E. Clifford, with whom I had labored at the Broadlands Conference, and in London, at Mr. Charrington's, Victoria Hall. He had been on a tour through Scotland, and hearing of my intention to

leave England for India, on his way home he came through Galishields and stopped off to see me. I shall never forget his untiring kindness. But he said he was afraid I was making a mistake in leaving England, for the Lord had blessed me so greatly there; everywhere I went He had given me blessing, which he thought ought to serve as a clear indication that my work was not yet done in England.

I admitted it all, for it was true; but down deep in my heart God had put a clear conviction; and then in answer to prayer had made outward circumstances very plain, and I knew well that it was He that was leading, though I could not explain.

So when he saw that I was settled in my decision, and when I told him that Miss Drake, the lady with whom I was going, was going overland, he said, "By all means, go overland; and, you must see all of Paris, and Rome, and the continent that you can."

When he rose to go he gave me a five pound note and said, "Now, I give you this to spend going about, to as to see all you can. You may never have another chance."

That was true. I never expect to have another such opportunity. I thanked him kindly, but thought to myself, "I don't mean to spend twenty-five dollars sight-seeing."

We went through on a more economical scale. But I saw what I called many wonderful things, through the kindness of this gentleman and other friends, for I had asked the Lord definitely to open a way for me, that I might get to see Paris and Rome, that I had heard so much about.

My going to India came about in this way: I was at Eastbourne, England. Dear Miss Mason has a very pretty home at Eastbourne, by the sea, where tired Christian workers may go for a little change and rest, just as she has in London. To this she invited me for a little rest, as I was weary and needed the change. The charge was very moderate, and then the spiritual help was what one needs so much. Praise the Lord for this oasis in the desert. Then to think that I should be thus highly favored. But it is the Lord's doings, and it is marvelous in our eyes.

While at Eastbourne I had a letter from my friend, Mrs. Dr. Bordman, in London. She said, "Who do you think is in London, and at my house? Lucy Drake. She is on her way back to India. She was delighted to hear from you, and wants you to call and see her on your way to Doncaster, as you have to pass through London."

I had known Miss Drake well years before; and I was so glad to see her again. I called, and we had a good old-fashioned chat, and a season of prayer. She said she had a conviction that the Lord wanted me to go to India. I told her I didn't see it in that light at all. She told me of all her plans, and told me to pray earnestly for light on my own path; "For," she said, "I'm quite sure the Lord wants you to go."

"I have I so much work to do here In England," I said, "and calls are coming in constantly from all directions, so that I could not go."

"If the Lord wants you He will make it clear."

"All right."

So we parted. I went on to Perth, Scotland. A few days after, I had a letter from Miss Drake, saying, "The Lord has made it clear to me for you to go to India, and I have told some friends, and they have handed me some money for you for your expenses."

"Well," I said, as I read the letter, "Miss Drake needn't do that, for I am not going to India at all."

I had never prayed a bit about it, although she had told me to do so. A few days later a letter came, saying, "It is wonderful how the Lord is answering prayer about your going to India. Dr. Mahan has just come in and handed me twenty pounds from Lord Mount Temple toward your expenses."

And I said, as I stood by the mantel shelf, reading the letter, "I know the reason Miss Drake thinks the Lord wants me to go with her to India; she is alone, and she doesn't like to travel alone, and it is easy to see the Lord in it; and I don't care, I have work enough to do now, without going off to India; and I'm not going."

Just then a voice seemed to say to me, clear and distinct, "You have been saying you would not go to India all the time, and you have never asked the Lord what His will is."

"That is true," I said, "Oh, Lord, forgive me."

There was no one in the dining room, and just in the corner by the mantel, stood an old-fashioned Scotch arm chair; I turned and knelt down by it, and burying my face in the cushion, and weeping, I prayed the Lord to forgive me for my impertinence, and if He wanted me to go to India, to make it very clear and plain to me, and I would obey Him, and leave all and go. Only I wanted to be sure that it was Himself speaking.

I cannot tell how, but as I waited before Him, He made it as plain as day to me that I was to go. I praised Him, and rose from my knees, without the least shadow of a doubt in my mind.

I had an engagement at Aberdeen, which I saw I would have time to fill before leaving. My other engagements I canceled, and explained how the Lord had changed me about. I wrote Miss Drake and told her I would go, and that I wanted to go overland. Then she wrote to say that she had enough means if I went all the way by sea. I could go to Liverpool and take the steamer and meet her at Suez. I wrote and told her I believed the Lord would let me go overland, and so see Paris and Rome. My! how the letters flew!

I went on to Aberdeen, and took up my week's services. Then I had a letter from Mrs. Bordman advising me to go by sea from Liverpool, and so save a hundred dollars; but I must let Miss Drake know by return mail whether I would go overland or by steamer from Liverpool, as she must telegraph and secure the staterooms.

After I had read this letter, and thought it all over, I arose and got all the little money I had, and counted it out; it was fifteen or sixteen pounds.

I wanted to send home to my daughter, who was in school, three months' board, and that would take it nearly all; and now I must give an answer by return mail. So I took Mrs. Bordman's letter, and the money, and spread them on the bed, and got down on my knees, and there seemed to come over me a spirit of desperation and faith as I told the Lord. I said, "Lord, Thou knowest my heart; how I have longed to see these great cities and the continent. And now, though it will cost more to go overland than to go all the way by sea, yet all the means are Thine, and I am Thy child; and if it can please Thee, grant me this desire."

And as I waited before the Lord, the Spirit whispered these words distinctly: "All things whatsoever ye ask in prayer believing, ye shall receive." And I said, "Lord, I believe you will give me the money to go overland."

And I arose from my knees, and sat down and wrote by return mail and said, "Please tell Miss Drake to secure my stateroom; I will go overland with her."

My heart was as light as a feather. My dear friend, Miss Morris, on her way home to Doncaster, stopped in London to see Miss Drake, before I got there, and made up all the deficiency, and then she wrote and said how sorry she was that I had not told her my need.

"For," she said, "you know, Amanda, I have always told you to let me know when you really needed any thing. I went to see

Miss Drake, and she is very nice, and I like her very much. I was very much interested in all she told me of her work in India. I asked her to tell me frankly if she needed any help for you in any way, and she told me what was lacking on the expenses, and I was so glad to give it to her."

So the Lord in this, verified his promise, "All things whatsoever ye ask in prayer believing, ye shall receive." I think I can see now that God wanted me in Africa, and He had to send me to India to educate me a little before He could tell me to go to Africa. I'm sure if He had told me in Scotland He wanted me to go to Africa, I should have made a bee-line for the, United States. But, oh, how good the Lord is. I shall evermore praise Him, and thank Him for all the great privilege of seeing what I did on the continent and in Egypt. How wonderfully He answered prayer through these instrumentalities. First of all, Miss Drake, and then Lord Mount Temple, and Miss Morris, and Mr. Clifford, and others. How wonderful it all seems.

CHAPTER XXII.

IN PARIS—ON THE WAY TO INDIA—FLORENCE—ROME— NAPLES—EGYPT.

Saturday, September 4th. We go around to see something of Paris. My! The wonders; not strange, perhaps, to others, but to me; the statuary, and parks, and buildings were lovely to behold.

Sunday, 5th. A beautiful, bright morning. My heart was full of praise as I woke and looked out upon the beauty. But how sad I was in a little while as I saw the buildings going up, men hauling stones, laundries open, everything just like Saturday. Others were going to church.

"Oh," I said, "is this fashionable, wicked Paris, to which the eyes of the Christian world are turned for their first fashions and imitations?" And as I thought of it I felt sad. At church time we attended the Wesleyan Church. It was communion Sunday The minister preached a grand sermon from the words: "Christ gave himself."

Monday, 6th. We go sight-seeing again. One of the places which interested me a great deal was the porcelain works. There I saw where this beautiful china is made. And as the man turned the different articles that he wished to make, from the finest little cup to the largest vase, I thought what complete power the potter had over the clay. There was no dictating from the clay. The potter had full control. At one time he would take a piece of the clay and make one kind of an article; then he would turn the same piece of clay into another kind of an article; sometimes a beautiful pitcher, then a mug, then a basin, and in all shapes whatsoever he willed he made the clay. And then he showed us some with the most exquisite flowering on them that were to be put in the furnace at a certain time, and the fire would bring out all the fine pretty marks and colors.

As I stood and heard his explanation, my heart caught fire; and I thought how much that is like the blessed Master. Sometimes what brings out the beautiful character is the furnace. And I said, "Oh, Lord, help me to be in Thy hands as this clay is in the potter's hands; and even when the furnace comes, to submit, and not dictate."

> "Pains, furnace, heat, within me quiver;
> God's breath upon the flame doth blow;
> And all my heart within me quivers,
> And trembles at the fiery glow.
> Yet I say trust Him as God wills,
> And in His hottest fire hold still."

In one of the avenues not far from this place (I'm sorry I can't remember the name), a very wide avenue, with beautiful trees on either side, almost making an arch, there were long rows of gypsy wagons, with everything to sell; a kind of fair—"Vanity Fair." The minute I saw this it brought to my mind a dream that I had had twenty-three years before. Oh, how marvelous! Everything was almost just as I had dreamed it, twenty-three years before!

We leave Paris at two o'clock in the. afternoon, and travel all night.

Tuesday, September 7th. Reach Turin to-night at eight-thirty.

Wednesday, 8th. Leave this morning for Florence. Reach there at nine at night. Spend the next day sight-seeing. As we traveled by what is called Cooke's coupon system which is very convenient, and gives you every information of places of interest, etc., and as Miss Drake had all that part of the arrangement to attend to, I did not even as much as note the names of the hotels where we stopped in my diary, only, perhaps, once, though I was familiar with all the names and places at the time.

We had a guide given us. We first visited the great Uffizi gallery, with its wonderful collection of works of art, such as I had never seen before, and never shall again. Here was the first time I ever remember hearing the name of the great painter, Michael Angelo.

There was so much that was beautiful, that I could take in but a very little of the whole. I was wonderfully struck with the bust and head of Negro when a boy of ten or fourteen. His countenance was sullen, and I could almost see him as he decided against Christians.

The next place we went to was the National Museum and gallery of fine arts. Here again was pointed out to us the bust of the great sculptor and painter, Michael Angelo, who is held in loving, if not sacred remembrance. It was he who furnished the model for the great dome of St. Peter's of Rome. All this was new to me, and some things I had heard of by the hearing of the ear. But could it be that I, Amanda Smith, was really living, and at Florence, Italy? Many times while they were talking, and the man would be explaining things, I was lost in wonder, love and praise at the Lord's dealings in giving me the privilege to enjoy so much that I never expected could come to one like me. Surely it is His doings, and very marvelous.

Our next visit was to the Baptistry of St. John's. There were those beautiful bronze gates. How magnificent! I can almost see them now as I think it all over. Just as we got there a priest was about to perform the ceremony of baptism to two lovely babies. Two carriages drove up. In the first were the father and mother, with the baby, and the priest. In the second was the party with the other baby. They were exquisitely dressed. I thought I never saw such lovely looking babies in my life. I would like to have just taken them up in my arms and kissed them. They looked more like angels than children. They didn't seem to offer any objections to us looking on. When it was over I saw the fathers pay the priest quite a sum in gold. My heart was sad for the little things, after all; for I thought they will live and die without the true light and knowledge of the glorious Gospel of the Son of God.

Thursday, September 9th. We leave this morning for Rome. Arrive about five P. M. How accommodating and courteous they are at the hotel. We got on splendidly. Here in this great old historic city there is much to admire, and much to be sad for. Poverty and wealth seem to rival each other. I think I got some little idea what it meant for a country to be priest ridden. Everywhere you go, up and down, every few stations on the railroad, every train you get off of, or on, priests; all through the streets, in every turn you make, you see a priest coming or going; or two or three or four; scattered in every direction, priests. I never saw so many priests and monks in my life. Old men, with gray hair, who had never done a day's work in their lives; large, well, strong looking men. Some of them looked almost like idiots; their brain, and muscle, and thought had never been developed. They had never worn stockings, or shoes. They wore sandals, and just straight gowns of the coarsest material, with a cord, a piece of common clothes line, round the waist, and the ends, which were tied in knots to keep it from untwisting, hung almost to the bottom of the gown; the sleeves were long, and came over the hands, something like the Chinese we see here.

You could see these men, in any numbers, walking about. Sometimes you would see them leading a donkey, with a load of grass, which they had gathered, and were bringing into town to sell. They generally visited the hotels, with a little bunch of parsley, and an onion, and a carrot, to sell as pot herbs. How I pitied them when I first saw them. I gave them some pennies. Of course, I didn't take the pot herbs; I didn't need them. But I soon found out that that was their business. I never saw one look clean. Oh, how horrible!

And these are the men they call holy, because they give up the world, and practice such rigid self-denial. How glad I am that God nowhere teaches that men have to go into filth and indolence in order to be holy. But He does say: "Cleanse yourself from all filthiness of the flesh and spirit and perfect holiness in the fear of the Lord." This is always the way when men change the truth of God for a lie, and begin to worship and adore the creature more than the Creator.

Sunday, 12th. Miss Drake was tired, so she did not go out to church in the morning. But I wanted to have it to say that I had been to church in Rome. So I started off alone to the nearest English church. The schedule of the principal hotels and churches hangs in the office; so I had no difficulty in finding it. So I went.

I found it was a High Church, almost Roman Catholic. They had candles, and choir boys, and they turned toward the east and bowed, and the atmosphere seemed like a vault. All this was new to me, for I had never been in a Protestant High Church before. How unsatisfying all this to one who knows Christ. For Him there is no substitute.

Monday, 1st. A grand day sightseeing. We had our carriage and our guide. What I was most anxious to see was St. Peter's. So to this we went first. The magnificence of this great historic old church cannot be described by me. As we walked through its large corridors and halls, and as I stood and looked up at the great dome, I was almost awe-stricken. It seemed as though it was a mile away, in the sky. What stupendous thought had been put into its architecture, coloring, and statuary.

A little to the right of the main entrance was a statue of St. Peter, in bronze, life size. I had heard that it had been visited by thousands of people, and that the great toe on the right foot had been kissed till it had been worn quite smooth. I went up and examined it, and found its smoothness really a fact; but whether the result of constant kissing, or whether from some other cause, I cannot say. I had no inclination whatever to kiss the toe; but I laid my right hand on it, and it felt cold. I said to myself, as I saw many come in and stand before it, and cross themselves and pray, "That is all they get in return for their long pilgrimages, and their prayers and tears." How sad! How glad I am that the lines have fallen to me in a more pleasant place, and I have a goodly heritage. Praise the Lord!

The next visit was to the Vatican and we walked through the great corridors, and admired the statuary and paintings, and my head ached with seeing so much. As we were passing down through a beautiful walk we heard someone shout out to us in a language we did not understand; but they motioned to us to get out of the way, and we stepped aside, and there came the Pope in his sedan chair, with his body guard seven or eight men, returning from his morning outing; some were walking in front of him, some by his side, and others behind. And I thought to myself, "It was only a few years since that I heard the infallibility of the Pope was declared." And I thought if infallibility had to be guarded like that, what would be my safety in trusting in it. No. My faith is in the infallibility of God only.

The next was the Coliseum, with its ruined walls. As the man went on telling us the great stories, and pointing out things of interest and explaining, I sometimes wondered if all he said was real fact, in every instance. But no one questions the veracity of the guides when one is sight-seeing. They are supposed to know everything you ask them, of course.

He told us of the great arena where the Christians were thrown in and devoured by the starved lions, while thousands of spectators were gathered in the amphitheater, to look on, with delight. And then I thought of Fox's Book of Martyrs, that I remember reading when I was quite a girl, and sometimes I wonder if much of the spirit of the age is not akin to it. Christianity has done wonders. Hallelujah!

Then the Appian Way was pointed out to us, and the guide said, "That is the very road on which they brought Paul front the prison to the court." There was the very floor, inlaid in marble, like a pavement, on which he said Paul stood before Nero.

The next was the Catacombs. We went down about six feet underground, and entered a little narrow passage, and then he lighted tapers and grave each of us one. Then we entered a very large room; and on the clear, solid wall were beautifully painted a pulpit and altar, and nearly all the ritual of an English church service. The colors were as perfect as if it had been done but a little while; and yet it was more than two hundred years old. There were shelves, or niches, cut out in the rock, where their dead were laid; then these were closed up by masonry. A number of the bodies had been taken out by friends, and these spaces were open; but some remained still closed up. They had to go in and out by these subterranean passages, quietly. How much they must have suffered for His name in those dark days of persecution. As I thought it all over, I said, "Oh, will history repeat itself? May God in mercy deliver us."

I was foolish enough to start off in a different direction from the others, alone; though the guide had said to me when we first went in, "Now keep close to me;" but, as he stood explaining and talking to Miss Drake, I turned into, as I thought, another room. But the turns were very intricate to one who does not know. It all seemed to me as the same hallway. But when I found myself I was out of the hearing of the others altogether. I kept turning, but didn't seem to come near them. Then I began to get frightened. Then I thought I would stand right still; and so I did, and prayed the Lord to help me. In a little while they came, looking for me.

The guide said I did quite right to stop, for then they came and found me. If I had gone on turning they might have missed me entirely.

My! I shudder as I think of it. But he never had to tell me to keep close after that. What a lesson I learned. I shall never forget it. I had the lighted taper in my hand, but I should have obeyed my guide, and kept close, as he had told me. God gives us His Spirit, but we must walk in the light of the Spirit; then we will not fulfill the lust of the flesh, going in our own way. May He help us. Amen!

Wednesday, September 15th. We leave Rome to-day for Naples. The little prayer I breathed just as we were starting, was, "Oh, God, for Christ's sake, send upon Rome the mighty power of the Holy Ghost. Let the people be awakened."

We reached Naples at about half past five or six o'clock P. M. The hotel where we stopped was very fine. We preferred stopping at a hotel where English was mostly spoken, as neither Miss Drake nor I were familiar with the French language. We noticed the city abounded with churches; and, on our way up from the station in the 'bus, as we passed several, the doors being open, as is usual, we could see persons in the confession boxes; some would be coming out, and others going in; and so many poor people seemed to be going hither and yon; and monks coming and going, as we saw at Rome. After we had our supper, as we were very weary, we soon retired.

Thursday, 16th. Up early this morning, feeling quite refreshed from our journey. As we had but a day to spend, we thought we would do some sight-seeing; so we got a carriage and a guide, and drove to some of the principal points of interest. The most interesting, to me, was the great museum, which is quite elevated, and off in the distance we could see Mt. Vesuvius quite distinctly. One could see it very plainly on a clear day; but it shows very much better on a clear night. It looks like a great burning furnace in the distance. Then we went through the museum, and there we saw Pompeii in statuary, as it was, and as it is, in ruins.

I had heard of excavations from Pompeii, and had read some little about them, but now I stood by them. Many of the things which were explained to us have gone from my memory since then, but some are very distinct. I remember one figure showed a baker; there he stood by the oven, seemingly just in the act of putting in bread; there was the table, with the bread and pans, all perfect. Another was a person lying on a sofa, asleep. There were policemen standing at the gates going into the city, all perfect. All this seemed to me so wonderful; and when the man was explaining all these things to us, sometimes it would thrill through me with sadness.

Naples is situated at the head of the bay of the same name. The bay is beautifully shaped, something like a horseshoe. Round about is quite mountainous; so at certain points as you ascend these mountains, when you get to the top, you can look off in the distance, and around, and see all the great city below and about you. I thought it was very beautiful; and I kept the great Mt. Vesuvius in my mind and thought for days together. When they told me of the red hot lava which this historic mount belched up and sent rolling down its sides, I wondered how it was that the people seemed to be in such peace and quietness as they were. There were houses very near the base of the mountain as we looked off, with patches of green that had been tilled for gardens, or what not.

No one seemed to be annoyed or thoughtful about it; and I thought how easy it is for us to get used to horrors and sadness.

After we had gone about a great deal, we drove back to our hotel, had our lunch, and a little rest, and then took another short drive; but the clouds gathered, and a little misty rain came up, so we did not go very far. Then Miss Drake began to get a little uneasy to know when the steamer would leave for Alexandria, though they had told us they would send us word; but as we were out we went to see, and there I lost my beautiful umbrella. A lady in England had given me a sovereign, and said, "Mrs. Smith, you must get you a nice umbrella;" so while I was at Eastbourne I saw a very pretty umbrella, and I thought I must do as I was told, and I got it, though I didn't pay quite that amount for it.

After we had been to the office and made inquiries about the steamer, and were satisfied, we returned to the hotel. The rain had stopped, though it was not clear yet, so I set my umbrella down in the carriage beside me, and when I got out I never thought of it. The next day, just as we got on board the steamer to leave for Alexandria, I thought of my umbrella. I paid a man a dollar to go back for it. It was an hour or two before the steamer would leave. He was very polite and kind, and was surely going to bring it; but when he came back he said he could not find the man, but if I would give him another dollar he would go where he thought the man had gone! But I saw there was game in that arrangement, so I told him he needn't mind. Then he said he would send it to me, and I saw there was more game. I was very sorry to lose my nice umbrella, but it was so good that the Lord kept my heart very quiet.

Friday, Sept. 17th, 1879. We are on the steamer for Alexandria. They said if you made up your mind not to be seasick, you would not be seasick; and so I made up my mind, and my mind made up its mind that it would not hold still, and I was just as seasick as I could be.

Sunday, 19th. A lovely morning; so quiet. I am better, praise the Lord. They told us when we were leaving Paris that we must not touch water on the continent; that the water was very bad, and everybody drank wine. And on the steamer they drank wine like water; the children and all drank wine; I expected to see everybody drunk, and I had a little queer feeling come over me. I thought, "Dearie me, what a time we will have if these people get to rowing."

Ladies and gentlemen, children, fathers and mothers, all drank wine, but they didn't seem to get out of the way. When we sat at the table and chose water instead of wine, they looked at us in astonishment. Then I asked how it was they could all drink so much wine and not get drunk. They said it was light wine and would not intoxicate. And then I wondered if that was not the snare so many got in; beginning with the innocent light wine, and ending up with that that is full of weights that hold them down. so that when they would rise they cannot.

Well, Miss Drake and I got through without touching either the light or the stronger wine, and we never had a moment's sickness, outside of the simple seasickness, with all of our fatigue and weariness, for sight-seeing is wearisome, especially when done in a rush, as we did it, and the like of which I never want to do again. Our steamer was due on the twenty-fourth, so we had no time to delay.

Monday, 20th. The morning is bright and pleasant. My morning thought is, "Oh, Christ, Thou art a reality; make me more like Thyself."

How balmy the air, and how bright the sunshine! So different from England. The passengers on board are very kind and polite. I think the French have the first rank among all the nations in this particular. As far as I have seen it seems to be natural to them, children and all. It is no effort to be polite and courteous. Even in Rome I noticed in the railway 'bus, where it was rather crowded, when I stepped in a beautiful little lad arose and, with a smile and tipping his hat, he pointed me to his seat.

In Paris I was walking through the park one day and there were numbers of children playing, and one little fellow sitting on a seat near by, and as I stood looking at the beauty around, he at once arose and, with a beautiful air and tip of the hat, offered me his seat. It was so beautiful, so different from what one sees at home. I came near shouting right out, "Praise the Lord!"

Tuesday, 21st.

"Precious promise God hath given
To the weary passerby."

Praise the Lord! "My soul, wait thou on God. My expectation is from Him." We are nearing Alexandria, Egypt. The great old historic Egypt! Egypt that I have read of in the Bible! Can it be possible?

Ten A. M. Here we are in the bay. Praise the Lord. And who are these men coming off in the boats? There are four or five boats, all manned, each with six, eight, ten or twelve men—black men—my own race. I had been so long without seeing any of my own people that I felt like giving three cheers!

I never saw such scientific rowing in my life. They stood up instead of sitting down, but, Oh, how perfectly they bent to their oars. They had on little red skull caps, with black tassels on the top, and neat black alpaca coats. I presume they were Mohammedans, as they dressed just like the Mohammedans in India. Many of them were fine looking men, black as silk and straight as arrows, well developed, and independent as kings. They moved about and did the business intelligently, and with promptness and ease. They didn't know what it was to crouch to any man. I felt proud that I belonged to that race when I saw such nobility in ebony. Then I thought of the passage in the Old Testament history: "Princes shall come out of Egypt." Then I remembered it was the birthplace of Moses, and the hiding place of the infant Jesus from the cruelty of Herod, the king. And out of all the world round it pleased God to bestow this great honor on the black race, which ought to be held in everlasting remembrance. And I prefer being black, if for no other reason than to share this great honor with my race.

After a good night's rest we went to visit the great pyramids, which was a drive of, I think, about four miles out of the city of Alexandria. We made all our arrangements overnight.

Next morning everything was prompt and we were called in time, and our breakfast was ready promptly at five, so that we had plenty of time, and at six we were off. I thought Alexandria—we saw of it—was a beautiful city. Many of the houses were large and spacious, and there were large, fine hotels. I forget the name of the hotel where we stopped, and on what avenue it was, but it was a wide avenue through the center of the town. Just opposite this hotel was a much larger one; it covered almost a half block. There were large ice cream parlors below, and the awnings came out over the sidewalk. It was beautifully lighted and they had exquisite music, and English ladies and gentlemen were sitting out round the ice cream tables, and it really seemed more like England or America than Egypt. How sorry I was, when in Africa, to hear of the sacking and burning of Alexandria at the time of the great Afghan war.

We were told that there were some missionaries who had got pretty well established, and were doing good work. But, Oh, war is so destructive and demoralizing in its sweep. And probably all that had been gained at this time was lost again.

On our way to the pyramids our drive was over the same road that had been especially built for the Prince of Wales when he visited Alexandria a year or two before, and but for this royal visit our drive to the pyramids would have been very rough.

This was the first time I ever heard of, or saw, the eucalyptus tree. All along the royal highway, on either side, were these trees; they had grown up and formed a high archway; it was very beautiful, and one felt inclined to linger in its shade out of the hot sun.

I think I got a little idea of what Paul meant when he said, "Lay aside every weight and run the race with patience." I never saw such pretty, scientific running in all my life, as certain men there did. They were tall, lank looking fellows; on the head they wore a simple white skull cap, and around the body a light, white cloth, of about three or four yards in length, the weight of which would be very little over a pound; under this would be, fitting close to their bodies, a little jacket with long sleeves, and made of the same material, or perhaps a little bit stronger. Their business, or profession, was begging. When our carriage had got just outside the city there started after us a half dozen or more of these gentlemen, shouting as they ran, "Backsheesh" (give me a penny), "backsheesh, backsheesh."

Our guide, who sat with the driver, to point out and explain everything to us, warned us against giving these gentlemen anything. He said if we encouraged them the least bit they would annoy us so we could not get rid of them.

But then they were so very polite, and bowed so gracefully, and ran so nicely, and they patted their stomachs and opened their mouths to say they were hungry, and their stomachs were empty, and I pitied them. The guide saw I was rather stuck on them, and he kept his eye on me pretty close for a while; but he turned his head, when he thought I was pretty thoroughly converted after all he had said and explained, and I dropped a few pennies for these poor fellows—about five cents of our money—and such a rush and yell I never saw or heard. Then I did get a little scared. He said, "I told you that if you gave them anything you would be annoyed."

Poor Miss Drake didn't know what I did; she declared she hadn't given them a cent; and I tried to look strange and blank. She said, "Did you give them anything, Amanda?"

"Oh, I only threw out a few pennies," I replied.

So the cat was out; and though our horses were under good speed, our driver touched them up, and we went on faster; and these gentlemen touched up, and came on faster, but they did it so gracefully and beautifully.

"Well," I thought, "I have done it now."

Finally they began to drop off one at a time till we were left with but two; these accompanied us to the pyramids, and offered to run up to the top for sixpence, if we would give it to them. I thought it was about worth that to go up to the top of that huge pile of stone, for that was what it seemed like; but I couldn't make the offer, for I had done enough; so they ran up a little ways and came back.

We walked about it little, and looked into the tomb where they said the wife of a king was buried; there was nothing in the looks of it that was specially interesting.

Then I saw the great sphinx. I used to wonder what it was; but now my curiosity was satisfied. We spent about two hours, and then drove back to Alexandria, and at two o'clock in the afternoon we left for Suez.

Suez, Egypt. The hotel where we stopped was kept by an Englishman, and most of the guests were English. I had no difficulty

on account of my color; everybody acted naturally and with common sense.

At dinner I noticed two gentlemen, who sat opposite us; they looked familiar to me. I thought they might be Americans. I noticed they looked at me very sharply, and as though they would like to speak, but they did not, and I felt like I would like to speak to them; but then I thought, "They are strangers; they seem as though they know me; but can it be that anybody in Egypt knows Amanda Smith?"

I said to Miss Drake, "I am sure I know those gentlemen, but I don't like to speak to them."

The next morning we met again, and Mr. Leech (for that was the name of one of the gentlemen) came up and spoke to me, and said, "Is not this Amanda Smith?"

"Yes," I said.

"I thought last night it was you; indeed, I was quite sure; but after dinner I went to the office and looked at the register and saw your name." They were two ministers from Newcastle-on-Tyne; one, a Presbyterian, and the other a Congregationalist. Both of them had helped me in the meetings that I held at Newcastle, at Mr. Lambert's hall. I introduced them to Miss Drake, and they were so nice they made it very pleasant for us.

They had been to Alexandria, and now were in Suez, on their way home to England. They took this little trip of two or three weeks on their vacation. They told us of the great Mahommedan school at Alexandria, which they had visited, of eight hundred students, studying the Koran. It is the largest college in the world where all the students study one thing. They said it was a wonderful sight to see them; they all sit on mats on the floor (all men or boys), and they rock themselves back and forth, and study aloud, so that the din is something fearful! They are supposed to commit the whole of the Koran to memory. How I should like to have seen that school. But we hadn't much time. So that was one of the things we missed.

These gentlemen, whom I have mentioned, had a day with us before their steamer came; so they walked out with us, and showed us different places. What was very interesting to me, was the way they did their irrigating. I had never seen it in this fashion before There were large plots of ground laid out, as far as your eye could see. There were old-fashioned pumps, such as they had a hundred years ago, I suppose; then there were long, wooden troughs leading to the trenches, about five and ten feet apart; they would pump the water into these troughs, and it would run and fill up all the trenches, and then the women and children would stand on either side of the beds, and with their hands throw the water, and so water the beds. Oh, how hard and tedious! But then they never thought of doing any other way than the way their fathers did. That was all they cared to know.

The onions and salads and water cress raised in these gardens were very green and nice. How my heart turned to God in prayer for poor Egypt. Only God can change the hearts of these people here, and make the desert blossom as the rose. Lord, once more, send light and help to Egypt!

When God called Jesus out of Egypt from the wrath of Herod the king, and when the light had gone out, darkness settled down on Egypt, and still lingers. If the light that is in you become darkness, how great the darkness!

Our steamer was due at Suez on Thursday, but it did not come until Sunday. We had these days to wait. I was rather glad, for I thought I never was so tired in my life. But still if we had known the steamer would not come till Sunday, we could have gone up to Jerusalem. These gentlemen told us we could go in twenty-four hours by stage.

Parties went up that way often; but they made all the arrangements a day or two ahead; which we might have done, and got back by Saturday night. That was the nearest to Jerusalem that I ever was, and ever will be again, until I get to the Jerusalem above,

I suppose. However, there is nothing impossible, and now that the railroad is there I would not be surprised to find myself going up on the train some day, especially if God said so.

CHAPTER XXIII.

INDIA—NOTES FROM MY DIARY—BASSIM—A BLESSING AT FAMILY PRAYER—NAINI TAL—TERRIBLE FLOODS AND DESTRUCTION OF LIFE.

We sailed from Suez Oct. 26th, 1879, for Bombay, and arrived at our destination Nov. 12th. I remained at Bombay until Jan. 1st, 1800, visiting, in the meantime, various places where M. E. Churches have been established, and holding meetings as opportunity offered.

Miss Drake remained in Bombay, and I had for a traveling companion for some time afterwards, Miss Jennie Frow, a missionary stationed at Chauldah, who had been on a visit to Bombay, and now was returning to her work.

January 1st, 1880. The Lord's Word to me this morning is, "Lo, I am with you always." I leave for Cawnpore. Watch night at Dr. Thoburn's church at Calcutta. I dine with Brother Goodwin, and the Stones, of Ohio.

Monday 5th. Cawnpore. Praise the Lord for this quiet day of rest. A nice drive to Memorial Gardens. What a sad fate that of those who sleep there! How dreadful the story of the Cawnpore well, where so many were massacred and thrown in at the time of the great Indian mutiny.

Wednesday, 7th. Conference opens to-day. A solemn but blessed time. The meeting of so many friends. How much it seemed like home to me. Praise the Lord! My head is very tired, but my soul is fresh.

Thursday, 22nd. Allahabad. Spend the day with Brother Dennis Osborn.

Saturday, 24th. My last Saturday in Alahabad. We go to the Maila. It is like what we would call in this country a fair. Oh, the hundreds of people. Oh, to see the heathen idol worship!

MARKET PLACE, BOMBAY, INDIA.

How sad to see the different idols they worship displayed on their flags and in every possible shape and way. My heart ached, and I prayed to the Lord to send help and light to these poor heathen.

Friday, Feb. 13th. Dear Jennie Frow is not so well to-day. God bless her! It is now Jennie Fuller. She was married since then. We leave to-day for Nagpore. Praise God for His great care over us during the night. We had to drive with the bullocks this fifty-one miles back to Acola. They had been mending the road, and there was a great deep gutter about a quarter of a mile in length. We had to change our bullocks three times; and the third time we thought we had got a very stupid driver; we got to a place where the bullocks would not go on, and the man seemed to be stupid. Poor Miss Frow remonstrated, and told him to go on; but the bullocks would not go; so we thought we would get out, and see what was the matter. It was very dark, and there were no lights; and when we got out and walked ahead two or three yards we saw the great danger we were in; if the bullocks had gone on, they would have surely broken their necks, and we might have been killed. Oh, how we praised the Lord when we saw the danger that God had saved us from. Then we had to turn the bullocks down on the lower road.

There are generally two roads; a native road, and an English road; the English roads were better, as a rule; they generally kept in their provinces good roads; we were on the English road, so we had to turn out and go down on the native road, which was very rough, because they never mended them, or made any repairs on them.

Sunday, 22nd. A meeting at Camp Te to-night. The Lord helped me this once. He led me to give my experience, and I had great liberty, and he made it a blessing. We leave for Elegepore. I feel I ought to stay. There was such an interest manifested in the grand aftermeeting.

Col. Whitlock was a very earnest Christian gentleman; he had a very beautiful little daughter, and one night when we were holding meeting in a large hall (he always took an interest in any religious meeting, which was not very customary among English soldiers), his little daughter, about ten years old, became very much interested, and when I asked them to rise for prayers, among others in the great congregation, this little girl rose; and the Lord blessed her; she seemed very happy and bright. Her father was delighted with her decision; the mother, too; but still she was afraid she did not understand what she was doing. But the little thing persisted, and had the sympathy and help of her father. So she would have her mother come to me next day, and I had a very nice Christian talk with her, and told her how she might help the little child, and she seemed very much pleased.

The child acted out her position by beginning to do something. Her mother kept a Hindoo derzy; a man who does all the sewing and mending and everything of the kind, in a family. Some of them have two or three. You will find them in almost every family in India. All the clothes to be made or mended are given to these men, and they sit down in a corner that is arranged for them, and do the sewing. They come and go, morning and evening, and are very quiet. They never pass about through the house only at their work. This one had been living with them a long time, and was a pucka Hindoo; that is, what we would call strong, or rank, or staunch in their faith.

So little Ethel began to tell him about what Jesus could do; and as she could talk the native language as well as a native, he listened to her; and she kept it up till he got so interested he asked her for a Testament; and so she got a Testament, and made the old man promise that he would read it. He was greatly pleased with it.

Who knows but what that child, though but ten years old, who was the means of getting that Hindoo to read the Testament, was sent by God with light to this poor, dark mind.

> "It may not be my way,
> It may not be thy way;

> But yet, in His own way,
> The Lord will provide."

When we went to leave, Mrs. Whitlock gave me a very handsome India shawl, and prepared us a beautiful lunch, and in so many ways was kind. In the lunch, she put two loaves of bread, a half dozen boiled eggs, six bottles of lemonade, a bottle of champagne, a bottle of wine, and I don't know what all else; but she sent a man with a note on Sunday afternoon, and this beautiful basket of lunch.

My! what a time I had over it. I couldn't send it back. The shawl was an elegant thing. It was about a twenty-five dollar shawl. The only objection I had to it, was, it was scarlet. But, still, that was not much, for I could get it dyed. But, I thought to myself, "What will I do with this wine and brandy?" I knew Miss Frow would not touch it, and I was a staunch teetotaler. "If I take it and say nothing about it, she may think, and tell somebody, that I was a good woman, and yet I accepted it," and I didn't know what to do.

So I prayed about it very earnestly. The enemy wanted to make me believe that she would he greatly offended, and that now I would undo all the good work that I might have done. Oh, how terribly tempted I was over that!

Sunday night was my last night. I spoke at the hall.

And that was the night I had promised to speak more especially of temperance. But then I had received a bottle of wine and a bottle of champagne. So the Devil suggested to me that nobody would know it, and now if Col. and Mrs. Whitlock were there, it would be better for me not to say anything about it, after they had been so very kind, and that they did not see it like I did. So I reasoned.

At last I resolved by the grace of God I would tell Mrs. Whitlock that I could not have it, and would go on and speak on temperance in the meeting, as I had intended. So, when the time came, I went to church.

Just as I got to the door going in, I met Col. and Mrs. Whitlock, and little Ethel; so I very kindly thanked the lady for the elegant shawl, and for the lunch which she had sent me; but then, I said, "Now what will I do with the bottle of champagne and the wine? for I am a staunch teetotaler; I never touch it."

"Miss Frow looks so pale," she said, "I thought a little wine would do her good."

"But, Oh," I said, "she would not touch it for the world. She is also a staunch teetotaler."

Then she laughed, and said, "You do with it, Mrs. Smith, anything you like."

I thanked her very kindly, and told her I would.

The Lord gave me liberty in speaking that night, and I was very strong on the subject of temperance. No one was offended. Everybody seemed to be much interested and pleased.

We went from there up to Chaculdah. That was Miss Frow's station. Mr. and Mrs. Sibley were there in charge of this station, and she was their assistant.

What a pleasant time we had at Chaculdah. There was a poor, old, native Christian woman who was very ill. She had been a very faithful servant in a Eurasian family for years; but because of great persecution from her own people on account of caste, though she believed in Christianity, she never came out. But when she got feeble, and sick, and very bad off, she went over to Mrs. Sibley's instead of going to her own people; she wanted to be a Christian; and they put her in a little house where she was very comfortable.

She was very fond of Miss Frow. So the first thing we did after we got home and rested a little, we went in to see this old woman. Oh, how emaciated she was! so worn; and she was dying; but she seemed to be happy. Miss Frow talked and prayed with her.

When we went out I said to Miss Frow:

"How would it do to give this woman (she is dying anyhow) a little of that wine?"

"Oh," she said, "I wouldn't dare to do it. She used to like it very much. They used to have it, of course, in the families where she had been so long, and she had got to like it, and it might be the means of diverting her mind. I had rather she would die without it."

So there I had it to contend with.

In a few days the old woman passed away. That was the first native Christian funeral I had seen. They dressed her nicely, and then the natives came and embalmed her, and then we carried her to the grave.

I shall never forget how pretty and nice it looked in the grave. She was the first native Christian that had been buried in that part of the country at that time, so it made quite a sensation. The grave was dug down a certain depth, and then dug out in the side so as to form a kind of niche, or shelf, and she was laid in this niche, then the earth was thrown in; so that the earth was not thrown on her, like we do here, and I thought how nice it was; I wouldn't mind being buried there myself. I think it is a much better way than putting the earth right on top of the coffin.

There we left her, to rest till the morning of the resurrection, when the trump shall sound, and when the dead in Christ shall rise. The grave die not seem to have gloom and sadness, even in India, with Christ.

PREPARING A MEAL, BOMBAY, INDIA.

From Chauldah I went to Lenoula. I kept this wine and champagne in my lunch basket, well covered up. I was so afraid somebody would see it, and if the natives saw it, I would not be able to explain. I thought I would take it to Bombay and give it to old Sister Miles, who was a grand, good woman, in the hospital at Bombay and, like Dorcas, "full of good works all the time."

"Well," I said to myself, "Mrs. Whitlock said I could do with it what I pleased, and I will give it to Sister Miles. She is so judicious and careful, she will know whom to give it to—the very weak and faint ones who are about to die; I don't think it would be any harm to give it to them."

Brother Fox was Presiding Elder, and it was Quarterly Meeting at Lenoula. So after resting all day, they had meeting Friday night. At first I thought I would not go out, as it was quite a little walk from the house to the church. Then the moon was so beautiful and the evening was so pleasant, that I decided to go.

The Lord's hand was in it. He had a great lesson to teach me. Brother Fox preached. A number of natives were taken in. Then we had an after meeting. It was full of interest and spirit.

Just as Brother Fox went to close the meeting, a man rose in the rear of the church, a fine looking Englishman; how well I remember him; I can see him now. He was a man that weighed about a hundred and fifty, and was about five feet and something in height; he was dressed in pure white, and had a full, round, flush, English face, with black hair and black eyes. I had noticed he had sat very seriously looking and listening all through the service. But now he was on his feet, and he called out:

"Brethren, I want to speak a word."

"Go on, certainly," Brother Fox said.

And he said, in a most deploring, pleading way, "Oh, brethren, brethren, whatever you do, be careful about strong drink. Don't ever advise any one to take it, under any circumstances," etc.

My! I trembled. I thought, "There, now, everybody knows I have those bottles."

They were in the lunch basket, well covered up, away back under the bed in my room. But it seemed to me somebody had found it out.

Well, I heard the story of this man. He said: "I have been a man that has been addicted to strong drink, and I have been overcome. It has been my ruin. But I came here and was converted, and for two years I went on, and the Lord blessed me. But I was not here at the last Quarterly Meeting; and why? Because I had been overcome. I was sick with diarrhoea, very bad, and a good brother came in to see me, and he told me if I were to take blackberry brandy it would cure me. I took it. The diarrhoea stopped, but it brought back the old appetite, and for six weeks I was in the gutter. For God's sake, don't advise anybody to take it. Better let them die."

And then he sat down.

"Lord," I said, "help."

There was a sad feeling that went over the house. Then Brother Fox got up and emphasized what he had said, and told an experience similar that he knew of, and then another, and another.

One man stated another case: He said that he knew a man who was very ill. They took him to the hospital. He was about dead, as they thought, so he prayed and gave himself to the Lord, and was very peaceful and happy. It pleased the Lord after awhile to restore him so that he became quite convalescent, and one day a friend went to see him and he looked so weak and pale that he thought that just a little wine might refresh and strengthen him, so he got some wine and took it to him. It brought on the old appetite so strong that that night this man slipped away from the hospital and went into the town and got some cheap whisky and got so terribly drunk that next morning when they found him he was in the gutter dying.

"Lord, deliver me," I thought, "can it be that they know I was going to take this wine to Sister Miles? By the grace of God I will never do it. Though she is judicious and careful, it might not be the thing."

On Monday morning, about five o'clock, I left Lenoula for Bombay. I never told anybody about what I had. They all supposed it was nothing but lunch in my basket, as everybody carried a lunch basket. And after the train left the station and we got pretty well under way, and there was nobody in the compartment but myself (the Lord helped me to be alone, for I said, "Now, Lord, help me to get rid of this champagne and wine"), I took the bottle of champagne, and just as we were crossing a very deep cut, about fifty or a hundred feet deep, I threw out the bottle and heard it rumble and gurgle as it went down.

"Dust to dust, ashes to ashes," I said, then out went the other bottle.

No one saw me, and I expect they are there yet, for the cut was so deep that no mortal would ever go down after them, I think. And that is the way I got deliverance from my champagne and wine.

The day we left for Chaculdah we prayed around—Miss Wheeler, Miss Frow, and I, last. I had been so deeply touched at seeing the sacrifice and need of these poor girls. They were there all alone. Fifty-one miles was the nearest railway station. And but two or three English families within two miles of them, except some English officers' headquarters.

Two of these officers had their wives there some of the time, but they are often, both husbands and wives, far from being Christians, and have but little sympathy with missionaries and their work. So these two girls, being there alone, were looked upon with a kind of suspicion. No woman had ever been known to build a house before. But Miss Wheeler had been her own architect and superintended her work, bought her lime, and tiles, and thatch, and everything.

I have known her while I was there to be out counting tiles from six o'clock in the evening till nine and sometimes ten o'clock at night.

The native men whom they had to deal with, felt like some of the English officers who were there. They thought that a woman had not sense enough to build a house, and if she had she ought not to do it, for it was lowering her dignity as a woman.

So the men gave them a great deal of trouble. They would come and make fine promises, then you must pay them so much money before they brought the things you needed or ordered. Then they would go away, and you might see them again in two or three days, or a week, or maybe not all. All this time you could do nothing, but you must wait.

A thing of that kind might happen two or three times during a month. So the work was delayed, and they had much to contend with.

It was three miles to the nearest village, of more than two thousand inhabitants, where Miss Wheeler used to go almost every day and do her missionary work in the zenanas, or preach to a crowd in some open space in the village, or under a tree. Then they had a room where she dispensed medicines two or three times a week, as the case might be.

Miss Lucy Drake, now Mrs. William B. Osborn, of Hacketstown, with Miss Wheeler, was the first to start the work at Bassim, under the auspices of Dr. Cullis, of Boston, but after a year or so Miss Drake's health failed and she returned to America, but Miss Wheeler remained. She has never been home since she left. She is a marvel. Her powers of endurance and stick-to-it-iveness and deep heart loyalty to God have made her rightly called one of God's noble women.

If they needed a loaf of bread, or a pound of sugar or flour, or the most trivial article, if they didn't happen to have it in the house, they had to go, or send, fifty-one miles for it, which generally took about three days, with a slow-going ox cart, as we would say, but bullock wagon, as they say in India.

Those were the pioneer days. God has wrought wonders since then. Praise His name. How I did pity and sympathize with these poor girls.

So while I was praying the morning before I left the Spirit of the Lord came upon me in a wonderful manner, and I was led to pray, "Oh, Lord, put it into somebody's heart to build a railroad through this part of the country, so it will not be so hard for those who are isolated to get the things they so often need."

I shall never forget how I felt as I prayed. And these words came to me: "Therefore I say unto you, all things whatsoever you ask in faith believing, ye shall receive." And I saw a railroad as really as I ever saw a railroad, by faith.

When I rose they laughed at me, and said, "You think we will have a railroad?"

"Yes," I said, "God will do it. You will see."

And it did come to pass in less than two years after, that the East Indian Railroad Company put a railroad right through that section of country and, I was told, a station within two miles of Bassim Faith Mission House. That was the name inscribed on the front of the building.

While I was in Africa a Mrs. Wills, from Bassa, Liberia, was in London on a visit. She went to a meeting at Miss Mason's House of Rest, and there she met a lady who told her to tell me when she got back to Africa that the prayer I had prayed in India for a railroad to Bassim had been answered, and the railroad was finished.

That was the first I knew of it from the time I prayed, and I said, "Praise the Lord. Is there anything too hard for God?"

Naini Tal, India, Wednesday, September 15, 1880. The morning is beautiful. Miss Fannie Sparks and I take our men and go up to what is called the snow seat. It is about two miles, I suppose, right up hill. The men who carry you in the dandies, when they get to a certain point on the hill, turn you round, and carry you up backwards. I don't know why they do this, but I think they have an idea that you are not so heavy carried that way. Miss Sparks had four men and I had four. When we got up to the top of the hill we found it very broad, a kind of tableland. You can look for miles away, and the hills are covered with snow.

When they put us down, and we stepped out of our chairs and turned round, we looked right on the great mountain ridge of snow, beautifully white, and the sun shining on it like silver. Oh! I thought I never saw anything so beautiful. I wanted to shout right out, and wave my hat.

But then one has to be so careful, because the natives watch you, and they think that it means you are worshiping the snow or the great mountains. So I had to restrain myself from shouting and dancing.

Oh! the sight was glorious to behold! Miss Sparks and I walked about, and then we sat down and had a nice little Bible reading together, and then we knelt down and had such a blessed prayer meeting. I shall never forget that morning.

That night, Wednesday night, was our prayer meeting. We were not very spiritual, still we had a good meeting.

Thursday, September 16th. The day the great flood began. It rained all day Thursday. Sometimes it would lighten up, and seem as though it was going to clear off; then a heavy cloud and fog would set in, and the rain would pour. All day Thursday, all night Thursday night, all day Friday, and all night Friday night.

By that time we began to get serious; we wondered; for the water ran in torrents; great trenches would give way in the ground; banks were falling in; and we did not know but danger was coming to us.

Miss Sparks, and dear Miss Leighton, who has recently gone to her rest, were staying at the Mission House, with Mr. and Mrs. Mudge, and we were expecting to return to the plains the following week. Mr. G. N. Cheney was pastor of the Methodist Church. Rev. Mr. Buck was pastor of the native work. I stayed

with Mr. and Mrs. Buck, at their home. I shall never forget their kindness to me.

Friday night we didn't sleep much. Mr. Buck was up most of the night, working; he and the boys. I had four boys and Miss Swain had four. We generally had to keep these boys by the month, so as to have them when we wanted to go anywhere; for we could not walk up the hills, they were so steep and long. We didn't pay them much wages; we didn't have anything to do with finding their food, or anything of that kind. We gave them a suit, which was their outfit.

In this, the Lord was good to me, for dear Mrs. Fleming gave my boys their suits, and made them; and they didn't cost me anything, I remember so well what they were, and how nice they looked; they were of a kind of brown flannel; the pants just reached to their knees; the coats were bound with red round the bottom and sleeves; and a little skull cap bound with red; they were very picturesque. There are always outhouses where the servants stay. These boys used to get wood and sell it days when they did not have anything else to do; so they kept along very nicely; I used to buy the wood from them sometimes.

Well, Mr. Buck and the boys worked all night almost. When Mr. Buck came in in the morning, he was very much exhausted.

How pale he looked. We could not get any breakfast; nobody seemed to want anything to eat.

He said we would have to pile up all the things in the house. So we began. The people up at the Mission House had piled their trunks outside. The water began to come in on them.

Between three and four o'clock in the morning Miss Sparks and Miss Leighton came down to our house. We had got our things out of one part of the house, and piled them in the parlor; then we took them from there and piled them on the veranda outside.

When morning came we were all in the parlor having a little rest. Someone said we ought to have a prayer meeting; so we got down and prayed as best we could; then we rose, and were quietly thinking what was the next thing to be done.

I went to my room, for I felt I could pray a little better alone. After a while Miss Sparks came in, and she knelt down by the bed beside me, and we prayed. I shall never forget Miss Sparks' prayer.

HILL MEN, NAINI TAL, INDIA.

When we arose she said, "The Lord has given me the assurance that this house will not go down." I said, "Amen."

After we went out, the engineer, who had been examining the hillside, came by and said to Mr. Buck, "I think this end of your house will go; but the other end is on the rock, and I think it is safer."

About nine o'clock the baker came. We got several loaves of bread, for that was about all we could get to eat. I bought two loaves for my men; they had not had anything to eat, and they were shivering with the cold, and were wet and hungry; but their caste feeling was so deep, that, hungry as they were, they would not touch the bread. One of them seemed for a moment to have forgotten; and just as I picked up a loaf and handed it to him, the other shouted to him, "Don't you do it!" and he threw it down as though he had had a snake.

Poor fellows, how I pitied them! One day one of my boys was suffering with a pain in his stomach, and came to me for some medicine, he said. I had some Jamaica ginger, and I mixed some with some water and sugar, and brought it to him; I never thought but he would drink it right down; but, no, he said, he could not.

"Well," I said, "what are you going to do?" And he went to a tree and got a leaf, and shaped it, and I had to pour the liquid in the leaf, then he drank it out of the leaf. If he had drunk it out of the glass he would have broken his caste.

Oh, how they are anchored to that caste feeling! But God is delivering them. The door is open. Light is coming. Praise the Lord.

The hotel was a very short distance from the mission house: perhaps a half block. There was a lady, whose name I have forgotten, who had come up from the plains a few days before, and was staying at the hotel (her father's), with her two children, and her native nurse. The youngest child was about a year old; the other about two years old. The nurse was giving the baby his bath in their room, and the mother had taken the other little boy, and gone out in the breakfast room to breakfast. She had not more than got out of the room when the side of the hill came down and buried the nurse and baby.

Mr. Buck and I were standing on the veranda. Mr. Buck said, "Well, Sister Smith, this is terrible."

"What will we do?" I said.

It would be as dark almost at times as six o'clock in the evening. Then it would lighten up, and you would hope that the sun was coming out; but, no.

After awhile Mr. Buck looked up the hill toward Government House. Government House was a large house where the Governor lived. It stood on a beautiful hill; and, though it was quite a ways up to Government House, it was beautiful to look from; the sight, when you got up, was charming, every way you would look.

So, standing on the veranda, we could look eastward and see Government House quite distinctly, though it was about two and a half or three miles away. And, as Mr. Buck stood looking, he said to me, "Why, Sister Smith. just look at those trees."

And just as I turned to look, the trees were swaying first one way, then another, and all at once there was it crash, and they went down so gracefully, and the earth plowed like a great avalanche.

Well, there was a panic. Everybody left the house, and got out as quickly as he could; the news spread rapidly, and in a little while there were a hundred and fifty or two hundred men, many of them English soldiers, digging, trying to get out this child and nurse; and while they were digging away as hard as they could, and we were lamenting, and feeling the sadness that had come upon this family, the earth gave way again, and buried them.

They didn't see the danger, and we couldn't alarm them; their heads were down as they were digging; and it struck the other part of the hotel and swept on, then it passed on like a great moving mountain; I never saw such a sight; it moved on, carrying great boulders on its face!

The next was the large reading-room and postoffice that stood on the lake, the Hindoo Temple, and Bell's large store.

I had just seen from the veranda some ladies and gentlemen go into the reading-room, and they had not come out; and there were persons in Bell's store whom I knew; one, a lady who was a very earnest Christian. I said to Mr. Buck, "Oh, Bell's store," and I had hardly got the words out of my month when it was swept away! Then "The Reading Room," and I had no more than said it till it was taken! "And there goes the Temple next" and there it was in the lake!

The lake was about a half-mile wide, and, perhaps, three miles in length; but the whole thing swept into the lake, and the noise was like the blast of a cannon, and the smoke ascended upwards; it swept everything clear; and there was not a brick of the chimney, or a piece of wood left. The horror of that hour I never want to see again!

Then the men came and said we would all have to leave the house; so we started. We thought we would go to the Methodist Church; but the native Christian Church had been swept away, and so they had taken refuge in the church.

The first native Christian had died on Friday night. She had been sick for quite a while, and Mrs. Buck and all went and did everything they could for her.

She was in one of the outhouses on the hill. So Mrs. Buck and I went up and prepared her for her burial. Mrs. Buck dressed her in a nice, white gown, combed her hair, washed her, and got her all ready to bury, and we left her lying on her bed and went down to the house; and about an hour and a half after it seemed like the Lord buried this woman Himself; for the house gave way, the ground opened, and she went down, bed and all, and was covered up. I never heard that she ever had any other burial!

Well, when they told us we would have to leave the house, we thought we would go to Mr. Sasha's; he was it photographer. Everybody had to look out for himself; and I felt I was alone, and everybody had so many more cares, and so I had to do the best I could for myself. Miss Sparks and I were the last to leave the house.

As we started down to Sasha's I thought I would go over to Mrs. Fleming's, which was about a quarter of a mile further along from our place. Mrs. Fleming had a large dressmaking establishment. Her men, who worked for her (for the native men do all the dressmaking, pretty much, there,) are called derzies; sometimes she would have twelve men, all sitting down on the floor in a row, sewing. She did the cutting and fitting, and these derzies did all the other work; the trimming and fixing of all kinds.

Her men were all gone. They had sent the children away, and Mr. and Mrs. Fleming were the two last to leave the house, and they were going on horseback. I said to Mrs. Fleming, "I don't know what to do, or where to go."

"Well," she said, "go with us as far as Sasha's."

The sweeping away of the Hindoo Temple had made the Hindoos so vexed; they felt, mid thought, the Gods were angry with the missionaries, and so had destroyed their temple; and there was an expression of indignation on the countenance of every one.

I remember as I was going along I would put my foot on what seemed to be a piece of turf, but it would give way, and sometimes I would go down almost to my knee; sometimes when I would step on it I would stick in tight; once or twice I thought I was stuck fast; two or three of these men passed by, and with a scornful sneer they grinned as though they hoped I could not get out.

I prayed to the Lord to help me, and finally I got to Sasha's. I went in. Miss Sparks, and Miss Leighton, and some others, had gathered there. Mrs. Sasha had a very sick baby; but she had had the servant get them a cup of tea, and they were getting a little refreshed; so when I got in they gave me a cup of tea, and Mrs. Sasha got me it pair of dry stockings; and just as I got my stockings on, and drank part of my tea, Mr. Mooney, an Englishman, came and said, "You will have to get out of here as quick as you possibly can; all the houses on this hillside are falling down."

Mrs. Sasha picked up her baby, supposed to be dying, in her arms, and started; we begged her to wait a little. She said, "It is easy for you all; you have got religion, and something to comfort you; but I have not."

Then clasping her little baby she ran. Mr. Sasha got the hammock and sent the boys after her, with some other things, for she went without a bonnet.

I was the last to get out of the house. I was so weak I trembled from head to foot. I was not excited; I was just weak; and it seemed to me I could never get my things on. But when I did get them on, Mr. Mooney—God bless that man; all the rest had gone—took me by the arm, and literally dragged me. He was a very strong man. As I think it over now it seems I can feel the grasp of his hand on my right arm.

We went from there to a Mr. Frazier's, about a mile away, on the other side of the hill altogether.

As I went along I said to myself, "The idea of running away from God." I said to Mr. Mooney, "I don't mean to go another

NAINI TAL, BEFORE THE LAND SLIDE.

peg; all the people can go who want to go; but I am done running; by the grace of God I shall not run anywhere. Running away from God! Lord, help me." And He did.

We got over to Mr. Frazier's, I suppose about five o'clock in the afternoon.

Mr. Frazier was a Scotchman; a very nice man. He had a large house, and he and his sons were there in some kind of government business. So we were all very comfortable. They got us a very nice supper, and we were all enjoying it. But the sorrow and sadness among the poor soldiers' wives and their companies, and the weeping, were very touching.

After we had had supper, and were sitting talking, each one telling how he got out, what he thought, what he did, etc., Mr. Buck began to feel anxious to know what had become of the poor, native

Christians, and he said it was so dark he didn't know what to do. Mr. Mooney said, "I will go and see what has become of them." Mr. Buck said he would be so glad if he would. So Mr. Mooney started off. About a half hour or more after he had gone, all at once there came over me a horror of darkness and awful sadness. I could not account for it. I left the room and went off to myself, and knelt down and prayed. Oh, how I prayed! I said, "Lord, there is no use going anywhere, but somebody is in awful danger."

It seemed to come to me as though somebody was in danger; and so I prayed the Lord to deliver somebody from danger. My heart seemed to get a little quiet then, and I got up and went out into the room again. I looked at everybody, but no one seemed to be unhappy; they were peaceful and quiet; so I sat a while, and they talked on.

Finally this agony came over me again; then I said to the brethren and friends, "Let us pray; I feel that somebody is in great danger; Oh! let us pray!" and we all knelt down and began to pray. When we got through we arose, and about a half hour afterward Mr. Mooney came back, and told what a narrow escape he had had from death; and looking at his watch, and comparing the time of the danger with the time I had had the agony, the time was identical.

A flash of lightning saved him from going down into the lake; though he knew the road so well, the trees and boulders had so piled up across the road that he missed his way, and just as he was going to step into the lake a flash of lightning came, and instead of stepping forward he stepped back, and to one side, and so was saved.

Now, that seemed to be a strange coincidence, yet it was God. I shall never be able to tell anyone the awful agony that came over we to pray for somebody that was in danger. This man was my savior a few hours before; and, in answer to prayer, God helped me to be his savior a few hours later. Praise the Lord! He still moves in mysterious ways His wonders to perform.

CHAPTER XXIV.

THE GREAT MEETING AT BANGALORE—THE ORPHANAGE AT COLAR—
BURMAH—CALCUTTA—ENGLAND.

This was a blessed time. We should like to have stayed a few days longer; but previous engagements being made, we had to pass on with praise in our hearts to God that He gave us the privilege of sowing, if only a little, for Him, and with prayers and tears to be watered, and in due time the harvest will be reaped. May the Lord help us to believe as we pray.

Miss Anstea came to Bangalore to attend the meetings. She came, she said, for a definite object, and that was, for a renewed baptism of the Spirit; and, after waiting several days, the Lord helped her, among others, to claim by faith what she had asked for; and she returned to her home and work, filled; and when I got there and saw the work, I said in my heart, "If ever there was need of such an anointing and empowering, dear Miss Anstea needed it."

Three hundred helpless souls God had committed to her care; and they leaned upon her as they would upon a mother. You have no idea of the care and anxiety and responsibility of such a position unless you were there to see it.

In connection with the orphanage there are two farms: Nazareth and Bethany. Miss Anstea is the head of all this work; and while she was so anxious that they should know all that would help them on in life, temporally, she had the greatest concern in the salvation of every soul; for this she labored and prayed daily; and, according to her faith, so it was unto her.

I am more and more convinced that to succeed in God's work everywhere, one needs to be filled with the Spirit and mightiness of God, and especially so in India and Africa.

Superstition and idolatry, and infidelity, are so rampant it seems the very air one breathes is impregnated with them. Oh, how the dear workers all over, need constantly the fresh anointing of the Holy Ghost, which can and does reveal the almightiness of Jesus to save from all unrighteousness.

Sunday was their Communion Sunday. It was a beautiful sight to see so many remembering the Lord's death, till He come again. It was very solemn and impressive. A sight like this means more in India than it would in England; these are poor orphans redeemed from heathenism. I expect to laud and wonder at His grace through all eternity. Amen.

Miss Anstea had invited me to come to Colar and visit her mission. So, on my way from Bombay. I stopped at Colar for a week. Colar was a large, native town, and Miss Anstea's mission covered a large area, in which she had a chapel, and a very nice, commodious mission house, large, comfortable apartments for the boys and girls, separate, and several very comfortable houses for missionaries, all nicely situated and well furnished.

I held meetings in the little chapel every night. Our morning prayer was similar to a service; at the ringing of the bell the boys and girls would file in and take their seats, and we would have prayers before they went to work.

The Lord gave us great blessings during the week's services. At night the church would be crowded; large numbers of the heathen from the outside came in; many of them seemed to be deeply interested. The Lord wonderfully helped me to speak to them every night; and several of the children professed to be converted.

One Sabbath morning we were at prayers at the Mission House, a poor woman came and sat on the veranda, outside, with a beautiful baby in her arms, about three or four months old. When prayers were over, she was asked what she wanted. She said she wished to see Miss Sob. That is what the unmarried ladies are called in India by the natives; a married lady is called Mame Sob.

Miss Anstea had several helpers, English persons, a man and his wife, and two unmarried ladies. Always after the prayers with the boys in the chapel in the morning, they had their family prayer at the Mission House.

So, when Miss Anstea went to this woman and asked her what she wanted, she said that she had had nothing to eat for two days, and she was starving, and she wanted her to take her baby; she

had come a very long way from a native town; she said she had three other children, and had nothing for them to eat; and if she would give her fifty cents and keep the baby, she would go and get something for the other children; but she could not bear to see the baby starve to death before her eyes.

It was a beautiful child, it little girl. By that time we were all a round her. Miss Anstea questioned her in every possible way to find out if her story was true.

She told her she was afraid she had taken somebody's baby and wanted to pass it off for her own; but at this the poor woman wept bitterly and declared the baby was her own, but that they were starving, and it was her last resort to save her baby, to bring it to the Mission; the others, she said, were older, and somebody might help them; but nobody wanted the baby.

Miss Anstea told her there was no one there who knew anything about taking care of so young a baby, and that she herself knew but very little how to manage a young baby.

As we all stood around looking and listening, my mother heart ached, and I would have gladly taken it myself, but I had no where only as the Lord gave me friends who would invite me to their homes for a while, as Miss Anstea did. But we prevailed on Miss Anstea to take the baby.

One of Miss Anstea's Christian girls said she would look after it. I think Miss Anstea offered to pay her a small sum; or some of the rest suggested that; another said they would milk the goat so the baby would have milk. I said, "I will give the woman the fifty cents;" but I gave her a little more than fifty cents.

She laid the baby down on the mat. Of course, they have no clothes on them; they are perfectly naked. She put her hand on her heart and sighed, and then ran away out of the compound. When she got to the gate she turned and looked back; poor thing! she was so thin, and looked just like what she had said, that she was starving to death; you could see she was weak; but, oh, that look when she got to the gate! I shall never forget it; it was full of a mother's love and tenderness for her baby. My heart ached for her; and to save my life I could not keep back the tears.

How often the missionary in different foreign fields comes up against heart rending scenes, before which they often stand helpless. All they call do is to weep with them that weep, and pray with them that don't know how to pray for themselves.

We took the baby in, and Miss Anstea adopted it, and we named it "Amanda Smith."

I left on Friday. Up to that time the baby had got on very well, but cried a good deal, nights; there were plenty to look after it in the daytime, but at night everybody wanted to sleep, but the baby. Dear, little Amanda Smith!

I went from Colar to Bangalore, then to Madras I never heard whether the poor, little thing pulled through or not; if she did, I know it was hard, after the novelty had worn off with the children.

Miss Anstea was a grand woman, and did a noble work in that province. How they have missed her since she has returned to England. She spent many years in India, and established and run the missions mostly at her own personal expense.

When she broke down, and was obliged to return to England, she turned the work over to Bishop Thoburn. So the work at Colar is still being perpetuated.

Madras, January 7th, 1881. I spend a few days at the home of Brother Shaw, pastor of the Methodist Church. Miss E. and I visit three zenanas and speak to a very nice family of girls; read, and explain the Word; then I sing; and as I sing, though they do not understand the words, the Spirit seemed to touch their hearts, and they weep. May God bless them.

Wednesday, January 12th. A meeting at eight A. M. The Lord was in the midst of us. A number of good testimonies, and a number rose for prayers, as they did also at night. Still there's more to follow.

Here I saw the great juggernaut car, so well known in the history of sacrifices in India, whose wheels have crushed so many infants at the hands of their poor mothers. How my heart ached as I listened to the story, told by the Chief of Police. How dreadful is heathen blindness. Thank God that the car of the juggernaut for such sacrifice has come to belong to the things of the past; has been superseded by the glorious light of Christian civilization, and judicious Christian legislation.

Tuesday, Jan. 18th. I leave this morning for Punrooty, to see Miss Reed. How God has kept His dear servant here, and made her a blessing and a succor to many! The Lord has sent her help from England just at this time, Miss Bloom and Miss Thurgood. Mrs. Fred Bowden and her dear mother came with them for a little visit. A beautiful company of Christian workers.

Wednesday, 19th. My first day at Miss Reed's. His word, how sweet: "Ye are all one in Christ Jesus." I give a little talk in the chapel this morning to the orphans who are redeemed from heathenism and starvation. Miss Reed took up this work at Punrooty during the year of the great famine, when hundreds perished from hunger.

Some of the scenes of suffering in those days, as she described them to us, would make one grow faint.

Saturday, 22d. Arrived at Bangalore late in the afternoon. Stopped with Brother Carter, pastor of the Methodist Church.

Tuesday, 25th. Oh, Lord, revive Thy work. A blessed time at family prayer. I go with Brother Carter and make some pastoral calls among the people. At night we have a good meeting, a crowded church.

But the good Plymouth brethren were much disturbed, because I was a woman, and Paul had said, "Let your women keep silence in the churches." So they had nice articles in the daily papers; then they wrote me kind letters, and bombarded me with Scriptural texts against women preaching; pointed out some they wished me to preach from. I never argue with anybody—just say my say and go on. But one night I said I would speak on this subject as I understood it. Oh, what a stir it made. The church was packed and crowded. After I had sung, I read out my text: "Let your 'men' keep silence in the church," quoting the chapter and verse (I Cor., 14: 28) where Paul was giving directions so as not to have confusion— one to speak at a time, while the others listened. And then one was to interpret, and if there was no interpreter, they should keep silence in the church. So I went on with my version of it. We had an excellent meeting, and the newspaper articles stopped, and the letters stopped, and I went on till I got through.

I have wondered what has become of the good Plymouth brethren in India since the Salvation Army lassies have been so owned and blessed of God. Their work has told more practically on the strongholds of heathenism than all that holy conservatism would have brought to bear in a thousand years.

Oh, that the Holy Ghost may be poured out mightily! Then shall the prophecy of Joel be fulfilled. For are we not living in the last days of this wonderful dispensation of the Holy Ghost?

Sunday, Feb. 6th. A blessed Sabbath morning. My last at

Bangalore. After a good day, I spend the night at Major Orton's. Praise the Lord for a good rest.

Monday, 7th. The word of the Lord this morning is, "Behold, I set before you an open door." Amen. In the afternoon I take a drawing room meeting at Mrs. Orton's. The Lord was with us, and gave me great liberty in speaking.

Wednesday, 16th. I leave Dr. Jewett's this morning for Rangoon. Very sick, but peaceful. Praise the Lord.

Saturday, 26th. We get in at three in the afternoon. As I look I see a boat nearing us, with three men in it—Brother Robinson and some others. Brother Robinson takes me to his nice home. I was entertained there for several weeks God bless him and Sister Robinson.

Wednesday, March 16th. Leave Rangoon to-day on the steamer for Maulmain. Kindly received by Mr. Norris and Miss Barrows, Baptist missionaries. Hold my first meeting at the Baptist Church this evening at seven-thirty. It is a new thing in the Baptist Church for a woman to speak. We had a large company out.

After Mr. Norris had spoken to them, he introduced me. The Lord helped me to sing, and talk. On Sunday we commenced meetings again, and went on for a week. The people came from far and near. The Lord was with us and blessed us.

Friday, 25th. Miss Barrows and I leave to-night for Amherst, in the boat. It is slow, but rather pleasant and cool going down the river. Get to Amherst at five A. M.: go ashore at six. A fine, large mission house, roomy and pleasant all about. Oh, Lord, I will praise Thee; Thou hast dealt so bountifully with me. How beautiful this place, and the quiet is so restful.

Sunday, 27th. Go to the Burmese service in the Baptist Church. A native minister preaches. At five P. M. the Lord helped me to speak to the people.

Wednesday, 29th. We leave this quiet place for Maulmain. We make our last visit to the grave of Mrs. Judson, hear the story of her life, and I breathe a prayer to the Father for His Spirit more fully in my own heart, as these words come to me: "Let me die the death of the righteous, and let my last end be like hers."

March 30th. Get to Maulmain in time for it meeting for women, and speak at night. Called to see several of the old Christians. One old man was baptized by Dr. Judson. What a grand work this mission has done for this part of Burmah. How I admire those grand heroes of missions in the days when it cost more and meant more than it does now. Surely, "Their works do follow them." Amen.

Rangoon, British Burmah, April 4, 1881. "Praise God, from Whom all blessings flow." This has been a precious day. Dear Mrs. Boyd sent her carriage for me, and I went and spent a few hours with dear Mrs. Bennett and Miss Watson, Baptist missionaries. The Lord helped me as I told them of His dealings with me, and how He had sanctified my soul. The Lord gave light, and when I arose to go, dear Mrs. Bennett said, taking my hands in hers, "Now, I want to say to you that this has been the happiest hour I have spent for years, and when I think that the Lord has raised you up and sent you here to teach me of these wonderful things of God, I praise Him. Now, I do trust He will bless you and keep you."

And then opening the door of a little closet near her, she handed me a donation to help me, as she said, in God's work, and regretted she had no more by her.

This good woman of God has given her life to the heathen in India. She has been abundant in labors for more than forty years. And now her eyesight has failed her, and also her physical health, and she is laid aside. And no doubt it is a great trial, for her life has been such an active one. But, thank God, she is finding His grace sufficient for her.

One of the first things I was struck with was the pagoda, or Burmese temple. You can see its dome for two miles away, as you look off, before you get into harbor. The streets of Rangoon are wide and rectangular, like those of Philadelphia, and the shade trees over the city are very graceful.

After being in Burmah a few days I wanted to visit this great temple. So I started, in company with some friends, and after walking some distance from Brother Robinson's house, we came to what I suppose would be called the park. There was an ascent of about seventy-five feet up a series of steps into the pagoda; a gentle ascent, not tiresome. On either side of the way were devotees at prayers, or beggars wailing for their rice; or booths where you could buy false pearls, imitation diamonds, beads, packages of gold leaf, flowers and cakes. The trinkets and flowers are given as offerings to Buddha; the gold leaf was sold for acts of piety.

Oh, how horrid this all seemed to me. I looked at the sad expression on the faces of the poor women devotees, and then I thought that they would go on, and live and die and never know that Jesus died that they might live and have life add happiness in Him.

Inside of this park where the pagoda stands, are thousands of gods, of all sizes. I thought I would count them, and when I got up to a hundred of those that were not broken, I quit. And then to think of the many, many years that the religion of Buddha and Brahma has gone on, and holds such sway yet. To me this is among the incomprehensibles.

The Burmese ladies walk about in the street; their dress is very pretty; a very handsome figured cloth, almost always silk, and just wrapped about the waist and tucked in at the side. They do not fasten them with pins and hooks and buttons, as we do, and yet they look very neat.

You never see a Burmese woman with her hair uncombed; but they use no hairpins; how they put it up I don't know; but it is as straight, every hair, as it can be. It is done like the Chinese women do their hair.

They are very shrewd business women. I saw them unloading wood and marketing, just like men; and in any kind of business you will see Burmese women sharp and active.

I was so amused to see the Chinese and Burmese carpenters. I watched them one day as they were building a house, and there would be a half-dozen men, and they would be sitting down using their planes, holding the board with their toes. They have some very large and fine buildings there.

Their funerals are something like the Hindoos'. A big man had died; I heard a great sound of music, such as they have there; I can't describe it; it couldn't be described by music that we hear here; tin-pans and tambourines, and something like the noise that a stove pipe, or something of that kind would make. Oh, it was a jingle. Mrs. Robinson called me to look out at it; it was on the main street of the town, and it was a large funeral. Dozens of men would go before the hearse and lay down cloth; the hearse would drive over this cloth; and so they went on, the music following this procession.

When a poor coolie man dies they carry him around till he becomes so offensive that I was told sometimes the authorities

NATIVE CHRISTIAN FAMILY, INDIA.

NATIVE CHRISTIAN FAMILY, INDIA.

have to interfere. They give them all the chance they can to come to. But, poor things! they are dead, three times dead; plucked up by the roots.

Brother Robinson, pastor of the Methodist Church, has done a good work in Burmah, and his influence has been felt. He was much thought of by all the other denominations.

I was given a sketch of the Burmese religion. One of the strong points in their religion is the transmigration of the soul. Guadama was the last great man born. He was born six hundred and twenty-five years before Christ, and lived in this world about eighty years. He was the son of Thokedaucareh, king of Burmah. He had previously lived in four hundred million worlds, and had passed through innumerable conditions of each. He had been almost every sort of worm, fly, fowl, fish or animal, and almost every grade of human life. At length he was born, son of the above-named king.

The moment he was born he jumped upon his feet, and spreading out his arms, exclaimed, "Now I am the noblest of men. This is the last time I shall ever be born."

His ears were so beautifully long they hung on his shoulders. His height was nine cubits. When grown up, his hands reached to his knees; his fingers were of equal length, and with his tongue he could touch the end of his nose!

The only sacred books of the Buddhists are the laws and sayings of Guadama.

When this was told me, and explained in points that I could not pretend to give, it seemed incredible; and yet, when one is there, and mingles much with the people, one can see how tenaciously they hold to just that superstitious belief. Oh, how darkness has covered the land, and gross darkness the people.

Among other interests in Burmah I had hoped to distribute about eleven Bibles among those who wanted them. I knew God would bless His own Word. But when I got to Calcutta, where I hoped to be able to get the Bibles, as I could not get them at Burmah, I found that Bibles in the Burmese language were very large, and very expensive; so that I was only able to send one, to a very interesting case, a Burmese man, with whom I think the Spirit of the Lord was working, and he was very anxious for a Bible.

How much good anyone with a missionary spirit could do here in Burmah, or India, and especially if he or she had an aptness in acquiring the language.

I had wished that my own daughter would have such a desire to do something for her fellowmen. I have prayed and asked the Lord to thus incline her heart, if He would have her. I have educated her, and done all I could, as far as I was able, to prepare her for a useful life; and now I leave it with her and her God. He knows my heart. I long to have her do what I know she could do if she was only fully consecrated to God. I would not have her come to this country without a full and entire consecration. And in her own land I fear she will do but little without it, like so many others. When I think of what God has done for me, and how He has led me since I gave myself fully to Him, I am encouraged to praise Him for all that has passed, and trust Him to guide my child that she may work for Him. Amen.

At eight o'clock one night I held a meeting in the Methodist Church for colored men especially, as there are a number in Burmah, and Rev. Mr. Robinson, who is pastor of the Methodist Church, was very much interested in these men. Several of them had families; and he had tried to get them to come to church.

Being an American, he seemed to sympathize with them, and to know how they felt in that country where customs are so different from what they are in the United States. So he said while I was there he thought it would be nice to call them together and have me talk to them, which I was very glad to do.

There was a nice company of these men gathered; some were from the West Indies, some from the west coast of Africa, and some from Boston, Philadelphia, and Baltimore. One man from the West Indies had been in Burmah for twenty years.

They were all men of average intelligence, clean, well-dressed, and sober; there were but three men in the company who acted a little as though they were under the influence of strong drink; one of these was from Boston, and his name was John Gibbs. He had been in Burmah sixteen years; another was a Mr. Jordan, a man of good position, a stevedore; he had been here sixteen years, also; and another, a fine looking young man from Baltimore, by the name of Jenkins.

There were about twenty of these men in all. They sang, just like colored people can sing. I spoke to them from the fifty-fifth chapter of Isaiah. I dwelt mostly on the words, "Let the wicked forsake his ways, and the unrighteous man his thoughts." The Lord helped me, and His Spirit was present.

I asked before I began who amongst them was converted. Only one man answered: he was a grand, old man. He had walked in the light of full salvation, and followed the sea, for fifteen years.

After I had got through speaking I asked him to pray; he did; and how the Lord helped him! He said he had been in Burmah twenty-five years. His son was with him; a nice young lad; may God save him! When the prayer was over, I said, "Is there anything you would like to sing?"

"Yes," said one young man, from the west coast of Africa, and who had been here only three days, "Sing such a number."

I found it; it was, "Stand up for Jesus, Christians, stand." As soon as it was announced they all seemed to know it, and they sang it well. After they were seated I talked to them a while. I said, "Now, who of you would like to have us pray for you? Hold up your hand."

And six or seven said, "Pray for me." Then Brother Robinson, the pastor of the church, spoke to them. Then after another season of prayer I said, "What shall we sing to close?" when young Gibbs, from Boston, said, "Please sing 'God our help in ages past.'"

He started it, and they sang it as if they knew how. Oh, it was good. How I have prayed that God would get glory out of this meeting to Himself, and save those men. Amen.

In talking I told them I believed that God meant they should live in a heathen land as Christians, and as colored men they should show the heathen with whom they came in contact that their God, whom they are taught to believe, is able to save them out here, as well as at home.

We arranged to have them come together on Wednesday evening for a little tea meeting. May God help us. Would to God that He would anoint someone who would work his way to this land, rather than not to come at all, and see after the flock here that stray and wonder and have no shepherd. I saw this need in Liverpool, England; and also in Bombay and Calcutta.

These were colored men; my own people. Some of them had left good, Christian homes, and started out Christians themselves. But they get into these ports, and there are no colored churches or missions to go to, and they feel lonely, and often give up all hope in Christ.

How my heart has ached for them. How I wish that my people in America might feel that they had a mission in this, looking after these poor men that brave the stormy sea. I wish they could think and feel about it, and put their thoughts and feelings in action, as the white people do; for in every port there is work done among white sailors; and if any men deserve to be looked after, and comforted, and helped, and cheered, it is these brave men, white and black.

I hardly ever hear the wind blow at night that my heart does not breathe a prayer to God for sailors. How many young men, and old ones, too, leave their homes converted, and many times get through the voyage all right; but they have no place to go to but these sailors' boarding houses, and they are thrown in with all sorts of sin and wickedness, and they finally drop into those ways.

How my heart has ached for them as I have seen them in London and Liverpool; they could go to church and be better treated there than in the white churches at home; but the old feeling of prejudice follows them, and they seldom venture to Church. If there were a church or place of worship where they knew their own people were assembled, they would feel free to go, I think. That is why I think our ministers at home should take this into consideration.

A good many of our American men, when they get to England, or India, or Burmah, or any other country, if they stay, feel they must get a wife, of whatever place they are in; if in England, an English wife; if in Burmah, a Burmese wife, and so on: and, in so many of these instances, when these sailors do marry, whether it is a white woman in England, or whether in Burmah, or anywhere else, it is generally somebody that likes whisky; and that is the sad part of it.

In Burmah it seemed that these men were better off than the most that one meets on foreign shores; some of them were engineers on railways, some conductors, some in government service, and they all had good positions, and made money. Some of them had nice families of children; but their wives didn't go to church, and their children didn't go to Sabbath School; so they generally were a hindrance to their husbands, instead of a help, in that respect.

One has no idea of what these things mean, unless they are just where they can see and know it.

The Lord blessed me very greatly in Burmah. The Baptists were very kind, and I held meetings in their several churches. At one church, where a Mr. Norris was pastor, we had a week's services, and the Lord gave us great blessing in the work. The Baptist missionaries in Burmah have done, and are doing, a grand work. I stayed at the Mission House, with a Miss Barrows. It was there I heard more of the great Dr. Judson, and Dr. Cary, those noble pioneer missionaries, than I had ever known before. I was sitting by Mrs. Judson's grave, and looking upon it, as Miss Barrows told me some of the story of her life, and, for a relic, I took a very smooth pebble that lay on the head of that noble woman's grave. And I thought of the blessed Word, "He that goeth forth weeping and bearing precious seed, shall doubtless return again, bringing his sheaves with him."

Wednesday, April 6th. We leave to-day by steamer, for Calcutta.

Monday, April 11th. Arrive at Calcutta. Thank God. Dr. Thoburn and Dr. Stone come off for us. Get home and have a little rest, for which we are very grateful. I shall never forget the Christian kindness of this blessed man of God. I spent so many pleasant days in his comfortable home. What a blessing God has made him to the church, and to the thousands all over India, and in the United States as well.

To-night at six, I spoke to the baubaus, in the public square. God, I believe, blessed His Word. We had an after meeting, and several English soldiers came forward and sought the Lord.

It is wonderful to hear Dr. Thoburn preach a sermon in English, and turn right away without saying so, and preach the same sermon, word for word, with energy and power, in three other different languages, according to the company gathered— Hindustanee, Bengalee, and Maratee—preaching the wonderful story of Jesus to the great multitudes that gather. God bless him.

Sunday, 17th. Easter Sunday. Somehow I always have a peculiar love for this day. It is the Christian's victory day. For, if

Christ be not risen, then have the people heard in vain, and our preaching is vain. But, glory to God, He is risen.

> "The rising God forsakes the tomb;
> In vain the tomb forbids Him rise;
> Cherubic legions guard Him home,
> And shout Him welcome to the skies."

Hallelujah!

Wednesday, 20th. I go with Dr. Stone to Hastings, A good temperance meeting. Then with Dr. Thoburn and some others, breakfast with Miss Hood, at the Presbyterian Mission School. How very kind they have all been to me. God bless them.

Friday, 22nd. Mrs. Meyers and I go to do a little shopping. I need some things, as I am getting ready to leave for England, and how wonderfully God has supplied my temporal needs.

Sunday, May 8th. My last Sunday in Calcutta. In the morning I speak at Dr. Thoburn's Church, and at night in Carson's Theatre. This was my first time in a theatre, but God helped me to speak for Him that night, and I trust good was done.

Saturday, May 21st. Leave at half-past five for the steamer.

Sunday, 22nd. We are out on the ocean and all sick.

Wednesday, June 15th. We enter the English channel this morning; not too hot and not too cold.

Thursday, 16th, 1881. Praise God, we arrive all safe. God has answered prayer for the sick child that was on board, so it is better. My dear friends, Mr. and Mrs. Stavely, meet me at the landing and give me a hearty welcome. Amen.

CHAPTER XXV.

AFRICA—INCIDENTS OF THE VOYAGE—MONROVIA—FIRST FOURTH OF JULY THERE—A SCHOOL FOR BOYS—CAPE PALMAS—BASSA—TEMPERANCE WORK—THOMAS ANDERSON.

I arrived in Monrovia on the 18th of January, 1882. I left Liverpool on the 31st of December, 1881. On the 7th of January, 1882, I arrived at Madeira; spent a few hours with Mr. Wm. G. Smart, of the British and Foreign Bible Society. He is a missionary to the sailors. He came on board our steamer. I was introduced, and, after he had had some conversation with the sailors, he asked me if I would like to go ashore. I told him I would, and when he was ready he called for his boat, and away we went.

We had a little stroll through the very primitive old town, to the post office, then to Mr. Smart's house. He showed me some repairing they had already done, and a large place was then under repair for a school and sailors' reading room. Formerly it had been a store-house for spirits. When he told me of the change I was glad; and sang as I stood in the street, "Praise God, from whom all blessings flow."

Then we went into the house. Mrs. Smart was ill in bed; but, oh, such a sweet, earnest, out-and-out Christian, one don't often meet in a foreign land. I spent three hours with them, and had an elegant dinner, and sang and prayed.

Madeira is almost all Roman Catholic. The window of the priest's house looks right into Mr. Smart's Sitting room. His windows are often hoisted mornings and evenings when they have family worship, and they say the priest is not bigoted, and they often see him listening to the songs and prayers. May the Lord mightily awaken him! Amen!

About eight o'clock the boat took me to the steamer again, and I was much refreshed and encouraged on my way.

On Monday, New Year's Day, we were at Grand Canary. A very pretty looking place from the ship. Here we got vegetables. This is the home of all the canaries in the world, I am told.

The captain and some of the officers and passengers went ashore. It was a magnificent, moonlight night. The captain asked me to join in the party, but I declined; I quite preferred quiet and the lovely moonlight. After a few hours the whistle blew, the anchor lifted, and we were off. Oh, this narrow bunk, and this dreadful rolling! I shall be so glad when I am through.

The next stop is at Sierra Leone. And now three days to Monrovia. This is a very busy looking place. A great many come on board to get work. They are called coolies. Some of them opened my trunks and helped themselves. There was a white Wesleyan minister that came on board who was very kind, and as we were there for a day, I would like to have gone ashore. I asked him about the prosperity of the work and the churches. He didn't seem to speak very favorably. He said that the colored missionaries were not men that could he depended upon to advance and develop the work as one might suppose.

At this I felt quite indignant, and thought it was because he was a white man, and simply said that about colored men. But after I had been there awhile, and got to understand things better, I quite agreed with what the missionary told me on my first arrival on those shores.

The captain and purser were very kind. They were greatly annoyed to think that my trunks had been interfered with. They stopped at Sierra Leone to take on coal. My largest trunk was down in the hold, where all the large trunks were, and these coolies were loading coal all day, and so were down in the hold a good deal, where the trunks were.

The first I knew of it was, I was up on deck, and as I went to look over on the lower deck, just at the side of the ship, where the steps go down, I saw one of the officers have a pair of shoes in his hand, and I thought they looked like my shoes; but I knew my shoes were in the trunk. Then I thought somebody had come on to sell things, as they did. All at once I heard a great outcry of "Thief, thief, thief!" And then I saw them bringing a man along from aft; a nice looking fellow, tall and clean looking; and he was declaring to all that was above and below that he had not touched anything, and that he was not the thief.

COOPER'S WHARF, MONROVIA

I felt so bad for him. The head man had hold of him, declaring he did have the things, and he declaring he did not. Then I thought the head man, being a black man, too, was very hard. But he let him go, and the storm was lulled for a while. Just then someone said in a low tone, "Look under his shirt." So the head man jumped at him and lifted his shirt (which was outside his pants), and there, if that fellow didn't have twelve yards of flannel wrapped all about his body!

Then I said to the man below, "Maybe those are my shoes."

"You had better come down," he said, "and see."

So I did; I put my foot in the shoe, and sure enough, it was my shoe.

"There," I said, "my trunk has been opened."

So I had them bring it up; the catch in the lock had been broken, then it had been filled up with pitch, so it would stick; it looked as though it had not been touched but there they set it on the deck, and all stood around while I went down into it. The tray had been carefully lifted out, and just what they wanted had been picked out, and they were gone. Some of the things I got. Others, and among them some very choice ones, I never got. But the Lord kept my heart very quiet; the captain and officers looked perfectly astounded because I didn't rave. The captain said to me:

"Mrs. Smith, I don't see how you do keep your temper."

"Well," I said, "Captain, I am sorry to lose the things, and if losing my temper and getting in a rage would bring them back, you would see me cut a shine."

"Well," he said, "I don't understand it, Mrs. Smith; it is too bad."

They did everything they could for me, and wanted me to go ahsore and give my affidavit against the man. But they had enough, because there was another passenger whose trunk had been opened, where the flannel, and soap, and quinine, and all these things had been taken out; so I thought I got on very well, and I told him that I wouldn't go.

Wednesday morning, Jan. 18th. Monrovia. We are in the harbor. The beautiful palm trees in sight. We are anchored. Breakfast at nine. And now here is Miss Sharp. Glad to see her.

We are soon off for the shore. The tide is very high, and crossing the bar, just before we get inside, I sing the Doxology and the rest join in the chorus. Five minutes more and the kroomen, being attracted by our singing and not paying attention, let a great wave break over us and we were wet through. I was glad we sang before we got wet, for not one of us sang afterward!

There was one white man in our boat, a German, a Mr. Amyre, and Miss Sharp and myself. I went to her house at the Seminary and stayed three weeks and three days. Then the Lord led me forth. Amen.

My first Sabbath I was asked by the pastor of the Methodist Church, Rev. Charles Pitman, to take the service. I did so, and spoke to a crowded house, and the Lord wonderfully helped me; and the following Tuesday, Wednesday and Thursday nights I was asked to continue, and did so, and some, I trust, were saved.

Friday, Jan. 20th. I took my first boat ride, up the St. Paul river to the Muehlenberg Mission, Rev. David Day, of the Lutheran Church. I had a delightful time at Brother Day's.

Sunday, 22d. Communion. I speak three times, to all that can be packed in the little chapel. The afternoon was for the children, as they had been crowded out in the morning, but the big folks crowded in after the children were seated. So we had a good time. Praise the Lord.

Monday, 23d. I leave for New Georgia, Rev. Mr. Hargrave's appointment. I speak in the Baptist Church to a large company.

Tuesday, 24th. I leave this morning for Monrovia. Go to Dr. Stanford's for dinner. Call and see Dr. Garnet in the evening.

Friday, 27th. Call to see President Payne. And on Monday I saw him for the last time on earth. I was taken down Tuesday night with fever, and it was ten days before I was able to go out again. On Monday night, the 30th, Mr. Payne died.

Tuesday, Feb. 7th. I leave Miss Sharp's, and am invited to Mrs. Payne's, a home I feel God Himself has given me. Oh, how I do praise Him! I am comfortable, and have every care.

My first "Fourth of July" in Monrovia, Africa, must not pass without a brief notice, only they celebrate the 28th instead of the 4th, as we do in America. A tirade was given on that day by the Hon. R. H. W. Johnson, against the churches. He said:

"Liberia should be independent in her religions as well as in her politics. But what does the foreign church bring us? They don't come with the pure Word of God. They come with some old traditions about the wickedness of Nimrod, and other old customs handed down by the Jews, who relegate to hell everybody but themselves. They come with some old pro-slavery traditions that assign all negroes to inferiority and eternal perdition. They come with all kinds of 'isms,' and 'schisms,' and doctrines, and disputes, and contentions, of more than fifteen hundred years' standing; contentions that have caused rivers of blood to be poured out on the earth; contentions and doctrines which not only the people of Liberia do not understand, but which have never been understood by those who bring them to us. You may be sure that any religion that teaches the inferiority of the negro never came from heaven."

This was the first big speech that I had heard, and I was astonished beyond measure. The church was filled with the best people of the capital and of the republic, ladies and gentlemen.

This address was received with enthusiasm and delight. And yet every one of them knew that no such religion had ever been taught in Liberia. But these are some of the things you meet on your first arrival. I think I discovered a change before I left, and trust it is still growing better.

While here, I saw a great need among the native boys that lived in Liberian families. Some of them go to Sunday School, but many, like in this country, did not go at all. I thought if I had a place of my own I might do something for them. I saw how they could be gathered in for an hour or two after the regular Sabbath School was over. I thought they might be helped a little. They would gather together and go in numbers to walk about as they would say, or go to Krootown, where they would not be any better for so doing. I saw this, Sabbath after Sabbath.

I thought if I had the money I might get some place. There were no houses to let there as here. There was an old seminary building and it was much out of repair, but still there were several rooms in it that could be used if they could be cleaned. There was a large garden that was all grown up with weeds.

All this would take money to clear up. I did not have it; so I began to pray the Lord to put it in the heart of some of my friends at home to send me money. I had been around in America to so many camp meetings and in different churches, and so many different parts of the country, east, west, north and south, and everybody seemed to know Amanda Smith, so many had helped me often, while there, and they would remember me now in Africa, and so help me.

Up to this time no one had sent me any money from home, but God wanted to teach me a lesson that I must needs learn, so now on good faith I began to pray as I had always done, for I never tell people my need; I always make my needs known directly to God. I prayed the Lord to put it into the hearts of some of my friends. I would think of one in New York, then another in Philadelphia, another in Boston, another in Ohio, and so I prayed the Lord would influence the hearts of these to send me the needed money for this work.

Week after week passed on and no money came. I still prayed on; I knew in so many hundreds of necessities where God had heard my prayer for temporal things. I told him He knew I was not asking for myself, I had a comfortable home with dear Sister Patsey Payne, of precious memory.

While in her home I was well nursed and cared for when I was sick with fever. My own mother and sister and brother could not have been kinder to me than Sister Payne and her daughter Miss Clavender, and her dear brother, B. Y. Payne. I feel to say as one of old: "Let my right hand forget her cunning and my tongue cleave to the roof of my month." if I ever forget the loving kindness shown to me in their home while in Monrovia. But for the care I had while passing through the fever I believe I should have been dead and in my grave to-day. How dear Miss C. watched over me and nursed me. I saw she was worn and weary and I got a friend to come in and stay with me one night. When I told Miss C., she said:

"No, auntie (for they all called me Auntie Smith), I would rather watch myself; I will not sleep though I know you have some one with you."

She was a splendid nurse. One might have thought she had been trained in some American institution; but I insisted on having this person come in, so she came in. It was not long till the poor thing fell asleep. I was nervous and restless, so asked her for something, and dear Miss C. came and handed what I wanted, and said Mrs. T. is asleep.

She did not go out of my room all night, so after that I said, "Well, if you are not going to lie down there is no use in my having Mrs. T. come in."

She was delighted, and said I told you not to do it. I thank God because of good and proper care. Though my attacks of fever were severe they did not keep me down long, two weeks would be the longest. As soon as I was able I would be at my work holding meetings, and out at night, which is not the wisest and best thing for a new-comer going through acclimating fever.

MISS C. PAINE, MISS CORRIN PAINE, MR. B.Y. PAINE, MRS. PATSY PAINE.

Again to my subject. I still prayed for the money, then waited, weeks went on, steamers came and went, letters came, but no money. Sabbath after Sabbath passed on; there were these native boys I wanted to help, and still it did not come, so one day I went to the Lord and asked Him what it meant, that He knew what I wanted to do for these poor native boys, and He seemed to say to me:

"You are not trusting in Me, you are trusting in America; you are looking to America for help more than to Me."

I saw it in a moment. Yes, it was true, I really was leaning on America.

"Lord," I said "forgive me and help me to give up every hope in America and trust in Thee the living God;" and I let go and rose, praising the Lord for showing me my mistake.

About two weeks after this a letter from my good and very faithful friend, Mrs. Margaret Davis, of Ireland, whom God hath raised up to help me as surely as He ever raised up a prophet in Israel. Oh, what that Christian lady did for me while in Africa tongue can never tell, eternity alone has the record.

In her letter was a five pound note; so God, in His own way, began to help me. Then shortly after this another token of another answer to prayer, a friend in India sent me five pounds: then after I had learned my lesson well a letter from the Western Christian Advocate from America came with five dollars in it, and several times from the same source came small sums; then some friends from Mrs. Carrie Judd's home, in Rochester, sent me a small sum; then some friends sent me some through Mr. Richard Grant.

So God showed me when I had learned to let go of human help and expectation, and trust in Him alone, that He could take care of me without America if He wanted to, for He had sent me to Africa Himself and I must trust Him to see me through.

I went to Brother Cooper, who then had the old seminary building in charge to look after, and got permission to use one of the rooms. I got a man to whitewash it and have the rear and garden cleaned of weeds, and the brush burned, then myself and one or two whom I could get, washed the windows and scrubbed the floors and I covered the chairs with some of the cloth that Mrs. Davis had sent me in a box, and put curtains to the windows and had some glass put in, and after days of hard work I got things in order.

Mrs. Davis had sent me in a box a number of cards and Scripture texts. Whenever she sent me a box it seemed she thought about everything. If I had sent an order myself I could not have been more explicit and thoughtful of what I really needed than was Mrs. Davis. So I had those nice mottoes for the wall. Oh, it did make it look cozy and nice. Different friends would come in and greatly admire them.

My first meeting was held on Friday afternoon, it was a Bible reading, a number of persons came out. Then on Sunday morning at six A. M., we held our band meeting that I had reorganized months before, and Sister Payne, my hostess, was appointed leader.

In a week or two after this a vessel came in—the bark "Monrovia," and the Librarian Conference was to be held at Bassa. I wanted to go to the Conference, so this was my only chance. I took this opportunity, and, though it would bring me there a week in advance, it was better to go then, than not to go at all; I want to stay three weeks, so I thought; when I got there the Lord seemed to direct me to go to Cape Palmas. I had been trying to get to Cape Palmas for two years, but was hindered time after time. so I gave up all hopes of going.

Now, when I got to Bassa, and found that Bishop Taylor was going, after the Conference, direct to Cape Palmas, I said to him, "Bishop, I have been trying so hard to get to Cape Palmas, and I heard you were going direct from the Conference to Monrovia."

"No," he said, "I am going straight on to Cape Palmas."

"Well," I said, "now, as I have been trying so hard to get there, it seems that this is my chance, what do you think about it, Bishop?"

"Well, Amanda, I think the Lord will have you go now, and I am just as sure the Lord is in it is I ever was sure of anything."

I had left my little native girl at Monrovia, so I asked Brother Palman if he would take Frances to his house. They lived at Paynesville.

Mrs. P. was very kind to native children, and I knew it would

ASHMAN STREET, MONROVIA, LOCATION OF FIRST M.E. CHURCH.

be a good home for Frances; then, it was out of town. Brother Patman at once said, "Why, yes, Sister Smith, Frances will be just like the other children, if you will be satisfied, we will see after her and do all we can for her."

Then I was confirmed, for this was the only difficulty I had; when that was settled, it was all clear, so I went to Cape Palmas with Bishop Taylor.

I will not stop to say now about the meeting and the first work, but will, later on.

I did not get back to Monrovia again for two years and three months, so that ended my work that I hoped to do for the native boys, but the Bible readings and the Sunday morning meetings, Sister Payne kept up till she died; then Sister Julia Sanders, one of

God's noble women, was appointed, and has led on the little band which is the spiritual bone and sinew of the church even to this day.

I have never seen a nobler band of Christian women anywhere, considering what they have to contend with, many of them in their own homes as well as outside. They have been a lighthouse and source of salt to all the marshy places around about them.

Thank God, even in Africa, there are those who have power to keep the banner of holiness unfurled and sing as they march:—

> "All hail reproach or sorrow,
> For Jesus leads me there."

And these shall walk with God, for they are worthy. Amen.

July 1st, 1882. Clay-Ashland. Just two weeks ago I came to Clay-Ashland, and my stopping place is on the St. Paul river, with Mr. Henry and Miss Martha Ricks, or "Uncle Henry" and "Aunt Martha," as they are more accustomed to being called. They are both devoted Christians.

I am very comfortable and feel quite at home with them. And cousin Sarah is a jewel. God bless her.

Rev. Mr. Richards is pastor of the Methodist Church. He asked me if I would take the service on Sabbath morning. I chose the words for the basis of my remarks, "Awake thou that sleepest and arise from the dead, and Christ shall give thee light." These are the words the Lord seemed to impress on my mind from my observation of the feeling among the people. The Lord helped me to deliver the message and blessed the people; and there seemed to come upon them a spirit of revival, and there was a prayer meeting appointed, and on Thursday evening I took the service again; then they appointed a prayer meeting for Friday afternoon; one seeker came forward for prayers; then there was another meeting appointed for Monday afternoon. On Wednesday and Thursday I gave some Bible readings.

July 25th, 1882. On Thursday night the Lord was with us in power; the altar was crowded, and a number professed to have found peace, there were some grand cases of real conversion. Praise the Lord.

We went on holding three meetings a day, in the morning at six o'clock, in the afternoon at four, and in the evening at eight, until Sunday. Being just the time of the rainy season, sometimes we were hindered by the torrents of rain. Sunday night was one of those wet nights, but the people came out; there were twenty-six in all who professed conversion during this week of revival services. Several native boys, who were servants in the families, were converted; these, to me, were the most interesting cases. Poor things, how my heart went out toward them! No one thinks much about them, or pays much attention to them. But it is wonderful when they begin to pray, to see how they will stick to it; and in their darkness, feeling after God, if happily they may find him.

Sunday evening I spoke to the children at the Sabbath School, on the subject of temperance, with good effect, I trust. At night, Brother Richards preached and I gave an exhortation. and the Lord greatly helped us. On Thursday night I spoke on prayer. On Sunday I spoke in the Presbyterian Church. We had a good congregation, and the Lord helped me to talk to the people, from the fifteenth chapter of John: "The branch and the vine."

Then I go to Virginia, and stop with Mrs. Fuller. I go to the Love Feast on Sunday morning. It was very wet and rainy, but we had a good meeting all day. What we need most is more of the Holy Ghost power. I had great liberty in speaking in the afternoon to a crowded house, from Romans 12.

On Monday, Mrs. Fuller and I go to Clay-Ashland in the canoe, and make some calls. We go to see a poor, sick, widow woman, and give her a word of cheer, with prayer and song. Then to see Brother Capehart, and then home, to my dear Aunt Martha and Uncle Henry Ricks'. It is so nice to get back; and I finish a long letter to my friend, Mrs. McDonald, Malden, Mass.

Bassa, Lower Buchanan, W. C. A., Feb. 8, 1883. Mr. Johnson asks me about a Mr. Declaybrook, who was here about two years ago, and said he came to raise funds for a girls' school. He wanted to see what the people were willing to do, and then he was to go back home and report, and they were to send the teachers out at once.

Mr. Crusaw, who was quite able, put down his name for a thousand dollars, Mr. Johnson for a large amount, and many others.

He went all through the county at Clay-Ashland and Arthington, and there were many who gave the money who were afraid they might not have it when he came again. He represented himself to be a pastor of a Baptist Church somewhere in America.

That is the way our people are humbugged. Good schools are so much needed, and these deceptions hinder greatly.

I asked the Lord to give me a word about Cape Mount. I opened at the fifth chapter of Luke, and my eye rested on the last line of the tenth verse; also the tenth verse of the fourth chapter: "Fear not; from henceforth thou shalt catch men." And, "He shall give His angels charge over thee, to keep thee."

My third Sabbath in Lower Buchanan, Bassa. Preaching in the morning by Rev. Mr. Briant. Sabbath School. Mr. Briant addresses the children. He spoke fifteen minutes, but said nothing! At half past seven I take the service—a Bible reading.

On Monday evening I began a series of services. I spoke on Monday evening, and gave a Bible reading consecration; a few people present, but the Lord helped me to speak for Him; so we went on, and the interest increased each night. Wednesday night and Thursday night a number came forward to the altar seeking sanctification. Friday evening we had a Gospel Temperance meeting. Four signed the pledge, while there were two seekers at the altar for salvation.

My last Sabbath. I spoke from John 17. The Lord helped me. The balance of the day I was ill. Lord, make me strong.

Upper Buchanan, Feb. 23, 1883. I leave Lower Buchanan to-day for Upper Buchanan. Stop at Mrs. Horris'. A pleasant walk late in the evening. This is a beautiful place. I have a nice room fronting the sea, with a fine view. And this is Africa, and I am here! Praise God for His goodness and mercy to me.

I expect, God willing, to walk to Congotown to-morrow to preach. God bless the dear people; and sanctify the message God may give me for them. The people are very kind, but the spiritual indifference among the people at Lower Buchanan is sad. Oh, God, awaken them! Awaken them!

On Tuesday I visited Mrs. T.'s school. There were about twelve or fifteen pupils present. Oh, the lack of life!

There is great need of good books. In this the government is very slack; and until we do our whole duty in this, our country is doomed. Education is our country's great need. There is so little attention paid to the education of girls; not a single high school for girls in the whole republic of Liberia. It is a great shame and a disgrace to the government.

Upper Buchanan. I am stopping with Mrs. Rebecca Horris. She has a nice, large house, which has been a first-class one; but it has gone down greatly.

Yesterday morning, Sabbath, I went to Brother Thomas' charge, a Congo village, to Church. Had a pleasant walk. Rode part of my way in the hammock. Spoke in the morning from Luke: "Have faith in God." The Lord helped me.

In the afternoon I talked in the Sabbath School, and got fifteen signers to the Gospel Temperance pledge. The Superintendent of the Sabbath School and the local preachers and class leaders would not sign the pledge. Oh, what hindrances they are in the work. Lord, save them, or move them out of the way.

Had a poor night's rest, but feel better this morning, thank God. Sister Thomas gets an early breakfast, and I start home to Upper Buchanan. Brother Thomas walks with me. Sister Toliver and Sister Marshal call, and we have a pleasant chat. The Lord is making away for His people. Oh, Lord, give us the whole city!

Send on the people the awakening spirit, the deep, awakening spirit of the Holy Ghost! Send it, Lord! Amen. Amen.

Edina, Grand Bassa, West Africa. On the 12th of April, 1883, in the evening I spoke in the Methodist Church, on the witness of the Spirit. I had been much in prayer all day.

My heart was greatly burdened for a precious soul, a Thomas Anderson. He was a young lawyer of great promise, but strong drink had been his ruin; so that his brightest prospects in life had been dimmed. But when he heard of Gospel Temperance he was glad, and the first week I held Bible readings he came and seemed to be much interested. He came also to the night services. The Spirit of the Lord got hold of him, and he yielded himself fully to God, and on the morning of April 15th he was clearly baptized by the Spirit. He felt the Spirit of God bearing witness with his spirit that he was fully accepted of God.

It was the Friday appointed by the President as a Thanksgiving Day; so at six o'clock in the morning we had prayer meeting, and the power of the Lord was present to heal backsliders and sanctify believers. Anderson had signed the total abstinence pledge, and when the society was organized he was made vice-president; but he was not permitted to serve very long.

With honor he delivered his first address, on April 25th, at the Baptist Church. He began, after addressing the congregation, by quoting the verse of an old familiar hymn:

"I once was lost, but now am found
Was blind, but now I see."

All felt the force of his remarks, for they knew full well what they meant. The address was powerful; broad and comprehensive; he handled it as a master from two standpoints, experience and observation.

His wife, who had shared all the hardships of a drunkard's wife, but never left him, signed the pledge with him. And though she was a professing Christian, yet being oppressed, and so often in sorrow, she had grown weary and cold in her spiritual life; but she gave herself anew to God.

In a few days after this she was taken very ill; and, after suffering for ten days, she passed away to her final rest, on the 26th, and was buried with the honors of the newly organized Band of Hope Gospel Temperance Society, from the Baptist Church, on Friday, the 27th.

This was a great shock to poor Anderson. He, himself, had not been well for weeks. But he was the teacher of the school there, and so kept about. He was taken to his bed about the first of May. After his poor wire was taken he seemed to break right down. They had no children, fortunately. I say fortunately, for of all the sad things that can happen, the worst is for a child to be left with the heritage of a drunken father.

Strong drink does not only destroy the soul and body of men, but robs them of every comfort of life. And now this was his portion; and those who were his friends in prosperity, were not to be found in time of his great need. Oh, how he suffered from want and neglect. I did all a stranger could do, for I had only known him and his wife for a short time. But I think I never saw such heartlessness in a Christian community all my life. My home was in the family of Mrs. G. Williams, almost opposite where Mr. Anderson lived. So I would run in and see him.

On May third I went in the morning. He was all alone. Mrs. Williams sent him some breakfast by me. At night a little native boy was left to look after him, and that was all that stayed with him at night. Late in the afternoon he had a chill. He wrapped himself up in a blanket as best he could, and prayed and asked God to show him clearly that he was fully His, and help him to give himself unreservedly to Him. He had longed to die and go to His home in Heaven, as his wife had gone, he did not want to stay; but for fear he might have too much of his own will in the matter, he asked the Lord to help him resign himself completely to Him. After he had prayed, he had turned over, and was meditating, and this hymn came into his mind:

> "On Jordan's stormy banks I stand,
> And cast a wishful eye
> To Canaan's fair and happy land,
> Where my possessions lie."

He said as he went on, the Lord Jesus began to manifest Himself to him, and fill his soul. Wave after wave went over him. And when he got to the verse:

> "Sweet fields beyond the swelling flood,
> Stand dressed in living green;
> So, to the Jews, old Canaan stood,
> While Jordan rolled between,"

the Holy Ghost came to him in such power that he cried out so loud that the people in the street heard him and went in. I went in, and said to him, "Anderson, what's the matter?"

"Oh, nothing's the matter. My Jesus has just passed by, and has left such a blessing. Oh, such a blessing!"

"Do you want anything?"

"Oh, no," he said. "Sister Smith, I don't want anything. Jesus is here. O, glory to His name."

"Amen. Praise the Lord;" I said, and left him, rejoicing in the very joy of Heaven.

I went to see him every day. He was always calm, and cheerful, and trustful. I gave him Wood's book, "Purity and Maturity." He read it through twice. His heart drank it all in. I believe the baptism that the Lord gave him was the full sanctifying baptism of the Holy Ghost.

On Sabbath morning, May 6th, Brother Rush preached at the Methodist Church. It was Communion Sunday. At the close of the service we took the communion over to Brother Anderson. I am glad to say we were able to celebrate this communion with unfermented wine. It was a time of great blessing; his first and last communion on earth. But, oh, how soon he renewed it with Him in the Kingdom.

Tuesday, May 15th. I left Edina this morning for Beulah. I shall always regret it; for I think, just then, I got out of the Lord's leading, and went myself, rather than wait for pure light from God. May God forgive me.

Miss Scott, the white Episcopal missionary, had been down to Edina, and had given me a very pressing invitation to come to Beulah at this time. But, oh, didn't I see my mistake afterwards? I thought it was all real. But, oh, how many things one has to find out by personal experience that they never could find out otherwise.

On Saturday, the 13th, a Mr. Lloyd came down the river, went to see Mr. Anderson, and told him he could cure his rheumatism; and though he was in so weak a condition, he had no friend to say, "You had better not go," and he went; it was in the rainy season, and, being uncomfortable and poorly clad, he got very wet, and cold struck in; and, instead of Mr. Lloyd's taking him into his house, and putting him in a comfortable bed, he was put in a hammock, and swung in an open kitchen, until two o'clock Monday morning, when they took him into the house, and at seven o'clock, when Mr. Lloyd went to look at him, he found him dead!

They said that all day Sunday they found him very happy, and that he spoke much of going home to God. And now the time had come, and the hard struggle of life was over. Thoma Anderson was not. For God had taken him.

> "Safe in the arms of Jesus,
> Safe on His gentle breast;
> There by His love o'ershaded,
> Sweetly his soul finds rest."

CHAPTER XXVI.

FORTSVILLE—TEMPE RANCE MEETINGS—EVIL CUSTOMS—THOMAS BROWN—BALAAM—JOTTINGS FROM THE JUNK RIVER—BROTHER HARRIS IS SANCTIFIED.

Hartford, Africa, July 1st, 1883. I have spent a pleasant time at Mr. Coy Brown's. Have gone on with two weeks' meetings. The Lord has given some blessing. Three have professed to find peace in believing on the Lord Jesus Christ. There are some five or six others seeking, but, oh, there is such a lack of faith on the part of the church. Zion travails, and comes to the birth, but has not power to bring forth. Lord, send us down the power they had at Pentecost.

One civilized native, a young man who has been converted, was baptized on Sunday, the 5th. God bless Isaac Cassie, and make him a burning and shining light. And may his father and mother, who are still in heathen darkness, soon be brought to God, and saved by faith in Jesus Christ.

I went from Hartford to Fortsville. I stopped with a Mr. Wiley Fort. After a little rest, I began some meetings; Bible readings, first, at the Methodist Church.

It being the rainy season, the people didn't come out very well; and then I arranged to have them at Mr. Fort's house in the afternoon, and go to the church in the evening, when the rain didn't pour too severely.

The meetings held were very interesting, and the Lord was with us. There has been some interest on the subject of temperance, and a number have signed the pledge. We hope to organize a society in this settlement on Wednesday night, God willing. May

He give us His presence, and enlighten the minds of the people, for we are very dark on this subject. And the merchants are flooding the land with this accursed fire, and men and women are being devoured by it.

One merchant, a foreigner, a Mr. Attier, I am told, is ordering a hundred thousand cases of gin, so as to escape the law of high duties, which goes into effect in September. The law goes in for high duties on the importation of strong drink. Then I see how many ministers there are in the country who stand aloof from the work of temperance, and are afraid to open their mouths against this great Zerubabel that shall become a plain. May God put a book in his jaw. Oh, Lord, work quick! For Jesus' sake, speak! Arrest this flood tide, and awaken the people to a sense of their duty.

What a dreadful snare this trade is. Of course, the doings and customs are all new to me; I have never seen it in this wise before. Preachers and laymen all think there is nothing they can do but trade. Some of the men go off in the country for fifty or sixty or a hundred miles; there they stay for years; two, three, five and eight, right along. Young men, and married men; they will leave their wives and children. Some start towns, and buy native women, and have large families; this is not an uncommon occurrence!

A fine looking young man, who owns his own house, and has a nice wife and one child, has left everything and been away in the country two years. His wife stayed at the place as long as she could; but he sent her nothing to live on, so her parents had to take her home. He has several wives in the country, and, of course, he cannot support all.

I am stopping with a lady now, whose brother, a young man, is in the country, and has been there over a year. Here is where our loss is in the perpetuation of our church. If they would try to teach and instruct the heathen, or teach school, or do something to elevate, and civilize, and Christianize the poor natives, then it would be well. But they at once fall into all the customs and habits, and turn from Christianity easier than they turn the heathen from idolatry.

Oh, what a blight is on our whole country because of this sin. We have degraded ourselves in the eyes of the heathen. And now the blind lead the blind.

On Saturday a poor woman came to me in great trouble. Her husband had been away in the country for six months. He came home and brought several boys with him. After several days had passed he seemed very unkind and quarrelsome. Nothing was

right. She could do nothing to please him. So he got drunk and beat her severely, and chased her from the house with a gun.

The secret was, he had become infatuated with a country wife, and his own home and wife had lost all charms for him.

Greenville, Sinoe Co., W. C. A., January 11th, 1884. Yesterday was a sad day. Two of the oldest men in town died, and one was interred at eleven and the other at four P. M. Both were good men; one a member of the Methodist Church for nearly half a century; a class leader and trustee, and also sexton and grave digger. His name was Thomas Brown. He emigrated to this country forty years ago. His life was not a life of comfort, after the style of the world. He had much to contend with; but the joy of the Lord was his strength, and he triumphed by faith, anyway! His last sickness, which lasted but a month, was very severe, and the dear old man had such few comforts; but not a murmur escaped his lips. A few months before he died, Brother Draper said to him:

"Brother Brown, you are almost home."

"Oh, yes," he said, "I shall be home directly," and he thanked God for the last little acts of kindness done; then he closed his eyes in peace, and went to God.

My heart said, "Oh, let *me* die the death of the righteous, and let my last end be like theirs."

He was a member of the Band of Hope Gospel Temperance Society; one of the first to join when the work began here in Sinoe, in December. His membership was of short duration; we had his happy "amens" to cheer us only a short time. But he stood true to his pledge, and the principles of total abstinence, and was a strong advocate.

The other was Louis Sherman. He also was a member of the Gospel Temperance Society. Each leaves a large family to mourn his loss.

A strange incident connected with this was, while the services were going on in the house over the remains of the men, the dogs, numbering six or seven in the different houses, howled in the most distressing manner; then they would cease, and begin again, as though they were directed by someone.

The Band of Hope formed a line and led on, the others following. At five P M., all was over, and the families returned to see their husbands and fathers no more till they all meet beyond the river.

MY FIRST SUNDAY SCHOOL, PLUKIE, CAPE PALMAS.

I have been visiting Frances Craten for almost a week. She is in a dying condition, but is clinging tight to life, and has not a ray of light, or joy, or thanksgiving, or praise. I seem to be shut up. I can't get hold of Him in prayer or in song. All is blank. God save me in the dying hour from darkness and doubt.

I have had much to contend with since I came to Sinoe. I have never had any such trials in all my travels as I have had here. I have never met with such deception and such planning to overthrow the work as I have met here. But not with standing all this, there are some good people here, and God is my friend, and has given me a few that are real and true, and I thank Him. He has delivered me out of the hands of the most subtle enemy—though always under the garb of real friendship—that I have ever met. Thank God for His wonderful and speedy deliverance. Now, Lord, keep me delivered, ever and always, and help me to watch and pray, and on Thyself rely. Amen.

I have found a good and true friend in Mrs. Sarah Marshall; a genial spirit, and a comfortable home, and plenty to eat. Not more than others, I deserve, yet God has given me more. "I will take the cup of salvation and call on the name of the Lord."

On the eve of the tenth of January, at the Presbyterian Church, Sammy Ross, Jr., gave a very interesting address on "Stand to the right." I see a noble man coming out of this temperance boy. God bless him.

Our next meeting is expected to be held in the Episcopal Church. I went to see Mrs. Craten. She is very weak; but she has got all her business arranged satisfactorily. God helped me to push them up till all is settled. Now the way is clear. May God come in with a flood of light, and show her what she still needs to know. Thank God for this gain.

Saturday, January 12th. I am not well this morning. I was at Mrs. Craten's late last night, and she seemed very restless, and as she was disturbed in mind, I sang and prayed; but she had no light or access to God. Oh, how she fought death to the very last. She never yielded one inch to God.

She could not die in the house she lived in; she made them carry her to her sister's, and in five minutes after, her breath was snatched from her.

She lived in the church, and lived in malice of the bitterest kind with her sister, her only sister, and died the same, not even mentioning her name in her will, and without it house over her head. She bade good bye to all, and they said she went to Heaven. But, oh, how dark!

January 13th. She was buried on Sabbath morning. Rev. Munger and Rev. Kennedy spoke over her. But, oh, that deceived soul, to the last deceiving, and living deceived! The Lord seemed to shut me up so that I had no word for her. "Oh, mistaken soul that dreams of Heaven and makes its empty boast!"

I was not out all day, except to the funeral. I hope to be stronger by and by. God help me. Amen.

Monday, January 14th. Praise God for His goodness and mercy to me. I am feeling rather weak, but call to see Mrs. Harris, and Mrs. G. Craten, and Mrs. Louis. They are all well. Then I take Brother Kennedy one pound, which makes up the balance of the eleven dollars I promised to get. There were fifty dollars subscribed. Some paid; I promised to pay the eleven dollars if no one else did. I walked all day on Monday and got six dollars, and waited a week and no one paid a cent; so I paid the five dollars myself. In all, I paid out of my pocket eight dollars.

Selfishness is killing us. God, have mercy. Paying the minister is a thing hardly thought of. The church here agreed to give the minister two hundred dollars; in a whole year they gave him fifty dollars!

This year, when he was getting ready to go to the Conference, he told them if they would give him fifty dollars he would give them the one hundred; and of that fifty on last year's salary they had only given thirty dollars, and eight dollars of that I gave myself.

Sinoe, January 15th. Tuesday. I make bread, and write a ten-page letter to my friend, Mr. Ester. Oh, precious time, how you fly!

Wednesday, 16th. I was very miserable and weak all day yesterday and to-day, but was better in the afternoon, so that I went out to the temperance meeting, held at the Episcopal Church. We had a very interesting meeting. Sammy Ross did nobly. Mr. Munger, the pastor, has not signed the pledge, but we asked him to speak, and he gave us a good talk, just to the point, and said he would do all he could for the furtherance of the work, and also offered to give us an address next Wednesday night. I believe the Lord will help him. Oh, Lord, save our land.

Sunday, 20th. I go to early prayer meeting; a good many out. Then I go home and have prayers. At breakfast, word comes that there is to be preaching and quarterly meeting at the Baptist Church, Brother Huff's. I go. The distance is about a mile and a half. The Lord gives me strength for the day, and I go to a baptizing. Hear two sermons; one, by Brother Roberts, at the church, the other at the water side, or pond.

I did not stay to the afternoon meeting. Having a little rest, I walked home. The sun was very hot. I was dripping with perspiration. I lay down and took a little rest, then went to church. Brother Draper preached. Text in Psalms, "Keep back thy servant from presumptuous sins."

I asked the privilege of making some remarks, and explained why I was not present the Sunday before (I was not well), and reported the money I had collected for Brother Kennedy, eleven dollars. I paid in all I had given. May God bless him, and me.

Monday, 21st. Sister Draper and I go to Jamesville to-day to see her niece, Miss Brown, who is sick. We have a pleasant time. Have a season of prayer, and read and sing. Sister Brown seems to enjoy it. But, oh, the coldness and death chill! No life, no power in prayer. Oh, God, awake the people, for Jesus sake!

Then we called at old lady Brichadenn's. This is a dear old saint, and is ripening for glory. After hearing her tell of the Lord's dealings with her, which were marvelous, we sang a hymn, and then knelt down and prayed.

The Lord met us there under the trees, and blessed us; and the benediction that old lady pronounced on me I shall never forget. May the Lord grant this, and more, according to His sweet will. Amen.

Went to Sister Kenney's. Had another song and season of prayer. There the Lord blessed us again. Then we returned home about two o'clock. After a little rest I went to Mrs. Harris' and took dinner, with some others. Had a pleasant time. Praise the Lord for the blessings He giveth.

Tuesday, January 22nd. I am well this morning. Praise God. And I am asking for the baptism of the Holy Ghost. Oh, how I need it. My soul cries out for the living God. God, help me. I have a good deal of writing to do, and a good many other things. But He has said, "My grace is sufficient for you." Mrs. Marshall and I have a nice call from Brother and Sister Munger.

Wednesday, January 23, 1884. This is my birthday. Oh, how the Lord has led me, and loved me, and watched over me for forty-seven long years.

> "All the way my Lord has led me,
> Cheered each winding path I tread
> Gave me grace for every trial,
> Fed me with the living bread."

I was born on the 23rd of January, 1837. My mother died when I was thirteen years old.

On my first birthday in Africa I was at Greenville. In the prayer meeting that night I gave the history of my conversion and sanctification. The people seemed much interested. Then I called all to the altar for consecration. We had some prayers, then I closed the meeting. The hymn sung while on our knees was the old familiar hymn, "Forever here my rest shall be." Oh, for the baptism of the Holy Ghost!

I spent the day at Greenville. Gave an address, and held a prayer meeting. About thirty in number came out. The darkness of mind here among the people is very great. God, send help, for Jesus' sake. Through ignorance there is much opposition to the temperance work.

Lexington, Monday, February 4th. Mrs. Birch, Sister Smith and I make some calls, and sing and pray at each house, in turns. Oh, Lord, revive Thy work. My first Gospel Temperance meeting held in the Baptist Church. The Lord helped me to speak from Mal., third chapter.

Tuesday, 5th. Second Gospel Temperance meeting. Surely the Spirit of the Lord is with us, and He is blessing us greatly. Not so much liberty in speaking, but God is with us, and we are expecting great things. Oh, Lord, for Jesus' sake, answer prayer, and send us the Holy Ghost to quicken and revive us.

Wednesday, 6th. We have a good meeting to-night. The pledge is offered and a number sign.

Thursday, 7th. I go to Greenville this morning to be at the installation of officers in the Order of Good Samaritans. Call at Brother Day's, (a Congo), who is an earnest Christian man, and a deacon in the Baptist Church. God bless him. He knows the Lord. We have a good time singing and talking over His Word. Called at Sister Wink's, then at Sister Mine's. The sun is very hot, but the Lord has given me strength. Two o'clock. Mrs. Marshall's, Greenville. My room is all arranged so very prettily; everything is so nice. God bless Mrs. Marshall. I go to church, sing and pray.

HOME OF PRESIDENT JOHNSON, MONROVIA, LIBERIA.

Sunday, 10th. Lexington. I preached at the Methodist Church this morning, from Romans 12: 1. The Lord helped me, though I felt so bad when I first began. In the afternoon I addressed the Sabbath School at the Baptist Church. The pastor and the superintendent were present.

Monday, 11th. Have a good Bible reading this afternoon, on the ability of Jesus, and a grand temperance meeting to-night.

Tuesday, 12th. Regular stated temperance prayer meeting. I make several calls, and take the meeting this evening. The Lord blesses us, and a number sign the total abstinence pledge.

Wednesday, 13th. We had a Bible reading to-day. The Lord was with us. At night we organized our Gospel Temperance Band.

Thursday, 14th. I do not get up till seven; so, much of the fine morning is gone. But, Oh, I felt so weary. He remembereth I am but dust.

Greenville, Sinoe, Sunday, February 17, 1884. I was at Lexington to quarterly meeting. We had a good meeting. I came home on Monday to Mrs. Marshall's, Greenville.

While at Lexington I went to see an old man, a Mr. Smith, a local preacher, and deacon of the Baptist Church. He was about sixty-five or seventy years old. He was much afflicted and could not walk. But I was told that this man was a very spiritually minded man, a man that people generally went to for spiritual advice. He claimed that the Lord revealed things to him in dreams, and people all about believed in him.

I was anxious to see him, and as I always went to see the sick and the poor, no matter when, or how weary and tired out I was, I went to see this old man; and I thought I was going to be refreshed by his counsel, as he had been in the way so long. He talked about religion, but really, to me, he did not seem like a man who possessed much of what he talked about. How dark and blank he seemed.

I talked and prayed with him, and asked him if there was any text of Scripture he would like to have me read for him. He seemed not to think of the Bible at all.

"Is there no Word of God that has been blessed to you," I said, "since you have been afflicted?"

"Oh, yes," said he, "if you can find about Balaam."

"Yes," I said, "I know what you mean; but what in that has been a blessing to you? I know Balaam was a very wicked king, and I cannot see what help came from it to you."

I was told that he had a great deal of prejudice against women preaching.

Just at this point he rallied, as though he was going to teach me something wonderful.

"Well," he said, "I will tell you Balaam had a cart, and the cart got stuck in the mud; and he had an associate, so he called his associate and asked him to help him pull his cart out of the mud. 'But,' he said, 'how are we going to get it out?' 'Well.' said he, 'if we can't get it out any other way, we will cuss it out!' "

"Well," I said, "of all the Bible reading I have ever heard or done, I have never read any such thing in the Bible in all my life."

"Oh, no," he said, "it's not in the Bible; but this is what the Spirit revealed to me."

"What did the Spirit purpose to teach you by such a revelation?"

"Well," he said, "the cart in the mud was his wicked heart, and the associate was the wicked trying to lead the innocent astray."

And after fifty years of being a Christian, and preacher and teacher, this was all he had to comfort him in his affliction. What a blind man! And the people at Lexington letting him go on into an unknown eternity. Oh, that God would awaken him in time.

I have not seen so much ignorance as there seems to be among many of the people of this county. How I wish the Lord would send some good missionary to be a blessing to the people.

Lexington, Sinoe Co., Africa, Sunday, Feb. 24, 1884. I had spent some months in the home of Brother Calvin Birch, whose faithful kindness, and that of his wife, I shall never forget. Mrs. F. Smith, another good sister of the Methodist Church, had invited me to spend a week at her home.

I went on Saturday, and on Sunday I was taken very ill with bilious colic, and came very near dying. After suffering terrible cramp and purging for about three hours, the Lord, in mercy, gave me ease. But I was not able to go out all day. After that I

had chills and fever every other day for a while, when I began to miss them, and soon began to gain strength.

On Tuesday, the 26th, I went to Louisiana. We had a fine temperance meeting; twenty-one signed the pledge. On Wednesday, the 27th, we had a fine meeting at Thankful Baptist Church, Lexington. On Thursday, 28th, I went down to Greenville.

Sunday morning, March 2. Went out to early prayer meeting; had a good time. Also at the Congregational Church there was a good prayer meeting. Poor Mr. Harris got a great blessing. May the Lord in mercy keep him. Rev. Mr. Frazier preached in the Congregational Church, and administered the Lord's Supper. The sermon was well read, but very void of spiritual power for such an occasion.

March 6. In the afternoon I went to Mrs. Morgan's to meet the lodge of Good Templars, and Daughters of Temperance. It is perfectly wonderful how all these old societies, which had once flourished, but had well nigh died out, began to be revived all over the republic as soon as I had begun the Gospel Temperance work among the young people and children, so that when I asked for co-operation and help, I was told that they belonged to this society, and to the other society, it had gone down, but that they were going to commence again. So to show them that I was with them in anything that was for the well-being of the people, I joined them, and helped what I could. But, Oh, how hollow, and empty, and unreal.

After all it is not the tinsel and show, but it is the real heart work for God and souls that Africa needs, especially.

Friday, the 7th, I went to Mrs. Bonner's and then off to the Baptist Association held at the Court House.

Sunday, March 16th, I went to Louisiana, preached in the morning. When we started home, and got to the river, the tide had gone out, and we could not get our canoe up; so we had to be carried through the mud to it. If some one had been near by where they could have taken our pictures I know they would have sold well. Imagine our position, on two Kroo boys' shoulders, while we hung down all about in spots!

Well, we got through the slime, anyhow, and that was quite an item. Brother Bonner went ahead, on the boys' back. I was obliged to do the best I could to keep from laughing, for fear they would let us go in the mud together; and that was my heaviest task. But my time came after awhile.

We got back in time to go to the Baptist meeting. Brother Rocker, a licentiate in the Baptist Church, preached. He was a good preacher, but, Oh, how he needed the Holy Ghost. Poor man, how often I have prayed for him. I called to see Mr. Rice. The poor man is dying. I spoke to him of Jesus, who is the only truth and life. How sad that any one should put it off until the very last moment; it does look so mean to live on God's mercy all through life and health, and then a few minutes before the breath leaves you, when you cannot serve the world, and yourself, and sin, any longer, possibly, turn to the Lord. How foolish! God help us.

Before I went, a temperance meeting was held in the Episcopal Church, Brother Munger. Had a grand, good meeting. Gospel Temperance took well there. The Lord seemed to be blessing the people with a spirit and interest, that, if continued, would be a blessing to them.

On Tuesday I started early and walked to Lexington. Young Jenkins put me across the stream with his canoe. Wednesday I walked to Louisiana, then out to Cherry Ridge, held a temperance meeting at the church, and a number signed the pledge. We organized. Thursday I preached, from John, 9th chapter. After suffering much with my back all day, I went to Lexington, and then expected to go to Farmersville to another meeting.

Monrovia, April 22, 1885. Rev. James Deputie and myself leave fifteen minutes past eleven for Mt. Olive. The distance is about seventy miles, taking the shortest cut.

We take passage in a canoe at the waterside, and after a slow pull in the hot sun for three hours we come to Paynesville, the first stop. There we rest an hour or more. No one asked us to eat, but the friends had given me a small lunch before I started, so we took a snack, and then started on foot across the Old Fields, a distance of about five miles.

The sun was warm, and I got very tired before I got to the end of the five miles. I was glad to rest, and had a short nap for ten minutes. We had hoped to get through to the creek, and so reach Marshall by seven o'clock; but the boys worked slowly, and the tide fell before we got off; so we had to remain all night.

We took refuge at the house of a Mrs. Clark. Brother Deputie asked her if she could take us in for the night: she said it would be very inconvenient, but as there was no other house within five miles, we told her we would stop and make the best of it.

NATIVE SOLDIERS, MONROVIA, AFRICA.

It was now about seven o'clock, and I suppose the supper and dinner were over, and not a word was said to us; I would have been so glad if she had offered me a roasted casava, or anything. So I ate a few dry biscuits and drank a cup of cold water, and was very thankful.

I had a little talk with Sister Clark about her condition; she said she was converted in America; she did not know the year or month; she seemed dead clear through; I tried to draw her out; but she seemed to stick fast on every side; I sang and prayed about Jesus, and I hoped that she would respond somewhere; but not a word; so I gave up and went to bed.

This poor woman was there, pretty much alone, no church nearby, and her nearest neighbors five miles away, and she in darkness equal to that of the heathen round about her, though born in a Christian land, and had heard the Gospel message. How often we find this.

I did not change my clothes when I went to bed; I thanked God for a cover over my head, and a corner to he down in; though I was very wet with perspiration, somehow I slept well. At three in the morning, Brother Deputie sang out:

"Sister Smith, it is time to go."

It didn't take me long to arrange my toilet. After prayer, we were soon off to the waterside. There was no moon, and as it had been raining it was quite dark; so with lantern in hand we marched off. The boys were a little stupid, but about four o'clock we got pushed off; it was dark, but having a good lantern we got out of the creek all right; the creek was long, and in some places very narrow.

We got to the head of the river just at daylight. The morning was pleasant; about ten o'clock the sun was very hot. We got to a friend's house, and stopped for a rest; the sister gave us some coffee, bitter and black, and not a bit of bread; poor thing, she didn't have any. I took a sip or two of the coffee, and ate a dry biscuit.

While there the Lord sent us a good shower of rain, which cooled the atmosphere; we left there and went to Grassdale, and spent an hour at Sister Brown's. From there we went on to Mt. Olive, Brother Deputie's station and home. We reached there about half past five P. M., and had a cordial reception from Sister Deputie and the children; a comfortable home, and every part of the house as clean as a pin, and his wife and children the same. I was thankful for it good bath, and a good dinner, as I had not had much for two days.

Brother Deputie had been going up and down this river so long that he did not think these hardships, but pleasant; well, I did not think them the worst that ever was, but I did thank God they were no worse. One thing there is, they have plenty of fine oysters.

I had a good, quiet rest from Thursday night till Sunday, before I was called upon to take a service. Brother Deputie's church was a good sized thatch church, the members mostly natives, but, being the only church, it accommodated others as well. We walked about a half mile, and I spoke to a good company that had gathered. I gave the Word from Hebrews, 12:1-23. The Lord wonderfully helped me. Brother Philip Harris, native interpreted. I was much pleased with this brother, and thought if a little encouragement were given he would make a faithful servant in the church. I remained for Sabbath School, and spoke a word of encouragement to the teachers and scholars, and sang a hymn: "Bringing in the sheaves;" then I walked home, weary, as I was not feeling very well all day.

Monday I was not well, but took some medicine, and so got better. On Thursday I went with Brother Deputie and made four pastoral calls. We called on a Mrs. Johnson, a very interesting woman, who is quite sick, has a houseful of children, and is not converted. I spoke with her, and urged on her the necessity of accepting Christ, then and there. We prayed with her, but she seemed blank. May the Lord be merciful to her.

April 29th, Brother and Sister Deputie and I took a nice canoe ride, of about a mile. Called on Deacon Kink. He was quite an old man; his wife, a very pleasant, sensible woman, from Pennsylvania, U. S. Brother King was a Southerner, one of the old type. We spent a pleasant hour with them; had a season of prayer; they were delighted. How those poor souls off in the desert enjoy a little call like that. How I do thank the Lord when it is my privilege to sing and pray and cheer the weary traveler along the lonesome road.

We called at the house of one sister who was not at home. Then we went on to Brother Artists. This brother was Chief Magistrate. He had been afflicted for years; could not walk; but sat on the floor. His right arm is withered; all the fingers of his right hand are off, only the stumps remaining; his right side is withered all the way down; he is a great sufferer, but seems happy. He was quite an intelligent man; much above the average young man in the neighborhood or country; his wife, also, was an intelligent woman, and an industrious one; she kept school in their house; I heard the children in spelling and multiplication, and they did well.

I hope to leave to-morrow for Marshall, on the Junk River. On Monday I go to Paynesville, and if Brother Pitman can arrange a service, I will speak at his church on Tuesday night. On Wednesday morning I get off for Marshall; got there about two P. M. Preached Friday night, Saturday night, and three times on the Sabbath, and left on Monday at six-twenty for Monrovia.

Virginia, Africa, November 16th, 1884. This was a glorious victory. I had been holding a meeting here every night for a week. The Lord poured out His Spirit, and there was a great awakening among the people.

Old Brother Jacob Harris, who was a member of the Methodist Church, and had been for years, and was much interested in the subject of holiness, by faith was enabled to see the way clearly, and claim the blessing of cleansing, and receive the witness of the Holy Ghost. It was about eleven o'clock, A. M., when he called to see me, where I was stopping, at Sister Watson's. Sister Watson was a grand woman, and for several years had enjoyed the great salvation, and was a power in the church and neighborhood.

Brother Harris came in to see me that morning, and, as I was trying to show him the simplicity of faith, he said:

"Yes, Sister Smith, I see it, and I have been trying and praying for this sanctification for over three years; and, somehow, I don't know how to take hold. But I have given my self all up, and I have put myself in the hands of God; and I am resolved to trust Him as long as I live; I never mean to stop; I want the blessing of sanctification."

The blessed Spirit was all this time overshadowing him till he could hardly speak sometimes for the flood of tears that rushed in upon him.

"Now, Brother Harris," I said, "can you accept Christ as your full and complete Saviour, now? He is made unto you wisdom, righteousness, sanctification and redemption; now, right while you are sitting on that chair, on this veranda, at this very hour, before you move from that spot, before you eat another morsel, before you drink another drop of water; now, Christ is made unto you wisdom, righteousness, sanctification, and redemption, and His blood cleanseth from all sin; will you take Christ now?"

Looking at me, he lifted his hand and said, "Sister Smith, I am determined to fight for this till I die. I give my life all into the hands of God, now."

"Brother Harris, you have been up to the point many times before, and gone right back; will you, do you, here and now, do it?"

He was looking right at me. I repeated, "Do you here and now, take Christ as your wisdom, Christ as your righteousness, Christ as your sanctification, Christ as your redemption, and believe His blood does now cleanse you from all sin, now, right now? Not because you feel, but because God has said so, and, in the authority of His Word, do you stand and declare to the dying world, not doubting, the conditions all being met, and trusting the eternal God, do you declare that 'The blood of Jesus Christ, His son, cleanseth you from all sin?' Now, do you do it?"

"Yes, I do;" he said, and as loud as I could I shouted, "Amen."

The old man buried his face in his hands, and, weeping, said, "Glory to Jesus."

"Trust Him," I said, "and do not doubt. He does save you now."

"Oh, praise the Lord;" he cried, then sprang to his feet, grabbed hold of Sister Watson's hand, and then hold of my hand. Brother Watson was in the house; he went after him. "Oh, glory! I am free, as I never have been before in all my life. Oh, how sweet! Glory!"

After about fifteen minutes of shouting and praying, he took his hat and cane and started for home. He said, "Pray for me, that I may ever be kept on the rock."

I stepped into the parlor, and said, "Let's all pray now."

We were all so full of praise and thanksgiving it was a little difficult to pray; but I tried to pray as best I could, then I asked Sister Watson to pray. Poor Brother Watson had been seeking the blessing so long; may God help him, and quickly.

Brother Harris had been a member of the Methodist Church for thirty years; and he said that Sister Watson's testimony after she first got the blessing first stirred him up to pray; so she has been praying for him and helping him all she could ever since.

"I knew this child," he said, "when she was a little girl; and she has grown up, and been converted, and sanctified, and here I have been in the church all these years, and what have I done? So I started out to pray, and glory be to God, He has heard me. Oh, Sister Smith, she did help me all she could, but I could not see it;

oh, I thank the Lord He sent you, and you seemed to make it so plain, the points you went over I could see, and I thank God."

"Of victory now o'er Satan's power,
Let all the ransomed sing;
And triumph in the dying hour
Through Christ, the Lord, their king."

CHAPTER XXVII.

CONFERENCE AT MONROVIA—ENTERTAINING THE BISHOP—SIERRA LEONE—GRAND CANARY—A STRANGE DREAM—CONFERENCE AT BASSA—BISHOP TAYLOR.

Monrovia, Jan. 1st, 1885. The morning is lovely, and my note of praise is, "Oh! Lord, I will praise Thee, and in the great congregation I will tell of Thy wonderful works. Thou hast brought me through deep waters the past year. I will praise Thee while I have being. Praise the Lord!"

The ladies are holding a bazar in the parlors of the mansion of Mrs. President Roberts. They don't hold their bazars and fairs in the churches in Africa. That is one good thing. I go down and spend an hour. Feeling very weak and bad, I go home.

Friday, Jan. 9th. Praise the Lord for this day. The President vetoes a bill for taking the duties off imported gin and whisky. Amen. Thank God. A great triumph for our temperance people. It is a noble act, and it took a man of courage to do it just at this time. There has been much prayer among the people, and especially in our band meetings. We are expecting the Bishop, and think we are in good condition for a blessing.

Wednesday, Jan. 21st. How glad I am to be here just at this time, and so to help the Bishop a little. It appears that somehow Brother Ware and the official brethren have had some little misunderstanding; so the end of it is to be the paying of a large sum for the Bishop's board. He has arranged this matter with Mr. R. E. Sherman, who is a merchant, and has a fine large house—the next in rank, for size, to the President's mansion.

Mr. Sherman is one of the leading Deacons in the Presbyterian Church. So it is with him Brother Ware has arranged that the Bishop shall stop. He is to have his boats and crew all ready to go to meet the Bishop, as soon as the gun fires, and the steamer is

in. Mr. and Mrs. Sherman are among some of the best friends I have in Monrovia. How kind they are to me. God bless them.

Mr. Sherman does not object to taking the Bishop, but thinks it would not look so well, when there are men in the Methodist Church who have good houses, and are amply able to entertain the Bishop, or anyone else. Brother Henry Cooper is the leading Steward; he and his son, Jesse, both have their own large brick houses, and are prosperous merchants, and they have their own boats and crews. Then there is Brother Campbell, also a Class Leader and Steward in the Methodist Church, with a beautiful home. But they do not know anything about Brother Ware's arrangement. After he has thus completed all his arrangements, he goes up the river.

On Wednesday night we had a very precious meeting. I had given a talk on the message of holiness; well, it is a kind of lecture from that grand little book, called the Believer's Hand-book of Holiness, by Brother Davies. I gave this talk to the people; and then we closed with a consecration meeting. The Lord helped us very greatly. As we were going out from the church it was whispered to me:

"Did you know that Brother Ware had arranged for Bishop Taylor, when he comes, to stop with Mr. Sherman?"

"No."

And then it went, just like a thing will go in Liberia. So off I started for the facts in the case. As I got to Brother Sherman's gate, he was standing talking with someone. He spoke to me very kindly, and said:

"Well, Mrs. Smith, I hear your Bishop is coming."

"Yes," I said, "so I have heard; and that he is to be your guest."

"Well, yes," he said; "how is it that you folks can't take care of your Bishop?"

This remark was meant as a joke, of course.

"Well, now," I said, "that is a pity, when we have such men in the Methodist Church as Brother Henry Cooper, and Mr. Gabriel Moore, and others. But I think we can relieve you of that task, Mr. Sherman. Though I think it is very kind in you to be willing to entertain the Bishop. But I'm going to see Brother Cooper about it."

"Well," he said, "Brother Ware came to me before he went up the river, and made the arrangement. But I think you would all feel better if the Bishop stopped with some of your own church people."

"Certainly," I said; "and when there are those who are so able to do it, without troubling you."

So I thanked him, and off I went to Brother Cooper's and told him all about it.

"Yes, Sister Smith," he said, "we are expecting the Bishop here. But Brother Ware, had said nothing to me about his arrangement."

"Well, that is the way it is. And the steamer may come to-night or to-morrow. So you get your boat and everything ready, and then tell Mr. Sherman that you or Jesse will see to getting the Bishop ashore."

"All right."

So all was arranged, and I went home and left the rest with the Lord. The people were glad that I did what I could.

The next morning was a lovely morning, as mornings in Africa generally are. I was very busy all day. In the afternoon I went up town and made some calls. About seven o'clock in the evening, a messenger came to Mrs. Moore's, where I was, and said the Bishop had come, and had gone to the church. It was our regular preaching night; so the Bishop, when he arrived, made his way straight to the church.

My! when I heard it, I went on double-quick down town; went to the church, and there was the Bishop in the pulpit. He preached a powerful sermon, from the text: "Thy will be done." And, as the people generally turned out well Thursday nights, the Bishop had a good congregation, and the people generally were delighted. I was delighted beyond expression. I had seen him before and knew him. Praise the Lord.

"Well, how did he get ashore?"

When the steamer arrived, she didn't fire her gun signal, as usual; she had no cargo for that port; only came in to let the Bishop off; so the captain sent him ashore in one of the steamer's boats, with the chief officer; so that Brother Cooper did not have to launch his boat, though he was all ready, and Jesse had seen the steamer, and was at the wharf getting ready to send off, when lo, and behold! there was the Bishop before him.

What a beautiful victory this was. How often I have stood

HOME OF THE LATE PRESIDENT ROBERTS, OF LIBERIA.

still and seen God overrule things of man's device, and work His sovereign will. Amen.

So Bishop Taylor's home from that day has been at Brother Henry Cooper's house, when in Liberia. Sometimes he has had to stop there three weeks, before he could get away. And God has always helped Brother Cooper, and always will.

How well I remember that all day holiness meeting, when God so wonderfully sanctified Brother Cooper, and, a few days later, his dear wife. How well I remember the morning she came to Sister Payne's, singing her song of victory, for she had got the baptism in her own home. She came up to Sister Payne's, where my home was. I saw her when she was coming in. Her face was all a glow of light. Oh! I shall never forget it. The first thing she said as she came in, was:

> "Glory to His name!
> Glory to His name!
> There to my heart was the blood applied;
> Glory to His name!"

And she has been singing it ever since; in the midst of trials and storms, for she has had them, and so will everybody that goes into the fountain straight. God doesn't often develop on any other line than that of trial, and sometimes suffering, in various ways; "For the trial of your faith is more precious than gold, though it be tried with fire."

Saturday, January 24th. The Bishop and I were invited to take breakfast at the United States Legation, American Consul, Hon. John Smyth. Prof. Brown, who was a guest of Mr. Smyth's, was also present. We had a most elegant breakfast, served in real American style, and we thoroughly enjoyed it.

I think the Bishop had no thought of any such reception in Africa. But Mr. Smyth, who is so thoroughly qualified for his position, is always quick to perform the courtesies due to strangers, and especially those from his own country, America.

The Bishop and I made a number of calls together in the different places. He never objected to going anywhere, among the poorest of the poor. He would go in and sit down, sing, pray and talk, and leave his blessing. He never seemed to give the impression to anyone that they need to stand off from him, or be afraid of him, because he was Bishop. He was always congenial and kind to everyone.

The Conference convened on the 29th. The Bishop preached every night, and on Sunday morning, and then addressed the Sabbath School in the afternoon, and at four o'clock preached at Krootown. The Lord wonderfully poured out His spirit, and there was a gracious revival. Sinners were converted, backsliders reclaimed, believers sanctified. Oh, what a tidal wave swept over us! So the Conference convened in the midst of the flood-tide of revival. Praise the Lord.

Sunday, February 1st, 1885. The great ordination. Ten Deacons and nine Elders ordained by Bishop Taylor. Glory to God. It was a wonderful day. Such had not been seen in Monrovia before.

Monday, February 2nd. I am very weak in body, but my faith is strong in God. I make some calls, and go to see William Potter, whom everybody is afraid of, for he is a very wicked man. But I never was treated with more respect by anybody than by him. I talked to him, and told him how wrong it was to treat himself and his wife and children as he did. He listened to me kindly, and thanked me. Poor, old William Potter. May God save him.

Wednesday, February 4th. I am asked to take the service to-night. The Lord helped me wonderfully. I spoke from the fourteenth chapter of John. Several professed to be saved. At six o'clock I invited the Bishop, with some of the leading young men of the place, to tea at Mrs. Payne's. There were but one or two of the young men Christians, and I wanted them to see the Bishop, as he was so fatherly, and I thought a nice, good talk from him would do them good; so in every way possible I tried to help. If Israel is not gathered, Jacob will not lose his reward.

Thursday, February 5th. I am invited, with the Bishop, to take breakfast at Mr. Gabriel Moore's. His Honor, the President of the Republic, Hillary Johnson, and Mrs. Day, a white missionary of Muhlenburg Mission, of the Lutheran Church, are present. Mr. Day is not able to be present. God bless Mr. and Mrs. Day. What a sanitarium their home at Muhlenburg Mission has been to those who have been weary and worn. How many pleasant days I have spent at their home. It was there I had one of my fiercest attacks of fever, and I thought sure I would die. How kind Mr. and Mrs. Day were. They did all they could, and they made me so comfortable. May God ever bless them, is my prayer. Amen.

Sunday, February 8th. The new pastor is installed. Thirty-seven join the church this morning. Praise the Lord. I take the service at night. Speak from John, fifteenth chapter: "Abide in Christ." The Lord helps me, and gives us blessing.

Monday, February 9th. This has been a very busy day. I called to see Mrs. Van Harmon, a white lady, the wife of one of the merchants. She had been sick with fever. She was glad to see me, and I found her a little better. Then I called to see Mrs. Day, and go with her to church. She proposed having a picnic, a little outing, for the Bishop's benefit. She went around among the ladies, and it was arranged for.

Wednesday, February 11th. We all go to Mr. Johnson's farm; Bishop Taylor. Prof. Brown, Hon. John Smyth, Mr. Moore, Mrs. C. A. Moore, Miss Payne and a number of others.

Friday, February 13th. Mrs. C. A. Moore and daughter, and Dr. Moore and myself go to Madeira, or Grand Canary. Mrs. Moore had not been well for some time, and her father-in-law thought that a trip would do her good. Her mother consented to her going, if I would go with her, as she was not accustomed to traveling much. They are very kind, and pay all my expenses, and I go. How much I need the change and rest.

Sunday, February 15th. Sierra Leone. We got in early on Saturday afternoon, and went ashore. This morning we went to the Cathedral and heard a grand sermon from the new Bishop, Ingham. We went again this evening. The sermon was on "Consecration and Holiness." But the people didn't seem to know what he was driving at. A beautiful congregation; a number of white persons are present, mostly government officials.

Monday, February 16th. We leave at ten this morning and go on the steamer again. And now we are off. Thank the Lord, I am feeling a little better.

Tuesday, February 17th. We are all a little seasick to-day. I'm the best of the party. Thanks be to God for His loving mercy, for it is wonderful.

Wednesday, February 18th. Praise God this morning for His goodness. Mrs. Moore and I purpose to read the Gospels through while on our voyage. May He help us for His name's sake.

Thursday, February 19th. Head winds. That means seasickness. How mean one feels. But, Oh! how grand the ocean. How majestic and God-like. As He holds and moves the mighty ocean, so may He hold and move me.

Friday, February 20th. Trials begin. But, Lord, Thou hast been my dwelling place in all ages, and such Thou art to-day, and my soul doth magnify Thee.

Sunday, February 22nd. The swell is not so strong to-day, so we are all feeling better. Thank God. We hope to reach Grand Canary by Tuesday.

Tuesday, February 24th. Praise the Lord! I am glad that we are at Grand Canary. It looks beautiful from the steamer. We will go ashore in about two hours. First night ashore. Everybody speaks French. We don't understand anything anyone says, and they do not understand what we say. We manage to get on by motion—almost perpetual motion—but we get through.

Wednesday, February 25th. Praise the Lord for His goodness so far. If we were where we could speak in our own tongue, wherein we were born, with all the kindness shown us, strangers among strange people, we would feel quite at home.

Thursday, February 26th. The redeemed of the Lord shall dwell in safety by Him, How very near He has seemed all day to-day. The lady of the house goes out with us. She understands a good deal of English, but can speak but little. She takes us to a store where a gentleman can talk English quite well; so that we get a little shopping done, and go through the motions of talking Spanish.

Saturday, February 28th. The Lord has helped us, and a little lad about ten years old, a very bright little fellow, formerly from Mexico, comes to us as interpreter. We are feeling glad and thankful to the Lord for His love.

Sunday, March 1st. There is no church service here, except Roman Catholic. So we have a quiet rest in the morning; in the afternoon we take a little walk, and come to a very fine Catholic Church; we go in, and I spend a half hour with tears for the poor people. Oh, Lord! How long! How long! The ignorance of the people, and the arrogance of the priests, is something appalling.

Tuesday, March 10th. We have had some very pleasant walks and drives since we have been here. The scenery all about is beautiful. The balmy air and the beautiful flowers and fruits of all kinds are delightful. They tell us the month of September is the finest month to be here. We go out to-day and finish our little shopping. I have been deeply wounded to-day. I have made a mistake in purchasing what I need not have done. But I did it

KATE ROACH, SIERRA LEONE, AFRICA.

without first telling the Lord. I feel He forgives. With Him is mercy and forgiveness.

Tuesday, March 17. We have spent twenty-one days, and we leave to-day for Monrovia on the steamer "Vaulter," Captain Haynes.

Wednesday, March 18th. Seasick all day. The port hole was left open, and the water floods the ladies' cabin. I bail till I am quite exhausted. I do all I can to help and make it pleasant for my friend. But I find I fail. Oh! how my heart aches at the spirit manifested. But God has undertaken for me, so I rest in Him. A night or two before I left Grand Canary, I had a remarkable dream. I had had a day of trial. I prayed and wept before the Lord. That night I dreamed of seeing a beautiful brown snake. It was not long, and it had the face of a woman, very placid and nice. I seemed to know the face. And, what was more strange, it had very black, wavy hair; and I thought to myself, "How pretty that snake is. It ought not to be killed. But then it is it snake, and it is one of the poisonous kind." Then the face seemed to change just a little, and I tried to get out of the way; and as I stepped back from it, it seemed to watch to see which way I went; and I kept on going back till I got to where I made a spring to get out of the way, and this woke me. How I watched that dream. And how very real it turned out. When I saw how it would likely turn out, I trembled from head to foot, and only found relief from my heartache when I would kneel in prayer.

Monday, March 23rd. Bathurst. We shall not leave here probably until five o'clock. So I make the acquaintance of a Mr. Taylor and his wife, missionaries of St. Louis, Senegal. They are very nice people. She called to see some friends, and took me with her; among others, Mrs. Nickles, Rev. Nickles' wife. He is colonial chaplain. She is the daughter of Bishop Crowther of the Niger. I was glad to make her acquaintance, and we had some pleasant correspondence. They now live at Freetown, Sierra Leone, where I had the pleasure of seeing them frequently.

Sierra Leone, Friday, March 27th. The steamer has much cargo to leave at this port, so we all go ashore. We dine with Mr.

Boyle, Liberian consul to Sierra Leone, Had a very nice dinner. As there were several courses, it was very late before we got through. Prior to this we walked about; made several calls at different places. Then we went to Mr. Boyle's, had our dinner, and between nine and ten o'clock at night, started back to the steamer. Dr. Moore went with us to the wharf, and saw us in the boats, but we women had to go alone with the crew. How I thank God. It was a lovely moonlight night; such as is only seen in Africa; for I think the moon is more lovely there than anywhere I ever saw it. I thought it was beautiful in India. But, oh! the moonlight in Africa. It was still and light.

The steamer lay a good ways out, but we got there in safety. The captain was surprised when he saw us alone, and said we had run a great risk. But we did not know it. Praise the Lord for His goodness. We left Saturday about four P. M.

Sunday, March 29th. The day is very pleasant. There is not much we can do. I have a few tracts, so give them here and there to the men on deck, and say a word as best I can, trusting the Lord will bless it.

Monday, March 30th. Eight o'clock. Here we are in Monrovia harbor. Praise the Lord. We are all well. How good the Lord is to bring me home in safety and peace. After a little refreshment I make several calls.

Thursday, April 2nd, 1885. The Lord's Word to me this morning, is: "I am the way, the truth, and the life." A good, quiet day, and much peace and joy in prayer. I preach to-night at the Methodist Church, from the 5th chapter of Amos. The Lord help me.

Friday, April 3rd. (Good Friday). The Lord is my light, and my salvation. This is one of my fast days. My soul takes on new strength. This morning I go to the Episcopal Church, as it is a little nearer, and hope to hear a sermon on the resurrection of our Lord and Savior, Jesus Christ. But I am disappointed in the subject. All right, Lord, I rest in Thee. Thou hast risen in my soul. Hallelujah!

Sunday, April 5th. Praise the Lord, He lets me live to see another Easter morning.

Tuesday, April 7th. Praise the Lord for this day's privilege. What a good, sensible talk I have listened to at the Baptist Church. Elder Jordan, just out from America, brings the truth. Oh! Lord, I thank Thee. How he has confirmed the Word that the Lord has helped me to give. Of course they will believe it, for he is a man, and a Baptist at that.

Wednesday, April 8th. I am very sorry, but the work is hindered because of custom. The Baptists are not accustomed to having speaking in a general way. So, Elder Jordan, after speaking to-night arranged a general meeting, and says it is free for anybody to express themselves in regard to the work.

Thursday, April 9th. Of course, as it was not a close meeting, several of the Methodists went. But there were not a baker's dozen of the Baptists there. They were frightened, I suppose. It was too broad. He went on for several days, but nothing very special was done.

Tuesday, April 21st. The Lord is good, a stronghold in the day of trouble. I have called and had a talk with Brother Capehart, the pastor of the church, about holding an all day holiness meeting. He is favorable, and will do all he can to help. Thank God.

Wednesday, April 22nd. I leave Monrovia with Brother Deputie for Mt. Olive. We leave at eleven o'clock in the morning, and in three hours we get to what is called "The Old Fields." We stop that night, and start at three o'clock in the morning, and reach Mt. Olive at five. We have to go by canoe. The creeks are low, and we have to manage so as to catch the tides.

Sunday, April 26th. Praise the Lord, I am better this morning and walk a mile to church and take the service. This is the first native church I have been in since I have been in the country. The Lord helped me to speak from Hebrews, 12:2. The Lord blessed. There was one native man who said he would join the church if I would stay. Poor fellow! Sister Deputie and her family have stood very true to the temperance cause ever since it was organized.

Monday, April 27th. I am not well at all to-day, but I rest in the Lord, and can wait for Him. In the afternoon I have a good talk with Sister Deputie and Sister Artist. I tell them my experience of holiness. May God make it a blessing.

Tuesday, April 28th. A little more strength this morning. I go with Brother Deputie, and make four calls. Sing and pray at each place, and then walk home, and pray at family worship. Many times, work like this would average seven times a day.

Wednesday, April 29th. I am troubled with fever again today, in my back. I am wonderfully saved in God. Oh! how He has blessed me in my private devotion, and while at family prayer.

Friday, May 1st, 1885. Brother Williams sends his son to Mt. Olive for me, to bring me to the canoe, and we start off at nine A. M. for Marshall. We stop at Grassdale, a very pretty little place, having a number of Liberian settlers, and some very good houses. I call to see King Tom. Sing, and pray with him. He is a good, old man, and is struggling for light. God save him. I believe He will.

Sunday, May 3rd. Marshall, on the Junk River. I took the service at the Methodist Church this morning. Spoke from the 1st chapter of the 1st Epistle of Peter. I had great liberty in speaking, and I believe the Lord blessed the people. I spoke in the Sabbath School in the afternoon, and spoke again at night.

Monday, May 4th. Leave Marshall for Sheflenville, at six A M. and arrive at eleven. Stop at Mrs. D.'s, have breakfast, and then pass on to Paynesville, which is twenty miles further on; then got out of our canoe and walked seven miles. Arrived at Brother Pitman's at seven P. M. If it had not been that Brother Deputie knew all this route so well I don't know what I should have done. When I had almost given out (for it seemed to me we never would get to Brother Pitman's, that long walk from the mouth of the creek across what they called "the Old Fields"—it was old fields, indeed), I said to Brother Deputie, "Dear me, Brother Deputie, aren't we almost there?"

"Oh!" he said, "Sister Smith, don't you know the Presbyterians believe in final perseverance? That's what we must do. We will get there bye and bye."

And so we did. I think it was about eight o'clock in the evening when we got in. Brother and Sister Pitman were glad to see us, and soon had us a good supper, which was very acceptable, for I was hungry. We had a little chat, and then went to bed.

Thursday, May 7th. I leave Brother Pitman's to-day for Monrovia. Have a walk of two miles, then get into the canoe, and in three hours and a half am in Monrovia. Praise the Lord.

Monday, May 11th. A number of letters written. Oh! how they accumulate, and what a tax this is. And yet, how nice it is to receive letters from our friends at home; and one feels it is right to answer them; and I thank God for the many friends He has given me.

I left Monrovia for the Conference at Bassa, in January, 1886. I had only arranged to stay three weeks—not longer; allowing, as I thought, for the delay in getting back to Monrovia. I did not take

ON THE ST. PAUL RIVER.

my little native girl, Frances, with me; I left her at my home, at Mrs. Paynes', where I staid in Monrovia, where she would be well looked after and cared for until I got back.

I had not heard directly from Bishop Taylor, but as the Conference was to be held at Bassa, we heard flying reports of the Bishop's movements: he was to stop at Monrovia, and he was to spend three months in the regions round about, go to Bopora, etc.

Not that the Bishop had given it out, or knew anything about it; but then some people feel they have a right to draw on their imagination, or invent just whatever will suit the case; and many times one will find himself all at sea; for when you think you have a fact, lo! it is not there. But amid all this, there are some facts that remain, and will to the end of time.

An American vessel came in—the bark Monrovia—and as it was going to Bassa, though it was a week before the opening of the session of Conference, I thought I had better go, as I wanted to go, and this might be my only chance; for though a steamer was due, it might not stop at Monrovia.

The captain of the vessel was kind enough, through a good word spoken him by my son (for so he was to me all the time I was in Liberia, God bless the dear young man), B. Y. Payne, and put himself out considerably to accommodate me, and my friend who went with me, Mrs. Emma Cooper. I think we were about twenty-four hours on what they called a "good sea."

Well we had a week before the Conference opened. As I had not been there for some time, I spent the week in visiting among the people—the poor and sick, and others on all sides.

I remember one morning I called on a poor, young German, who was sick with fever. He had not been in Africa long. He was a young man who was well raised and trained, well educated, and bore about him all the marks of a gentleman. He had charge of a German store in Bassa. As he was alone and lonesome, he would often in the evening come over and talk with Mr. Gus. Williams, who was his neighbor, and kept a large store on the same street.

Poor fellow! how glad he was when I called to see him. He said that he was better; but I saw from his looks that he needed help, and good nursing, and medical attention quick, or he would not stay long; the poor fellow tried to be cheerful, and I said nothing to alarm him. I encouraged him to do all he could for himself, and put his trust in God. He was not religious, but very

respectful. He had been several times in our Gospel Temperance meetings, and told me he was much interested. I told him I would like to pray with him; I saw he was greatly embarrassed, but he did not object. The Lord helped me, and I left him with a mother's pity in my heart.

In the course of a week or two he was dead. How glad I was that I had gone and done duty by this poor man. I was laughed at and criticised at the time. "The idea of your going and praying with that white German trader!"

Well, I know that as a rule they only have respect for Africa for the money they get out of it.

"But, Oh!" I said, "he has a soul, and a poor mother somewhere; I believe she would thank me for going to see her boy if no one else did."

Oh, how often I have pitied these young men; some of them were well bred, and well raised, from Scotland and Germany. I have seen them at Calabar, and also at Lagos. I believe they sign a contract to stay a certain length of time; and, being young, and unused to the climate, and having no one to look after them but their native men that help around, many of them in a short time die. How my heart ached as I stood in the grave yard at old Calabar, on a beautiful hillside facing the great ocean—the missionaries' burying ground. Some missionaries from Scotland, and Jamaica, West Indies, and young men from England and Germany.

As I stood and looked as they were pointed out to me—their friends have sent many of them beautiful tomb-stones—I wept as I thought of the song that Bishop Taylor taught me sitting in the boat on the Cavala River; I shall never forget it, how he sang it the first time I ever heard it:

> "At the sounding of the trumpet, when the saints shall gather home,
> We will greet each other by the crystal sea;
> With the friends and all the loved ones that are waiting us to come,
> What a gathering of the faithful that will be."

> "What a gathering, gathering
> At the sounding of the glorious jubilee.
> What a gathering, gathering,
> What a gathering of the faithful that will be."

But to return to my story. I think the Conference was to convene on the 29th, and the Bishop got in several days before the time, also. It was well that I left Monrovia on that vessel, for the steamer that brought the Bishop did not stop at Monrovia; only at Bassa; so I should have missed it, if I had waited for that steamer.

I was at Lower Buchanan, and did not know the Bishop had arrived until several hours after: and I went up to Edina, the seat of the Conference, and there was quite a stir. The Bishop had arrived. The brethren were coming in from their different stations, and several had got in, taking their opportunities as best they could. It was not very convenient for them always to get to Conference in Africa. Sometimes they had to go two or three days ahead in order to be there in time.

Brother Rust, Sr., was pastor in charge of the church at Edina, and the old gentleman was a little peculiar; and as the Bishop had come unexpectedly, and he had not got a notification in due time, as he thought he ought to have done, he was feeling quite out of sorts. And besides, he was getting his house shingled; and he being pastor, of course the Bishop, when he arrived, was sent to his house.

I was told all this, and how unpleasant they were feeling, so as I knew them very well, I thought I would go up and help a little bit. So I went to the house and found that the old gentleman, and his wife, too, were feeling just as I had heard. They began to tell me how unprepared they were, etc. I talked to them, and told them the Bishop was very plain, and would not expect them to do any extra fixing for him. Of course I talked quietly, for the Bishop was in the room near by.

They thought someone else could have accommodated him better. But this one was afraid because he was "Bishop," and another one did not like to do it, because he was "Bishop." So as I was talking and explaining to Brother and Sister Rust as best I could, the dear Bishop overheard what we were saying, and he called out:

"Oh, brethren, don't trouble about me; I can sleep outdoors; I would prefer to do so."

And when I went into the room, there he sat, smiling, and mending his mosquito net.

"Well," he said, "Amanda, how are you?"

"Very well, Bishop; God bless you."

"Have you got a thimble? I cannot get on so well without a thimble."

So I got a thimble and helped him mend his mosquito net. But he didn't have to sleep outdoors.

As the Bishop had arrived several days before the Conference he had an extra Sunday, and Brother Morgan, who had charge of our church at Hartford, came down to Edina and insisted on the Bishop's going up and preaching for them on Sunday at Hartford. Edina was a larger town, and the Bishop would have preached on Sunday to a larger number of people; but as the people had never seen him up in that part, Brother Morgan was very anxious that he should go up, and he asked me if I would accompany the Bishop.

Of course I went, and if he had not asked me I should have gone anyhow, because I knew all the people up there. I had been up there about six months, and I knew I would be of some service to look after the Bishop a little, and do all I could; and having been up there before, I had the hang of things a little, and I was quite sure I would be of service.

So on Saturday afternoon Brother Rust, the Bishop. myself and several others went to Hartford.

It was not as convenient for Brother Morgan's folks as it would have been for some others that I knew to entertain the Bishop, but he thought as he was pastor, and had invited the Bishop, it was his duty to entertain him. So his sister-in-law, Miss Barclay, and myself arranged the room the best we could. I stopped with a friend not far away, and went back and forth and did all I could.

The dear old Bishop was as kind, and gentle, and pleasant, as if he had been in a palace. He sat and conversed, and made the poor things feel comfortable, because he saw they were doing the best they could.

My! as I think it over now, I wonder what some of our Bishops at home would have done. There are no hotels in Africa like there are here, but there are some pleasant and comfortable homes. But these are not always the people that take the Bishop. Brother Morgan was a grand man; a black Englishman, born, raised and educated in the West Indies; a very intelligent man. His wife, also, was a West Indian—a Miss Barclay.

The family of Barclays are as fine a family as there is in Liberia. Mr. Arthur Barclay is a leading lawyer in Monrovia, a young man of high moral character, and a real, true standby in our Methodist Sunday School, and also an earnest worker in the temperance cause; or was when I was there.

The Bishop preached at Hartford Sunday morning and evening in our little church. On Monday we went to Fortsville, and he preached there Monday night. Tuesday we came back to Edina, had a rest of a day or so, and then the Conference.

CHAPTER XXVIII.

OLD CALABAR—VICTORIA'S JUBILEE—CAPE MOUNT—CLAY-ASHLAND HOLINESS ASSOCIATION—RELIGION OF AFRICA—TRIAL FOR WITCHCRAFT—THE WOMEN OF AFRICA.

Old Calabar, West Africa, May 29, 1887. To-day I made my first visit to the King's Yard at Duketown. Mrs. Lisle and I, with a native Christian woman for interpreter, visited the women in the native town. Oh, the sadness, and the deplorable condition of these poor women. The wives of the kings and chiefs are not allowed to go out to church, or to go out at all without permission.

The first yard we visited was that of a big chief who has about twenty wives, and that number, or more, of slaves. The first court was the quarters and houses of these slaves. Passing out of this, up a dingy alley into a small court, then through a door into a large, open courtyard, we come to the quarters of the wives.

At the entrance of the first door are planted in the doorway four human skulls. I tried to step aside, but every way I stepped it seemed to me I stepped on one. It was a very uncomfortable feeling, but then I knew I had not done anything to the poor souls.

In the center of the yard of this large court was a tree with a little, low frame-work around it. Within this frame-work was a large American dish, such as we would use here to put a turkey on, with a human skull on. As I looked at it I thought of Daniel Webster. It was a skull quite resembling that of the great statesman; of such marvelous shape and proportions.

To the right, and very nearly in front, was the head of a goat. All had been sacrificed. I said, "When was this done?"

"Oh, years ago, men and women were offered for sacrifice; but since the missionaries have been here it has been stopped, and the skulls are a remembrance."

My second visit to the King's Yard was Sunday, June 12th. We went to four houses. I sang, and talked through an interpreter, and prayed, and told them how I found Jesus, and how He saved me. Poor things, how interested they seemed; and I saw the great tears in their eyes.

Some of the women were very good looking; good features and beautifully formed, as are also their children. Oh, how my heart longed after them for Jesus.

At the house of Ironbar, who is a big chief, the first thing, we saw on entering was in one corner of the courtyard a large juju, the head of an elephant, which represents a superstition they all believe in, and which they all have, in some shape or form, in their houses. They also have the skulls of goats, numbers of human skulls, turtle shells, chicken feathers, lots of long strings, or bits of rag, hanging in strings and tied in different knots and loops, and plenty of dirty grease poured over them.

This was a big chief. He dressed like a gentleman, in English clothes, and was my first escort to the Presbyterian Church.

He had a train of servants behind him to carry his umbrella, which was large, and of different colors of silk; blue, yellow, green, red, etc., and a brass knob on top as big as a good sized teacup; two men could manage it quite well; then they would take turns. Ironbar went to church nearly every Sunday; and yet he was as full of superstition and heathenism as if he had never heard the Gospel.

At the third yard, buried at the threshold, there was a human skull, over which one must walk to get in. Oh, what horror! a human graveyard. But what about all you have not seen and heard of, of horrors? I said, "Oh, Lord, how long shall the dreadful night of heathenism last? Oh, that the day may break, and that right early. Amen."

At the fourth yard, as we passed the king's palace, to go to the court where his wives stayed, we looked in and saw the table, on which were bottles of champagne and brandy; and some eight or more of the lords, and princes, and rulers gathered around, while their servants stood ready to do their bidding; and as they drank their wine and smoked, I thought of King Belshazzar and the writing on the wall. May God hasten the time when this kingdom will be taken from them and given to the King of kings.

At the fifth yard we saw the queen; a great, fat woman, with most regular features, handsome brown skin, beautiful hands and arms, and very small feet; her hair was done up in beautiful style; she was very dignified, and tried to be pleasant, but I could see she was in no sympathy with Jesus. I ventured to give her a few words, sang a hymn, and left her. She was in full costume; about three yards of beautiful cloth about her loins was all she had on! She has slaves by the hundred.

A few days before one had hanged himself, supposed to have been kidnapped and brought in, and the horror of slavery there is, to many, as it was here, and they often kill themselves, by drowning and hanging; his head was cut off and taken to the queen as a relic. Some of the wives are girls of about fourteen.

Duketown, Old Calabar, June 20th, 1887. This is a great day in England and the Provinces; the jubilee of the fifty years reign of the good queen. I should like to have been in England, and could have gone; but I thought how many poor missionaries would have been glad to be there, just for a little change and rest, as well as to be at the great royal anniversary, but their work, and, with some, the want of means, kept them from going; and I thought, though I needed the rest so much, and the doctor had told me I would need to get out of the country, and have an entire change of climate, before I could hope to be much better, that it was right to deny myself this great and only privilege that I should ever have of seeing such a demonstration, and in doing it the Lord blessed me, and I trust will answer the little prayer. He put in my heart for the queen, whose reign for fifty years has been of such a beautiful, high moral, Christian character. May her life and health be very precious in His sight may she live long to be a blessing to all nations; and when her reign is ended here, may she reign with Him, who is the Lord of all nations, and out of all has redeemed unto Himself, by the blood of Christ, kings and priests unto God. Amen. Amen.

Clay-Ashland, Liberia, West Africa, July 12th, 1888. For a long time there has been a good deal of interest manifested among a number of Christians, on the subject of personal holiness; and since the revival, which has been going on for the last three weeks, this interest has been intensified, and under consideration at different times with several of the members, and with some of the leading Stewards of the church.

GENERAL SHERMAN'S HOUSE, MONROVIA.

I suggested the propriety of having a stated meeting once a month, for the promotion of holiness, and for the benefit of those who were specially and definitely interested on the subject. And in order that the object or this meeting might be better understood, we thought it well to organize it into an association, to be called the "Clay-Ashland Holiness Association." It has the endorsement of the pastor of the church, Rev. James Cooper, and also has the benefit of his own personal experience of the blessing of entire sanctification.

It was decided that the pastor should appoint an assistant to Sister Martha Ricks, as she always had an assistant at her Friday afternoon prayer meeting; and then Sister Ricks might call anyone else to assist whom she might choose.

In order that we might help each other more, spiritually, we thought it advisable to suggest that we be very watchful, very prayerful, and devoted to God; and endeavor to lead a life of self-denial and fear of God, and, as much as lay within us, to live consistent lives, and by all means endeavor to avoid appearance of evil; in praying for the blessing, be definite; in testimony after receiving, be definite and God will strengthen your heart, and strengthen your faith; stand together; and, with a firm faith in God, you may not fear; but trust ye in the Lord forever, for in the Lord Jehovah is everlasting strength. Amen.

I had prayed, and asked the Lord for guidance about going, and had been disappointed so often; then I had been down with a severe attack of fever, and was quite weak; but the opportunity to go to Cape Mount, and I thought I would go. Mr. Sherman's boat was going up, and they told me I could go in it. As I opened my Bible, my eyes fell on these words, which I took as an assurance to start with: "I shall not die, but live, and declare the goodness of God."

After we had got started, about three o'clock in the afternoon, a storm came upon us about nine o'clock at night, and raged fearfully; it seemed every minute that the boat would be capsized; a strong head wind, and we were dreadfully sick; I was so sick I could hardly hold up my head.

But all the time, as the little boat dashed to and fro, and it seemed every moment as if it would go to pieces, the Lord kept my heart very calm by repeatedly bringing these words to my mind: "I shall not die, but live, and declare the goodness of God." And so it did come to pass. Hallelujah!

On the 3rd of June, 1889, I made another attempt to go to Cape Mount, just before leaving Liberia for America. This was my last opportunity and as I had visited all the other towns in the republic, I felt I must see Cape Mount. As this was a very beautiful day, I went around to see if I could get some good sister to go with me. I asked several, but as it was not a very pleasant time of year to go, no one was able to go with me. I went to Mrs. Sherman and asked her if she could not suggest someone. She said she thought Amanda McCrumidy would go.

Amanda was a good friend of mine, and had a sister who lived in Cape Mount, and as she was in charge of Mrs. President Robert's house, in Monrovia, I thought probably she might be able to go; so I called and asked her, and at once she consented. She was not a very strong body, but very brave hearted; I could not have got anybody from Monrovia who was better suited for this trip, (for we had an open boat), than was Miss McCrumidy.

I went to Mr. Isaac Dixon, who was a large trader in Monrovia, and also had a business at Cape Mount, and asked him if he could send me up in one of his boats; of course I was to pay for it. He was very kind, and gave me a good boat and a crew of his best men. We were to start on Tuesday morning. Monday afternoon, about four o'clock, the clouds gathered black, and we were threatened with a dreadful storm. As I looked out and- saw the clouds, my faith quivered just a little, but I looked up to the Lord, and in a moment all was calm. On Tuesday morning, June fourth, the Lord had confirmed the assurance in my heart that I was to go. At six A. M., the clouds were black and lowering, the thunder rolled, the winds blew, but my faith never wavered; that was my time to go. So about eight o'clock my friend, Amanda, came, and said: "Are you going?"

"Oh, yes," I said. A few moments later Mrs. Dixon sent her little boy to say for me not to go; she was afraid we would have a great storm. But I said, "No, this is my time to go."

I found when I got down to the waterside that Mr. Dixon's heart had failed him; he was in hopes I would decide not to go. But they built a kind of booth over the boat to protect us a little from the sun and storm, and off we started for Cape Mount. We were out all day and all night and reached Cape Mount at seven o'clock next morning. We praised the Lord again and again.

Thursday, June 6th. Made several calls, and preached to a

full house at night, and the Lord gave me great liberty in speaking, and helped the people.

Friday, 7th. We arranged a hammock, and walked three miles to a new settlement to visit the emigrants; and of all the sad sights I ever saw, it was those poor people; how my heart ached for them; destitute, and sick, and ignorant; there was not a house among them, that I visited, that was anything like comfortable.

Saturday, 8th. I visited at Mrs. Briley's station, the Episcopal Mission. This lady was a white missionary, and has spent a number of years in Africa, and I suppose will be there the balance of her days. This used to be a very prosperous station; but from what I saw of it, it seemed to lack about everything, and need about everything.

Sunday, 9th. I preached twice, and addressed the Sabbath School.

Monday, 10th. Six A. M. We are off to our open boats again to Monrovia. Out all night. Oh how good the Lord is. A storm overtakes us and threatens us heavily. As I looked up to my Father, God, and called on Him to help us, He answered me speedily, and in a little while the wind seemed to subside, and the clouds passed away.

Tuesday, 11th. Still in the boat, and sick; but the morning is lovely. Praise the Lord. We get to Monrovia about eleven o'clock.

I am often asked, "What is the religion of Africa?" Well, where I was they had no real form of religion. They were what we would call devil worshipers. They say God is good; He don't make an humbug for them; so there is no need of praying to Him. But they pray, and dance, and cook large dishes of rice and fish, and set it out of a night so that the Devil can have a good meal. They think if they feed him well, and keep on good terms with him, he will give them good crops and good luck, and keep away sickness. If smallpox, or any sickness of that kind comes to their town, they say it is because somebody has made the Devil mad.

While at Baraka with Bishop Taylor, I had my first experience of their laws and customs. Sister Betty Tubman, Aunt Julia Fletcher, and I, went, in company with the Bishop, to open a station at Baraka. It is a large, native town, and years ago the Methodist Church had a flourishing station right near this same town.

As Bishop Taylor had come to Africa to help my people by establishing missions and schools, I felt it was my duty to do all I could to help, and stand by the Bishop, and do what I could by looking after the little necessities.

I had a large canteen, as they call them in Africa; we would say lunch box here; so I would fill it with food, the best I could get; I would bake a large pone of bread, and get some tinned meats, and a ham, when I could. Five dollars was about the cheapest a ham could be got, for at Cape Palmas, but even at that they didn't have to hang on the hands of the merchants; for when it comes to food, the Liberians are not stingy, and ham is not a rarity, though they don't have them every day; but generally manage when they want them specially. They can often get things of this kind, that are expensive, in trade, with coffee or palm oil. But, of course, I had nothing of this kind, and had always to pay cash for what I got at the stores.

Then I had a little kerosene stove that I took with me, and cocoa, and coffee, and a tin of condensed milk, and biscuits, or hardtack, for bread don't last very long; if you attempt to keep it, it will sour or mould; so we generally use it up while it is fresh, and fall back on hardtack.

The Lord was so good that I generally had a little cash by me. But often it was not a question of cash, and you couldn't get the things you needed; they were not to be had. But it was wonderful how I learned to manage and get on. It is said that necessity is the mother of invention; and Africa is certainly the place where it can be developed.

We used to get up in the morning early; I would boil some water and make the Bishop a cup of cocoa or coffee, and so give him an early breakfast.

The natives were always kind and hospitable; they would have their meal about nine or ten o'clock; but we would be very faint by that time, not being used to it; and, as the Bishop was a very early riser, I knew it was best for him to have something to eat before that time. And then I always took at least a cup of tea, or something before it was late in the day.

The natives would bring in, perhaps, a chicken. They didn't scald them and pick them as we do; they would kill them and swing them over a fire; and, of course, all the feathers they didn't get off, we would have to take off ourselves; then they would bring great calabashes of rice, and pepper, for they use everything very hot with pepper; that was one of the things I never could get used to, the hot pepper. But the dear old Bishop would help himself to the rice and fowl, and goat, for they would often kill a goat in the morning and cook it for breakfast.

We would set a box in the middle of the floor, and I would spread a cloth over it, and they would set these calabashes on, and we would sit down. Sometimes they would bring in three or four calabashes; we would have to eat some out of each one; they wouldn't feel pleasant at all if we sent one back without eating out of it; so we generally had plenty, if we could only eat it; one often has to acquire the taste before he can really like it. I was in Africa a whole year before I really enjoyed or relished my food. Everything seems to taste different; but some get used to it very quickly, and others take some time. I always had plenty to eat in Africa. I never saw a day but what I had plenty, though it was not always what my appetite relished.

I thought when we got to Baraka that we would make a fire outside, and we would have a real picnic time. We would cook everything the way we wanted to cook it, just as they do at picnics; for Aunt Julia and Betty, were both good cooks, and on that line I was expecting just to show the Bishop how nicely we could treat him.

But, lo, when we got there we were not allowed to make a fire outside at all; whatever cooking was done, must be done in the native house we occupied. No fire was allowed outside, except a kind of kiln, where they burned their pottery—all sorts of vessels made of clay which are put in the fire and burned.

It is wonderful how clever they are in those things; they make all their cooking utensils; we would call it earthen ware; some of them are very pretty; they are strong and well made, and of all sizes; jars that will hold one, two, three and five gallons of water; then there are smaller utensils.

We stayed in the king's best house; a large, native house; mud floor, but dry; no windows, no chimney; there was a space in the floor where we made the fire, and did the cooking, and the smoke would ascend and go all through the thatch. I don't know how I stood it, but I got on beautifully. When the wood was wet and would smoke a good deal, I would suffer with smoke in my eyes; but, somehow, I have all idea that smoke was healthy in Africa!

The custom was that every house in the town in the evening had a little fire outside in the front of the door, and many times a piece of tobacco and a pipe would be laid by it; that was for any of their friends who were dead, or the Devil could come and light his pipe; (of course they suppose the Devil smokes); they thought it was a good thing, and would please him. This was why they would not allow us to build a fire outside. I thought it was nonsense; but they told me I had better not persist. So, when I sent word to the king, and he said, no, we could not make a fire outside, and when I took a walk myself all through the town, just about dusk, and saw, sure enough, by every hut a little bunch of wood that had been burned and was ready to light again, I just did as I was told, and did my cooking in my own native house.

While we there the old king's head wife, who was the queen wife, was tried and condemned as a witch. That meant that she was to die by drinking sassy wood.

One of the other wives of the king accused the head wife of bewitching her child. The child was a girl about fourteen years old, and while in the casava farm digging casavas she was bitten by what is called the casava snake, which is as poisonous as the cobra of India. When this child died they said it was because the head wife had bewitched her; and when any one is accused of being a witch she must die.

This poor woman ran away and was gone three months, to her people. And being the king's head wife it was what they called a great "shame palaver;" anything to happen to the king's wife —that was very bad indeed.

As the king's wife was of a very high family, they all came together, and it took them three months before they could settle it. But it was settled and she had decided to drink the sassy wood.

She had two sons, splendid young men; they were tall and graceful, just like their father, the king; they were very bright young men, and one of them could speak good English. So they told us on Friday that the mother was to drink sassy wood on Saturday again; she had to drink it twice. So we asked them to come and tell us when the time came, and they said they would.

The mother stopped at another little native town about a half mile away from this big town. So on Saturday morning about eight o'clock the young man came and told us. Aunt Julia had gone out to look for some wood; so Betty and I went with the young man. Betty Tubman could understand the native language and talk it very well.

Just as we got to this little town we found the men and the woman going to the place of execution. The town was enclosed by a stick fence. The old woman walked through the gate into the open space just outside.

She was a woman not very tall, but very black, beautiful limbs, beautifully built, small feet, as a lady would have, and beautiful hands and arms; her head was shaved and something black rubbed over it; and she had a little grass hip cloth like a little skirt just around her loins.

As we passed through the gate I thought of the Lord Jesus, who had told us to go forth bearing his reproach. Outside the gate there was a kind of a grove, and an open space just beyond this grove. When they got to the place they stopped. There were four or five old men, and two young men.

The old men stood as witnesses. They set down a mortar. One had a calabash, and another carried the sassy wood, which is a liquid decoction. I don't know as any one has ever found what the composition of this sassy wood really is; but I am told it is a mixture of certain barks. There is a tree there which grows very tall, called the sassy wood tree; but there is something mixed with this which is very difficult to find out, and the natives do not tell what it is. They say that it is one of their medicines that they use to carry out their law for punishing witches; so you cannot find out what it is.

Though it was so warm, I felt myself got cold as I looked at the scene. My heart seemed to stop beating. Oh, how I prayed to God to save that woman. We couldn't do anything to help her; her husband couldn't help her; her sons couldn't help her; her people couldn't help her. No, she was accused of being a witch, and she must pay the penalty; and the penalty was to drink the sassy wood. If she throws it up she has gained the case.

Sometimes they do throw it up, and then they stand very high; they are raised to a higher state of dignity than ever they held before. So I prayed for the poor, dear woman, that God would make her throw it up.

I thought once I could not bear to see it; but then I held on. I remember how I clutched the limb of a tree near by when she was about to take it; and I held on and prayed. Her son stood with us and looked at his mother drink the first dose; and then ran away. The two young men dipped this decoction out of the mortar into the calabash, and set it on the ground, and then she had to pick it up and drink it.

When they had filled the basin she stood and looked at it and then picked up three pebbles, and said something like a little prayer; then she struck on the side of the basin. I could understand when she said "Niswa, Oh, Niswa," which was to say "Oh, God." I didn't know what else she said. But she struck one of the stones on the side of the dish, threw the other in it, and the other one she threw away. Then she drank the sassy wood. She had two gallons to drink.

I turned to Betty and said: "What does she say, Betty?" And she told me the part that I could not understand. The whole prayer was this: "Oh, Niswa, if I have made witch, and this child has died, when I drink this sassy wood I must not throw it up. But if I have not made witch so that this child has died, then I must throw up the sassy wood."

So that was what she said all the time she was drinking the sassy wood. After she had swallowed the first dose they dipped out another basinful. Oh, I trembled. I said, "Lord, do make her throw it up." And just as she was going to stoop down to lift up the second basinful, I saw her give her shoulders a little twitch, and open her month, and if you ever saw a water plug in the street throw out water—she threw up that sassy wood, in a perfect stream!

Well, I could have shouted. I said, "Thank God." But I didn't say it very loud, for those fellows looked vengeance, and I was afraid they would drive us away.

Then she drank the second basinful, and then the third, and threw it up, and she was victor. My! didn't I come home out of that place jumping? I cannot describe how I felt.

The next morning was Sunday morning; and about eight o'clock we heard such singing and playing and beating of drums, and we wondered what in the world was up. We looked out, and here came through the town all the women, and this same woman, the king's wife, with two escorts on either side, and beautifully dressed; she had a handsome country cloth, with all sorts of colors, like Joseph's coat, wrapped about her; she was bathed and greased; she had rings in her ears, and bracelets on her wrists; her fingers were covered with rings, and rings on her toes and ankles. She looked beautiful!

They have some kind of grass they dye black, and it looks very much like hair; and she had on a head dress of this, beautifully curled, and she looked as beautiful as she could be. Then she had a great, big umbrella, red, and blue, and green and yellow striped. Oh, but she was a swell! And they took her through the town; they danced and sang; children, little boys and girls, and women.

The next day, on Monday, the men burned powder, as they called it. About five o'clock in the morning we heard a great gun firing. We didn't know but war had begun. But it was the men's day for their jollification over the victory the king's wife had gained.

I shall never forget how the poor old king came to me and wanted me to drink wine.

"No, king," I said to him, "you know I am a temperance woman. I no drink wine."

He seemed to be quite indignant. He said, "What is the matter? When my woman no die you can't drink wine a little bit with me when my heart is glad cause my woman no die?"

"Well," I said, "king, I am very glad, and I did pray, and believe God helped your woman so she no die. But myself I no drink wine."

Then as he went to turn away, almost with disgust, I said to him, "I tell you king, I give you cup cocoa. I make it for you. So you drink cocoa with me."

"Yes," he said, then he smiled.

So I went to work and made a nice bowl of cocoa, and put sugar and condensed milk in it, and gave him a hardtack and some meat, which pleased him greatly. So we were friends.

The poor women of Africa, like those of India, have a hard time. As a rule, they have all the hard work to do. They have to cut and carry all the wood, carry all the water on their heads, and plant all the rice. The men and boys cut and burn the bush, with the help of the women; but sowing the rice, and planting the casava, the women have to do.

You will often see a great, big man walking ahead, with nothing in his hand but a cutlass (as they always carry that or a spear), and a woman, his wife, coming on behind, with a great big child on her back, and a load on her head.

No matter how tired she is, her lord would not think of bringing her a jar of water, to cook his supper with, or of beating the rice; no, she must do that. A great big boy would not bring water for his mother; he would say:

"Boy no tote water; that be woman's work."

If they live with missionaries, or Liberians, or anyone outside of their own native people, then they will do such things; but not for one another.

The moment a girl child is born, she belongs to somebody. The father, who has a son, makes it the highest aim of his life to see that his son has a wife; so he settles, and begins to pay a dowry for a girl for his son. Sometimes they are but a few months old, when you will see them with their betrothal jewels on.

If the fellow who buys the girl is well off, she will have about her little waist a thick roll of beads; sometimes five or six strings together; or she will have bracelets on her little wrists, sometimes of brass, sometimes only made of common iron by the native blacksmith; she will have the same on her ankles, with a little tinkle in it, like a bell, so it makes a noise when she walks.

As they grow up, they have their tastes, and their likes and dislikes. The marriageable age is from thirteen to fourteen, and sometimes younger. All these years the boy's father, or the man himself, is paying on the girl. That is why it is hard to get the girls. It is the girls that bring big money; so the more girls a father has, that much richer he is.

Girls who are bought with a bullock are high toned; that is about the highest grade. Then the next is brass kettles, and cloth and beads. The third is more ordinary; tobacco, cloth, powder, and a little gin is not objectionable. To all of these he can put as much more as he likes; but what I have named are the principal things used in buying a native girl for a wife.

Poor things, they are not consulted; they have no choice in the matter. If they don't like the man, they are obliged to go with him anyway, no matter how illy he may treat them; and sometimes they are cruelly treated. But their own father could not protect them. The laws in this are very strict. A man's wife is his wife, and no one dare interfere.

One morning at Sinoe, about six o'clock—I generally got up at that time, and often earlier, especially when washing; five or six o'clock in the morning was the most beautiful part of the day in Africa, especially if one had a big day's washing or ironing to do, or any thing else; it is very pleasant and cool then, but as the sun rises it gets stronger, until sometimes it is almost unbearable— I heard someone crying most piteously in the street, and there seemed to be a number of voices shouting and talking; but mingled with all I heard this deep, piteous crying.

FRANCES, MY NATIVE BASSA GIRL.

I went and looked out of the window, and there was a poor girl, I suppose about fifteen or sixteen years of age, and as pretty a colored girl as I ever saw; she had a dark brown skin, was of medium size and beautifully formed; her hair was done up prettily, as they can do it, and her hands and arms were as plump and as delicately shaped as if she had been born a queen.

There were five or six men, and the same number of boys. The old man was as ugly as a monkey; he was her husband; he had hold of her arm, and was jerking her along, and beating her; then the boys would run up and give her a slap on her bare shoulders which you could hear quite plainly.

I ran down stairs and called Mr. R., and begged him to go and se if he could do anything for the poor thing. He said it was a woman palaver, he supposed, and that is the biggest kind of a palaver in Africa, and nobody can help settle them, but themselves. However, I begged him so hard that he went.

He came back in about an hour, and said she was the wife of this horrid, old man, and she had run away from him because he had beaten her, and had been gone several weeks; and these other men had found her, and had held her for the old man, but she did not want to go to him.

"Well," I said, "can't anything be done to help her?"

"No," he said, "there is only one thing; if some one of these younger men would coax the old man to sell her, and he consented and they paid him a good dowry, they could have her. But if the old man was contrary, and should refuse, he would torture her to death right in the presence of her own father, and he could not help her."

But he said the old man was rather good natured, and he thought one of these young fellows would buy her.

Sometimes these old fellows do these tricks to get money. I really hope they did buy her.

Now that is the reason it is so much better for the missionary to buy the girls, at the price of a bullock, which is twenty or twenty-five dollars; that is the price of a girl. And they are very honorable in this. If a girl has been bought by a missionary, she is free as long as she lives; no one will ever claim her; but if otherwise, she can be claimed years after, by anyone of her people who chooses to make trouble. Even, if she was married and settled it would not save her, if she could not say she was bought.

I was not asked to pay anything for my Frances, a Bassa girl, though that was their custom. Her father gave her to me, and so did Mrs. Brown, to whom he had first given her without any dowry. Her mother died, and I told Mr. Brown if her people wanted her, they must pay me two bullocks; for it had cost me that with the care and trouble I had had with her. After that I never heard any more about it.

The boys are free; no dowry for them. They can go and live with missionaries, marry and settle, just as they like.

CHAPTER XXIX.

HOW I CAME TO TAKE LITTLE BOB—TEACHING HIM TO READ—HIS CONVERSION—SOME OF HIS TRIALS, AND HOW HE MET THEM—BOB GOES TO SCHOOL.

When I first went to Africa I saw there was much to do, and I felt I could do but little. At that time there was no real medical doctor within twenty or thirty miles of Monrovia. Of course there were plenty of patent medicines to be had, such as pills and quinine, and other helps. And then the natives helped in fever cases, and all kinds of sickness, by the use of herbs, which, when skillfully administered, as many know how to do, in my opinion are much better than doctors' medicines, except quinine.

But I had never been where a doctor could not be called in a case of emergency.

So I thought it I could get a nice little boy, I would train him for a missionary, and a doctor as well. I saw how he might do much good. So I felt led to pray, and ask the Lord to open the way that I might get a boy.

I saw three boy that I liked. They lived in different Liberian families.

One was the son of a king, who lived with Mrs. Crusoe at Hartford. He was a nice lad, and I would have liked to have him.

Another was at Edina, Bassa. He lived with Mrs. Moore.

The other lived with Mrs. Horris, at Lower Buchanan, in Bassa.

The were very bright, smart boys, and only needed a little help, as I thought. But non of these parties would consent to my taking them. They wanted I should take a Liberian. But I did not feel led just that way, and I plead with them for one of the boys. But I could not get them; so then I gave it up. I thought the Lord knew my heart, and what I wanted to do was for His glory only.

In 1887, while at Cape Palmas, though I had given up all hope or desire of getting a boy, little Bob and a little playmate of his used to come to Mrs. Harmon's. They were very little fellows, and as I did my own housekeeping, and so often had bits of food left, I would call these children and give them to them. My! they were pleased; and I became very fond of them, and often would talk to them as best I could. I could not understand them so well as they could understand me. Ma Harmon could talk the Gredebo language just like a native, and they almost idolized Mr. Harmon. They knew they lost a true friend when he was taken.

Ma Harmon had told these children that they must always speak to me; say "Good morning, Mammy."

So one day I was going downtown, and little Bob and his friend were hanging on the gate as I passed. When they saw me coming they began shouting, "Good morning, Mammy! Good morning, Mammy!"

I went up and put my hand on Bob's head. I always admired him so much; he was so black, and his skin was so soft and smooth, like a kid glove.

"Well," I said, "are you fine boy to-day?"

"Yes."

He understood what I said.

"True, you be fine too much," I said.

To a native child that means everything we mean when we say, "You are a good boy," or a "nice boy."

My! they were so pleased. I had noticed, as I was passing, a man and woman who stood talking together; and when I had gone a few steps away the man called out, "Mammy!"

I turned, and he said, "Mammy," (for you must know that all foreigners and Liberians are called 'Mammy' and 'Daddy;' and in the sense it is used in America, one would feel like drawing up their shoulders sometimes; but when the natives use it, it is as we would use 'Mr.' and 'Mrs.'), "I want you to take that pick'n and teach him God palavar," pointing to little Bob. "Myself, I be fool; I no sabe God. I don't want my pick'n to be fool all same like myself."

"Jack," I said, "is that your pick'n?"

"Yes."

"For true? You be his daddy?"

"Yes. I want you to take him; all that place you live to come when you catch England and big America, you teach him, so he can sabe God proper."

"Well, Jack," I said, "myself don't be well just now; dem fever humbug me too much. I be weak plenty. So when dat steamer live to catch here, with Bishop Taylor's missionaries, myself I go down the coast a little bit. Jack, why not give him to some of the Liberian people? He will teach him."

"No, Mammy," he said, "if you left him on his hand, he no sabe nothing."

And strange as it may seem, there was much more truth than poetry in this statement.

This was on Tuesday; and on Saturday the looked for steamer arrived with Bishop Taylor's second party of thirteen or more missionaries for the Congo.

I had been down with fever for three or four days, and was very weak. I hardly knew how to get ready. But the kind friends came in, and my old standby, Betty Tubman, and Rosetta Cole, took hold and helped me get my things together; and the dear old Bishop, God bless him, got hold of my trunk and helped out with it, then rolled up my things in the rug and carried them down, and I can hear him say now:

"Come on, Amanda."

Oh! but wasn't I weak! He saw and knew it, and I could see the great sympathy in his eyes. But, Oh! he did not know how much he helped me when he went ahead and said, "Now come on, Amanda." I said, "Lord, help me." And He did, and we reached the boat. They helped me in, and we were soon off to the steamer.

Now aboard the steamer. Thank God. How nice to see a lot of home folks, and all so happy. I seemed to gather strength. We had a pleasant time.

I was away for months, and returned with but little gained, if any; for my trip of seven days from Calabar to Cape Palmas was so sad that whatever I had gained I lost, and was so weak I could scarcely get out of the boat.

"Well," I said, "it is no use; I see I have got to go home."

For three years I had been planning and hoping, but could not seem to get clear light from above, and I was so sure God Himself had sent me to Africa that I felt I dare not leave without His permission; although the doctors at Lagos and old Calabar both said that I should come home. So I kept my few things packed so as to be ready for a homeward steamer that would stop at Cape Palmas and at Monrovia, for I must stop there for my little girl, Frances.

I waited one week and no steamer stopped. Two weeks, three weeks, and no homeward steamer stopped. How tiresome. But then, what will you do? and what could you do?

I worked away, as usual, doing all I could by day and night. The latter part of the third week brought a letter, by an outward bound steamer, to Brother Pratt, Bishop Taylor's agent, that thirteen missionaries would be out soon, giving the date that they would leave Liverpool; and the Bishop had asked me to help Brother Pratt in looking after the missionaries when they arrived. Brother Pratt came to me and said;

"Now, Ma, you can't go. These missionaries are coming, and the Bishop said he wanted you to help get them settled."

So I felt that delay to me was of the Lord, though I seemed to be of so little use. But, though I say it myself, I really don't know what Brother Pratt or the missionaries would have done if it had not been for the little help I was able to give; and this, I believe, dear Miss Whitfield and Miss McNeil would say, too.

"Well," I said to Brother Pratt, "all right; I'm in for it."

So we went to planning as best we could. Jack was not home when we first got back. So I thought it was all over about taking the child. But one day I met Jack in the street.

"Mammy," he said, "howdy; I glad for see you. You be well now."

"Thank you, Jack, but myself don't be well. Weak, weak, all time."

"Mammy, I be sorry for you. You goin' take that pick'n?"

"Well, Jack, that boy be very small boy; he live to give somebody plenty trouble; small boy, so."

So I spoke to him in what we call broken English. He could speak it well, and understand it very well if you would break it up.

"You See, Jack, if I take him I must be all same as his mammy. All same like if I born him myself. My heart must be big like his own mammy's heart; and this fever bother me all time; so I am weak."

"Well," he said, with a sad face, "Mammy you promised to take him."

BOB.

BOB.
"Well, Jack, I go home; I look my head; then I will speak to God, and if my heart lay down I will call you."

So he said "all right," and went. Several times he came to see me to see if I had got light.

"No, not yet."

He and his wife came, and I still said "No."

So I said one night, "Now, Lord, this must be settled. I must say something to these people when they come again."

Then I prayed, and asked the Lord to show me His will in the matter. "Oh! Lord, Thou knowest I have no money to support this child if I take him; and I don't want to take the care and responsibility of this child, with nothing to help myself, or him. But if Thou dost want me to take him, and wilt make it clear that it is Thy will, and I should do it, it will be all right; and I know Thou wilt help me to take care of him. Now, Lord, make it clear what I must do. I will wait until Thou dost speak to me."

Then a few moments' quiet, as I knelt before Him. And these words came to me, clear:

"Is not Ethiopia stretching out her hands to God?"

"Yes, Lord."

"Cannot you help a little?"

"Lord, Thou knowest I am very weak, and I don't know what I can do."

Then these words came clear and distinct: "You do what you can, and where you leave off, God will raise up somebody to do the rest."

"Well," I said, "that is reasonable, and I will trust the Lord, and take the child, and do the best I can."

In a few days Jack and wife, Bob's own mother, came, and brought Bob; and they both signed the agreement, relinquishing all claims. Bishop Taylor and Betty Tubman were witnesses.

The following is a copy of the agreement:

CAPE PALMAS, February 16, 1888.

We, Jack Smart or Na we, his father, and We a de, his mother, do give our son, Bob, to Mrs. Amanda Smith to raise and educate as her own child. And we relinquish all claim to him from this time forth.

JACK SMART (his X mark).
WE A DE (her X mark).

WM. TAYLOR, Bishop.
ELIZABETH TUBMAN,
Witnesses.

Now there was Bob; a little, naked heathen, but he was as happy as a prince.

His mother had given him his bath in the river; so I gave him a nice red kerchief to put on around his loins, and he was dressed! A day or two more, and I had made his first pants, out of a half yard of calico.

When he got them on, oh! if you had seen him strut! He was the proudest little darkey that ever got into pants, and calico at that!

Next thing was his lesson. Mrs. Margaret Davis, Foxrock, my ever faithful, untiring friend, had sent me a box, and in it were some A, B, C cards, and several little primers.

I had given them all away but one little primer, and one card; so I must begin my work at once; for I was so miserable I thought I could not live long, and the little I could do, I must do quickly. I prayed the Lord to help me, and bless Bob, and help him to learn quickly. I thought if I could get him so he could read the Bible for himself, that was about all I could hope to do.

In two weeks he could say his A, B, C's, and knew every letter.

One day he got a little stubborn, and did not want to say his lesson. I coaxed him, and reasoned, but he had "spottie" on him; he would not learn. I saw that would not help any. I thought, "Well, I cannot give it up now; so I must doctor him a little bit." So I went out and got a little switch; when he saw it he said;

"Oh! I can learn; I can say it."

"All right," I said; so he did; and his lesson was all right.

Now the next. I had no little spelling primers, nor could anything of the kind have been got in the republic anywhere, at that time, whatever there may be now. The little primer Mrs. Davis had sent was good, large reading, only. The first lesson began:

"God is good. He gives us our food every day."

Now Bob knew every letter when he saw it; so I had him use this book for a spelling book and a reader. After he would spell the word out, "G-o-d, i-s, g-o-o-d, h-e," etc., I would have him stand up on the floor, and I would give it out, "God," he would spell; "is," "good," and so on.

Finally, I told him he must learn to read. I would start off myself to show him what I meant; then I would say, "Now, go on."

He would begin, "G-o-"

"No, go on."

"G-o-"

"No."

"God."

"Ah! that's right."

"I-s."

"No."

"I-s."

"No."

"Is," he would read.

"Ah! that's right. Go on."

I felt he caught the idea of what it was to read. And so he went on. And in six months he had learned to read a little, and spell most of the words, though he did not know what they all meant; but I stuck to him, and prayed the Lord to help him.

I do not know how old he was when I took him, as the natives do not keep dates, as we do. The only thing I had to go by was his teeth; a child is about six years old when he cuts his back teeth; he was just cutting his back teeth when I took him, so I thought he was about six years old.

He was short, and fat, and very strong. He had learned English remarkably fast, so that months before I brought him to England he had got so he could read in the Testament, and, at family prayers every morning, he and I would read verse about; and he could read almost as well as I could in the Testament when I brought him to England.

The people were astonished. They could hardly believe that a little while before, he was a little, raw, naked heathen, and could speak but two words of English when I took him: "Good morning, Mammy," and "Drink water."

When he would want a drink he would take hold of my dress, and lead me where he could see the pitcher or pail of water, then he would say, "Mammy, drink water."

Now, when all is considered, I don't believe there is a child in this country, born of Christian parents, that would have shown a capability beyond that child's. It is nonsense to say that a native African is not capable of learning.

It was in March, 1891. I had been invited to Folkston, England, to hold a mission. On my way from Southport to Folkston, we spent a day or two in London, with Mrs. Dr. Bordman, who had arranged a nice reception for us at her home, Highbry, London. She had invited to meet us, Mrs. Hannah Smith, Mrs. Mark Guy Pierce, and a number of other friends. We had a blessed time of fellowship, and then we passed on to Folkston.

I had arranged in April for Bob to go to school at Southport. I had become very much attached to him, so I felt I hardly knew how to let him go away from me, and yet, for his good, I knew I must do so. But I was anxious that he should become converted. I was very much burdened for him. I had taught him all about the way, simply as I could, and he and I often prayed together. Dear little fellow!

Sometimes when I would be so weak, when we would get down to pray, he would pray for me so earnestly, and say, "Oh! God, bless my ma. Make her well, so she can be strong, so she can walk about."

I used to suffer a great deal with my back. So he would say, "Oh! Lord, oh! God, make my ma's back well."

And then he loved to hear Bible stories. He would sit for hours and listen to anything you would say about Jesus.

Before he could speak English at all, when at family prayer, he seemed to have such a love for the words "God," and "Jesus." He used to kneel beside me and those two words were all he could say in English. So, as we would kneel down, while someone would be praying, he would pound on the chair with his little hand, and say, "Oh! God. Oh! Jesus. Oh! God. Oh! Jesus." I could not understand what else he said, but there was something religious in him.

One night I got greatly burdened for him, while at Folkston.

I slept very little all night. Oh, how I prayed that God would save him.

Next morning, at family prayers, just he and I, we read our chapter over, and I preached a little sermon to Bob, about an hour and a half long. I read, and explained, and illustrated, by what I knew he could understand, things he knew of in Africa. I took my time to explain it, so he could give it back to me in correct answers to my questions, so that I knew he had clearly in his mind what I tried to teach.

"Now, Bob," I said to him, "you know that I have always told you that if you ask Jesus to do anything for you, you must believe He will do it."

"Yes," he said.

"You know I never told you a lie, did I?"

"No."

"When I told you I was going to do something, I always did it, didn't I?"

"Yes."

"Well, just so you must believe Jesus. When you ask Him to make your heart good, believe that Ho will do it, because He loves you, and wants you to be good. So now He can give you a new heart this morning, if you will just tell Him what you want, and just believe Him, and trust Him. Now, we will just kneel down, and you pray for yourself. Tell Jesus just what you want. Tell Him in your own way, just the best you know how."

So we knelt down. Dear, little Bob! He waited for a few moments, thoughtfully and sincerely, and then he began to pray. He said;

"Oh! God, I come to you. I beg you to make my heart good. Take all the bad out of my heart, so I won't lie; so I won't steal. Oh! God, put your good Spirit in my heart, so I can always obey my ma; so I can be good. I beg you, Jesus. I will believe you. Help me. For Jesus' sake. Amen."

I felt sure God heard that little prayer, for my heart went with it; and when Bob stopped praying, I took hold of God. Oh, how I prayed, and how I believed. And I claimed Bob's conversion with him. that God had done what we asked Him. I felt peace in my heart, and assurance, and I rose up and we sang Praise God!

This was on Friday morning. In the afternoon I was invited to take a service at the Rev. Mr. Toke's church. He was an Episcopalian clergyman, and a grand man of God, and was what they call in England "a Low Churchman."

We had a wonderful meeting that afternoon. God gave me great liberty in speaking, from the 12th chapter of Romans. A number of people came to me at the close, and told me that they had received help, and blessing, and light, as they never had before. To God be the glory.

On our way home we met a crowd of six or seven little boys, and they began to call out to Bob:

"Oh, there goes a little black boy."

And I began to pity Bob so, because I knew he was sensitive, and I knew how he hated to be looked at, and hear such remarks made. Of course he was unaccustomed to it. When in London, if he would be looking out of a window, and boys would come by and make remarks, he would get down on his knees to hide from them.

I felt very sorry for him, and would tell him they were not accustomed to seeing little black boys. I was very weak, and they were taking me to my lodgings in a perambulator; and when I heard the boys call out to Bob, I began to say: "There, now, poor Bob." So I said:

"Boys, boys; that little boy's name is Bob."

"Oh, Bob, hello," they said; "Hello, Bob; how do you do?"

Just then little Bob came running up to me, and said to me;

"Oh, ma, the boys like to look at me, don't they?"

"Yes, they are not accustomed to seeing little black boys, you know. There are not many in this country."

"Well," he said, "I don't mind if they do look at me now; since I told Jesus this morning, and he made my heart good, I don't care if they do look at me now."

His face was beaming with delight; and I said: "I know Bob is changed. The old things have passed away, and the things that he hated, he has begun to love."

And the word from him in England now is, that he is a good boy, and trying to be a Christian. Why should it be thought a thing incredible, that God should convert a little heathen child? Amen.

One day, while in Liverpool, Bob and I started down street to take a little walk. Bob was carrying my handbag, and I walked slowly, and he was behind me. As we were going on, we met a crowd of rather rough boys, and they hallooed out:

"Look at the darkey! Look at the darkey!"

And by and by I heard one of them say, as though he was going to strike somebody, though I didn't look around:

"Look out! I'll knock your head off."

I knew Bob had done something; shook his fist at him, or made a face at him. It was in him, and he was full of pluck. After awhile I turned around, and, oh! such a face as Bob had on him; long, and sour. So I said to him:

"Bob, what's the matter?"

He was very pouty. I stood still till he came up to me. Then I said to him: "What ails you?"

"Ma, didn't you hear what those boys said?"

"Yes; didn't they say it to me, too?"

"Yes, ma'am."

"Did I say anything to them?"

"No, ma'am."

But still he was frowny and sulky. Then I said to him: "Bob, did you sleep in bed last night?" For he always slept in the bed with me, and it was as much as I could do to keep him covered, for he would kick the covers off, and I was afraid he would freeze.

"Yes, ma'am."

"Did you have your breakfast this morning?"

"Yes, ma'am."

"Have you got your boots on?"

"Yes, ma'am," he said, looking down at his feet.

"Have you got your pants on?"

"Yes, ma'am."

"Have you got your coat on!"

"Yes, ma'am."

"Have you got your cap on?"

"Yes, ma'am."

"Did what those boys said to you hurt you?"

"No, ma'am."

"Well, what is it? You have had your breakfast, and you have your boots on, and your pants on, and your coat on, and your cap on, and you are not hurt. What is the matter?"

So he saw the point, that nothing the boys said to him had done him any harm. He smiled, and we went on.

Now this was before he was converted; and so the change, in my mind, when he was converted was very clear. Praise the Lord, for He is good, and His mercy endureth forever. Amen. Amen.

The question has often been asked me, how I got Bob in school. This, too, was the Lord's doings.

We had been at Southport, and I had an engagement in Liverpool, and was to leave by a certain train. My friend, Mrs. Stavely, was going to the station with us, and I mistook the time. She had gone out for a few moments, and said she would be back in time to go with us to the station. But I got a little nervous, and felt I must not miss that train; the carriage was at the door, and I said: "I will just get into the carriage, and drive on to the station; I am so afraid I will be late." So off we went.

I sent the carriage back immediately, but when I got there I found I was twenty minutes too early; and I thought to myself, as I sat in the waiting-room, "What does this mean?" What will Mrs. Stavely think of me for driving off in the carriage as I did? Oh, dear, I'm so sorry. But what does it all mean?" Then I said, Lord, there is some lesson in this; teach me what it is."

A few minutes later a lady came in, and looking at me, she said:

"This is Mrs. Amanda Smith, is it not?"

"Yes, ma'am."

"My daughters have been to your meetings, and they enjoyed them so much. I would like to have attended myself; but other duties have pressed me so, I was not able to come; but my daughters have enjoyed them." Then turning, she said to me, as she looked at Bob, "Is that your little boy?"

"Yes, madam."

"What are you going to do with him? Why don't you put him into school?"

"I have been looking to the Lord, but no place has opened up yet. I would like to get him into a good school somewhere."

"I will tell you of an excellent school, right here in Southport;" she said, "a good Christian school where he will have good attention and care; just as good as if you were with him yourself; and you might go thousands of miles away, and leave him, safely; and they have had several of your people from the West Indies, and they understand how to care for them, coming from those warm climates."

I thanked her very kindly, and she gave me the lady's name, and said, "I will go and see her about it, and let you know. I will go at once."

"I am going to Liverpool," I replied, and gave her my address, where she could write me. And sure enough, she did so; and so in April I took Bob to Miss Hobbs' school, at Southport, where he has been ever since.

They made a reduction for me, as I was a missionary, from their regular terms, so as to make it as easy as possible for me, which is another token of God's loving kindness.

I went on paying for about six months; then I got a letter from a friend, saying I needn't send any more money for Bob; it was all attended to. Since then no bills have come to me for him.

And this winter has been the first time he has been sick, anything special; he has had a sore throat, and cold, but the Lord has taken wonderful care of him.

How I thank God for the dear friends He has given; and how true His word; surely he has raised up friends, and I have done the little I could. Praise His name forever. Amen. Amen.

CHAPTER XXX.

NATIVE BABIES—VISIT TO CREEKTOWN—NATIVE SUPERSTITIONS — PRODUCTS OF AFRICA—DISAPPOINTED EMIGRANTS.

One day, while at Careysburg, I heard a poor, little, native baby crying most piteously, and I looked out to see what was the matter. It was just across the street from Brother Hagins'. The mother was sitting in front of the house.

She had given her baby its bath; they are very particular about bathing them and keeping them clean; of course they wear no clothes, not a stitch, and they bathe them every morning, and sometimes oftener, during the day; their skin is generally as clean as can be; really I never saw a dirty native baby.

The mother was sitting with this little thing, about six months old, I suppose. and a beautiful child in form, with features regular and well ordered, and she had a little iron pot, that held about a quart, full of soft boiled rice setting beside her, and a little tin cup that had been used for condensed milk, full of water; the rice was boiled very soft, and hot with pepper, with a little salt, and she was stuffing her baby; we say feed, but she was literally stuffing it; they generally stuff them till their little stomachs stand out.

She held the little being between her knees, and filled its mouth, and it scrambled and hollowed, and almost choked; but when it did choke a little she would shake it till it caught its breath, then put a little water in its mouth, and it would strangle and choke and kick till you would think it would go into spasms.

I went over and thought I would beg for it; I felt so sorry to see the little thing; to me it looked like brutal punishment. I went up to the mother, and said to her:

"Mammy, you do that baby too bad; don't do it."

She looked up at me at first with a kind of a frown; she didn't quite understand what I said; but when I made her understand, she laughed and said:

"Mammy, it do him good; it make him fine." And sh seemed to pity me to think I was so weak as to want to save a baby from growing fine!

I stood and looked at her; when she was done she had put nearly every bit of this rice into the baby's stomach. Then she greased it all over from head to foot with palm oil, and then laid it on a mat in the sun, and it kicked and cried till it got tired, and then stopped and quieted down, and went to playing with its toes and hands, as happy as a cat in the ashes!

"Well," I said, "it is wonderful."

They think that to let a baby cry and kick gives strength to its muscles and lungs, and helps it to grow. It kicks and exercises, and after all I don't know but there is pretty good logic in it, when you see how the little things develop, and grow strong and straight.

At another time, while I was at Tatakai, with Bishop Taylor, I heard a baby early in the morning and late at night, in the next native house to where I stayed.

It cried so pitifully one night that I was tempted to go and see what was the matter; but then I knew I could do nothing, for they would not understand me; so next morning, I asked Aunt Julia, who was with me, and who was a Liberian, but could speak and understand the native language quite well, what was the matter with the baby; it was a little thing about a week old.

She said that the mother was giving it its bath; and then after bathing it would rub it with pepper; and that was why it cried so dreadfully. I asked her why they did it, and she said to keep it from taking cold. The weather was damp, and their houses have no floors, and that is a preventive from taking cold. And they often put pepper in their eyes, they say, to make them strong.

Whether this be true or not, there is one thing, you seldom see a native heathen with sore or weak eye; you hardly ever see one blind; sometimes, it is true, but they are not nearly so general as you see them in civilized countries.

Now, so far as a preventive to taking cold is concerned, I am in for that; but, Lord, deliver me from that means!

At Old Calabar they used to sacrifice twins, but this is stopped, so that if they can get them to a missionary they save them. Dear, old Mother Goldie, whose home is in Creektown, and who has spent so many years of her life in Africa, was one of the first who began to save the twin children. How sad, and yet interesting, were some of her experiences, which she related to me.

It is considered a mark of very bad luck when the mother has twins, and the father and mother feel alike about it, and think it is quite right to let them perish.

At Duketown a pair of little twins were brought to the mission house to Miss McFunn, in a small basket covered with plantain leaves; they had been born about four hours, and had never been touched; one was dead, and the other living, and both lay in the basket together, the dead and the living. Miss McFunn took the living child and washed and dressed it, and rolled it in a nice blanket; they tried to feed it; but the poor little thing was so weak it could not nurse; so it lived about three hours and died, which was a great relief to the mother and father, who both sat down and mourned together that the Lord should send them such bad luck.

A Mr. Henderson, one of the chief merchants, who was most kind to all the missionaries, and who always kept very nice, large boats, and a full crew, took Miss McFunn, Mrs. Lisle, Mrs. Jaret and her husband, and myself, for a little trip, of a distance, I suppose, of twelve miles, to Creektown.

It was the first time that I had seen dear old Father and Mother Goldie, as they were called, the heroes of thirty-five or forty years. How glad I was to see them. God bless them.

Creektown is a very pretty settlement; a very nice, large church, school house, mission house, out-houses and other houses where the missionaries live, besides some very nice, large, native houses.

Miss McFunn and myself were invited to dine with Mr. and Mrs. Goldie. Mrs. Lisle was invited to dine with Miss Slicer, who is also a Scotch missionary, and has done a grand work. God bless her.

She has about twenty or thirty children to teach. She speaks the language as well as if she were a born native. It is perfectly wonderful. She might be called an expert. She gave me the history of a little baby which she had had only three months.

The father stole a dog and killed it and cooked it, and of course the wife helped eat it. It was found out rather soon; for

just as they had finished eating, the man who had owned the dog came and threw down his curse on the ground before them, and said that who ever ate his dog should die. The poor woman, being frightened, I suppose, was taken sick and died in a few hours; and the poor baby, only a few weeks old, was left. Of course. no one would touch it. The father did what he could for a week, and then took it, dying, as they thought, to Miss Slicer and begged her to take it. She did, and with much care and strong faith in God, she saved its life, and it was growing finely. It had got fat, and was as bright, and Miss Slicer was as fond of it, as if it had been her own child.

Miss Slicer is the kind of a missionary for Africa. May the Lord bless, and send scores of such. Amen. Amen.

One thing which is peculiar in the Sierra Leone people is that they seldom let go of their superstitions. They have the fetich in charms on their persons, or hidden in their houses. I was told there were but few houses but had some charm buried in their yard or under their doorstep.

One day I was admiring a handsome gold chain a gentleman had tastefully arranged on his person. A friend said to me, "Would you believe that that gentleman has four charm fetiches in gold? He has the strongest kind of belief in fetich."

So it is everywhere you go. I visited the hospital while at Bunth. There I saw an old man who was a Christian, and had been sexton in the Episcopal Church for twenty years, and a regular communicant He was very intelligent, and interesting to talk to; spoke good English, and though he was feeble, he would get out of his cot and kneel down while I prayed with him. As I went to help him up after the prayer, I saw under his loose gown, or shirt, a string of cowries around his waist. Poor old man!

In this the Liberians are different. You see there but very little of this, though here and there are some relics. Then, as a rule, the Liberians all speak good American English, which is quite noteworthy.

I am often asked what are the products of the country? And what the people live on? And if the soil is good?

In Liberia the soil is generally rich; some places better than others; and they can raise about every kind of vegetable there that would grow in California or Florida. I have seen as fine cabbage, melons, cucumbers, tomatoes, beans and sweet potatoes raised there as I ever saw raised anywhere.

Then there are various kinds of fruits. They are different from what we have here. There are no apples, or peaches, or berries like ours. The mango plum is most abundant, and is very nice in every way you can prepare it. When in Cape Palmas I dried some, just as we dry apples.

Some of the people thought I was wild; the idea of drying plums. But it was not very difficult; the sun is so hot that in two days they were as dry as bones. I found them most convenient when the rainy season came on; and some of the folks that laughed at the idea learned a good lesson.

As a rule they do not dry any of the fruits. Sometimes they will make preserves, but not often. They just use the things as they come round in season, and when the season is done they are done, until the Lord brings the season for them around again!

There is a nice fruit called petanga; something like a cherry; quite tart. These make a very nice jelly, something like currant jelly. I didn't see Irish potatoes grow, but I was told they had been grown there, but were generally small. For them they depend on the English steamers that bring them, generally from Madeira.

If they get fresh seed imported every year, their cabbage, and melons and other vegetables grow large, and to the same perfection they would here; but if they plant from the same seed, they will be a size smaller each year. They seem to degenerate. No one seems to be able to account for it. They have the same soil and attention, but they are smaller.

In bringing seed across the ocean, unless it is put in sealed tins, air tight, no matter what it is, the salt air affects it, and very often it does not come up at all; and if it does come up, it will die away.

The proper time of year for gardening is September. Everybody that makes a garden at all, or puts seed in the ground, must do it then, so that at Christmas and New Years they have the nicest kind of vegetables and melons.

Then there are coconuts, bananas, oranges, pineapples and such as that. No one plants them specially; they grow almost everywhere. I did, just before I left, get some cocoanut scions, or young plants, and set them out, some five or six in number, in Ma Payne's lot. I named them all. The last I heard they were growing nicely, and the one I named "Amanda Smith" was flourishing.

Cotton grows nicely, with but little care. They could grow acres of it; but I never saw a dozen plants or bushes anywhere. The most I did see at any one place was four nice, large bushes which grew in the yard at old Sister S.'s, at Sinoe. They use a good deal of this for quilts. Everybody has quilts. They don't put as much in them as they do in quilts at home; they do not need to be as heavy; yet they don't raise a sufficient quantity of cotton to supply all the people who would use it.

All these things that I have spoken of are possibilities in Liberia that are yet to be developed on a larger scale. For why should they not manufacture goods there as they do in England and America? In the good time that is coming they will.

Then they raise a great many fowls. So do the natives. They have eggs for their own purposes. Then they have cattle and pigs and goats; and while these are essential, and a blessing to those who own them, to others they are a great annoyance and trouble.

For instance: one has a good garden made, and a strong stick fence as they could get around it. These native stick fences do not last longer than one season, as a rule. After the first year someone is most always sure to break them out for wood to burn, and as soon as they begin to break them it is only a matter of time when they will be all gone.

Then, as these pigs and goats and cows all run at large, just as you get your garden made, or just as the things are beginning to come to perfection, you go out some morning and a goat or cow or pig has been in, and your whole garden is gone.

If those who own them in different neighborhoods would arrange to keep them up, then the people who make the gardens would have enough for themselves, and could help their neighbors. But this is one of the drawbacks. Then, if you had no more seed to put in, which is very likely, you are out; often this is the case. In different parts of Liberia, in every county I was in, the people complained of the same trouble; consequently, many that might have fine gardens did not bother to make them.

I advised them to form companies, as they do in India; each man who had land, to give so much for grazing for two or three months at a time, then hire a man or boy to take the cattle and bring them back every day. spoke of this everywhere I went, and they thought it a good thing; but who would start it, and who would get the most money out of it? But I am sure it would be the best thing for all. I think the time will come when they will see it so. But the time is not yet.

Mr. Johnson, with whom I stopped several weeks, in Bassa, told me he had lost eight or nine bullocks in a few years; and pigs and goats, as well. He was a merchant, and had what they call a farm, some two or three miles away from where he lived. But he let his cattle run at large, just as other people did; if he would make a fence, it would be destroyed in a little while, and his cattle would be shot, or chopped with a cutlass, and maimed so they would have to be killed.

One day while I was there, one of their cows (one Mrs. Johnson had raised from a little calf), came home with three large arrows that had been shot into her, still sticking in her. That is the way Mr. Johnson came to tell me about what I have just said.

At Sierra Leone, and down the coast, I think they are more advanced. They have large markets both at Sierra Leone, and at Lagos, so the steamers take on a supply. Then all along the coast after they leave Liberia, they are supplied with fowls, eggs, pigeons, bananas, pineapples, peppers, water cress, and all sorts of vegetables in abundance; large fowls, sixpence apiece.

Further down the coast the natives make very handsome cloth. They are very clever in making their dyes; it is wonderful how they do it. They have very strong dyes, with fast colors, green, blue, red, yellow, and various colors; it is marvelous how they blend them; and some of the native cloths are really beautiful. They bring them on the steamers and sell them for different prices, ten, twenty, twenty-five, twenty-six shillings, and some for more. I bought an elegant cloth at ten shillings; but one of the officers got one at twenty, and he said it was very cheap.

Chillicothe is the place where you generally get these handsome country cloths. I also got one or two very nice pieces at Monrovia; but nothing like those that you get down the coast. They weave their cloth in strips about four or five inches wide; then they sew it together to any length or breadth they want it.

The natives are great geniuses in this way; and it is wonderful to see the number of things they can make.

Then the Liberians have other products besides those which I have named. Their coffee is very fine, and of rich flavor. There are some large planters who raise and ship thousands of pounds. Among these are, Mr. Moses Ricks, and Senator Coleman, of Clay-Ashland;

Sanders Washington, of Virginia; June Moore and Saul Hill, of Arthington; and Jesse Sharpe. These are all on or near the St. Paul River. They are men who went from this country years ago, when young; men of sterling worth and push. The Ricks' were three brothers—Moses, Henry, and John; they were staunch Baptists, and good men. They always stood together, and were the stay and the backbone of the church at Clay-Ashland.

In developing mission work among the natives, so far as my observation went, the Baptists were ahead. And their churches and mission work are all self-supporting, that is, they have no foreign help, as they used to have. Then at Arthington, June Moore and Saul Hill, were classed among the men of large means. Both of these were earnest Christian men, and Deacons in the Baptist Church.

Mr. Moore, in his outward appearance, was very plain, but a man of more than ordinary intelligence, and unquestioned veracity, and moral character; and a strong temperance man. His is a beautiful character I wish I could have found it more general.

Mr. Moore was a very good preacher. He had charge of the Baptist Church at Arthington, and had the confidence of the people,

Liberians and natives. Through his sympathy and co-operation we held a temperance meeting in the Baptist Church at Arthington, and organized a Gospel Temperance Band, and, I think, made him President. Of course, the majority there, were not far advanced on the line of woman preaching. It was all right at other churches, and they would go and hear, and get what benefit they could. But they were generally in favor of Paul's assertion: "Let your women keep silence in the churches."

The more liberal believe that the other statement of Paul should be considered as well, viz.: how a woman should be adorned when praying or prophesying.

The Lord blessed me very greatly, and I had my friends among them all. I was never asked in a Baptist Church to take a service, while I was there; only to address a Sabbath School.

I spent a very pleasant time at Mr. June Moore's home, and immensely enjoyed the conversation we had together. He was full of information on all points of interest in the republic, and country, both the natives and Liberians.

After the family prayer was over in the evening, we sat and talked till twelve o'clock. He told me all about the much talked of Richard Morris school, of which he had charge at that time. This I was very anxious to know about, as I had met Mr. Richard Morris in England, before I went to Africa, and had heard some of his interesting lectures, and about the school that he was establishing for the education and training of the sons of native chiefs! But when I got there, and saw and heard for myself, oh, how different. So far as the sons of native chiefs being in the school, there never had been one. The native boys who did go to the school, were the boys who lived in the different families in the neighborhood. Mr. June Moore had several native boys. These went to the school during the rainy season; when this was over they had to work on the farm.

The little school house was formerly a Methodist church, with a seating capacity of about fifty, when it was packed.

Poor Mr. Morris meant to do Liberia good; and no doubt he did help the people greatly, by introducing their coffee at the great Centennial Exposition. But the pretty little steamer, costing six hundred pounds, which he sent out from England, and the three large iron soap kettles, ended up pretty much like the hanging of the gin at Virginia; that was a sad failure.

I think that often these things are misleading to those who purpose emigrating. They hear of these things, and they sound well; they have gathered a little together, by dint of hard work, and much self-denial; they sacrifice it and go off to Liberia. When they find things so different from what has been represented, they become discouraged, and disappointed, and often disgusted. They have no means to get back to this country, and if they did, they could not recover what they have sacrificed, and so would have to make an entirely new start; so that many give up and die, or make up their minds to do the best they can, and that is often a grievously poor do.

I remember when that large emigration came to Cape Palmas, the citizens called a mass meeting in the Episcopal school room, to which these strangers were invited. Papers, and addresses of welcome, were read.

As it was but a short distance from where I lived, when I heard of it I said I would go. I was glad of it, and thought it would encourage and help the strangers. But I was told, a little while after, that no women, were to go; it was only for men. Then

I was more anxious than ever; and, womanlike, I became suspicious, as well as curious. I thought, "Why can't I go? These emigrants are from my country, and I have a right to go, and I will."

Just before the meeting someone called and asked me if I were going.

"Yes," I said.

"Oh, my husband says there are no women going, and he will not let me go."

"Well," I said, "you have a husband to obey; but I have not; so I am going."

"The seats will all be full," she said.

"All right, I will take my own chair."

So I did. They all knew I was a kind of privileged character anyhow, and generally carried out what I undertook.

I noticed, when I went in, they began to look at one another. Sure enough, I was the only woman there.

I went and took my seat in the middle of the aisle. I think they thought that I wanted to talk; but that was a mistake. There was talking enough done to have built a tower, if there had been anything in it. Mr. James Tuning was the speaker of the evening. He had a very lengthy paper about Jacob receiving his brethren. And of all the big talk that anyone ever listened to, they had it in that meeting.

I knew that more than half that was in the papers was only worth the paper it was on. I was quite sure it didn't mean more than that; but the strangers didn't know it, All the prominent men of the place were present—His Lordship, Bishop Ferguson, the Hon. J. Gibson, Mr. J. Thorne, Mr. Ashton and a number of others.

When they were all through expressing themselves, and heartily welcoming the emigrants to their country, this free country where they were not oppressed by white men; the country where they could be *men*; where they had the rights of the law, and were independent, and all the other big things we can say, then they asked the emigrants to speak.

As it was getting late, there were but three of these emigrants who made speeches. The leader was a young man, a Mr. Massie, who had been the chief in getting up this emigration and leading them out. He was the Moses. He talked well, though his speech was not lengthy. But of all the raking of white people! It seemed as if their chief aim was to say all the hard things and vent all their unpleasant feelings against the white people; which is very much admired by the Liberians, and is a mark of real race loyalty.

Each one, in turn, expressed himself the same way. The home folks laughed and smiled and looked at me. I felt very sorry for this. It is the wrong spirit to be cherished and cultivated and perpetuated. I have never seen any good from it. Somehow or other, though I cannot explain it, it is not the spirit that has the sanction of God. It is wrong in those who have caused these grievances, but it does not help us any to forever keep looking at the wrongs, and never see any of the good, which has always gone along side by side with the wrong. The good has not always been the strongest or the most prominent, yet it has been there.

I could not help thinking, as I listened, that before these poor emigrants had been there half as long as I had been, if they needed sympathy or help, they would find it quicker right among those whom they had held up that night as being their worst enemies, than they would among those who got up there and said such big things.

And I was there to see that same man, within six months, come to such absolute need that he came to me to borrow two gallons of rice. His wife was sick, his baby had died, and he had terrible sores on his feet and legs from the effects of the chigoes; and he was in a pitiable and helpless condition. He had been to one of the white merchants the week before and borrowed some rice. He could not get it from any of his brethren and friends who had read such noble papers and given them such a hearty welcome.

He did not like to come to me, because I had not failed to tell them that when they got to where they were in great need they would find very likely these friends would fail them. So he stayed away as long as he could.

I was glad when he came to me that I was able to help him. I said to him, "I am sorry for you. I could have told you that, that same night you were talking; but then if I had told you then, you would not have believed it."

Poor fellow, the tears were in his eyes. He said, "Ah, Sister Smith, I have learned a lesson."

And so he had. But as the old saying is, "Bought wit is better than taught wit," when you do not buy it too dear. This poor man's purpose was, after he got settled in Liberia, to come back to America and bring out a large emigration. My! what wonderful things he was going to do. But that little experience cooked him pretty thoroughly; so that his ambitions were not so high.

Poor Massie! I wonder how he has got on. I am simply speaking of this as what I knew and saw when I was there. Everything may have changed since then, for all I know. There were possibilities, but not many probabilities.

CHAPTER XXXI.

LIBERIA—BUILDINGS—THE RAINY SEASON—SIERRA LEONE—ITS PEOPLE—SCHOOLS—WHITE MISSIONARIES—COMMON SENSE NEEDED—BROTHER JOHNSON'S EXPERIENCE—HOW WE GET ON IN AFRICA.

Emigrants going to Liberia think they can rent a small house, or rooms, as they can in this country. People will come there, who have left a comfortable home behind, and think they will rent a small house for six months or a year, till they can get their own house built; but this they can seldom do. The reason of this, I think is, the climate is very hard on timber, and a house standing unoccupied for any length of time will soon be destroyed.

The bug-a-bug is a very large ant, which eats the wood to a perfect hull, and the most destructive insect in that regard in the country. If they get into a trunk or chest of clothes, and are not discovered in time, they will go through everything, books, papers, etc.; nothing stands before them. After you know this, a little watching may save you a great deal of trouble.

So that the most of the people in Liberia, or anywhere else in the republic, build, and live in their own houses. Houses that are built of stone or brick are the most durable; and the best houses there are thus built. But the frame houses have the hardest time.

Slate roofing, in one sense, would be better than shingles, especially for the rainy season, for the reason that the rain and sun do not affect it so much as they do the shingles.

During the rainy season there, it literally pours. I have often thought of Noah in the ark when I have seen the rain pour down without mercy for two or three days in succession, with just a little intervals of a slight break between. Then the sun would come out, sometimes for a half day, perhaps in the morning or

afternoon, then it would rain at night; but these little intervals help the people to get about and do their work. Nobody seems to stop especially. After you have been here awhile you do not seem to mind it. It is rather comfortable, for it is not so warm then, and you can stand a good little fire in the house to absorb the dampness.

As a rule there is a good deal of sickness and fever among the natives during this season; but people having comfortable houses suffer but very little inconvenience.

When the rainy season is over, and the blazing, hot sun beats down, the shingles curl right up and split, so that almost every year it is necessary to go through some repairing. On the other hand, the slate roof gets so hot that it makes sleeping almost impossible, unless the roof is high, and well lined under the slate.

There are some large houses, for stores; these are occupied by white merchants, or traders, so that if there chance to her a good house of any size to rent, they generally have the preference, for they always have the money, and that is the first consideration in Africa as well as elsewhere.

Now, in this regard Sierra Leone is different. There are almost always good houses to rent there; they build houses for that purpose. And so if you want a house with a store underneath, or a large private house, or one not so large, it can be got at a reasonable price, as a rule, and on a good, wide street.

The Sierra Leone houses are very substantially built, but generally of stone or brick, with yards enclosed by a good, high wall, after the English style, and nicely furnished inside. I have seen some as finely finished houses in Sierra Leone and Lagos as I have seen in America or England.

The people of Sierra Leone are greatly mixed, as to tribes; so much so, that I think it would be difficult to tell to just what particular tribe they really belong.

They have no real, distinct language. They speak a lingo of broken English, which all seem to understand; and when two or three dozen of them are together, especially the women and girls in the market places, it would remind one unaccustomed to it of the chattering of a thousand swallows. My! but they can talk. But there are hundreds who speak good English.

There are many wealthy merchants, both in Sierra Leone and Lagos, who often send their sons and daughters to England, and sometimes to France, to be educated. But somehow they never seem to lose this peculiar Sierra Leone idiom; so that they are just as distinct in their customs and manners of speech from Liberians and Americans, as Italians are different from Americans in this country; so they do not assimilate easily. They intermarry occasionally, but not often, and when they do, they seldom get on well together, their training and education are so entirely different.

But the country is no better off for this education. Of course they don't come home to do missionary work among the people; they belong to the upper rank; and so those of the same rank are a society among themselves; and the second and third classes of their own people are never the better for their higher education, only as they may serve them, as servants, or otherwise.

If it is a lady, she is either engaged, before she comes home, to be married to some rich gentleman, or very soon after she gets home you may hear that she has had an offer; sometimes there will be rival suitors for her hand, and you will wait with the greatest interest, for you are sure to hear of it, which of these has won the suit. As much of this depends on the weight of their pockets as anything else.

And then, when one of these weddings comes off, it will give you a little idea of what real black aristocracy is. It would compare favorably with the same kind of an event on Fifth Avenue New York, or in Washington, D. C. Fine cards and wedding presents, and all the outfit for four or five bridesmaids, as well as bride and groom, and best man, etc., etc., all imported from England and France. These people are not ignorant in regard to the highest style, and the greatest etiquette.

As a rule, I think the Sierra Leone people are generally industrious, there are merchants, tailors, carpenters, etc., among them. They have large markets where you can go and get, two or three times a week, all sorts of produce, at a good price. Then they have regular beef markets, from which they supply Government House, and the large barracks of English soldiers.

They are great traders, men, women, boys and girls; the women often surpass the men. They will go up and down the rivers, and in the interior, buying palm oil, rubber, camwood, and boys and girls, if necessary. I was told they do this sometimes, but for the purpose of setting them free, as the English law

BAPTIST MISSION STATION, LIBERIA.

does not allow anyone to own slaves, when it is really known. Thank God for that.

Formerly they had good schools in Freetown. This is one thing I admire in the English government; she generally looks well after the education of her colonists. Of course there is room for much improvement, even in Sierra Leone and Lagos.

All up and down the coast, wherever you go where the English flag waves, and there has been any civilization at all, you will find scores and hundreds who have a liberal education, and are fitted for most all professions and callings.

The Wesleyan Girls' High School, at Freetown, was once a beautiful building, with well furnished dormitories, and a staff of first-class teachers; but it has seen its best days, without a great change takes place. For several years it has been sadly declining in power and influence, being almost entirely under the control of one or two parties. I was told that when it was first founded, it was under the management of white people; the lady principal and teachers were all white, and they did a grand work. And then the boys' high school, which I also visited, and had the privilege, through the invitation of the principal, Mr. M., of addressing, was not what it once was, or should be. The Episcopal school, both for girls and boys, is good. The boys have a fine, large, commodious building, and a good staff of teachers.

Several of the Liberian families, who have not been able to send their sons and daughters as far as England to be educated, sent them to Freetown. I had the pleasure of going all through this building, on the day of the dedication of the new dormitory and recitation rooms, which had been added to the main building, accommodating, I think, probably two hundred in all. His lordship the Bishop, was in the chair, and gave a most excellent address, as did also Mr. N., who, I think, at that time had charge of the theological department, and who was a noble, Christian gentleman. His sister was the lady principal of the girls' high school, which I also visited, and had the pleasure of speaking a few words to the young ladies. Everything wag in good order.

I was greatly delighted with this school, especially the housekeeping department, where, in connection with their studies, each girl took her turn in the sweeping, dusting, making bread, biscuit, pie, or cake, and in washing dishes and attending the dining room. This, it seemed to me, was the most essential of all; it would certainly

be one of the "one needful things." For if, having the intellectual qualifications, the girls in Africa are remiss in this, the former is as good as lost, to a great extent, as their homes would not be what they might be otherwise.

Then, there are private schools. I visited a Mr. Leapol's school, which was a very nice school for boys. I suppose he accommodated about forty. Mr. L. was a very high type of a Christian gentleman; I think, a West Indian by birth. This school was of the higher grade. Teachers and helpers, I believe, were all colored.

There was a good government school, which, according to my American ideas, should have continued to exist. But when the new Bishop came, he, being a very conservative English gentleman, and invested with power, thought it best, as I was told, to disband the government school, and build a large parish school. So that many of the poor children, who were not able to pay, were shut out. This opened a good harvest for the Roman Catholics, which they lost no time in securing.

I am often asked if I think that missionary work in Africa prospers and develops better when under the entire control of colored people, or do I think it is better under the control of white people.

To answer this as best I can I will give my experience and observation at the several places I have been.

The schools at Old Calabar under the Scotch Presbyterian Missionary Society, and the schools and missions at Lagos, and the Episcopal, Baptist and Wesleyan Schools in the Republic of Liberia, and then in Sierra Leone the United Free Methodists, the Episcopals, the Lady Huntington Society, the U. B. Mission, and the English Baptist Mission, all were established, supported and superintended by white missionaries; but just in proportion as they have died, or on account of poor health have had to retire from the work, the schools and mission property have declined.

Many of them in the work have developed good native teachers and preachers, who are loyal, and faithful, and true; and the white missionary feels that he, or she, could not do without these native helpers. But when the whole work is left to them the interest seems to flag, and the natives themselves seem to lose their interest, which the teacher feels, but cannot help.

I do not attempt to make any explanation of this; I simply state the facts as I met them. And as I mingled with the people, old and young, and as the older people, who knew more about it, would tell me what it had been in former years, the remains of which were left, in the mission house and grounds, it was not difficult to see the difference.

BOYS OF MISSION SCHOOL, ROTIFUNK, AFRICA.

Then, the white missionaries, as a rule, give better satisfaction, both to the natives and to the church or society which sends them out.

I suppose no church or society ever gave a salary to a colored man, no matter how efficient he was, as large as they give to a white man or woman, no matter how inefficient he or she may be in the start; and I think they are generally expected to do more work. This I think is a great mistake.

I believe that the death of the grandest black missionary I ever knew, Rev. Joseph Gomer, of the Shanghai Mission, was hastened through over-work and pressing need, and salary and means for work being cut down, and great anxiety because of the urgent demand for the work.

For pure Christian integrity and untarnished moral character, and fatherly sympathy and love for the poor heathen, he had but few equals in Africa, if any.

"Then you think, Mrs. Smith, it is better that white missionaries should go to Africa."

Yes, if they are the right kind. If they are thoroughly converted and fully consecrated and wholly sanctified to God, so that till their prejudices are completely killed out, and their hearts are full of love and sympathy, and they have firmness of character, and good, broad, level-headed common sense, and are possessed of great patience and strong, persistent, persevering faith, and then keep up the spirit of earnest prayer to Almighty God, day and night. I do not say that it is necessary to be under a dead strain all the time not at all; but my own personal experience is that the more one prays and trusts in God, the better he can get on, especially in Africa.

Everything is so different from what you have it at home, that this is an absolute necessity; and the person that has not got the stick-to-itiveness on these lines, especially, whatever else he may have, will not make a good missionary in Africa, whether he be white or black.

I have known some white missionaries who have gone to Africa, who were just as full of prejudice against black people as they are in this country, and did not have grace enough to hide it; but they seemed to think they were in Africa, and there was no society that they cared for, and that the black people had but little sense, so they would never know if they did act mean and do mean things.

And I have known some who have done disreputable things, and it has had its effect on the motives and principles of the good missionaries, until they have had time enough patiently to live it down, and have proved to the Liberians and natives that there is a difference, even in white missionaries.

But thank God, He has sent some who have fully answered to what I have said before. There are one or two who come to my mind now, who, I believe, in every particular fill the bill. I refer to Miss Lizzie McNeil, who, it seems to me, is a born missionary, and to Miss Whitfield. There are numbers of others; but I speak of these because I know them personally, and know their work.

I remember the first party of Bishop Taylor's missionaries that came to Cape Palmas while I was there. The steamer got in on

Saturday afternoon; six of the men came ashore Saturday evening; the others, with their families, remained till morning, and they all got ashore in time for church Sunday morning.

Dear Brother Harnard preached a grand sermon. He was the leader, or bishop, of the party. They were all so full of hope and cheer. How bright and happy they all seemed to be. Brother Harnard had two beautiful children, about two and four years of age, I suppose; and the people, natives and all, were so delighted with them. Some of them have never seen white children so young; and then they were so beautifully trained; and Brother and Sister Harnard were so good and kind to everyone.

Brother Pratt, Bishop Taylor's agent in Cape Palmas, whatever he may be now, was certainly the best man that Bishop Taylor could have got anywhere to fill the position, at the time. Oh, how faithfully that man worked. How he sacrificed his home, and everything for the work. His poor wife was sick all the time; suffered—Oh! what a sufferer she was; but she was second in everything for the success and good of Bishop Taylor's work.

He took Brother Harnard and his wife and two children, and two of the other men, Brother Johnson and Brother Miller, to his house. Sister Harmon and I had arranged to take care of three of the brethren—Brother Cadle, Brother Ortlit, and Brother Garwood. I gave them breakfast and tea, and Sister Harmon lodged them, and gave them dinner.

MISSION SCHOOL, ROTIFUNK, AFRICA.

On Monday afternoon I invited Brother Johnson and Brother Miller to take tea with the other brethren. Of course, these were my own country people; they had left their home and went to work among my people in Africa. So we did our best for them.

I got Sister Harmon to make some nice, old-fashioned, Maryland biscuit (which she knew as well how to do as I did myself, and I used to be considered an expert, once upon a time), and we had nice fried chicken, and all else we could get, and that in abundance that is the way we generally had it in Africa, when we were in for a big thing!

Of course, we could not go at that speed every day. But thank God, I never saw a day in Africa that I did not have plenty to eat. And when at Ma Payne's, in Monrovia, for days my meals would be sent to me in my room, when I was not able to go down, and as nicely served on a waiter as if I had been at a nice boarding house, or at my own home in America.

After tea was over we were all talking and having a pleasant time; the brethren seemed so to have enjoyed their tea, and we were all pleased.

Brother Johnson had been expressing in the most flattering terms his delight and appreciation of the splendid tea, and especially the biscuit. He said the lady who made them must have been a wonderfully nice lady, and if she was not married, she ought to be; for a lady that could make such biscuit ought to have a good husband. Well, we all laughed, and passed it off in a joking manner. I felt pretty safe, as I had not made the biscuit.

Sister Harmon was a nice looking woman, but was older than I, and had sons grown and married, and grandchildren; so she had no fear of anything, save the embarrassment of the question and answer, if it really came to that. So Brother Johnson said to me:

"Mrs. Smith, I would like to speak to you privately."

"Very well," I said; "we will excuse these brethren, and you can see me just here."

So the three brethren arose and withdrew to the parlor. I had watched and listened to Brother Johnson, and had taken his measure pretty thoroughly while he was talking, and I felt in my mind that he was going to play the fool.

"Now, Brother Johnson," said I, "proceed. What is it you want to say?"

He straightened up and smiled, and acted a little embarrassed; then got red in the face and all down his neck, till his beautiful white necktie seemed as though it was about to get pink, too.

I thought, "Dearie me, what will he say?" For I looked him squarely in the eye, and with the look of the rock of Gibraltar, if Gibraltar ever looked. I said, "It cannot mean that he is going to propose to me; he has just come; has not been here three days." After clearing his throat, he said:

"Well, Sister Smith, or *Mrs.* Smith," (emphasizing the Mrs.).

"Yes," I said.

"Well, I have come to Africa, and expect to make it my future home. I have not come to go back. I expect to die here."

Then I spoke and said, "I don't think you need die here any sooner than you would in the United States. One need only use his common sense, and go a little slow while he is acclimating." Then I waited for the next shot.

"I thought," he continued, "I would ask you if you knew of any nice colored woman that you think would make me a good wife. I could have married before I left my country, or America," (he was a Swede); "but I chose to wait till I got here; and I thought it would be better for me to marry a woman of the country, who is already acclimated. If I were to marry a white woman, she would all the time be crying to go home to see her aunt or uncle, or her mother," with a pretty smile.

I groaned, being burdened, to give vent to my mingled feelings. But then I controlled myself; for, during the time he talked, I was reading him, and I said to myself: "There is nothing in this man; he is as full of self as he can be, and he is going to be a failure, if not a disgrace, to Bishop Taylor's mission here." For the work was just starting, and was new, and needed much careful guiding and management, with all the American and African prejudices against this new, self-supporting movement.

"Mr. Johnson, I know some very nice women here, who, I think would make good wives for somebody; but I would not recommend anyone that I know, to do what I would not do myself; and I, myself, would not marry you, or any other man, if you were gold; a rank stranger, just come from another country, and have not been here three days; no one knows anything about you; you know nothing about the people. You are entirely premature. You will need to be here some time, and know Africa and the people Then, besides, Bishop Taylor's self-supporting mission is in its infancy, and every eye is upon these first missionaries, both here and at home, and we must be careful that we do nothing that will hinder or hurt it in the start."

I saw that my version of things did not take very well with Brother Johnson. But I did not know until Wednesday what had gone before.

Mr. Pratt's wife's sister, a very nice girl, had gone to help in the house, as Mrs. Pratt was sick. She took a great fancy to Mrs. Harnard and the children, and had offered herself to Mrs. Harnard, to go with her, to take care of the children.

It appeared that when Mr. Johnson came ashore on Saturday, and saw this girl at Mrs. Pratt's, he was struck clear through at first sight, and had proposed; and she, poor thing, thought it was splendid. She judged from outside appearances; for Mr. Johnson was very nice looking man, nicely dressed, patent leather boots, shirt collar and necktie exquisitely beautiful, and she thought she had a fish of the first water. I suppose she had; but it was bony.

They were to be married on Thursday, and would have been, if Mr. Pratt had allowed it. When he found it out, he sent the girl home to her father, and managed to hold Brother Johnson in check for two weeks.

So that was the meaning of the private conversation that Mr. Johnson wanted with me Monday evening. But he did not come straight out and tell me. I was glad afterward that I did not know anything about it, and that I talked just as I did. And, notwithstanding all that, they tried to say that I was favorable to it.

They were married at I the Methodist Church, by somebody, I don't remember now by whom; but I know Brother Harnard did not marry them. I never went near; because I was so busy with my sick missionaries, and I did not care anyhow, to see the beginning the thing; I was more interested about how it was going to come out.

Well, it turned out just as I said. After a week or so he carried the poor thing up into the country to their station. She had nothing, and he had nothing, only his mission supplies; and they had used the best part of those for their marriage feast, no one

made them any feast, or gave them any presents, as they do in this country. In this they both seemed to be greatly disappointed.

Mr. Johnson seemed to think if he only married a colored girl, he being a white man, it would be such a standing proof to the colored people that he really loved them, that they would take him right into their arms, and lavish upon them their wealth and gifts; especially as he had married into one of the most respectable families in Cape Palmas; the daughter of the Hon. Mr. H. Gibson. My! he thought he had it. And so he had.

Poor girl! I knew her well. She had been converted and sanctified in one of the meetings that I had held, and bad grown in grace, and was developing so nicely, and was one of our good workers in the Band of Hope Temperance work.

When I knew that the decree was passed to marry Mr. Johnson, I confess I was disappointed in her; for I really gave her credit for having more sense. So I never opened my head to her on the subject.

Her joy and delight were of short duration. He got fever and was down sick. They came back to the Cape. I went to see him, and did what I could.

When he got better they went again up to their station. The natives received them gladly, and gave them a bullock. They had their mission house built to go into. But everything was so different from what it was in America. He got down with fever again, and again they returned to the Cape. I, with Brother Pratt, did everything I could for him till I left.

After some months of going back and forth, and getting down with fever, he came back to the Cape again, and took the first steamer for home, and left his wife there, to live or die. Poor thing! In less than a year she died.

And Brother Johnson—though everything was done for him that could be done, I saw him after this in Monrovia, going about from house to house, and the worst thing he could say of Bishop Taylor and his self-supporting mission was too good.

Of course, he and Mr. Hillman, and Mr. Astley, had all gone over to the Episcopal Church; and, it seems that one of the surest marks of true fidelity to that church is to ignore and denounce everybody and everything in the church that has fitted them for this church to receive.

The last time I saw Brother Johnson, was in July, '91, at the Episcopal Mission at Cape Mount; and of all the poor, forlorn looking creatures that I had seen for some time, he seemed most to be pitied.

I have said it was not always a matter of having the cash, in order to get on in Africa, for there were times when you couldn't get things even with the cash.

"Then what would we do when we couldn't get the things we wanted at the stores?"

Well, we would just have to wait, and do the best we could, till a steamer came, or an American vessel; sometimes it would be a week, or two, or three, just as it happened.

"How did we get on?"

Well, that is a difficult question to answer—how we got on. But we did get on; we would just call up the old mother of invention, and she always had some plan to help us out; so there was no necessity of getting homesick or backsliding.

I never was homesick but about five minutes the whole eight years I was in Africa; and that was one day when I was reading an account in the "Christian Standard" of a wonderful holiness meeting held at old John Street, New York, and I was so hungry for such a spiritual feast; and as I read I found myself saying, "How I wish I were there."

When I thought of what I had said I sprang to my feet and cried out, "Now, Lord, help me, for I know I am right in the place where you want me, and it is all right." And in a moment the homesick feeling left me.

Then once, while I was at Miss Sharpe's, I was very nearly homesick. I was just going through my first attack of fever, and suffered for a drink of cool water. Being accustomed to having ice in this country, or going to a spring or pump and getting a cool drink, I felt I must have some ice. In India they make ice; so while there I could get ice water; but they don't make it in Africa. Sometimes we could get a piece off the steamer; but only a small piece, which could not last very long; and generally when one wanted it most, there would be no steamer in; so one must do without it.

And the water is always warm. The only time you get it cool is very early in the morning, or during the rainy season. In the morning it would be a little cool, but if you drink it so very early you will be very apt to have a chill; so you must be careful on that line.

I was pretty well scorched with fever, and as the days and nights went on, and nothing cool to drink, and no appetite to eat anything I could get to eat, I craved what I could not get.

Plenty could be got, but not what I wanted. I wanted a nice broiled mutton chop, basted with some nice hard butter, not that soft, oily stuff that was in the tins. I wanted a nice baker's roll, with hard butter off the ice, and a nice cup of tea, with some fresh cream, not condensed milk.

All the nice things that I ever did for sick people when I lived in a rich gentleman's family came into my mind. I knew exactly how to do it; I had done it for others. And when I would shut my eyes there would be all the things right before me. I could see them just as plain as could be. When I fell into a little doze of sleep they would haunt me. When I would wake, Oh! how hungry I would be for just that; I wanted nothing else.

It was not the question of money; I had a little, and would have got all these things, but they were not there to be got.

So one night I prayed nearly all night, and asked the Lord to take all desire out of me for everything I could not get, and help me to like and relish just what I could get. About four o'clock in the morning I fell asleep, and woke about six; and every bit of desire for mutton chop, and rolls, and hard butter, and fresh cream was gone, and I was as free from the desire as if I had never had it. I laughed, and cried, and praised the Lord for His loving mercy.

No one who has not had the experience can tell anything about what it means to be weak, and sick, and hungry, and where you cannot get a little or what your appetite craves. But our God is a wonderful deliverer. And then the grand old text that He gave me when I first started, "My God will supply all of your need,"—how true. Praise His name. Amen.

CAPE PALMAS, LIBERIA.

CHAPTER XXXII.

CAPE PALMAS—HOW I GOT THERE—BROTHER WARE—BROTHER SHARPER'S EXPERIENCE—A GREAT REVIVAL.

I had been trying to get to Cape Palmas for three years before I reached there. Dear Mr. Harmon, then pastor of Mt. Scott Methodist Church, had so kindly written for me to come, and had arranged for me, and I had got my things packed. But no steamer called at Monrovia that would stop at Cape Palmas; so I had waited two or three months.

Then a rumor came that small-pox was raging at Cape Palmas; another delay for me. There were no railways, or cable cars running yet; neither were there livery stables, where one could hire a team. These are things that are yet to be; until then, we must wait, and of course pray a little. However, it turned out all right in my case.

Brother Harmon died, and after his death Reverend Ware had charge. He was so different in spirit and government from Brother Harmon. He had treated me most kindly at Monrovia, with some little exceptions, which I did not mind so much, for when it came to temperance and holiness, there are ministers and laymen in this country, who, notwithstanding their light and privilege, stand just where he, and others, stand on these points.

Then he was very bitterly opposed to a woman preaching, or taking any part in a public way. He had a very high appreciation of that especial text of Paul's: "Let your women keep silence in the churches, and if they would know anything, let them ask their husbands at home;" and, as I had no husband at home to ask, I thought according to my orders in John, I had my authority from the words of the Master:

"Ye have not chosen me, but I have chosen you, and ordained you, that you might go and bring forth fruit, that, your fruit might remain, and that whatsoever ye shall ask the Father in my name, He may give it you."

Brother Pitman was pastor at Monrovia in 1882. He was a prince of Israel. A great loss the church in Liberia has sustained, and one, I fear, that will not be easily replaced in Africa. Never shall I forget his fatherly kindness to me. Peace be to his memory.

So it was fortunate for me that I lived at Monrovia when he had charge. He received me as a Christian brother, and stood by me in all the work of the church, in the revival meetings, prayer meetings, and week night preaching services. The church prospered under his administration. The Lord was with us, and we had a blessed time.

Brother Pitman had lived in America several years—I don't know just how many—but he lived in the family of Dr. Gracy, who was the noble editor of the Northern Christian Advocate; so he was quite American in his ideas, but nothing of the pompous sort. He was simply a true, and a clear-headed, logical preacher. How glad we were when he preached. Somebody always got fed on the finest of the wheat.

He had sought, and clearly obtained, the blessing of sanctification. He enjoyed the fulness and lived the life, and when he preached, it was in demonstration of the spirit and power.

I remember one Wednesday night; it wits prayer meeting night. It was true I had been feeling weak and poorly all day. but somehow I felt especially led to go to meeting that night. The distance from Sister Payne's (my home) was not very long; about two blocks. I walked very slowly, but after I got in my back was weak, and pained me dreadfully, so that I said, "I wish I hadn't come." But I felt somehow that the Lord had sent me, so I prayed, and asked Him to strengthen me for the word He would have me give, if I spoke at all.

Brother Pitman was leading the meeting that night; there was nothing out of the ordinary way of things, but a good meeting. By and by the Spirit prompted my heart with these words: "With the mouth confession is made unto salvation."

I was impressed that God meant something by it, yet I did not know just how I was going to be led in speaking: so just before the meeting closed I a rose and said:

"Brother Pitman, I feel the Lord mints me to speak a word."

"Certainly, Sister Smith; speak on."

I spoke as the Lord led me on, confessing Christ and what He had done for a soul definitely. I did not know anything about Brother Pitman's experience; I had never spoken to him about it, and did not know he was interested in the subject of holiness at all, only I knew he seemed to possess the spirit of holiness; I felt it in his conversation and preaching.

After I was through I took my seat. Brother Pitman sprang to his feet in a moment, and said, "The Lord has sent that message to me;" then he went on with how, some three months before, as nearly as I can recollect, he had received this distinct blessing of sanctification, and was helped wonderfully to see the way clearly through the teaching in that grand, old, pioneer holiness periodical, "Guide to Holiness."

"I see as you have spoken, Sister Smith," he continued, "my mistake has been, I have not definitely confessed what the Lord has done for me. But I do here and now confess, before God and these people, that He has cleansed and sanctified my heart."

And from that time forth, he never swerved from preaching or testifying to this great blessing, definitely sought and received by faith.

God made him a great blessing to the people everywhere he went. I believe it was the power of this grace that enabled him to endure as he did; for, being a thorough native of the Da tribe, he had much to endure. He, like Paul, had false brethren to contend with. How my heart has ached, as I have seen and heard things that would have kindled a blaze that would have been unquenchable in the church and community; but he was patient and true, through all.

Then, I think it was in 1883, Brother Ware had charge. The change was great. Some were glad, but I believe most were sorry.

But he and I got on nicely. I always consulted him about my meetings; and, to my face, he would always give me the greatest liberty; and I would be led to think that we saw together; though he did not often take much part; he would say:

"I give you full charge, Sister Smith, whenever you want to have any meetings. Of course I will not be able to be present at all of them, but all the brethren will stand by you, and it will be all right."

I would have afternoon meetings for the young converts, to instruct them in Bible lessons; he would come in and sit way

back, and listen, but that was all. He would generally go out when I was about to close. I went on, carefully, but I went on. And God surely was with us, and blessed us.

I went to Bassa in 1885. after I got to Bassa and met the Bishop, I told him how we had heard at Monrovia that he was to spend three months in that region round about, take a trip to Bepora, etc. He said it was the first he had known of it; that he had made an arrangement, with a certain steamer that was to pick him up at Bassa, and leave him at Cape Palmas, and said this was my chance to go.

"I have not come prepared to go to Cape Palmas," I replied, "but I have been waiting for three years to go. Just when I got ready some months ago, word came that there was small-pox there, so I could not go."

"Well," said the Bishop, "this is your chance, Amanda."

Just then dear Brother Pitman came in. I told him, and he said, "I think, Sister Smith, this is your chance."

"Well," I said, "if you will take Frances (my little native girl) to your home in Paynesville, and keep her till I come back, I think I will go. Do you think Sister Pitman will care? I would go and see her myself, if I could."

"That will be all right, Sister Smith; Frances shall fare as the other children do, and if you are satisfied with that, I will take her."

Sister Pitman was a grand, good woman. She was a splendid housekeeper, and was also a dressmaker and tailor. They never had any children of their own, but all the native boys and girls they had in their family were well raised and well trained; and I knew Frances would fare as well there as if I had her myself.

May God ever bless Sister Pitman. How I sympathize with her in her loss.

So when he returned from the Conference in Monrovia, he took her with him to his home at Paynesville.

I think it was on Wednesday, February 17th, a steamer came to Bassa. The Bishop said we would go. I had but little to get together; only just what would do me as I thought, for the three weeks I had planned to be away. So I had to send for my things after I got to Cape Palmas.

When we went to get into the boat to go to the steamer, a messenger came to say the captain sent word he would not stop at

Cape Palmas, and for no one to come from the shore. "Oh, Bishop," I said, "what will you do?"

"Oh, we will just go."

"Shall I go, then?"

"Oh, yes, come on," he said, quietly, but with such perfect confidence. I just held my breath, and did as I was told.

The man remonstrated, but the Bishop said to the men, "Push off;" and off we did push. When we got alongside, the men aboard the steamer hailed us.

"Where are you going?"

The men gave the word, "To Cape Palmas."

"We are not going to stop at Cape Palmas," one of the officers shouted; "the captain sent word ashore."

When they saw Bishop Taylor was a white man they let down the steps. The Bishop said he wanted to see the captain. It was just dinner time—six o'clock—when we got on board. Of course they did not want that I should come up; but the Bishop said to me quietly, "Come right along, Amanda."

Brother Turner, one of the Bishop's missionaries, a genuine black man, who had been out but about two years, was with him. He was going to Sinoe. We kept close to the Bishop, for we knew if he succeeded, we would.

Oh! how vexed the officers were. But of course they said nothing to Bishop Taylor. They were civil to him.

The Bishop had no baggage; he never did carry any about with him in Africa; simply a small basket, and his bed rolled up. To look at it you would think it was a surveyor's instruments; that was generally his outfit. But some of the rest of us did have something, in the shape of a small trunk. When the officers saw this they said:

"We are not going to stop at Cape Palmas; don't lift the baggage."

So I stood quietly while the Bishop went in to see the captain; or rather send word to him, and there was a pause of fifteen minutes, or so. I stood trembling in my boots almost, for it was about five miles back to shore, and I thought, "Oh, dearie me, if I have got to go back in this darkness all alone!" So I said, "Oh! Lord, help the Bishop, and bless that captain, and make him let us go."

While they were gone with a message to the captain, I slipped softly up to the Bishop, and said:

"Bishop do you think we will have to go back to shore?"

"Oh, no," he said, in perfect confidence, "it will be all right."

And sure enough, word came to the Bishop from the captain:

"All right; we will take you."

My! didn't I whirl? Dinner! I didn't want any. I was full of joy and gladness. I hadn't any room for anything else until next morning.

Now, then, you may say what you please, explain it as you like, but if Bishop Taylor had not been a white man, not simply a Bishop, but a white man, as sure as this world, we would have had to come all that way back to shore in the night. And I did thank the Lord down in my heart for a white Bishop that time.

We were two nights and a day on the vessel and arrived at Cape Palmas about ten A. M. Friday.

I shall never forget the delight of the dear people when they saw the Bisop and myself. The children crowded around like he had been a father, more than a Bishop. He was so kind, and shook hands with them, and had a pleasant word for all. The little, native boys danced and laughed, and seemed so glad.

When I saw the Christian spirit so manifest among the people toward the Bishop and myself, I came nearly crying out. Oh! it was so different from what it seemed to be in Bassa.

We were conducted from the landing at Cape Palmas to Sister Harmon's; she received us gladly, and entertained us kindly.

Sunday was to be quarterly meeting; so it seemed to be such a propitious time for us to arrive just then.

Brother Ware had notified the brethren, and the Bishop held his quarterly conference Friday afternoon at four o'clock, and preached on Saturday night to a full congregation. Of course everybody turned out, Baptists, Episcopalians, and Methodists, (those were the only denominations at Cape. Palmas), senators, lawyers, deacons, etc.

Among the dignitaries I noticed his honor, Bishop Ferguson. It was the first time I had ever seen him.

But everybody seemed to be interested in this American Bishop. And he preached a grand, old-fashioned Holy Ghost sermon, as everybody knows he can. I think that Bishop Ferguson was rather pleased, until he heard the good Bishop speak of standing on a hogshead, in California, I think it was, and preaching to the multitude. The idea of lowering his dignity! He seemed to look almost disgusted.

But what capped the climax with them, after the Bishop got through, he told them who I was, and spoke some kind words of me, and of my work, and told them if they would stand by me I would do them good, etc. Then he said, "I will ask Sister Smith to speak a few words to you."

I lifted my heart and asked the Lord to help me. And He did. And the people were blessed.

Poor Bishop Ferguson! He hung his head all the time I was speaking, and went out as soon as he could; and I don't suppose he has heard Bishop Taylor since.

Poor Brother Ware had strong proclivities toward that church at that time. His eldest son, who had been brought up, and trained and converted in the Methodist Church, had left it, and gone over to the Episcopal Church.

And, by the way, that is one good thing the Methodist Church has done in Liberia; for if she has not done so much in the conversion of the heathen, she has certainly done her part in furnishing workers for the Episcopal Church. I don't believe they have a single worker, except a few among the natives; for the matron in their orphanage, the teachers in their schools, or the workers on their farms, come out of the Methodist Church; and those in the church that know anything about real conversion, have been converted or sanctified in the Methodist Church; so if ever a church ought to thank God for Methodism in Africa, notwithstanding her faults and failings, it ought to be this church!

But strange to say, they do not; but, like the Jesuits, they cease not day or night, in every possible way, to disturb and proselyte.

I tried my best to be as unselfish as I could, and show in every possible way that I was a Christian and had no other object than to help everybody I could, in every way I could. I did not advocate a new doctrine, or start a new church. I told the people this was not my errand in Africa. There were churches enough already. All that was needed was the spirit of full consecration to God, and a baptism for real service.

When I began my temperance work in Cape Palmas I wrote Bishop Ferguson, and the several ministers in his diocese, and sent them our pledge card, and tracts, and our constitution and by-laws,

so that they might see for themselves what I was trying to do; that it was nothing in the corner, or in the dark; that they might know exactly what I was teaching among the people; and I asked his honor, the Bishop, if he would be kind enough to preach a sermon and explain my object; as I knew how the people in general are given to extravagance in trying to tell anything.

As this was Gospel temperance, to help Christian men and women on to a higher platform of Christian character and Christian life, it never entered my head but they would be willing to co-operate on this platform, as it was purely undenominational, and had met such favor in England and America while On this basis.

But the good Bishop replied in a short note, saying he would consider the matter, and let me know later on. In a few days he wrote me a great, lengthy epistle of five or six pages; beautifully written, for he certainly wrote a beautiful hand. But I must confess the best thing about that letter was the beautiful handwriting. A regular General Conference document, saying he could have nothing to do with the subject I had written him about, and pointing out a clause in our Methodist discipline, saying that was all that was needful.

Well, I was ashamed to say anything about it except to one of two persons; for I had always heard him spoken so highly of; and I was proud of him, being a black Bishop; and knowing that he knew the condition and the suffering among the poor natives on account of strong drink, and among the Liberians as well, I thought I had a right to hope for, at least, sympathy.

Perhaps I would not have thought much about it if he had been a white man. But I find that human nature is the same in black men, even in Africa, as in white men in America. It is the same old story everywhere: "None but Jesus can do helpless sinners good."

Well, the Lord helped me, and I went on with the work, and men and women, young and old, some of all the denominations, joined in. But his position toward it had its effect, which is natural.

So, poor Brother Ware, with his Episcopal proclivities, and underlying all a strong desire to be a Bishop, had got all the official board so fully over to his side in regard to a woman taking a public part in a meeting, and had filled them so with prejudice, that if I had not gone to Cape Palmas with Bishop Taylor, I would not have had a shadow of a chance. But when God is on our side, you may not fear what man may do.

Away back in the years before, He had said, "Behold, I have set before you an open door, and no man shall shut it." How I proved His every word true.

Brother Ware was not well, so did not get to the Conference at Bassa. On Sunday morning we had a great Love Feast. The Spirit of the Lord was among us, and at 10:30 the Bishop preached. What a sermon! I suppose they had never heard anything like it. Surely the Lord of Hosts was with us.

Just after the consecration of the elements for the sacrament, as the Bishop was about to proceed in administering, or passing it, the steamer signalled, and the good Bishop was notified that he must leave. He had already announced that he was to preach to the young people and children at three P. M., and had asked all the other people to be seated in the gallery, and reserve the body of the church for the young people and children. So, when the Bishop had to leave, he turned to Brother Ware, and said:

"Brother Ware, if you are not well, Sister Amanda Smith will take the service this afternoon in my stead."

"Yes," Brother Ware said, "we shall be glad to have Sister Smith take the service."

I saw it was all awful pill, but he swallowed it as meekly as he could.

Oh! how the Lord did bless me that afternoon.

At night I took the service again. The power of the Lord was present among the people. One good sister in the Episcopal Church, Sister Tubman, got sanctified that night, as a seal to my first work at Cape Palmas. The Lord gave her light and help, as I went on talking from the fourteenth chapter of John, fourteenth verse: "If ye shall ask anything in my name, I will do it."

What a stir it made. The people were up in arms, and the cat got out!

"Great Lord, that woman can preach. That ain't no so-so talk. God is in that woman."

And so it went the rounds. They said, "What is the matter with Brother Ware? Why don't he let her preach?"

Then a number of the brethren called on him, and asked him to give me an appointment, as they all wanted to hear me speak.

But that, I think, made it worse. I called on him. He seemed pleasant and treated me kindly, but never said a word to me about taking a meeting. For two weeks then I went on quietly, holding afternoon meetings and giving Bible readings on the subject of consecration and holiness. This was the beginning of the wonderful blessing at Cape Palmas.

At the expiration of two weeks, Brother Ware was obliged to leave for Monrovia; but he called his local brethren, Brother Os Tubman, old Father Jenkins, Brother Dennis, Brother Thompson, who was Vice-President of the Republic and a local preacher, Brother Sharper, and Brother Bowen, who had the pastoral charge of the church at Mt. Tubman.

No one of these brethren were to give their appointments to any one, under penalty of having to answer at the quarterly conference. Some of them said:

"Brother Ware, we believe Sister Smith is a woman of God, and she came here with Bishop Taylor. He knows her, and endorses her, and we ought to give her a chance."

But his reply was, "I, and not Bishop Taylor, am pastor of the church."

So, according to the laws of the Medes and Persians, the decision must not be altered.

Another week had passed, and it had come Saturday. With all that was said, I kept quiet, and said but little to any one. Some of the people wanted to know if there was any misunderstanding between me and Brother Ware.

"No, nor there never has been, as I know of."

I must confess it was a little embarrassing to me; but it helped me to see God as I had never seen Him before. Out of all these brethren, there was not one of them who dared give me an appointment except old Father Dennis. He was a man of strong moral courage and good, broad common sense; a highly intelligent man; and he knew every weak spot in the whole government, as well as the strong; and he knew the discipline of the Methodist Church as well, if not better, than any other man in the Republic; and, notwithstanding all this, he was very peculiar, and, withal, eccentric. So he said to some of the brethren, that if Ware wanted to have him up in the quarterly conference for giving his appointment, he might do it. He did not care.

He came to me on Saturday, and asked me if I would go to

Mt. Tubman, which was about two miles from Latrobe, and take his appointment; he was not feeling very well, anyhow.

I told him, "Yes, I would."

"The brethren tell me that Brother Ware will have me up for it; and I told them I didn't care."

"Well," I said, "if you are willing to risk it, I will go."

So I went out on Saturday afternoon, Sister Harmon and I.

Mt. Tubman is a beautiful spot. How plain I seem to see the little church on the hill. What times of blessing I have had; and this man, and that man were born there.

I was not very strong, so they arranged that Sister Harmon and I should go out in the carriage. So, in a little while we were ready. The carriage drove up, with a nice little black bullock, and we were soon seated and off. But we had not gone far, when the bullock began to cut African capers.

First he backed and then he ran up on one side of the bank, and came near tumbling the carriage over. Then we got him down and he went on a little ways, Then he made another break at the other side of the road, and Then he stopped. I thought it was a good chance to dismount and so I did, and footed it the balance of the way, which was more than half way.

I went to Brother Bowen's and stayed all night. How kind Brother and Sister Bowen were. They did all they could to make me comfortable. I could see that Brother Bowen was a little embarrassed, as he was pastor. He said, "Brother Ware's orders were that the brethern should take their appointments in order."

But, Brother Bowen was a good man, and he had good sense, and was reasonable; but he was a little afraid of his superior.

I talked, and sang and told him many things about his own country for he had gone to Liberia when quite a young man.

Many of his friends would come in; then they would go out and seem to have a quiet talk together. I prayed. I knew I had not gone myself, but that God had sent me; and I waited to see Him get the victory.

Sunday morning came. There was a splendid congregation. Just as it was time to open the service, who should come in but dear, old Brother Dennis.

I saw Brother Bowen was glad. He at once asked him to take the service; and he got up and said he had asked me to come out there and take his appointment, as he was not very well; then, in the morning, as he felt better, he thought he had better come out and explain, for he knew the Methodist discipline, and he was not afraid of anybody. Everybody knew that was old man Dennis, and it was all true.

So that was my introduction. If ever I prayed for God to help me, I did that day. And He did. Then I stayed and took part in the class meeting after the service. Then I addressed the Sabbath School, and took the service at night. The church was crowded. Oh! how the Lord helped me to speak. I thought, "This is my last day here, so I will do everything I can."

After I was through speaking at night I gave the invitation to sinners to come forward and seek the Lord; and almost immediately eight men came forward; four were converted that night.

I thought that my strength was gone; but it seemed to me that God gave me a double portion. I had no further trouble with Brother Bowen.

The news spread like wildfire. The people came from all directions. We went on for two weeks without a break. We had several all night meetings, and all day. In that meeting some old men were converted that were never known to pray, or be serious before. I went to see them from house to house, and sat down and talked with them, and explained the way of faith. Oh! how God put his seal on the work. This was the beginning. In this meeting Charlie Gray and Brother Cox were sanctified.

I had worked hard, and was so weary I thought I must come home for a rest. So on Monday I came home to Sister Harmon's.

Now, the two weeks' Bible readings that I had held prior to going to Mt. Tubman, had laid a foundation, and God had blessed the people.

Tuesday night was the prayer meeting night. I had had a little rest on Monday after I got home, and on Tuesday night was the prayer meeting at Mt. Scott Church. Brother Thompson called and asked me if I would lead prayer meeting that night. I told him I was very weary and needed a rest. But he said he would be glad if I would take it. I told him I would do the best I could. I was so very weak, but I asked the Lord to strengthen me, as I did so often. Oh!

how many times He has heard and answered that prayer. Blessed be His name. That night the work began at Latrobe. And what a tidal wave swept all over Cape Palmas. Oh! it was wonderful.

I have gone to the church at six o'clock in the evening to hold a prayer meeting before preaching, and have never gone outside the door till six next morning.

When we did go in for salvation we didn't play, but went in. God converted sinners, reclaimed backsliders, and sanctified and established believers.

The Baptists fought a little. They were very firmly fixed. Once in grace, always in grace, no matter what you say or do. But with all the opposition, God's chariot rolled on; and many of them were brought to realize the power of Jesus, and were saved fully. Glory to Jesus.

How well I remember Brother Sharper, one of our old local preachers. He was a man of more than ordinary intelligence, and good, broad, common sense. He was one of the best local preachers we had. He had a nice, comfortable, little home of his own, and a very nice wife and baby boy. When I first held my Bible readings Brother Sharper became very much interested in the subject of holiness. The Holy Spirit convicted him of his need of a clean heart. He was a man of high moral character and Christian integrity, and stood high in the community and the church.

When the Spirit of God got hold of his conscience, he did like so many; he began to reason with himself: "I know I am convicted, and I have been a Christian all these years, and I will just go on growing in grace, and purity will come."

But, poor man, he had it wrong end first! The very best chance for growing in grace, really and successfully, is to get the cleansing and all obstruction to growth out. As the Psalmist suggests:

"The clean heart, then the teaching of transgressors Thy way." The Psalmist had it right. Praise the Lord.

Poor Brother Sharper used to come to the Bible readings, but all at once I missed him. He didn't come. I would call around at his house and have a little chat. I didn't bore him. He was always glad to see me, and always had a good reason for not coming to the meeting.

He was a most inveterate smoker, but he never let me see him with his pipe in his mouth. He was much of a gentleman in his bearing. On Sunday I had been calling on some friends on next street; on my way home I called in, and there was Brother Sharper in his nice little home, all alone, his Bible on a chair by him, and his pipe. He had read and smoked and fallen asleep. When I called to him, poor fellow, how embarrassed he was. I saw it, and tried to help him by asking him what he was reading, particularly. He laughed and said:

"Sister Smith, I didn't mean for you to see me with that old pipe."

"Oh, no matter," I said, "you and the Lord will settle it by and by."

So, after a little chat, I went home to pray and ask the Lord to deliver Brother Sharper. He began coming to the meetings, but seemed depressed. And he didn't stay till the close of the meetings. But one night at prayer meetings, I was leading, and I asked anyone who had the desire to seek the blessing of a clean heart to come and kneel at the altar. A number came; among others, Brother Sharper. He came like he meant business. He was not a demonstrative or emotional man, and when I saw him kneel and clutch the alter railing, I said to myself, "Sharper is in for it."

One and another prayed for themselves, and God set them at liberty. Oh! what a meeting it was!

Brother Sharper groaned and struggled. It came to a close about eleven o'clock. A number had got blessed, and we arose and sang the doxology. Brother Sharper had not moved from his position. But I knew the Lord would take care of him.

Just as we were about to sing, Brother Sharper sprang to his feet and shouted at the top of his voice:

"But you must go through! You must go through! Victory! Victory! Victory!"

He went over the tops of the seats like a streak of light. I tried to catch him. I was afraid he would kill himself. But he swung from my grasp as though he had been oiled. Oh! what a shout. When that tremendous wave had passed over, he calmed down as quiet as a lamb, and he smiled. He was a handsome man anyhow: but this night he looked beautiful.

He stood up in front by the altar and faced the congregation, and said:

"Sister Smith, I want to tell what the Lord has done for me. I have had an awful struggle for days over this question. I thought I would stay away from the meetings; but that didn't help me. And you know the Sunday you were around to my house, and caught me with the Bible and my pipe?"

"Yes," I said.

"Well, there was where I stuck; but I thought if I did everything else all right, the Lord would not require me to give up my pipe; and I did not know it was such an idol until I tried to give it up. Oh! how it held me. You know I love my wife and child; but I felt I could give up either of them easier than I could give up my pipe. I would smoke, the last thing before I went to bed, and the first thing in the morning, and sometimes I would get up two or three times in the night to have a smoke; and if there was not a match, or fire, in the house to light my pipe, I would walk a mile to get it.

"The other night I lay down and fell into a doze of sleep; and I dreamed I saw a great host marching. They were divided into two companies. Oh! such singing I never heard. It was wonderful! The sanctified host was ahead, and outsang the justified host. As they marched they sang. I stood and looked at them. I said, well, I will join the justified company. They will get in, too, just as well as the others. So joined the song with them, for I wanted them to keep up with the host ahead. Oh! how I sang with all my might; but the sanctified host seemed to out-sing us.

"In our march we came to a culvert in the road, and I thought 'I will watch and see how they get through there.' I saw when they got up to it, they all, with one accord, bowed low, and went through, and struck up their song on the other side. And when the justified company came up to the culvert, they stopped, and there seemed to be quite a contention about how to get through. But not one of them stooped. After a while they divided, and walked around on either side, and went on. When I came up to it I started to go round, first on the right; but a voice confronted me and said, 'but you must go through.' Then I made an effort to go to the left; and again a voice said, 'but you must go through.' so I tried the third time, and again the same words, 'but you must go through.' And glory to God, the tobacco is gone, and I got through!"

As he stood and told that wonderful experience, which beggars description, the spirit of the Lord fell on the people, and it was wonderful.

Poor Brother Sharper preached with a power and unction that he had not known before. And the last I heard of him, he was at one of Bishop Taylor's mission stations on the river, working for God.

The meeting went on, and many of the natives got saved. John Yancy got saved.

One night we were singing that victorious hymn, I call it (for when it is sung properly, it generally carries blessing with it)—

> "Ah! many years my longing heart
> Had sighed, had longed to know
> The virtue of the Savior's blood,
> That washes white as snow."

> "There is power in Jesus' blood,
> There is power in Jesus' blood,
> There is power in Jesus' blood,
> To wash me white as snow."

I had sung this hymn in the meetings, and the people had learned it, and they could sing it as only colored people can sing. John Yancy had been seeking the blessing for several weeks. He was converted, and had been a consistent member of the church for two years or more. But, as he said, "He felt that God had something more for him;" and as he sat in the church that night, while we were singing, the Holy Ghost fell on him. Oh! how he shouted.

"Oh! yes, there is power in Jesus' blood to wash me white as snow. Yes, there is power in the blood. Yes, there is power in Jesus' blood."

Every time he said it it went like an electric shock through the house, and the people seemed to be swayed by the mighty power.

Everybody believed in John Yancy's sanctification. The people all had known him from a little boy. He was raised right up there among them. And I never heard a soul express a doubt about John Yancy's life and testimony. He was a rank, native, heathen boy, born in heathenism. He had been brought out of the country, and the most of his raising, and where he took his name, was from Mr. Allen Yancy, a good man, formerly of America. God wonderfully sanctified him, and his dear wife, also, shortly after John got the blessing.

On Friday night, the last night of our meeting for the week, there were several very interesting cases who were seeking pardon; but they had not come out into the clear light. One was a Congo man. I felt very anxious about them, lest Satan should get the advantage of them. I was very weary in body, but on Saturday afternoon, I thought I must go and see after those seekers.

Where this Congo man lived, was on the back street, as they called it; and the people who lived on that street were nearly all Congos, with the exception of two or three families. It was not one of the prominent streets, but it was the prettiest street, I thought, in Cape Palmas. It was wide, and had several very pretty, little cottages on it.

I found the place where the man lived. He was sitting in his own yard, under a pretty arbor, talking to someone. He was quite surprised to see me. But I told him why I came. I told him I was anxious about him, as he was seeking the Lord.

So I sat down, took out my Testament, and began to read and explain a few passages of Scripture on faith, and how to exercise it. The Lord helped me, and helped the man. Then I sang; and in a little while I had a number of earnest listeners around me. Then I prayed.

This was all right out in the yard. When this was finished I thought I would go home; but a woman said:

"Mrs. Smith, there is some one in such a house, sick, who wants to know if you will come and pray with him."

So I went with the woman. I talked, and read the blessed Word and explained it as the Spirit led me; then prayed, sang a verse, and left.

When I got downstairs, a little girl came and said her mother was sick and had heard the singing, and had sent to beg me to come, if but for a moment. So I did. And so I went on and made eight calls of the same kind, and prayed, and sang, and talked.

The Lord blessed this poor, sick woman; and a short time after this she died. Sister Harmon and all wondered what had become of me; for I had left home at four o'clock to be gone only an hour or two, as I thought; but I didn't get home until eight o'clock in the evening. The cases were so interesting, and I got so absorbed and carried away, that I forgot all about my weariness and weakness till I got home and sat down. Then it came over me like a great wave; and I trembled like a reed in the wind.

As I think of it now, I wonder how I ever went through all I did. Sometimes I have started to church feeling so weak, and I have prayed every step of the way; and there have been times when I have stood up to speak, I have felt is it were a hand press my back, and seem to hold me up while I would deliver the message to the people. Blessed be the name of God. How well I know His mighty touch of strength and power.

There was a Mrs. Delia Williams, whose house I went into and prayed that afternoon, on this same street.

Just inside her gate, in the yard, there stood a beautiful broad fruit tree. As I passed out I said, "that would be a nice tree to hold a little meeting under."

"Oh! Mrs. Smith," she said, "will you come here and hold a meeting for us here on this street? We need it. These people do not go to church much. They will not go."

This woman was what you might call a kind of half way Christian. She belonged to the church, but she was not straight. She was always seeming to seek peace, but could not find it, because she did not give up to God. Poor thing, she was good-hearted, and wanted to see everybody get all the good they could. So I said to her:

"I will see about it, and let you know. Of course that bush there in the street would have to be cleared away."

"Oh!" she said, "if you will come, I will have that done. And I can put a table and some chairs out, and put some mats down."

"I might come Monday," I said; "but, however, don't do anything until you hear from me."

I kept very quiet. I never told even Mrs. Harmon's people. I knew if the word was said, the people that considered themselves not Congos would all come, and my purpose to do these non-church-going people good would be lost.

But somehow it got out; first thing I knew Monday, somebody came to me and said, "Mrs. Smith, I hear you are to hold a meeting on the back street this afternoon."

"Who said so?"

"Well," they said, "Delia Williams has had the bush all cut down, and they tire getting ready over there, and said you were to come, and all the people are looking for you."

Oh! dearie me how I felt. "Now," I thought, "there will be a great crowd. That was not what I wanted at all. I just wanted to go quietly and have a meeting for these poor Congo people."

By and by another came; and so it went. Mrs. Harmon said:

"Why, you never told me anything about it."

"No," I said, "for the very reason I was afraid there would be a great excitement about it."

She laughed and said, "You try to keep anything quiet here, and you will miss it."

So I got ready and went; and there, sure enough, under that pretty tree stood a table with a white cloth on it, a hymn book, a pitcher of water, and tumbler; chairs all around, and mats down, and there the people were. As I drew near I smiled to myself, and yet was fit to cry. I said, "Lord, help me this once."

I read and explained the Word as best I could on consecration and faith, pointing out some of the sins and hindrances to the exercise of faith for any blessing that God was willing to give.

The Lord did help me that afternoon as I talked. Several good sisters had come who had got the baptism of the Spirit, and knew how to pray; so I asked if there were any there who desired we should pray for them, and I asked them to stand up, and several did so. Among them was Brother Sharper's wife.

Dear Sister Sharper! I shall never forget her. She was a woman of no ordinary intelligence; and she was desperately in earnest. I asked them to come forward and kneel around the table (for we had no altar), and she came. Oh! how she prayed. And when the Holy Ghost struck her (for it did) she whirled like a top, round and round, and round and round! We could not touch her. She just went like a streak, through the bush, out into the street. I thought she would kill herself. Oh! I was frightened. As she rolled over, she kept saying, "Glory, glory, glory to Jesus! glory!"

The sisters followed after her, and tried to hold her, but they could not. By and by she sprang up all at once; and didn't she shout! She marched home, and there was not a scratch or a bruise on her. It was wonderful. I shall never forget the day when Jesus washed her sins away. Glory to His name!

These were some of the wonderful days at Cape Palmas. And still there's more to follow.

Brother Ware did not get back for six weeks; so we had full swing and God was with us. When he did come, how surprised he was.

Every Sunday, prior to his coming, a number were taken in. The first Sunday after he came he took in nine or ten; I don't know what number was exactly. I never like to number Israel. The record is one high. But I know one Sunday after this, one of the leaders said to him, just before the meeting closed (as he had not opened the doors of the church to receive any members), "Brother Ware, there are several persons who would like to join the church," and he brought them up; and he refused to take them in, because he had not been notified of their desire to join more than two or three days before, and said that he would not receive any more unless their names were given to him two or three days before, and he could see them, and have a talk with them himself.

It seemed to throw a damper on the work. Everybody seemed to understand what it meant. But the Lord of Hosts was with us; and the God of Jacob was our refuge; and we hid, and went on.

CHAPTER XXXIII.

EMIGRATION TO LIBERIA—SCHOOLS OF LIBERIA—MISSION SCHOOLS—FALSE IMPRESSIONS—IGNORANCE AND HELPLESSNESS OF EMIGRANTS—AFRICAN ARISTOCRACY.

I am often asked if I favor colored people's emigrating to Liberia, Africa.

My answer is, "Yes," and "No."

Yes, if the right kind of emigrants go. For in this country, if the right kind of emigrants come, we need have no fears. But it is the flood of ignorant Italians, uneducated and untrained, and poor Polish Jews, and Irish, and Germans, who have no interest in America whatever, only for what they can get out of it, have no love for its institutions, no love for its government, have not been taught any of its principles, don't know anything about them, and don't care to—these are the people that we don't want in America; women ignorant, men ignorant, and, of course, herds of children equally ignorant; worse than the heathen in Africa, and much harder to enlighten, because they have been steeped in Romanism, and the African comes only with his superstitions, which he soon drops, under the civilized and Christian influences. Now, without there has been a vast improvement since I was there, the Liberian government is very poor, but makes out to manage somehow. And if educated, industrious, intelligent black men, with money, would go there, for the love of the race, and with the love of God in their hearts, and go with no other object than to sacrifice their lives and their money for the good of the republic and their fellowmen (and it would take but a little while to do that; but this is the only way for black men to go to Africa; and *I* believe this is the proper way), then I say, yes, emigrate.

On the other hand, I say "No." For I don't believe it is right to take out men and women indiscriminately, and generally of the poorest that are in the South, or anywhere else, ignorant of the principles, and the need and duties of the Liberian government, as the poor, ignorant Italians, or Polish Jews, or others with no knowledge of the country or its customs, no love for it in any way, only what they get out of it, have not been taught, have no love of loyalty, only as they may borrow it for selfish ends, then I say, "No, No!"

God bless the Colonization Society. It was raised up at a time of imperative need; and so was John Knox, of Scotland; Wesley of England. It did its work. But from the standpoint I look at it, I would move its disbandment forthwith, and let white people who want the Negro to emigrate to Africa so as to make more room for the great flood of foreigners who come to our shores, know that there is a place in the United States for the Negro.

They are real American citizens, and at home. They have fought and bled and died, like men, to make this country what it is. And if they have got to suffer and die, and be lynched, and tortured, and burned at the stake, I say they are at home.

Like many of the foreigners that come, they are not all industrious; and to be poor, and ignorant, and lazy is bad enough at home. But to be seven thousand miles away in a heathen country, is ten times worse.

At first sight, it would seem all right; but one cannot know Africa in a week, or a month. It is quite easy for a stranger to go there and make a call or two, on some of the best people, have a fine dinner, big speeches, and all that (all of which they can give you), but, Lord bless you, that is not knowing the people, any more than it would be knowing the people in Italy because you dinned with the king. And there is where people are so often deceived about Liberia, and often the real state of things is misrepresented. What a pity! What a pity!

I believe that if the real facts in the case of that republic had been known twenty years ago, she would have been in a better condition, financially and commercially, and she would have had the sympathy, and respect, and admiration of the world. But the Liberians have a false that to speak of their failures or mistakes in any way, means to reflect upon them, because it is a black republic. But I never thought so, and told them I didn't believe

it. But my people often called me "White folk's nigger," anyhow. So I am in for it, and I don't care. All I care to do is to keep in favor with God and man as much as lieth in me.

During my stay of eight years in Africa there was not a government school building in the republic, and never had been, as far as I could learn; but their schools were held in churches, or private houses. I remember there was a high school talked of and arranged for during the session of the legislature in 1885 or 1886. A Mr. James Lewis, of Sinoe, was appointed by the government as teacher. I was in Greenville, Sinoe, when he returned home from the Legislature with his appointment.

Of course there was a great deal of talk about this new department of school work. Mr. Lewis was thought to be the man for the position. And I thought from the talk that they would erect a building for the purpose. But no; when Mr. Lewis opened his school, with quite a nice number of pupils, it was on the veranda of his own private dwelling; and his seat was a hammock!

Many times I have passed by, or from my window could see him, hearing his pupils recite, while he would be lying in the hammock. It was right in the public street, so it was not a thing done in a corner. I spent some weeks with his sister, Mrs. Marshall, almost opposite his house; so know whereof I affirm.

Then there were two other schools called government schools; one held in the Congregational Church, and another, said to be for natives, held in another part of town. This school was held about three times in a week, with an average attendance of five or six native boys, who lived in the families generally. The teacher was Mrs. Marshall's sister.

Of course the government had an inspector of schools; but you were a friend of the inspector, or if you had a friend who was a friend of the inspector, it had more to do with your keeping the school than any other qualification.

Then people say, "Well, but they have a college." Yes, they boast of a college. I often told them that it did not come up to a good high school in this country, not in any sense. I think there was a time when it was in a better condition than it was when I was there. Whatever that was, I don't know. I simply speak of what it was during the eight years of my stay. To call it a college, I think, is a misnomer; for it led the people to believe that we had graded schools, and every requisite preparatory to a college course. But that is really not so.

There was no standard school book in any of the schools. The children used any kind of books they could get—Sunday School books, story books, or any book. Everywhere I went I inquired about the schools, and found the same statement. I visited a school one day where I found a very nice lot of children, ranging from six to fourteen years of age. Many of them seemed to be very bright. They came to recite one at a time.

"Why don't you have them in classes?" I asked.

"Yes, that is what I would like to do," the teacher said. "But we haven't got the books. There are not four children in the school with books alike. Their parents send them with any kind of a book, and I am obliged to use it; and some of the children come and have no book at all; but they come."

"How do you manage?"

"I borrow a book from some of the other children, and hear the lesson."

"Then they can't study when they go home?"

"No," she said, "they just have to study in school."

"How long have you been teaching this school?"

"Two years," she said.

"Well, why don't you speak about it? Isn't this a government school?"

"Yes, but I have spoke, and have gone myself to Monrovia, and done all I could about it; but it does no good."

And that was about the way I would find it everywhere, unless there was a mission school.

As I was going to Liberia, in 1882, when we got to Sierra Leone, a Liberian young man, a very nice lad, I suppose about seventeen years of age, Mr. Eddie Lisles, from Bassa, got on the steamer. I saw he was a very nice, interesting looking lad, and one day as he was sitting smoking, I went up to him and had a talk with him. I asked him his name, and where he lived, and he told me. He said he had been away at school.

"Away at school?" I said; "where?"

"At Sierra Leone."

"Sierra Leone? Why they have a college at Monrovia, haven't they?"

"Yes," he said.

"Well," I said, "I'm surprised. I thought that the people would be sending their children from other places to Monrovia to the college."

He smiled as though he thought I was green. And I was, too. He said: "I have a sister that is going when I go home."

"Have they good schools in Sierra Leone?" I asked.

"Very good."

"And don't the people in Sierra Leone send their children to the college at Monrovia?"

"No," he said.

It was all a mystery to me. I could not understand it. I felt inclined to think he was not straight. But still I said nothing more. Of course I understood it after eight years' experience and observation.

The mission schools have done the most good, I think. The Presbyterian Mission, at Clay-Ashland, at one time had a flourishing school. They had a fine, large, brick house, and outbuildings. When I first went to Africa, these buildings were all in good condition, but were unoccupied. The school was held in the hall, on the opposite side of the river. Mr. Albert King was the teacher, and as his home was on the other side of the river, I presume that is why the school was changed over there.

However, the former house and buildings were all standing when I first went there. I have often passed it as I have gone up the river. What a pretty situation it was, and how nice everything seemed to be around it. But, like the Methodist Seminary at Monrovia, and the Ann Wilkins school at Millsburg, and the school up at White Plains, and the seminary at Cape Palmas, was once flourishing, but had gone down. And that is one of the good things that Bishop Taylor has done for the Liberians—restoring and manning their schools, and establishing schools among the natives, and supplying them with teachers, and so helping the government to fulfill their promise to them, which hitherto they had not been able to do.

I was told that that was one of the causes of the Gredebo war; that the government had promised to establish schools among the natives, and sen

CHAPTER XXXIV.

LETTERS AND TESTIMONIALS—BISHOP TAYLOR—CHURCH AT MONROVIA—UPPER CALDWELL—SIERRA LEONE—GREENVILLE CAPE PALMAS—BAND OF HOPE TEMPERANCE SOCIETY AT MONROVIA LETTERS—MRS. PAYNE—MRS. DENMAN—MRS. INSKIP—REV. EDGAR M. LEVY—ANNIE WITTENMYER—DR. DORCHESTER —MARGARET BOTTOME — MISS WILLARD—LADY HENRY SOMERSET.

Before I dismiss the subject of Africa, where I spent eight years of labor in the service of the Master, I wish to present a few miscellaneous papers—testimonials, letters, etc.—as specimens of the many that I have received from those who have known me, and my work, there and elsewhere.

It is not from motives of vanity that I do this, but because I am sure that my readers will be interested in the testimony of some whose names, for the most part, are familiar to the entire Christian world; and of others who, though not so well known, were on the ground and personally acquainted with my work in Africa.

I have many letters from Bishop William Taylor, of whom I have had something to say in the preceding chapters, but I withhold all but the following, which may serve as a sort of general introduction, although it was written simply as a letter of commendation to Ex-President Payne, of Liberia:

James S. Payne, Ex-President of Liberia.

MY DEAR BROTHER:—This will introduce to your acquaintance our beloved sister, Mrs. Amanda Smith. As you may know, Sister Amanda is one of the most remarkable evangelists of these eventful days in which we live. She is a member of our church, and well accredited, and everywhere owned of God in America, England and India, as a marvelous, soul-saving worker for the Lord Jesus.

I heard you pleading for Liberia at our recent general Conference. Your prayer will be answered in a great revival of God's work in Liberia, through the agency of Sister Amanda, with the working concurrence of your churches.

I am sure you will do all you can to open her way. God bless you all. Amen.

Your brother in Jesus,

WILLIAM TAYLOR.

MONROVIA, July 10, 1889.

Mrs. Amanda Smith, Evangelist.

DEAR SISTER:—Now, upon the eve of your departure from us, after a sojourn of eight years, we feel it highly becoming us (and it affords us great pleasure to do so), to accord to you this tribute of respect and appreciation, as a testimonial of your untiring labors among us as a Christian evangelist; of the purity of your doctrines, the earnestness of their enforcement, of the clearness of their illustration, and of the wonderful and happy results which have followed. These all you leave behind you as enduring monuments of your zeal for the Master, and of your unabated love for humankind; and we do accept it, that your mission to Africa has been from GOD.

Your life among us during these years of your sojourn, has been an even one, and one of untarnished moral and Christian rectitude and earnestness, nor needs any further defense, other than what it has borne along with itself, for it speaks for itself.

And this is the testimony of all honest hearts throughout Liberia. The children of Belial here, may rise up to asperse your fame, and to sully the lustre of your name, which they so much covet, but this were a vain attempt. And we accept it as a complete refutation of the theory emphasized by some, in their ignorance of the real character of the Negro at home, that white missionaries are preferred by them. The responsibility of such a theory rests solely on those who originate and sustain it.

Your extensive travels throughout the length and breadth of our land, your free and liberal intercourse and labors among all classes, civilized and heathen, Christian and Pagan, and the universal hospitalities extended to you, show but too plainly, when compared with the welcome and entertainment given our white brother, that the theory above mentioned is not so tenable as they have vainly and ignorantly supposed. With the Negro at home in his native wilds, when untrammelled and unsophisticated by unfavorable contact with the dominant race,

"A man's a man for a' that."

The higher plane of Christian experience, as preached by you, in its distinctiveness and definiteness, is a doctrine purely Scriptural; a doctrine recognized and enjoyed under all ages of the church. It first blazed forth from the altar upon which "Abel by faith offered a more acceptable sacrifice than Cain." In equal lustre it shone in Enoch, who, "By faith was translated that he should not see death." And then, in righteous Noah, who, "By faith being warned of things to come, not seen as yet, moved with fear, prepared the ark to the saving of his house." And all along the line, through the patriarchal, Mosaic, and prophetic ages, it blazed from the altar in an unbroken series. And then, under the fuller illumings of the Holy Ghost, since the advent of the blessed Savior, it was the theme of the Apostolic and primitive Christians. The middle ages, though an age of terror and of gross darkness, still preserved it in good tact, and transmitted it to the present age, baptized in fire and blood.

And we rejoice that it is our privilege to say that, though not so much in its definiteness and distinctiveness as preached by Christian evangelists in other lands, and by you in this land, in these latter years: yet, it was the doctrine preached, and lived, by many of the first founders of the church in this country, long anterior to this day. And while the zeal of the church in Liberia in its more universal proclamation and enforcement had abated, yet it was always hailed by many, as the central idea of Christianity and of Methodism. And your happy arrival to these shores served only to stir up the dying embers of a fire that had long since been kindled by the earlier Christians. We hail your arrival among us, therefore, as opportune and gracious, because, God appointed.

Return, Sister Evangelist, to your home, and friends, and loved ones, from whom you have long been separated. You need rest, for your toil has been long and unremitting. Rest in the assurance that you have done some good—how much none can tell; eternity alone will reveal. Rest in the assurance that many bear grateful and prayerful remembrance of you, and shall ever. Rest in the assurance that your motives will sufficiently apologize for, and excuse, any blunders you may have committed, in your zeal and push for the Master.

And now may the God of all grace grant you many years added to your life, and still greater peace. And when your sun goes down in the west, may it be without a cloud. Amen.

[Signed by the Pastor, Assistant Pastor and the Stewards and Leaders of the M. E. Church in Monrovia.]

UPPER CALDWELL, LIBERIA, July 16, 1889.

DEAR SISTER AMANDA SMITH:—Please allow us also, your little Sister Caldwell, second in the train in the point of birth, to bid you good-bye, as an assurance of our good will toward you, and also of our high estimation of your Christian character, and of your earnestness and untiring effort to preach a pure doctrine, and to lift up the standard of holiness.

Our fathers preached this, they lived this, and died this. They inculcated the idea of a holy life, as the central idea of Methodism, and laid it down as the corner stone and basis of Bible doctrines. And we hail it as an undeniable fact, that while there has been some declension among us from this base line of Gospel truth, yet there never was a time since the founding of the church in this country, when there were not witnesses, living, practical witnesses, to its truth. Not recognized possibly so much under the several titles as now preached by evangelists throughout Christendom in these latter days, as in its essence and power.

From the first of your arrival among us, you began to give your trumpet this certain sound, and its echoes have gone all over the land. The churches have felt the renewed impulse, and under its inspiration have moved on apace.

You have this testimonial also from us, that of the many who have come among us as missionary workers from the Mother Church of America, none have been more truly welcome, none more zealous, none more untiring than yourself, and returning to their home across the waters, have carried with them kindlier feelings, or more grateful, than you do now. And we wish to God that we could accord to others residing among us as missionaries, the tribute we now accord to you, a tribute of unselfishness, and of purity of life—uninfluenced by mercenary motives. And now, finally, "good-bye," my dear sister. May you have a pleasant and safe voyage back to your home and friends, and may many more years be added to your already useful life, in the enjoyment of restored health, and of increased peace, is the prayer of

Yours, in the Lord,

H. B. CAPEHART, *Pastor*.
J. D. A. SCOTT, *Assistant*.
THOMAS H. CLARK, *Lay Preacher*.
F. T. CLARK, *Steward*.

An Address Delivered to Mrs. Amanda Smith, by the Members of the A. M. E. Zion Church, Sierra Leone, on her taking leave of them.

DEAR MADAME:—We, the undersigned members, on behalf of the above church, and all the Christian public who are interested in our mission, beg most respectfully to forward you this address as a sure testimonial from a gratified society, that has had the pleasure of your visit, and among whom you have been laboring with unwearied zeal, for the short time you have been in Sierra Leone.

We cannot fully express ourselves as we would. We hope you should not think that we are flattering you, whilst we are declaring our sentiments; because we are candid in doing so; and we trust we are cautiously avoiding the use of any expression that will bear any resemblance to it. When the Rev. J. R. Frederick announced to us, shortly before your arrival, that you had kindly given your consent to come and labor amongst us, he spoke very much of your zeal, labors, and travels, in very many places. In our opinion, so far as our eyes have seen, and ears heard, we can say of you, that "the half was never told." In every respect, the information is correct.

We need not tell you that all have been greatly satisfied with your discourses. The great number of people that used to attend your services, will prove to you, that by all means, so far as outward successes are concerned, you have not failed in your work. We believe that God has answered your prayers in that way—you have been casting your net on the side of the ship, that Christ ordered; and you have gathered fishes.

The number of those who were willing to give up their sins, and with whom you have been wrestling in prayer for awhile for the help of the Holy Spirit, will also convince you of the success of your labor. Long after you shall have left these shores, the effects of your visit will still be felt.

We are thankful to Almighty God that we are privileged to witness the fulfilment of the prophecy of Joel, that, "It shall come to pass in the last days, that I will pour out my spirit upon all flesh, and your sons and your daughters shall prophesy," etc., etc.

We thank you also for the interest you have taken on behalf of the poor heathen in the adjacent rivers, where you have been laboring with so many disadvantages. We are also thankful to God that you have testified that your labor has not been in vain— the Lord has had mercy, on those on whom he will have mercy.

We are thankful, also, for your reproving the prevailing sins of the times, viz.: Superstition, adultery, drunkenness, slander, pride, disobedience to parents, hypocrisy in religion, sinful indulgences, etc., etc. We are very sorry that we are not composed of richer classes of people, who will cast in of their abundance to the treasury, as a donation for your services, but we trust that of our penury, the little amount realized from us and the generous public, will be received by you as Christ received the widow's two mites.

We feel very sorry to say to you, good-bye; but such is life. We hope and trust that though we meet here to part again, yet in Heaven we shall meet to part no more. We pray that God may raise up your successor, as he raised up Joshua before the death of Moses, to carry the souls to Canaan whom you have left by the way; and that a double portion of your spirit may rest upon her.

God Almighty bless you with many and happy days; that as His Heavenly hand has enriched you with many singular and extraordinary graces, you may be the wonder of the world in these latter days for happiness and true felicity; and that the everlasting doors will give way for the entrance of your soul with Christ in Paradise, on the other side of the grave, is the prayer of

YOUR BRETHREN AND SISTERS IN CHRIST.

[Signed by the Pastor and the entire membership of the church and Sabbath School, and accompanied by a testimonial amounting to over a hundred dollars.]

GREENVILLE, SINOE Co., AFRICA.

To the Christian Churches wherever established.

DEAR BRETHREN, SISTERS AND FRIENDS OF JESUS— Hallelujah! to the lamb forever. Amen!

This comes as a recognition of the wonderful work of God in our country through that most worthy and faithful handmaiden of His, the sainted evangelist, Sister Amanda Smith.

This sister crime to this country in the year 1882, laboring in Montserrado and Grand Bassa Counties as an Evangelist.

In the month of November, 1882, she came to Sinoe County, where she began with much zeal the evangelical works of her Lord; landing here in Greenville on Sabbath morning, four o'clock,

November 17th, 1883, she gave an exhortation that evening in the Methodist Episcopal Church. Then began the working of the Lord in this county.

Her first object was *Gospel Temperance*. After preaching a series of sermons she succeeded in organizing in Greenville a society, or Band of Hope, Gospel Temperance. She next organized a similar society in the townships of Lexington, Louisiana, Bluntsville, and Farmersville. About three or four hundred have now become temperance signers, including men, women, and children. Many are saved from a drunkard's grave, because there are in this number many who are real; nay, they would taste death before violating their pledge. Glory to God for this salvation! Amen!

Not satisfied with this alone, she began to cry, secondly, that without holiness of heart no man can see God in peace. She earnestly insisted on holiness, assuring those who were justified by faith the possibility of living holy lives on earth. The people began to seek a closer union with God. Sister Smith's prayers for holiness were real, earnest, and faithful. God heard, God saw, God moved!

In the month of May, 1884, the holy fire began to fall. It fell first by degrees in Lexington, then in copious showers. Next in showers it began to fall in Louisiana, in Bluntsville, finally in Greenville, and elsewhere. In the month of September a Holiness Camp Meeting was held, at which meeting a *National Holiness Camp Meeting* was organized, and at this place upwards of one hundred professed sanctification to the Lord, and are living for Christ alone, and are prepared to die for Christ, if need be.

Wherefore, in consideration of the wonderful works of God through our evangelist and worthy sister, and in consideration of her departure from us; therefore,

Resolved, 1st. That we recognize the wonderful works of God through this sainted evangelist, and her much faithfulness to God, and her Godly walks and Christian examples before us; and that the Lord truly sent her to Africa.

Resolved, 2nd. That we, on behalf of ourselves, and the Christian Church of which we are members, tender her our sincere thanks for her labor of love, and a high appreciation of her Christian society, assuring her of the deep sense of our feeling of sadness on account of her departure, and our sincerity and continuance in prayers to God for her protection and support wherever His Spirit may lead her.

Resolved, 3rd. That we recommend Sister Amanda Smith to the most favorable consideration of the pastors and members of the Christian Churches wherever she may go as a workman of God in reality.

Resolved, 4th. That we recommend her now unto God the Father, God the Son, and God the Holy Ghost, now, and forever. Amen.

In witness whereof, we have hereunto set our names officially.

WILLIAM P. KENNEDY, JR., *Preacher in charge of the Greenville Circuit, and Presiding Elder of Sinoe District.*
S. D. MAYSON, *Deacon Baptist Church, Lexington.*
JOHN L. FULLER, *Steward and Leader M. E. Church, Greenville.*
Z. B. ROBERTS, *Local Preacher M. E. Church, Greenville.*
J. W. BONNER, *Local Preacher.*
W. E. HARRIS, *of Congregational Church, Greenville.*
H. B. BROWN, *Leader and Steward M. E. Church.*
ALLEN PEAL, *Local Preacher.*
J. N. LEIN, *Sup't Presbyterian S. S., Sinoe County.*
GEO. B. DUNBAR.
Z. T. GREENE, *Superintendent Sabbath School, Greenville.*
R. P. MAYSON, *Local Preacher, Lexington.*
H. C. BIRCH.

Affectionate appreciation of the labor of Amanda Smith, the elect lady Evangelist, during her stay in Maryland County, Cape Palmas, Liberia.

CAPE PALMAS, LIBERIA, Dec. 17th, 1886.

God sends blessings, often, to communities and nations through feeble instrumentalities. When angels, the higher order of created beings are not employed, the message comes to us through earthen vessels—frail mortality.

Divine Providence has seen fit, of late, to visit these Liberian counties, through a female instrumentality, in the person of Mrs. Amanda Smith, the elect lady Evangelist of the Methodist denomination of America.

Her efforts among us at Cape Palmas, have, under the Divine Head, had no precedent in this county. The doctrine of Christian holiness has been most beautifully explained by her own Christian walks and teachings; and the result has been an addition of scores of members to the various Christian denominations of this county.

After an impartial examination of her teachings, and duly comparing them with the sacred Scriptures, we find them in perfect harmony with Scripture doctrines.

May her life be prolonged to preach Christ and Him crucified to the multitudes, who yet sit in the regions of darkness, as well as to explain the most wholesome doctrine of sanctification for the spiritual benefit of those who are already justified by faith. And may the Holy Ghost accompany her, and illuminate her mind more and more, unto the perfect day. Please receive this tribute of Christian respect, as a parting farewell from many who may never see you again in this life; and may the blessing of God rest upon you always. *Amen.*

[Signed by the Officers and Members of the M. E. Church at Cape Palmas.]

MONROVIA, LIBERIA, W. AFRICA, July 17, 1889.

THE BAND OF HOPE TEMPERANCE SOCIETY OF MONROVIA have heard with regret of the intended departure, in a few days, of Mrs. Amanda Smith from among us. They feel that it is but due to her to place on record the fact, that Gospel Temperance has had in her a faithful and untiring advocate and worker ever since her arrival in the Republic. In this, and other sections of the country, she interested many influential young men and women in the temperance cause, and everywhere utilized them as the founders and supporters of the Band of Hope. She leaves behind her a strong, temperance sentiment, which, under God, can, and we trust, will do much to paralyze and extirpate the curse of strong drink.

The band of Hope feels it also its duty to note the fact that Mrs. Amanda Smith has done her best to raise the standard of religious life and aspirations among the people of this country. In wishing her farewell and God speed, it expresses the hope that she may long be enabled to continue to bring in sheaves for the Master, and that her work may everywhere have abundant and fruitful success with the seal of the Holy Spirit.

The Band of Hope is having prepared an album, containing photographic views and portraits of places and persons in Liberia and West Africa, which it begs that Mrs. Smith will accept as a reminder of her visit to West Africa, and as a slight token of their appreciation of her efforts and labors while in this region of the Dark Continent.

>H. W. TRAVIS, *Pres. Band of Hope, No. 3, Monrovia.*
>ISAAC J. MOORT, *Rec. Sec'y Band of Hope Temperance Society, No. 3, of Monrovia.*

I gladly place on record the letters that follow, not only because of the kind appreciation of myself and my work expressed in them, but in the hope that they may prove a blessing to those who read them. The first is from Mrs. Martha Payne, sister-in-law of ex-President Payne, of Liberia; the second is from Mrs. Mary R. Denman, of Newark, N. J., of whom I have also spoken in a former chapter; and the third, from Mrs. Inskip, whose husband was so well known throughout the Christian world as a leader in the Holiness Movement. She also has been greatly honored of God in the same blessed evangelism.

MARTHA PAYNE'S EXPERIENCE.

A letter to Mrs. Amanda Smith.

MONROVIA, June 19, 1883.

My DEAR SISTER:—In compliance with your request I now conclude to give my religious experience. I was converted at the age of fifteen. The greater part of the time I was in darkness, because I did not have a daily witness of the Spirit. I believed that a Christian was to have a daily witness as a child of God. I had a fear of God hid in my heart, but no lasting joy, and this caused me much uneasiness. Sometimes I would doubt my conversion. Resolve after resolve was made to be true and steadfast, but I found I was utterly helpless.

My temper gave me much trouble, and caused me often to neglect my prayer. Then I would be filled with doubts and fears, and in a state of oscillation continually. As the cares of the family increased I sought for sanctification so as to be steadfast. I did not receive it, and became very dark. I lived only with the fear of God. Then a restlessness took hold of me, impatient to be freed from sin. As I prayed for grace and faith the hidden evils of my heart were made known. Then I resolved to look to Christ, and grew in grace, taking for my comfort the promise, "They that seek diligently shall find." I often read my Bible, and tried to cast my burden on the Lord, because I had learned to trust him through difficulties. The Spirit drew me and I followed on to know the Lord.

I had read "Upham's Interior Life." I was much encouraged and endeavored to be submissive to all things. Then I had severe trial, and my heart was much burdened. I arose at midnight and submitted all to God. From that time I was kept steady and more willing to acknowledge myself a follower of Christ than ever. About two years after, Mrs. Amanda Smith came to Monrovia and preached holiness. I was anxious to get light on the subject. I paid attention to all that was said. After her second discourse she called for persons to come forward to seek sanctification. I wanted to he sanctified; promised myself to seek quietly to grow into the blessed experience, and say nothing about it to anyone, for I had learned that great would be the gloom if the blessing was not found. Some months after, Mrs. Smith commenced her work again. Sickness weakened her so that she was unable to work as she desired. In December she commenced Bible reading every day. I gave all attention to her instruction, and did not allow her to know that I sought the blessing, notwithstanding my home was her home. In her instructions she gave us to know that we must be definite in our request to God. I had an aversion to the word "sanctification," and prayed all around it. Finally the middle wall of partition fell, and I was willing to utter the words, "Lord, sanctify me." I yielded all, and a stillness of soul followed for three days. I was determined to stand until light was given. The stillness was broken while I calmly sought, before retiring for the night, with these words: "The blood of Jesus Christ, His son cleanseth from all sin." It was reasoned with such force that I assented audibly, "Yes, it is so, because the word of God says so. The heavens and the earth shall pass away before one jot or title of His Word shall fail." My heart replied: "Yes, because the Word says so, and when Jesus Christ said it is finished, a full salvation was complete." Then, with all the earnestness of my soul, I said: "Lord, you know, now let the Spirit witness with the blood and apply it to my heart." Then I felt a sinking sensation pass through me. I fell to my knees to pray, but my prayers were turned to praise and thanks to Jesus. My soul was filled with humility, and my eyes with tears. My faith was established in Christ, my soul was quickened into new life, and I viewed Jesus Christ by faith as I never did before, with the promise, "I will abide with you." And no sooner did I confess openly that my soul was cleansed from sin, than it seemed to me, my whole being was changed anew. Glory to Jesus! I am saved! And ever since the twelfth of December, I have the witness within, and the way is more clear as I move on.

Your sister in Jesus Christ,

MARTHA PAYNE.

MARY R. DENMAN'S TESTIMONY.

The first time I ever saw this sister, Mrs. Amanda Smith, was in 1870, at a time that I, having a hungry soul, had learned that a party, called "Higher Life Christians," were holding meetings in the Y. M. C. A. rooms in our city.

I went to them to learn if they had something that would suit my case. At the first meeting I heard a brother giving his experience of the rest of faith, God had given him. At once I thought this was just what I wanted. So I followed them to one of their evening meetings, that was held in the Franklin Street Methodist Church.

Early in the meeting a colored woman arose, and began to speak and sing. I was disgusted, that a woman should be allowed to speak, and a colored woman at that, and felt she should be requested to sit down. But soon I became interested in what she was saying, and enjoyed her sweet songs, and at once felt that I wanted the same faith that that woman had.

From that time I sought something of the same kind, and found Dr. Palmer's meeting. Fifteenth Street, New York. There I heard other men and women give their experience, which taught me a great deal.

At last a colored woman, sitting the second seat from me, dressed in plain Quaker dress, arose (after a man from Ohio had spoken and thanked God for the light that had come into his soul during that meeting) and gave thanks to God for His answer to prayer in giving that soul to her in that meeting.

I have often thought since it was my soul that was given to her at that time, for after she sat down I felt I wanted her prayers, and putting by all my prejudice (I had lived in the South many years), in asking a colored person to pray for me, I reached my hand to her and asked her prayers. She turned to me, as I thought, very coldly, and said: "What do you want?"

I had made a more full consecration of myself during that meeting, and now knew just what I wanted, and said, in answer: "I want bodily strength to do God's will." She said, "I will." And for the glory of God, I wish to give my testimony that I have had more bodily strength ever since. I did not know then that this woman was the same one I had heard speak in Franklin Street Church, for at that time she had not given up her irons, and wash tubs, and was dressed in her wash-woman's garb.

When I saw her the third time, it was at Sea Cliff Camp Meeting, when I was glad to tell her of the answer to her prayers for me.

After passing through the ten days' meeting, without receiving the baptism of the Holy Spirit (having been brought up an Episcopalian, and not understanding the especial need of a clean heart, and this especial baptism), the dear Lord was very good to me, and came to me in the night with deep questions to my soul, that I could not answer in my own strength, and knowing that

Amanda Smith was in the next tent, and had just come in from a late meeting, I called her, and she came in and knelt down beside me, asking what my trouble was. She prayed with me, and made me fully to understand that our Heavenly Father would not ask anything of me that He would not give me strength to do, and that all He wanted of me was to say "I will" to Him.

When I fully understood this, it took all my will power to say "I will" to God, for I knew it was no light thing to do, for it was to be "*I will*" *to Him* for the rest of my life. But when the "I will" *was said*, the power came, and she sang that beautiful hymn,

> "'Tis done, the great transaction's done,
> I am the Lord's, and He is mine."

I can never tell that great peace that came to my soul at that time, and down in the depths of my soul has remained. The upper surface may be ruffled, as the ocean often is; but down below the surface the undying peace remains.

Dear reader, I am glad to give my testimony to the power God has given our dear sister, Amanda, to bring souls to Him, and to help them on to *keep steady* before Him, until He can finish His work of redemption in them. He is no respecter of persons, and is as willing to-day to give the baptism of the Holy Spirit to every soul who will come to Him in lowliness of heart, and ask Him for this blessing, and believe that He will give it. Wait for it. It will surely come, and you will be happy. When done with the up-and-down old Christian life, sinning and repenting, you will look to Jesus, moment by moment, for His guidance, which He will surely give, and then you call say to the Tempter when he comes (for he will never leave us while in the body), in Jesus' own words, "Get thee behind me, Satan." Jesus will open your spiritual vision when He comes in to dwell, and you will recognize the temptations of Satan from the blessed leadings of the Holy Spirit.

Respectfully submitted, praying God's blessing upon these few words.

MARY R. DENMAN, Newark, N. J.

2002 BRANDYWINE ST.,
PHILADELPHIA, PA., Dec. 22, 1887.

MY DEAR, DEAR SISTER SMITH:—Your precious letter came to hand, and it was too good to keep; I had it published in the "Standard," so your many friends would also enjoy it. It did my soul good to hear from you; many thanks for the same.

The beautiful tribute paid to my now sainted husband by you, was appreciated by me. My dear one often said he thanked God that he was the instrument, in God's hands, of bringing you into this beautiful light of full salvation, or entire sanctification. That day, at "Old Green Street," was never forgotten by my dear husband, and he spoke of it all around the world.

God has made you "A flame of fire" in this and other lands, and my dear husband rejoiced in the glorious work God enabled you to do, and he used to say, "Praise the Lord, Amanda Smith's success is mine."

Oh! with what interest he would watch every move you made.

He, with myself, felt anxious for you to go to Africa. My dear husband often would say: "That will be Sister Smith's crowning glory."

I have no doubt his spirit has been very near you as you have been pushing the battle. Bless the Lord for the glorious victories won.

I often feel that my dear one is looking over the "battlements of glory," waiting to welcome me into that mansion of glory prepared for us. Oh! Sister Smith, what a meeting, when the redeemed ones shall return and come to Zion, with songs and everlasting joy. I think I can almost hear the anthem of praise unto Him that hath loved us, and given Himself for us. To Him be glory and praise forever and forever. Glory! Glory!

My darling sister, God has wonderfully given me physical strength and spiritual enduement for the work he has called me to do. I promised God, around the casket of my dear one, I would give to Him all the strength He gave me in work.

You know my husband was a wonderful leader; strong and fearless, yet very loving. I have heard Bishop Simpson and Bishop Harris say he was the grandest leader to marshal the forces and lead them into battle they ever knew. I have often wondered why God took him and left me; but I know He is too wise to err, and too good to be unkind; so I must leave all with Him. What I do not know now, I will know in the sweet by and by.

God has helped me as never before. After coming from Ocean Grove, where I was kept busy with work, I attended the Holiness Convention in Wilmington four days. It was a wonderful meeting. Souls converted and sanctified. Brothers Thompson, Pepper, Gray, Smith, Todd, Mrs. Kenney, Nettie Van Name, Clara Boyd and mother, Mrs. Blackston, Bangs and myself went from Philadelphia. Orr, Smith, Kenney, Boyd and Van Name stayed the following week. I had to leave. I had an engagement with Rev. S. E. Searles, in Brooklyn, two weeks. God did reveal. Himself in the salvation of the people. Glory to God! We often spoke of you.

I had to leave in two weeks to fill an engagement at Wilmington, Del. I was there nine days. Over fifty converted; forty-three united with the church. Twenty were entirely sanctified, and twenty men and women (unsaved sinners) arose at the close and asked us to pray for them. The meeting we could not close till half past ten. Last Saturday will never be forgotten by the people present.

I have to leave on Monday morning to get ready to go South, where I am engaged, if my health holds out. I shall start for Florida in a few days. If the Lord brings you home we shall hail your coming with delight.

Brother and Sister Thompson, where I am stopping, say you must remember this is one of your homes. They unite with in much love to you. I will also say I shall welcome you to my cottage at Ocean Grove when I am at home. God bless you abundantly with the riches of His grace.

I am glad Bishop Taylor is doing such glorious work for Africa. How my soul goes out for that Dark Continent. I am glad God has used you. Praise the Lord for the work you have been able through God's grace to do. God is blessing Sister Kenney, Lizzie Smith and others in the work. All your friends send lots of love to you. God bless you forever. Love to all the saints.

Your loving sister,

MRS. J. S. INSKIP.

I have sent you the "Missionary Review," and paid for it myself one year.

The following letters from Rev. Edgar M. Levy, Annie Wittenmyer, Dr. Daniel Dorchester, Margaret Bottome, Bob, Miss Frances E. Willard and Lady Isabel Somerset, respectively, are personal, but will, no doubt, be read with interest;

MANCHESTER, N. H., Feb. 2, 1890.

MY VERY DEAR SISTER:—I learn through the papers that you are now in London. I am real glad that you are that much nearer to us —the many friends who wait to greet you. Let me thank you for the kind word you write of me, which I see in the "Standard" this week. I sincerely reciprocate your kind wishes, and hope soon to see you and renew our sweet fellowship of bygone years.

I have written you several times while you were in Africa, but I have received no answer. In the last two communications I informed you that you might draw on me for two hundred dollars. Not hearing from you, I concluded that you had decided not to do so until your arrival in England, and your readiness to embark for America. I have now in my care $214.21 awaiting your pleasure. If you will inform me as to your wishes, I will either send it all, or in part, to you at any time, or I will keep it till you reach home.

When you write me, please direct to the care of McDonald, Gill & Co., 36 Bromfield street, Boston, Mass., U. S. A.

When you return I shall take pleasure in helping to increase the amount, which would be but a reasonable return for all you have done for us under the burning sky of Africa. God, however, will reward you in a far richer manner—in the "Well done, good and faithful servant."

Remember Douglass. All I ask is that you give that camp meeting the precedence over all others; as much for dear Brother Morse's sake as anything else. He has been the largest contributor, and will cheerfully do more when you get home.

Our winter has been very mild, but now has become very cold. It looks like we shall have the winter in the lap of spring. I hope God will guide you in choosing the safest time to return to America.

Of course you have met dear Brother and Sister Pearsall Smith in London, where they now reside—44 Grosvenor Road, Westminster. We miss them exceedingly.

I am, you see, in New Hampshire; not permanently, but for a few months, perhaps, preaching for a Baptist Church—the most spiritual I have ever known. We are just now having a precious work of grace; conversions every night, and as many as forty seeking the blessing of a clean heart. Glory to God! I expect Brother Morse to come and help me next week.

Now, dear sister, I must close, commending you to God and the Word of His grace. I am,

Yours, in eternal and holy fellowship,

EDGAR M. LEVY.

SANATOGA, PA., Oct. 11, 1890.

MY DEAR MRS. SMITH:—I welcome you back to America. I thank the Lord for all your grand work, and rejoice that He has used you for His own glory for so many years, and has brought you safely back to us again.

I send this as directed in the Philadelphia Methodist, and hope it will reach you. *I want you to visit me.* I am thirty-three miles out from Philadelphia, on the main line of the Reading Railroad. I have bought a farm of sixty-five acres, on the Philadelphia Pike, one mile or less, from the Sanatoga station. If you will let me know when you are coming, I will meet you with a carriage. I have a big house and plenty to eat, and a warm welcome awaits you, and a good warm room will be ready for you.

My son, the little boy who was with me at Ocean Grove, is married; has a good, practical, Christian girl for a wife; and we all live together. There are only three in our family. They both join me in the invitation.

As ever, your faithful friend,

ANNIE WITTENMYER.

OFFICE OF SUPERINTENDENT,
DEPARTMENT OF THE INTERIOR,

INDIAN SCHOOL SERVICE,
STANDING ROCK AGENCY, N D., October 29, 1891.

MRS. AMANDA SMITH:—Your letter of August 8th, after many wanderings, has at last reached me here.

Was very glad to hear from you. I have sometimes wondered why the Lord keeps a person so full of faith, and love, and Christian zeal, so long out of Heaven; it must be, that you may be a blessing to this poor, sinful, needy world.

I shall never forget your earnest prayers, so full of faith, and the profound respect the good people of Salem, Mass., had for you and your Christian character. Your labors have been a great blessing to multitudes, and your reward is on high, and will not fail.

May God greatly multiply such laborers. The world needs them. With kind remembrances, yours, etc.

DANIEL DORCHESTER.

NEW YORK.

My DEAR SISTER AMANDA:—You know I always loved you. I think it was Chaplain McCabe that called you our "Palm Tree," in the years gone down into the past, when we met you at our National Camp Meetings. And now, in these latter days, you have come into our organization of The King's Daughters and Sons.

I am so glad to see the gleam of the silver cross on any Daughter or Son, but when I saw it on you, my princely sister, I was peculiarly happy. Many jeweled hands I shall forget, but never your dark hand, raised so high when singing:

> "My Saviour's promise faileth never,
> He counts me in the whosoever."

You are it real daughter of the King "all glorious within." How often I would have given a good deal to have heard the tones of your voice singing:

> "The wonder-working Jesus!
> The very same Jesus!"

Well, he has worked wonders through you. Many an owner of a white face would have been willing to have exchanged it for your white soul, but we are in a spiritual kingdom where there is neither bond nor free, white nor black. Christ is all and in all.

I am glad to think that wherever you go, you will bear the cross of our Order, and I do hope that many will follow you into the banqueting house where His banner over us is love. Some day we shall enter the King's palace, and I trust be presented faultless before the presence of His Glory; and the joy of all joys to my mind will be that of giving our King "exceeding joy" in the presentation.

Your loving President, "I. H. N.,"

SISTER MARGARET BOTTOME.

This letter from Bob—my Bob—is short, but will show how he is getting on, and that he is like other boys. I am sorry the sweet-shop was wrecked, and that it rained so they could not go to see the procession, but I am glad on account of the new boots and trousers!

SOUTHPORT, October 28th, 1892.

MY DEAR MOTHER:—I hope you are better than when you last wrote to me.

There was a shipwreck at Blackpool a fortnight ago. The storm destroyed a sweetshop, on the pier.

Miss Hobbs has bought me a new pair of boots, and made me a new pair of trousers.

I am trying to learn the books of the New Testament, but I cannot say them yet.

There has been a procession here; it rained so we couldn't go to see it.

The Exhibition closed on October 1st. Hundreds of people came to it. The fire-works were lovely.

The weather is very rainy and cold.

Mr. Walker sends his love. I met him in Chapel Street last Thursday. Miss Hobbs sends her love.

With much love, I remain,
Your loving son,

BOB SMITH.

WORLD'S WOMAN'S CHRISTIAN TEMPERANCE UNION, HEADQUARTERS AND OFFICE OF PRESIDENT, ALBANY BUILDINGS, 47 VICTORIA ST., WESTMINSTER, LONDON, February 17, 1893.

Mrs. Amanda Smith, 2940 South Park Avenue, Chicago.

DEAR SISTER:—We learn that you are about to bring out a book containing your experiences of life which have been so varied and remarkable. We are glad of this, and confident that great good will come of it to all who read it, for your cheery Christianity bears the stamp that should become universal, and every fresh example helps to bring that day nearer.

Believe us, your true friends in the love of God,

ISABEL SOMERSET.
FRANCES F. WILLARD.

CHAPTER XXXV.

RETURN TO LIVERPOOL—FAITH HEALING—BISHOP TAYLOR LEAVES AGAIN FOR AFRICA—USE OF MEANS—THE STORY OF MY BONNET— TOKENS OF GOD S HELP AFTER MY RETURN FROM AFRICA.

I left Sierra Leone in November, 1890. I was so miserable that I only gave myself three weeks to live; I thought I might possibly drag along about that length of time.

I did not go to any of my friends in Liverpool, or Southport, as they wanted I should do. I was so tired, and weak, and I thought of the care and anxiety I would be to them, and then the extra work for the servants—all this I thought of—though I never saw better principled servants in my life, than in England.

I suppose there is not a lady in England who would think of consulting her servants as to whether she should entertain a colored person in her home; I do not believe there was ever such a thing heard of in England. But such a thing in America would not be considered out of place. I have met the like more than once.

I was at a good lady's house in Philadelphia, not long since; she was very kind to me, and wanted to ask me to stay for tea, but did not dare to do so, on account of an old servant who would have been vexed if she had had to serve a colored woman, whom the lady herself had asked to sit at her table. It was night, and I only had to ride two and a half hours, from Philadelphia to Newark, my home, and I got my own supper, thank the Lord.

Well, I had no fears of this kind in England. But I felt that I wanted to be quiet, and simply let alone. I had it in my mind all clear as to what I would do with little Bob.

While on the steamer I had my first attack of "la grippe." I had not heard of it in Africa; it had not got there then; so that I did not know really what had happened to me. But the good doctor on the steamer seemed to understand how to manage it, and with little things I knew to do for myself, I got relief in a few days. Then it seemed to turn again; and, oh! the pain I suffered. I told the Lord not to let me die and be buried at sea.

I had seen poor Mrs. Beede, when on my way from Old Calabar, buried at sea. And I knew all that would have to be done, and I shrank from it. I said, "Oh! Lord, if Thou wilt only give me strength to get to Liverpool, I will not trouble Thee anymore."

For I was so tired of holding on, and trying to keep up; and for three weeks after I got to Liverpool I did not pray. It seemed to me the Lord had done all I asked Him, and now all I had to do was the little I could do for myself, and just wait and see what next the Lord would do.

I calmly looked over all my mind, and my work in Africa. I felt that while there was so much to be done, and I had only done a little, yet that I had God's approval that I had done all I could. I went to Africa at His bidding, and did not leave till I was sure I had His sanction. So I felt, if I were to die, my conscience was clear before my God. I had worked willingly, and suffered cheerfully, in the work, for His sake. And there was not a shadow between my soul and God, and I felt I had nothing to ask.

We got into Liverpool on Friday night. The stewardess said I could have lodgings with her. So she took me to her house. All night I suffered. On Saturday morning I felt a little rested; but the pains troubled me very much; so, as the evening drew near, I sent out and got some medicine, and thought I would go to bed early. But just about eight o'clock, my dear friend, Mrs. Stavely (whom I had written to say I had got in, but did not expect to see before Monday), and her husband came in. Dear souls, how very kind they were. They were delighted to see me, and said they thought I looked well to what they expected. I told them how miserable I had been, and how I had suffered. At once Mrs. Stavely said:

"Oh! why don't you trust the Lord to heal you?"

"Why," I said, "that is what I have been doing all along; and I believe if I had not done so I would have been dead long ago."

She had often written me on the subject of faith healing, while in Africa, and had sent me numerous papers; then I knew dear Mrs. Baxter, and Mrs. Dr. Bordman, and many others of those choice spirits. But somehow I did not seem to be able to see the teaching as they did. They could not understand how anyone so strong in faith as I seemed to be, did not see it; and they knew, and I knew, that the Lord was with me, and did lead me, and bless me. But, like them, I did not understand it myself.

"However," I said to Mrs. Stavely. "if an effort on my part is necessary, I cannot make it, I am too weak. But like the man we read of in the Gospel, I am willing for anybody to do anything for me that he can."

The man we read of in the Gospel was too weak to do anything himself, but was willing they should take the roof off the house and let him down before Jesus; and Jesus, seeing their faith said to the sick of the palsy: "Arise." So I said, "there is just where I am. I am willing, from the crown of my head to the soles of my feet."

"Oh, well," she said, "if you are willing, the Lord can do it."

"But, then," I said, "I have just swallowed a dose of castor oil and laudanum five minutes before you came in."

"Well," she laughingly said, "you can trust the Lord."

I knew how very conservative good Mr. Stavely was; that he was not an enthusiast by any means, though one of the grandest men I ever knew; and he spoke up:

"Yes, Sister Smith, why not trust the Lord to heal?"

"My," I thought, "if he has got to believing so, it is wonderful."

After a pleasant chat they went home. All day Sunday I suffered. There was a sick lady in the next room to me, and they called in a doctor for her. He was a good Christian man. So, as I was so very ill, my hostess said I had better have the doctor see me. I agreed, and he came in. He was very pleasant, and I told him I was just from Africa. He was much interested, and said that they had a large mission on the Congo. He was delighted to see little Bob, and said he would like me and Bob to come to Sabbath School in their church.

He left me some medicine, which did me good, and relieved the pain so that I was able to sleep a little on Sunday night. Then, as he had to call on the other lady on Monday and Tuesday he called each time to see me, also.

I took the medicine on Sunday and Monday, but did not take it on Tuesday.

"Now, I ought to trust the Lord—now as I am willing," I said, "but the doctor is so kind, he may not like it if he knows I am not taking the medicine; still, if he asks me, I will tell him I am not taking it." Then I prayed, "Lord, do not let him ask me anything about it."

So sure enough he called in on Wednesday, had a nice chat, and said, "Well, Mrs. Smith, I see you are better."

"Yes, Doctor," I said, "I am feeling much better. How much shall I pay you?"

"Oh! Nothing at all. I am very glad to do what I can for you."

So I thanked him, and he left.

On Friday, I heard that Bishop Taylor was in town, and would leave on Saturday. So I went down to Mr. Stavely's office, the Temple, Dale Street, Liverpool, and found that the office of Anderson Fowler, Bishop Taylor's agent, was next to Mr. Stavely's.

This was the first time I ever saw a telephone work. It was a new thing to me. But I soon heard from the Bishop. They said, "Yes, he was there; had just gone out live minutes before."

So I left my address, and asked the Bishop to call on me at my lodgings. But, as the Bishop was poorly, with asthma, his son, Mr. Ross Taylor, and Mr. Welch, the former editor of the "African News," called at my lodgings.

I was delighted to see them. We did have a pleasant time together. We had a little song, and then we knelt and had prayers. My! how Brother Ross Taylor did pray; and Brother Welch. They were in quite a hurry, so did not stop long.

Mr. Ross told me that his father was to leave for Africa on Saturday. So next morning I got a cab, and Bob and I went down to the pier to see the Bishop off. I got there before the Bishop arrived, and I saw him when he came on board; and I think I never pitied a man so in my life. It seemed as though he could scarcely walk, he was so weak and thin. I said to myself, "That is not the Bishop

Taylor that I left in Africa." Oh! how changed he was. After I had looked at him for a time (for he did not see me) I went to him and said:

"How do you do, Bishop?"

"Pretty well," he said.

How glad he was to see Bob and me. He saw us last at Cape Palmas, in Africa. Then I said, "What a dreadful cold you have."

"Yes," he said, "an attack of asthma. I have not had an attack before for (I think he said) thirty years. The other night I did not know but I was going. My breath was so short. But I told the Lord if He would spare me I would like to live a little longer for Africa."

And I saw the great tears in his eyes, and his lips quivered. Then he brushed the tears away, and said, with a twinkle in his eye:

"You know, Amanda, I have known men to die for want of breath."

"Yes," I said, "they generally die for such a want."

Oh! how I would like to have gone back with him. As I looked at him I said, "Oh! what a sacrifice, all for my people. At his time of life he ought to have his home comforts, with his wife to look after him, and his children around him. Now he is so weak and sick. And then he is going all alone on the steamer, and not a soul to do anything for him."

I cannot tell how sad I felt. I said to Mr. Ross, "Can't you go as far as Madeira with the Bishop?"

"No," he replied, "father says I must go home."

Then the Bishop said to me, "Well, good bye, Amanda. Take good care of Bob."

I bade him good-bye the best I could, and left. I never expected to see him again in this life. When I got into the cab, oh! how I cried! And for three days every time I thought of the dear old hero, I had a good cry; I couldn't help it. How good the Lord was to take him to Africa, and bring him back to his home land so well and strong. How like a God is He who doeth all things well. Amen.

Again I turn to my story. Going out at that time gave me fresh cold; I had not got my winter clothes yet; so a dreadful cough set in, and rheumatism in my left arm; and what I suffered, God only knows. But I had quit taking any means. I was willing to trust the Lord.

"Lord," I said, "there are all the things I have been taking, and they have helped me up to a certain point, and then I had to trust you. So I will trust you and do without taking anything."

Now this time, the Lord did not seem to test me as before. I just wanted a little relief from pain, for I was going to die anyhow. So I went on.

One night about two o'clock, I had not slept a wink up to that time, I was sitting up in bed crying with pain in my arm. Dear little Bob was in bed beside me, sleeping away. Everybody in the house was asleep; my cough was terrible; and I said, "Oh! Lord, help me. What shall I do?" and as though someone stood by me and spoke, I heard, "Put cotton batting on your arm."

"Thou knowest," I replied, "I have not got any; but in the morning I will ask the lady if she has any."

So I did, and she gave me some. I got down before the fire on my knees, and put on the cotton batting It did seem to relieve me, and the pain seemed to quiet down as I knelt down before the fire and it got warm, and I fell into a little doze of sleep. It was better next day, but, oh! so sore. I told my friends I believed it was the good Spirit that prompted me to put on the cotton batting. But they thought I should not have done it, but simply ignored the plan, and just trusted the Lord.

Well, I tried the best I could. They sent me books on the subject; but I said, "I will not read anything but the Bible. I am going to take the Word of God, and ask help of the Spirit."

All right. One night after this my cough troubled me so that I could not sleep. After a severe fit of coughing, I said, "Oh! Lord, do help me. What must I do?" And in an instant a voice distinctly said to me, "Beet root tea will allay the irritation." And I said, "Now, Lord, if that is Thy voice speaking to me, please keep it in my mind till morning and I will do it."

I remembered that twenty years before I was told this thing, and did it for a friend who was ill with cold, and it helped her; but I didn't remember that I had ever thought of it from that time until it came to me that night.

This was between three and four o'clock in the morning. About day-break I got a little quiet; and at seven o'clock a servant came in and made the fire, and it came to me about the beet root. I said, "Well, I am better now, and I needn't mind about it."

I got up at eight, and it came again, "Beet root tea." But still I did not heed. About nine o'clock the same whisper came to me again:

"You said if the Lord would keep it in your mind till morning, you would make the beet root tea."

"So I did."

And I called Bob and sent him downstairs to ask the lady if she had any red beets. She sent me two small ones, but very nice and red; I had a small sauce pan, and I put them in and boiled them and made a strong cupful and drank it, and it did allay the irritation so that I coughed but little after that to what I had done before; and I shall ever believe that God was teaching me not to ignore the use of all means in sickness.

I believe that God is honored as much when He tells me to do a thing and I obey, as when He says not to do it, and I obey. "Thou shalt not covet." "Thou shalt love the Lord thy God with all thy heart." To me obedience in both cases is absolutely necessary to honor God. I only receive blessings as I obey.

Rev. D. F. Sanford, of Boston, was so kind to Bob and me, and he and his wife were at the Berachia home, at Southport, and during the series of meetings he was holding he gave Bible readings on this subject; and it seemed so clear, and many seemed to get help and blessing, and I did too.

But many thought I was not half out of the woods. So one day two ladies called to see me, after I had returned to Liverpool. I had never seen them before, but they said they had heard of me; and one of them, Mrs. A., told me of her wonderful experience of how she was healed of dropsy.

I was deeply interested, as she went on narrating all the incidents in relation to it, and how she used oil and anointed herself, as she said she felt the Lord led her to do.

"Oh," I said, "I was out last evening to the shop, and it came to me to get some sweet oil."

"That is it," she said at once.

"But," I said, "I did not get it."

"Well," she said, "olive oil is the best; but I did not have that in my case. Haven't you got oil of any kind in the house?"

"Only a little castor oil that was left in the glass."

"It only needs a few drops, and that will do."

So I knelt down, and they anointed me with this oil, and prayed very earnestly. They both said they got such a baptism when they were healed; so I could not help expecting some assurance to this work of healing my body, as I did to my sanctification and justification.

They told me this was right for me to expect, for God had made the provision for the body's healing, with that of the soul; and I did honestly try to see it just its they did. But I could not. I went on for ten days waiting for this especial assurance that I was really healed. Oh! how I longed for it, but I never got any such assurance. Still I held on by faith.

Christmas came. My dear friend, Mrs. Stavely, had invited me to Seaforth. It was with great difficulty that I got there. When I did, oh! what a night of suffering. She prayed with me. Oh, how true and kind she was. Her faith held on to God for me.

Next day another dear friend, Mrs. D., came; and they two together prayed and encouraged me to still hold on; that all the pain I suffered was simply a temptation; the Lord would heal me. I made my will do the best it would; but I felt the pain just the same.

About noon I got up, and they helped me to get my clothes on. They were so anxious I should be down to Christmas dinner with them. So I was, and as best I could, endured the pain through dinner. When it was over I could not hold out any longer; I went up to my room, and walked the floor in agony. I tried to ignore the pain; but in spite of my will and faith, it would not be ignored a bit!

About day-break I got a little quiet and slept a little; and while the pain was not so bad as it had been, it was three weeks before I was able to get my arm above my head. And when I would use any means, or talk of it, my friends would feel so sorry for me, and say that it was not honoring the Lord to do so.

But I had sincerely prayed for light. And I believe God has given it to me; if for no one else, He does to Amanda Smith, and I feel quite sure I am not mistaken in God's leading me. I think He has saved me from bondage on these points. Amen. Amen.

As one of the little incidents that reached its culmination after my return from Africa to England, I must here relate the story of my bonnet—not a very important story in itself, but, like most stories, it has its moral, also, if we choose to see it.

How I did hate to give up my nice Quaker bonnet! I had no special feeling about putting it on, so far as feathers and flowers were concerned. I settled that when I was converted. All of those things were surrendered, though the love of them was deep in my heart, so that when I sought the blessing of cleansing I had no difficulty on the dress question.

I always admired the Friends' dress, so this was at once my choice, and at that time many of the Christian sisters among all the colored churches in Philadelphia, New York, and Baltimore, dressed like the Friends, and were generally called Band Sisters, and, as a rule, were noted for their deep piety and Christian character. I loved them for this, as well as admired their very plain dress, for the height of my ambition was to be a consistent, downright, outright Christian.

It was not a question of your belonging to the Society of Friends because you chose to dress like them. I remember that not only colored Methodists dressed like them, but white Methodists as well, so that I never dreamed of anyone questioning me on my plain dress. When I got to England I found it was different, dressing like a Friend and not being a Friend, and none of my people being Friends. They did not understand it, so as I went about I was often questioned, though in a very nice way.

I was with the Friends a great deal, and they were most hospitable and kind. They would sometimes say;

"Does thee belong to the Society of Friends?"

"No."

"Did thy father and mother?"

"No."

"And none of thy people are Friends?"

"No."

"How strange that thee should wear the Friends' garb."

Well, then I would go into a long explanation, tell of Americans being independent in what they choose; how no one felt bound to wear any set garb; that Methodists or Presbyterians, no matter who, if they liked to dress like the Friends, or anybody else, if they had the money, just got the article, whatever it was, and no one had any thought about it.

They would listen patiently, and then kindly say: "Well, I think if I were thee, I would not do it."

I didn't understand it at first, but later on I found out that no one in England would wear a Friends' bonnet who was not a Friend, if they did they would be suspected of pretending to be what they were not. When I first heard this I was frightened. I said, "Oh, deary me, is this why I have been so questioned?"

As I was going from place to place, everybody treated me most kindly, but, "oh," I said, "has this been the thought in their mind, that I have been pretending to be what I am not?"

I prayed and cried about it a great deal for the Lord only knows how I hate deception or sham in anything, but especially in Christianity or religion; but then, I could do nothing. I thought, if I take off my bonnet, and I did not want to do so, for I really loved it, but still if I should take it off, and see persons from America who knew me, that they would say, "Yes, that is just what we thought, Amanda Smith would take off her plain bonnet when she got to England!"

Then the people on this side thought I was representing myself, by wearing the Friends' dress, to be what I was not.

So there I was, between two fires, and the thought of sailing under false colors, this was more than I could bear, but I stood it until I got back to Liverpool, then I had to get a new bonnet. I dreaded going through the explanation again. I saw that the settled ladies were wearing little bonnets. I thought, "What shall I do, I can never wear a little bonnet."

I thought if I could find a Friends' milliner, I would get me a plain bonnet if it were not a real Friends' bonnet. I knew I could not get what I wanted at any ordinary milliner, and I did not know where to go in Liverpool to find a Friends' milliner.

I wrote to my friend, Mrs. Margaret Davis, of Fox Rock, Dublin, and told her my dilemma. She wrote and told me she thought I was quite right about getting the bonnet I wanted, and that she would find out where I could find a Friends' milliner in Liverpool. But before I got her word, two ladies called on me and would go with me to get some warmer clothing. It was very cold and I had only my African clothes, four double, but then I was not warm, so we went shopping, as we would say in England.

The ladies got me a nice fur cloak, warm under flannels, nice jersey jacket, stockings, gloves, etc., then they said:

"Is there anything else, Amanda?"

"That is all," I replied.

Just then one of the ladies said, "Oh, you must have a nice bonnet!"

Then I told them I was waiting for a letter so as to know where to go. They said, "You will not wear that big bonnet again."

I tried to explain to them as best I could, but they insisted that I must get a bonnet, "properly," as they said. So we went into the millinery department and got me a "nice bonnet," the largest one they had, and that was not very large, and the plainest.

So I went on all right until I came back to America, then here it was again, "Oh, what have you done with your plain bonnet?" I felt so sick of explaining that I felt like starting a new style and wearing no bonnet at all!

Scores of people have asked me about my bonnet that have never thought of asking me how my soul prospered, and this, after all, is more important in God's sight than though I wore a hundred plain bonnets.

I thought it well to give this final explanation. Amen.

I had a great many expenses during my stay at Sierra Leone. I had my two native children, Bob and Frances, with me, and the little girl was sick all the time. I did everything I could for her to get her well enough to bring with me.

She had been sick for three months before I left Monrovia; but I had got her well enough to get as far as Sierra Leone, where I hoped, through better medical attendance, she would get quite well enough for me to bring to England.

After spending three or four months in Sierra Leone, and doing all I could for her, paying doctors' bills and all, the doctor told me at last that the child could not stand the climate if I brought her, and that she would be a great deal of trouble and care, so I had to decide to leave her, as I had little Bob to look after.

Then I had to provide everything for Frances, so as to leave her comfortable, as I was going to bring little Bob with me. This made my expenses more; but I had quite enough to bring me to Liverpool, if I could live to get there, though sometimes I was a little doubtful whether I would. But the Lord understood my case.

It was not long after I got there before my loving Father, God, began to fulfill that blessed old promise, that He gave me when I left America: "My God will supply all your need according to His riches in glory, by Christ Jesus." Phil. 4:19. Different friends began to send in, as I have already shown; some, three pounds; then two pounds; others, one pound.

One week when I needed just four shillings to pay for my lodgings at Liverpool, before leaving for my friend, Mrs. Staveley's, at Seaforth, where I was going that afternoon, the postman brought a letter in the morning, and when I opened it it was from America, and contained one dollar. I did not know the sender—no name—only "God bless you; I welcome you back from Africa." That was all. So I praised the Lord, paid for my lodgings and left.

> "This, this is the God I adore,
> My faithful, unchangeable friend
> His love is as great as His power,
> Which neither knows measure nor end."

CHAPTER XXXVI.

WORK IN ENGLAND—IN LIVERPOOL, LONDON, MANCHESTER, AND VARIOUS OTHER PLACES—I GO TO SCOTLAND AND IRELAND —SECURE PASSAGE TO NEW YORK—INCIDENTS OF THE VOYAGE —HOME AGAIN—CONCLUDING WORDS.

My first work in England, after my return from Africa, was at Gordon Hall, Mrs. Stephen Menzies', Liverpool, where I spoke at a large conference and sang, and the Lord blessed me greatly. My next work was at Fleshfield, at Mr. Radcliff's. I began on Watch Night and spent a week. I was not well, but somehow the Lord helped me to speak to a large congregation in the little chapel. From there I went to Southport and assisted in some meetings held by Rev. D. F. Sanford, of Boston, U. S. A.

All this time I was miserable, but I would earnestly pray and ask the Lord to strengthen me, and He would always do it, but I see now the wise thing would have been for me to have rested entirely, for that was my real need, and the strength I used in praying I should have spent in resting. I believe this would have been pleasing to God. What a dull scholar I have been in His school and yet He has been so patient with me.

Then I held several meetings in Liverpool; then on to Doncaster, was entertained at the home of Miss Morris, Chequer House. I shall never forget her kindness to Bob and me. Here I had some rest, but held a number of meetings, some in the hall of the Y. M. C. A., and Mother's Meetings, and several drawing room meetings at Mrs. Richard Norris'; and various other meetings. From Doncaster we went to London on our way to Folkston. My dear friend, Mrs. D. Bordman, of London, had kindly invited me to stop on my way. She had also kindly arranged a little quiet reception. A number of friends were invited, among those that were present was Mrs. Hannah Whitehall Smith, Mrs. Mark Guy Pierce, and others. This was a surprise to me, but it was a blessed meeting and meant more to me than I have language to express.

From London I went on to Folkston, where I had been sent for, to hold a special service at the Railway Mission. Here Bob and I had nice lodgings provided; and it was here where little Bob was converted, one morning just after breakfast as we kneeled together to have our morning worship. Praise the Lord!

I shall never forget the blessing the Lord gave us at Mr. Tokes' church. He is a grand man of God, a staunch churchman, but what is called low Church; broad, but orthodox, so that he invited a woman to take services in his church, and God wonderfully blessed his work and people. One dear woman told me that she had sought the blessing of heart purity for several years, but she said somehow the Lord helped me to make the way so simple that she saw it, believed, and entered into rest. Her face beamed with delight. To Him alone be glory forever.

Then on Sunday night the Congregationalist minister invited the Railway meeting over to his fine church, which was just across the street, the crowd being so great we couldn't seat them in the hall. He threw open his pulpit; though it was a new thing under the sun for a woman to stand in the pulpit of a Congregational Church; and I must confess I did feel a little shaky myself to be up there alone; but I cried mightily to the Lord for help, and, if ever He did help me, He did that Sunday night, and blessed His own Word to the hearts of the people, and several entered in and found soul rest. Praise the Lord!

Then I spoke at several other meetings, including one of the Salvation Army, who were doing a grand work at Folkston. They had given me an urgent invitation to speak for them. I had but one night that I could possibly give, so I went in the name of the Lord and did what I could.

From Folkston I went to London, spent a few days with Mrs. Col. Finch White, at Louishem Hill. Here I held several meetings, including a drawing room meeting at Mrs. Finch White's. Drawing room meetings are not a rare thing as they are in America, I think, as I have never held any here, but did so often in England, and often with great profit, I trust.

Thursday, April 3, I leave London for Southport, and stop at Mrs. Stavely's Berachia Home. Monday, April 10, I take Bob to Miss Hobb's school, where he is now, and has been ever since.

How good the Lord was to open this door of mercy to this dear boy; thus the promise is true, "If ye shall ask anything in my name, I will do it." On the 16th I go to a Conference at Manchester, Mr. Crossley's, Star Hall. This was a blessed meeting, conducted by Rev. D. F. Sanford, to which I was invited and entertained at Mr. Crossley's home with Mr. and Mrs. Sanford, and though I did but little, the Lord blessed me. And when I was leaving, Mr. C. handed me a check for, I think, ten pounds— not quite sure as to the amount—but at all the places they paid me well.

Besides the meetings at Star Hall, I took a meeting at a large mission hall carried on by the Society of Friends. Here the Lord gave His blessing on the Word.

April the 23rd, I leave Manchester for Southport, attend to some little matters for Bob, then, on Friday, April 25, I leave Southport for London, stop at Mrs. Isabella Walker's, where I had had a very warm invitation to spend some time at her home. This lady was anxious I should go to some of the meetings held at the headquarters of the Salvation Army, Congress Hall.

This I was not able to do, but spent two very pleasant weeks with Mrs. Walker. at Clapham. How the grace of God was magnified in this lady's home life, a lady of rank and culture and position, but so fully consecrated to God. She was Mrs. Booth's warmest friend, and was with her through her last severe illness. It was here I had the pleasure of meeting Mr. and Mrs. Col. Clibborn, of the Salvation Army, whose work is in Paris. May the Lord bless them.

May the 1st, I was invited by Mr. Reader Harris and Rev. D. F. Sanford to be at their anniversary meeting, at Speak Hall,

Clapham. This is a great meeting, held every year, and has been a great blessing to scores of souls from all parts of England.

May 7th, through the invitation of Mr. Clifford, Honorable Treasurer of the Great Church Army, I speak at the anniversary meeting at Piccadilly. The crowd was very great, but the Lord gave His blessing; then I addressed several meetings at Miss Mason's House of Rest, Cambridge Gardens, London, West.

Saturday, May 10, at Woodgreen, Mr. Morgan, the editor of "The Christian," invited me to take some services at his hall on Sabbath and several week nights. Here again the Lord was pleased to give tokens of His favor, and a number professed to have found peace in believing.

On the 24th, I leave London for Scotland, stop at Carlisle, with Mrs. Walker's sister, Mrs. Johnston. What a lovely home this is. I was so tired and would so like to have rested, but I had not been in long before a number of dear friends gathered and I had to have a meeting. I felt I really could not, at first, but I asked the Lord to help me, and He did, praise His name. On Monday, the 26th, I leave Carlisle for Alloa, Scotland. Miss Patten, of Morris Hill House, through my dear friend, Mrs. Lisle, had kindly invited me to Alloa to have a little rest, God bless her, I shall never forget her kindness in every way to me. Before I ever saw her she wrote and sent me five pounds, which came just at a time when I needed it. God's word of promise did not fail. (Phil., 4:19).

After a little rest, I held several meetings at different places in Scotland, at Alloa and then at Crief. Here Miss Patten took me to the great Hydropathic institution, at her own expense, where I could well have spent a month, but because of an engagement for some meetings at Edinburgh, I could only spend one week. How kind the people were, and the baths and treatment that I received during the short stay did me the greatest good. I shall ever praise God for Miss Patten, and for the kindness shown me at this beautiful institution. I was asked to give a little missionary talk one morning in the chapel, which seemed to be very much appreciated.

From Crief I went to Edinburgh, after holding meetings a week, arranged by Mr. Govern, who had also arranged a series of meetings at Peble's, on the River Clide, and at a number of other places. Then, leaving there, I went to Blaine O'Chile, Dunblain. I went on Friday to stay until Monday. This lady, Mrs. Chapman, was a very dear friend of Mrs. Lisle, who had spent a number of years in Africa on the Congo and at Old Calibar, where I first met her, and worked with her a little while there. It was through her that I got to know Mrs. Chapman; since then she has gone to her reward. May God bless her memory.

Mrs. Chapman is a lady of large means, and I think I never saw one whose means and all was so fully consecrated to God. How many young men she has educated for foreign work, both white and colored, and has also been the help of many others. Her record is in heaven.

She invited me to come and see her before I left Scotland. I was getting ready to go home and I felt I needed the money, still I wanted to go and see this lady, so I told the Lord if He would have me go, not to let me be anxious about the means, but to open the way for me. I had a good quiet Saturday, and it was very stormy and rainy on Sunday, so that Mrs. S. said we would not go to church in the morning. In the afternoon she asked me if I would take a service and speak to the servants in the large kitchen. This I did, and spoke with great freedom from the 15th of John. We had a very interesting meeting. At the close Mrs. S. said, I think the meeting has been very profitable. She was very pleased, and as we went to the next room she said, "I want to hand you a little donation," so she handed me six pounds. I said, how the Lord has answered prayer!

On Monday morning as I was leaving she said, "I think I had better give you another pound." I thanked her and praised the Lord.

From here I went on to Grenock, spent a night and spoke to a large congregation in a hall. On the 15th I left for Belfast, spent a few days at Neury; held several meetings there. On the 18th I leave Neury for Fox Rock, Dublin; stopped with my friend Mrs. Margaret Davis, whom God raised up to help me so while in Africa; God bless her forever.

During my stay at this very pleasant Irish home I held several meetings at the Friends' Meeting House, Monkstown, then at different places in Dublin at the Wesleyan Chapel, etc., etc.

Then, July 30th I leave Dublin for Leeds, Eng. Thank God He has given me the strength and the intimation that I may start for home. Praise His name. How I have ever gone through with the work I have, I cannot tell, for I was not able to think of getting my things together till last Monday, the 28th. In the morning when I woke the thought came how I should get my things together, and when I had thought it all over I had found that the dreadful weakness did not overcome me as it had done before. I said, praise the Lord, I can go home.

I got up and wrote to Mr. Stavely, at Liverpool, to get me a ticket; this he could not do, as everything was engaged. So I had to wait till the 26th of August, when I left by the steamer Gallier for New York, and arrived Friday, September 5, 1890.

On the way over from England there were a number of ministers aboard and four or five Catholic priests. All had services on the Sabbath. The Catholics in the lower cabin, and the Protestants in the upper saloon.

In the afternoon there was a meeting among the steerage passengers. I went and listened to a young man talking in very broken English; but, oh! so earnest. He was a foreigner, and was speaking from the fourteenth chapter of John.

There was a number of Plymouth brethren among them, and they seemed to have the right of way, so that the poor young man was alone; for, as a general thing, they have but little sympathy or fellowship for anyone that does not say as they say and teach the truth as they do. All that I have ever met seemed to think and endeavor to impress it upon you that they only, know the Scriptures, and all teaching outside of themselves—true Plymouth brethren—is not safe, and ought not to be relied on. So they all started off from this poor foreigner except a few. When he stopped the Lord said to me as he said to Phillip, "Go up, join yourself to him." So I said, "I want to sing." I struck in:

> "I praise the Lord that one like me,
> For mercy may to Jesus flee.
> He says that whosoever will
> May seek and find salvation still."

And then the chorus:

> "My Saviour's promise faileth never;
> He counts me in the 'whosoever.' "

I sang out with all my ransomed powers, and the people came from all parts of the ship. There was a great crowd. The speaker seemed a little astonished, but said, "Hallelujah. Amen."

When I got through with my song I began to speak. O, how the Lord helped me. Then the people wanted me to speak in the saloon on Sunday evening. I felt God wanted me to do so, and the door was open; I see it now. I am careful, and never like to overdo anything—never like to do anything that looks like I want to push myself, so the devil took that advantage, and when I thought, I would do it, he said:

"Now, you had better let well enough alone, there has been enough for to-day, and to-morrow there will be nothing; why not do it to-morrow?"

"Yes," I said, "perhaps that is the best." But, no; it was not. I ought to have done it when the Lord bade me.

On Monday the saloon was full and they sang and played cards and other games. No shadow of a chance for anyone to speak unless he just broke right in with everything.

"Well," I said, "I will speak on Tuesday," but no, no chance.

Then I said, "I will the last night," for they said we would not likely get in until Friday.

"O," I said, "I will get ready and do it on Thursday;" but I felt I should have spoken Wednesday night anyhow.

A number of the passengers, ladies and friends, wanted that I should speak, but I said, "On Thursday night I will, without fail, speak and sing."

But, O, what a mistake! We got in on Thursday afternoon, four o'clock, instead of Friday. How ashamed and sorry I was I had not spoken on Wednesday night, as the Lord had showed me.

This is not the only time my courage has failed me under somewhat similar circumstances. Once, on my way front Calcutta, India, to British Burmah, there were a number of English passengers, and though they were respectable and all right as far as I know, they were not of the best type of English ladies and gentlemen. They were of an 'airish' quality, and that class of English or Americans, especially when traveling, are not the class that good taste would be apt to admire or fall in love with; and to do your duty in spite of these surroundings takes a good deal of pluck, especially for a colored woman.

There was a man, his wife and baby, and his brother, from San Francisco, California. The baby was the crossest baby I really ever saw. It cried night and day for simple amusement, it seemed, if for nothing else. Everybody was worn out with it.

These Californians seemed to avoid all Godliness. They laughed and jeered at everything that was said about religion; but they were anxious for me to talk on Sunday morning when they found out I was an evangelist; and I did pray God to make my duty plain to me; and I think He did very clearly show me that I was to speak on Sunday.

They kept up a laugh and joke about it all Saturday, and Sunday morning at the breakfast table, and all the steerage passengers had it, and they seemed as though they were looking forward to a menagerie. When I saw this, I began to question, and the Devil helped me.

"You know you are not to cast your pearls before swine," he said.

One might have thought he was careful of God's pearls. So I did not do it. I didn't feel that I did right, but still I didn't do it.

I believe God would have blest souls on that steamer if I had only done my duty. Then the Californians, after all, seemed disappointed, and were more taunting and sneering than they were before. O, how I saw my mistake, I wept before the Lord, and again sought His forgiving mercy. The mistakes of my life have been many.

O, the patience and loving kindness of the Lord, so infinite in power and might, to bear with such cowards. How true the words of this song:—

> "Were it not that love and mercy in my Lord abide,
> When my conscience is o'ertaken, where would I hide?
> How could I live without Thee, Saviour and friend,
> Thou art my only refuge, saved to the end."

Upon our arrival at New York I was kindly invited to the home of Mr. and Mrs. Gibson at their pleasant residence, 384 Union street, Brooklyn. Mrs. Gibson was sick in bed, but Mr. Gibson met me at the landing and took me to his home, where I was for two weeks. Then I took a room, the only one I could get; it was ten dollars a month; but this gave me a little chance to look around; then my friend, Mrs. Mary R. Denman, of Newark, N. J., kindly gave me a room in one of her small houses, where my home has been ever since up till last October, when I came to Chicago. Since then I have decided to make this my future home, but entirely subject to God's direction and leading.

And now I close the last chapter of this little book, which has been such a task to one so unskilled in work of this kind. There has been no attempt to show a dash of rhetoric or intellectual ability, but just the simple story of God's dealings with a worm. If, after all, no one should be brought nearer to God, and to a deeper consecration, I shall be sadly disappointed; for my whole object and wish is that God will make it a blessing to all who may read it; and with this desire and prayer I send it forth to the world. And especially do I pray that many of my own people will be led to a more full consecration, and that the Spirit of the Lord may come upon some of the younger women who have talent, and who have had better opportunities than I have ever had, and so must do better work for the Master; so that when I have fallen in the battle, and can do no more, they may take up the standard and bear it on, with the inscription deeply engraven on heart and life, "Without holiness, no man shall see the Lord."

THE END.